REDESIGNING THE WELFARE STATE IN NEW ZEALAND: PROBLEMS, POLICIES, PROSPECTS

Edited by

JONATHAN BOSTON
PAUL DALZIEL
SUSAN ST JOHN

D1566427

OXFORD
UNIVERSITY PRESS

OXFORD

UNIVERSITY PRESS

540 Great South Road, Greenlane, Auckland, New Zealand

Oxford University Press is a department of the University of Oxford.
It furthers the University's objective of excellence in research, scholarship,
and education by publishing worldwide in

Oxford New York

Athens Auckland Bangkok Bogotá Buenos Aires Calcutta
Cape Town Chennai Dar es Salaam Delhi Florence Hong Kong Istanbul
Karachi Kuala Lumpur Madrid Melbourne Mexico City Mumbai Nairobi
Paris Port Moresby São Paulo Singapore Taipei Tokyo Toronto Warsaw

with associated companies in Berlin Ibadan

OXFORD is a registered trade mark of Oxford University Press
in the UK and certain other countries

ISBN 019 558 3736

Edited by Alison Carew
Typeset by Archetype, Wellington
Printed by Kin Keong, Singapore

CONTENTS

Part III: Summary and Conclusion

PREFACE

After six years of radical economic reform by the fourth Labour government, the October 1990 general election produced a landslide victory for National. On 19 December, the new government announced its Economic and Social Initiative 'to translate into action the mandate it [had] received to redesign the Welfare State'. These announcements led to the social welfare benefit cuts from 1 April 1991, the Employment Contracts Act 1991, and the creation of a number of official committees and task forces to undertake comprehensive reviews of social assistance, accident compensation, housing, health and education. The motivation for the reviews was perhaps best expressed by Minister of Finance Ruth Richardson in her first Budget speech (1991, pp.7-8):

> The redesign of the welfare state is integral to our strategy for growth. We cannot make economic progress without reforming our social systems, nor can social and economic policy be divorced from one another. The only sustainable welfare state is one that is fair and affordable. Our current system is neither. Real welfare is created by people and families through their own efforts. Our redesigned welfare state will support those efforts and assist those who cannot assist themselves.

In response to the first wave of reforms announced in the Initiative and the 1991 Budget, two of the present editors commissioned a series of essays which were published as *The Decent Society? Essays in Response to National's Economic and Social Policies* (1992). We wrote in the preface that the book was 'prompted by a belief that some of National's key economic and social policies are seriously flawed and that, unless they are changed, New Zealand is likely to face increasing social and political strife'. We further argued that the next few years would be a critical time for democracy in New Zealand:

> At stake are not merely the details and direction of economic and social policy, but the *kind* of society in which we, as New Zealanders, wish to live. Do we want a society in which there are vast disparities of income, wealth, and opportunity? Do we want a society in which the poor must carry various health cards in order to secure access to health care, while the rich enjoy the advantages of private insurance, queue jumping, and better-quality services? Do we want a society in which large numbers of tertiary students have little option but to borrow substantial sums of money in order to pursue their studies? Do we want a society

v

that is unwilling to raise sufficient tax from those with the ability to pay to provide those who are sick, retired, or unemployed with an adequate income? These matters, and many others, need to be debated, and debated vigorously (p.xi).

There has been vigorous debate over the last seven years, and some of the policy changes that concerned us, particularly in health, have been reversed. Others were not implemented—most notably, the family social assistance accounts and global abatement rate foreshadowed in the 1991 Budget, and some announced changes in superannuation. The 1996 Coalition Agreement between National and New Zealand First committed the government to increasing its aggregate spending by $5 billion (reduced to $4.7 billion in the 1998 Budget) over three years, mostly on social services. Nevertheless, the overall thrust of cutting back the welfare state continues. Social welfare beneficiaries were explicitly excluded from almost all of the government's 1996 Tax Reduction and Social Policy Programme, so that while middle- and upper-income households gained significantly, the effects of the April 1991 benefit cuts on low-income households remained in force. Indeed, the 1998 Budget reduced the sickness benefit to the level of the unemployment benefit for new beneficiaries after 1 July 1998, and introduced extended work-tests for domestic purposes beneficiaries. That Budget also announced that private sector insurers would be permitted to compete with ACC in major areas of the accident compensation scheme from 1 July 1999. Greater targeting of social assistance continues to guide policy development. Housing assistance is now provided on a cash supplement basis (based on income and housing costs) rather than through income-related subsidised rentals. At the time of writing, the government was contemplating introducing health-style reforms into the tertiary education sector. Government leaders frequently make speeches that stress the importance of reducing top tax rates, already low by OECD standards, as a top priority for future policy.

There is no argument that New Zealand faces a large number of challenges in economic and social policy. The programme of reforms after 1984 involved substantial economic sacrifices without producing significantly better performance. By 1997, the balance of payments deficit and the level of overseas indebtedness had begun to raise questions in the international community about the soundness of the New Zealand reforms (*Economist*, 2 May 1998, p.74). From the perspective of 1998, the strong growth rates of 1994 and 1995 proved not to be a harbinger of a higher trend, but simply a familiar rebound out of a deep and long-lasting recession. Thus the extra resources needed to address the reform programme's legacy of increased poverty are not available from greater economic growth (see Chapter 4). Caps on government spending, including the 1991 benefit cuts, helped to eliminate

New Zealand's fiscal deficit, but a large social deficit remains as more New Zealanders find they do not have access to the same level or quality of income support, health care, education, housing assistance and accident compensation as in the past. Foodbanks, virtually unknown before 1984, continue to face high demand from desperate individuals and families, and many schools are now providing free food to some of their students. A number of publications by community groups and academics have highlighted the problems being experienced by the children of low- to middle-income households. Greater targeting is producing very high effective marginal tax rates for large numbers of low-income New Zealanders, creating sizeable poverty traps. The quest for social security is further threatened by the trend in recent years for new employment opportunities to be more heavily concentrated in part-time or casual jobs. It is possible to begin speaking of an underclass in New Zealand, as there is clear evidence of a polarisation of households, with those on high incomes receiving a disproportionate share of the economic benefits of the reform programme, while others remain trapped on the margins of New Zealand's society and economy.

These trends are by no means unique to New Zealand. Governments around the world are struggling with decisions about public spending and the welfare state, and there have been cutbacks in many countries. In countries like the United States, Australia and the United Kingdom, demands for reducing the role of government still further are based on arguments that anything beyond a minimalist welfare state undermines liberty, is inequitable, crowds out the private institutions of a civil society, weakens personal incentives and is economically damaging. However, there is also a robust international literature that highlights the benefits of a properly functioning democratic state in facilitating economic development, and in ensuring that the social inequalities created in a free-market society are moderated according to fundamental principles of social justice. This second point of view has struggled to be heard in New Zealand, as well-funded business groups and the dominant policymaking departments of the public service have promoted what is often called the 'New Right' or 'market liberal' agenda. The essays in this volume are a contribution towards redressing the balance.

In commissioning the essays, we chose to focus on the ideas behind, and the outcomes of, the policy reforms in New Zealand since 1990. Consequently, the book has relatively little to say about the combinations of interest groups and political forces that promoted each policy change; nor does it discuss the new currents of opposition and support that have appeared in reaction to the reforms. This is not because we think the political economy of redesigning the welfare state is unimportant. Indeed, the opposite is true. These issues, however, have been addressed in a number of recent books: for example, Boston, Levine, McLeay and Roberts (1996; 1997); Kelsey (1997a);

R. Miller (1997); and Rudd and Roper (1997). Rather than replicate that work, our aim in this volume is to analyse the conceptual and practical weaknesses in the current policy framework, and to offer suggestions for rebuilding an effective welfare state in this country.

The essays are presented in three parts. In Part I, the fundamental principles and key themes that characterise the international and domestic debate about the future of the welfare state are examined. In Chapter 1, Jonathan Boston surveys different models of the welfare state that have been introduced around the world, and places the New Zealand debate in this global context. Boston continues in Chapter 2 with an essay examining the critique that has come from the New Right concerning the fundamental values that have underpinned the welfare state, such as justice and social citizenship. In Chapter 3, Mānuka Henare draws on Māori worldviews and associated cultural practices to present a framework of ethical values for developing sustainable social policy. The impact of government taxation and spending on economic performance is analysed by Paul Dalziel in Chapter 4, which also documents the disappointing results of New Zealand's reforms on economic growth. Chapters 5 and 6 address two fundamental issues concerning government spending that have driven many of the social policy reforms over the last decade. In Chapter 5, Paul Dalziel and Susan St John review the literature on the extent to which governments should be involved in providing or funding public services, while in Chapter 6, Boston and St John revisit the debate on targeting versus universal provision of income support and subsidised services.

Part II focuses on specific policy areas: Pat Walsh and Peter Brosnan examine industrial relations and the Employment Contracts Act in Chapter 7; Toni Ashton reviews changes in health policy in Chapter 8; Susan St John analyses ACC reforms and the pressure for its privatisation in Chapter 9; Michael Peters and Mark Olssen address New Zealand's compulsory education system and Jonathan Boston comments on tertiary education in Chapters 10 and 11 respectively; Laurence Murphy assesses the radical changes in housing assistance introduced in 1993 in Chapter 12; Robert Stephens documents trends in poverty and the role of income support in Chapter 13; Jane Higgins reviews recent debates about social welfare and the government's community wage scheme in Chapter 14; and Susan St John summarises the history and ongoing issues of superannuation policy in Chapter 15.

In *The Decent Society?* we commented that writing about social policy in New Zealand is often frustrating because policies are continually being revised and reformulated within the public service and Cabinet system in a way that is not accessible to external analysis until after policy changes have been announced. This continues to be the case. When Jenny Shipley took over as Prime Minister in December 1997, she began her tenure by promising a major announcement in social policy in February 1998. That announcement was accompanied by the distribution to every household of the government's discussion document, *Towards a Code of Social and Family Responsibility*, and was backed up by some policy initiatives in the May 1998 Budget. It was not possible for the contributors to this volume to incorporate all these developments in their individual chapters, but the final chapter by the three editors, in Part III, contains a commentary on recent developments in the light of the principles and issues discussed in the rest of the book.

In conclusion, we wish to acknowledge again the considerable work undertaken by the contributors, all of whom have written their chapters in the midst of heavy teaching, marking and administrative pressures. Some of the text draws heavily on material first published in *The Decent Society?*, but all of the chapters have been thoroughly revised and brought up-to-date. Jonathan Boston would like to thank Victoria University of Wellington for a research grant that was used in part for preparing Chapters 1, 2 and 11. We are grateful to our editor, Alison Carew, to the anonymous readers who commented on either our initial proposal or the final draft for Oxford University Press, and to our publisher, Linda Cassells, for her support and advice throughout this project. While the merits of this volume are to be shared equally among the contributors, the editors take sole responsibility for the book's overall coherence and any errors contained herein.

Jonathan Boston
Paul Dalziel
Susan St John
(May 1998)

CONTRIBUTORS

Toni Ashton is a Senior Lecturer in Health Economics in the Department of Community Health at the University of Auckland. She has sat on a number of government advisory committees, most recently the Cervical Screening Advisory Committee, the Health Determinants Group of the National Health Committee and the Nursing Taskforce. She has written extensively on the topic of health care reform, and has co-authored two books with Susan St John on superannuation in New Zealand.

Jonathan Boston is Professor of Public Policy at Victoria University of Wellington. He has written and edited numerous books on New Zealand politics, public management and public policy, and has published more than 40 articles in a wide range of academic journals. He is currently a member of the New Zealand Political Change Project, which is examining the behavioural, institutional and policy consequences of MMP. This project is funded by the Foundation for Research, Science and Technology.

Peter Brosnan is a Professor of Industrial Relations at Griffith University, Brisbane. His current research focuses on labour market flexibility and inequality. He has written numerous journal articles. He and Pat Walsh are co-authors with David Smith of *The Dynamics of New Zealand Industrial Relations* (1990).

Paul Dalziel is Reader in Economics in the Commerce Division of Lincoln University. He is a frequent commentator on New Zealand economic and social policy, and has published more than 20 academic articles in this field. He is the author with Ralph Lattimore of *The New Zealand Macroeconomy: A Briefing on the Reforms* (1996).

Mānuka Henare is a Senior Lecturer in Māori Business Development in the Department of Management and Employment Relations at the University of Auckland. He is a regular commentator on Te Tiriti o Waitangi/the Treaty of Waitangi, and on economic and political issues impacting on Māori. He has published numerous articles on Māori history, biography, ethics and sustainable development.

Jane Higgins is a Lecturer in Sociology at the University of Canterbury. Her teaching and research interests lie primarily in the field of social policy—especially employment policy and New Zealand's welfare reforms. Her current research includes work on the impact of policy changes on the lives of sole parents, and a longitudinal study of changes in the youth labour market in Christchurch since 1976.

Laurence Murphy is a Senior Lecturer in the Department of Geography at the University of Auckland. He has published academic articles on housing policy and finance, property development processes and urban regeneration issues.

Mark Olssen is a Senior Lecturer in Education at the University of Otago. He is editor of *Mental Testing in New Zealand: Critical and Oppositional Perspectives* (1988), author with Elaine Papps of *The Doctoring of Childbirth* (1997), and editor with Kay Morris Matthews of *Education Policy in New Zealand: The 1990s and Beyond* (1997). He has also published numerous articles internationally and in New Zealand on education policy and philosophy. He is presently writing a book on Michel Foucault.

Michael Peters is Associate Professor in the School of Education at the University of Auckland, with research interests in education policy and philosophy. He has published over 70 academic articles in these fields and is the author and/or editor of over a dozen books, including *Individualism and Community: Education and Social Policy* (with James Marshall, 1996), *Poststructuralism, Politics and Education* (1996), *Cultural Politics and the University in Aotearoa/New Zealand* (1997) and *Virtual Technologies in Tertiary Education* (with Peter Roberts, 1998).

Susan St John is a Senior Lecturer in Economics in the Department of Economics at the University of Auckland. She has published widely in public policy and is co-author of *Macroeconomics and the Contemporary New Zealand Economy* (1996) with Robert Scollay, and *Economic Concepts and Applications* (1997) with James Stewart. She has been active in the superannuation policy area and was deputy chair of the Periodic Report Group in 1997.

Robert Stephens is a Senior Lecturer in Public Policy and Economics in the Faculty of Commerce and Administration at Victoria University of Wellington. His research interests cover the areas of taxation, social policy, and income distribution and poverty, with publications in each area.

Pat Walsh is Associate Professor in Industrial Relations and Public Policy at Victoria University of Wellington. His current research focuses on the implications for industrial relations and human resource management of organisational restructuring. He is the author of many journal articles and co-author of *Public Management: The New Zealand Model* (1996).

ACKNOWLEDGEMENTS

Chapter 1. The material in this chapter draws heavily on Chapter 1 of *The Decent Society?*

Chapter 2. The material in this chapter draws on an earlier paper by the author (Boston, 1993). The author wishes to thank the following people for their assistance: Bob Gregory, André Kaiser, Pat Moloney, Andrew Moore, John Myers, Bob Stephens and Amanda Wolf.

Chapter 3. The author is grateful to Judge Mick Brown, Professor Richard Benton, Ross McDonald and Ella Henry for general discussions on Māori development and sustainable social policy. The hospitality and generosity of the Rūnanga of Whangaroa deserve special thanks, and in particular Pat and Hiwi Tauroa, and the kaumātua, Te Uru Hone Heta and Poihākena (Syd) Kira, for sharing their time, history and knowledge.

Chapter 4. The author is grateful for very helpful comments on earlier drafts by Patrick Caragata and Ewen McCann, and to Patrick Caragata, Fraser Jackson and John Small for general discussions on the growth-maximising tax rate research programme.

Chapter 6. The material in this chapter draws heavily on Boston (1992a) and St John (1996b).

Chapter 7. The authors are grateful for the research assistance provided by Brigette Hughes and Catherine Scully.

Chapter 8. The author thanks her colleagues in the Centre for Health Services, Research and Policy—especially Peter Davis and Rod Perkins—for useful comments and suggestions on earlier drafts.

Chapter 9. Comments on earlier drafts from Ian Campbell, Devon Diggle, Grant Duncan, Diane Salter and Ross Wilson are gratefully acknowledged.

Chapter 10. The authors would like to thank Kay Morris Matthews for editorial assistance and corrections of some sections of the chapter. Much of the original essay was written while Michael Peters was a Visiting Scholar at the Research School of Social Sciences at the Australian National University in July 1997, and he would like to thank Barry Hindess for his kind support.

Chapter 11. The author wishes to thank the following people for their assistance with the preparation of this chapter: Rob Crozier, Jane Kelsey, Sholeh Maani, Andrew Moore, June Pallot, Bob Stephens and staff of the Ministry of Education.

Chapter 12. The author is very grateful for the cartographic assistance of Jan Kelly and Jonette Surridge.

Chapter 13. The author would like to thank Kay Goodger from the Department of Social Welfare for comments on an earlier draft. The usual disclaimers apply.

Chapter 15. Comments on earlier drafts from Michael Littlewood, Brian Easton, Petrus Simons, Angela Ryan, Roger Hurnard and Bob Stephens are gratefully acknowledged.

PART I

PRINCIPLES
AND
KEY THEMES

CHAPTER ONE

NEW ZEALAND'S WELFARE STATE IN TRANSITION

JONATHAN BOSTON

In September 1938, the first Labour government enacted the Social Security Act, thus laying the foundations of the modern welfare state in New Zealand. The aim of the legislation, to quote Prime Minister Michael Joseph Savage, was 'for the first time to provide, as generously as possible, for all persons who have been deprived of the power to obtain a reasonable livelihood through age, illness, unemployment, widowhood, or other misfortune' (quoted in Gustafson, 1986, p.223). In so doing, Savage hoped 'to make an end to poverty', to safeguard orphans and invalids 'against want and neglect', and to free dependent individuals from being 'an economic burden to relatives or friends' (p.226). While these high ambitions were never fully realised, New Zealand's new social assistance programmes attracted considerable international interest and much acclaim. Moreover, for at least four decades following the passage of the Social Security Act there was solid, bipartisan support for the principles underpinning the welfare state. Such support was no doubt sustained by a reasonable level of economic growth, low unemployment, relative social stability, and a perception that the various forms of social assistance provided by the state were effective, fair and affordable.

Since the early 1980s, however, support for the welfare state—both in New Zealand and in many other industrialised democracies—has been dissipating. In part, this has been the result of fiscal pressures, prompted in their turn by lower economic growth and higher unemployment, an ageing population, increased demand for health and education services, and changing family structures. In part, too, it has stemmed from public concerns over welfare abuse and fraud, and opposition to rising average tax rates. But this waning support has also reflected a significant shift in the intellectual climate, most notably the growing ascendancy of market liberalism and neo-conservatism, and a corresponding loss of confidence on the part of social democrats and socialists. Whereas Savage's description of the welfare state as 'applied Christianity' (p.216) would once have received near-universal endorsement, a

3

rather different view has become increasingly prevalent. In fact, many no longer regard the welfare state as a 'blessing' but as a 'curse'; not as the embodiment of sound economic and ethical principles but as a genuine threat to a nation's economic, social and moral vitality. Roger Kerr, one of New Zealand's leading market liberals and the Executive Director of the Business Roundtable, has even characterised the welfare state as one of the 'seven deadly economic sins of the twentieth century' (Kerr, 1997).

While few policy specialists take such an extreme position, there is no shortage of detailed critiques of comprehensive, state-funded, social assistance programmes of the kind operating in New Zealand (for recent examples see Green, 1996; Jones, 1997). Critics claim, for instance, that the welfare state has:

• failed to reduce poverty or overcome disadvantage;
• provided disproportionate assistance to those who need it least;
• encouraged dependency on welfare benefits;
• promoted 'provider capture' and generated large, insensitive and inflexible bureaucracies;
• undermined the traditional family unit;
• displaced private and voluntary welfare;
• undermined personal responsibility; and
• created perverse incentives, thereby discouraging employment and undermining economic growth.

According to Kerr (1997, p.310), the welfare state not only 'wastes money' but also 'destroys families and wastes lives'.

Whatever the empirical validity of such claims—and many are highly suspect—governments in a number of countries have embarked upon major changes to their systems of social assistance. In the United States, recent Republican and Democratic administrations have cut welfare programmes and imposed more stringent eligibility criteria. In Britain, the Conservative government (1979-97) made significant changes in key social policy areas, designed to reduce assistance levels and curb welfare dependency. More recently, the Labour government led by Tony Blair has announced plans for major social reforms, including a greater emphasis on targeted assistance.

In New Zealand, the various centre-right governments since the early 1990s have undertaken the most radical social policy changes in 60 years. While it would be an exaggeration to say that the welfare state has been dismantled, it has certainly been substantially altered. Major initiatives have included significant cuts in benefits and other forms of income support, changes in the means by which the state provides assistance (most notably in the areas of housing and health care), and a much greater emphasis on targeting. Such changes raise fundamental questions about the kind of society in which New Zealanders want to live. At stake are not merely questions

about the appropriate level of welfare benefits, but important philosophical
and ethical issues concerning the respective roles and responsibilities of
individuals, families, iwi, voluntary agencies and the state. For example, how
far should a society go in minimising economic insecurity through the
collective sharing of risks? What assistance should the state provide to those
requiring long-term residential care? What are the respective responsibilities
of families, communities and the state in relation to sole parents with young
children? What criteria should be used to determine the level of welfare
benefits? Should the receipt of social assistance depend on individual merit
(for example, whether the individual is a 'good' parent or citizen)? Should
social assistance in areas such as housing and education be provided in kind or
in the form of vouchers, and should it be tightly means-tested or funded
universally?

Such questions are not new. They have been the subject of vigorous debate
for over a century, certainly in the developed world. Moreover, they are part
of a much larger and more complex philosophical, political and theological
debate over the proper role of the state (see, for instance, Nozick, 1974; Rawls,
1972; Report of the Social Policy Committee, 1986; Royal Commission on
Social Policy, 1988a; and Treasury, 1987a). The debate is in many respects an
ethical one. It addresses such issues as the nature of a just society, the scope of
citizenship rights and welfare entitlements, the relative merits of individualis-
tic versus communitarian values, the nature and responsibilities of the family
or whānau, iwi, and voluntary agencies, and the obligations of individuals to
one another.

This chapter outlines three models of the welfare state and, against this
backdrop, briefly traces the development of social security in New Zealand. It
then considers the rationale for the major social policy initiatives in the early
1990s, summarises their content, considers their consequences, and outlines
subsequent policy developments.

Types of Welfare State

Many attempts have been made over the years to distinguish different types of
welfare state (see Castles and Mitchell, 1990; Esping-Andersen, 1990;
O'Higgins, 1987; Shannon, 1991; and Ware and Goodin, 1990). The criteria
used to make these distinctions include the level of expenditure on social
services, the range of social services funded and/or provided by the state, the
extent of income redistribution, the scope and quality of social rights, the
pattern of social stratification, the relationship between the state, the market
and the family, and the degree of targeting or selectivity. One helpful
approach is that adopted by Ware and Goodin (1990, pp.5-8), who distinguish
between three models of welfare provision or social assistance:

- a residualist, minimalist or needs-based model;
- an insurance or contributions-based model; and
- a social citizenship or rights-based model.

The first model, which has its philosophical roots in classical liberalism and has been espoused in more recent times by market liberals and neo-conservatives, expects individuals to provide for the bulk of their needs via the market, their family, or voluntary agencies and charities. The emphasis, in other words, is on self-reliance and individual responsibility. Those unable to meet their (narrowly defined) basic needs through their own efforts are entitled to state assistance, which would include education, housing, health care, and income maintenance. However, such assistance is rigorously means-tested to ensure that the state does not support those with income or assets above a certain level. The level of assistance available to those who meet the requirements is kept to an absolute minimum, in order to curb public expenditure and deter dependence on state handouts. Because social assistance is available to all those who satisfy the relevant criteria, a wealthy person who falls into abject poverty through foolishness or misfortune will be able to secure state assistance in the same way as the person who has always been poor. Although this model permits a degree of redistribution or inter-class transfer to those in need, such vertical redistribution is limited because the overall level of social assistance is low. Consequently, substantial inequality is likely.

As Ware and Goodin (1990, p.6) observe, the residualist approach was perhaps best exemplified by the Elizabethan Poor Law (1601) and subsequent British social policy, at least until the early twentieth century. In today's world, the model is not rigidly followed anywhere in the OECD. Perhaps the country that comes closest to it is the United States, but even there some important services, such as primary and secondary education, are not subject to a means test. In most OECD countries, however, there are examples of tightly targeted forms of social provision, particularly in the area of housing assistance and certain kinds of income support.

Under the insurance or contributions-based model, at least in its actuarially pure form, previous financial contributions (whether by individuals, their family, or their employer) provide the primary basis for social assistance. The size of the payments and the range of social assistance available (for example, unemployment and sickness insurance) thus depend on the level of a person's contributions rather than their financial need. In fact, some people may receive assistance such as a retirement income even though they have no need for it, while those in great need may receive nothing at all because they have no insurance cover (unless, of course, the scheme is compulsory and universal in its coverage). Under an insurance-based model, some *interpersonal* income redistribution will occur (for example, from those who enjoy permanent employment to those who experience periods of unemployment), but much of the redistribution will be *intrapersonal* (that is, over a person's life cycle—for example, from the period spent in the workforce to any period spent unemployed, incapacitated or retired). In its extreme form, such a model tends to discriminate against those who are unable to work or who spend much of their working life looking after children (most often women).

Elements of the insurance model are found in the social policies of most OECD countries, but are particularly significant in parts of Europe (for example, Austria, France, Germany, Italy and the Netherlands) On the whole, the insurance model was more important in the late nineteenth and early twentieth centuries than it is today, and even in those policy domains where it remains significant (for example, pensions, health care and unemployment benefits), it is usually supplemented by means-tested or universal social assistance programmes.

The social citizenship or rights-based model is the most recent of the three models under consideration, not emerging until the middle of the twentieth century. Under this model, which draws its inspiration from social democratic thinking, entitlement to social services and income transfers is based on a person's status as a citizen rather than on income, assets, prior earnings or contribution. Hence, all those in need of health care have a right (within certain limits) to receive the form of assistance they require free of charge (or for only a minimal fee), irrespective of their financial situation or that of their immediate family. One of the aims of this model is to provide good-quality public services for all, and to ensure that levels of income support are sufficient to enable people to participate in society, instead of merely surviving—as is the case under the residualist model. Again in contrast to the residualist model, the intention is not that the family should exhaust its capacity to provide assistance before the state intervenes, but rather that its costs should be shared, at least in part, by the whole community. Accordingly, an important goal of social policy is to enable people to become independent of their family, if that is their choice (see Esping-Andersen, 1990).

The most fully developed examples of this model are found in Scandinavia (Christensen, 1997). But even here, not all social services are available universally. For example, there is frequently a degree of means-testing in areas such as tertiary education and housing. The extent of income redistribution under this model has been the subject of considerable debate, with some scholars arguing that universal benefits often favour the middle class disproportionately. This issue will be addressed in Chapter 6. However, it is important to note that under a social citizenship model, even with a relatively proportional tax system, those on middle to high incomes are generally net contributors rather than net recipients of state assistance. In its more advanced form, the rights-based approach can be very expensive, both because of the range of assistance provided (for example, pensions, welfare benefits, tax-funded maternity leave, universal child allowances, heavily subsidised childcare, care of the elderly, health care and education) and the high levels of payment. Hence, it is only affordable if the economy performs satisfactorily, if the tax system is efficient in raising the necessary revenues, and if high levels of employment can be sustained.

In practice, most OECD countries use elements of all three models, with some social services heavily targeted, some funded (and often provided) universally, and others based on the level of contributions. However, countries vary in the degree to which they rely on any of these forms of social assistance. Broadly speaking, the general trend in OECD countries between the mid 1930s and the late 1970s was away from the residualist and insurance models towards the rights-based model. In most of continental Europe, for example, means-tested benefits generally account for no more than 5 per cent of total transfer payments or social security budgets (Barry, 1990, p.73). Since the early 1980s, however, some countries, under the influence of fiscal constraints and/or market-liberal political movements, have begun moving in the opposite direction. Interestingly, social assistance programmes have generally been more vulnerable where the rights-based or insurance-based models have been the least well established (Ware and Goodin, 1990, p.9).

The Evolution of the Welfare State in New Zealand

Developments in social policy in New Zealand have largely reflected broader international trends. On the whole, policymakers have drawn to only a limited degree on the insurance-based model, and the contributory principle has therefore remained weak. Instead, the social policy regime has been based primarily on a mixture of the residualist and rights-based models (see Castles, 1985; Cheyne et al., 1997; Easton, 1980 and 1996b; Rudd, 1997; Shannon, 1991; Stephens, 1996b; Thomson, 1991a and 1991b). Even the first Labour government's approach to income maintenance embraced a degree of means-testing. By contrast, its health and family assistance policies were largely universal in nature. The family benefit, for example, was non-means-tested and in the immediate post-war period was very generous, being worth the equivalent of 31 per cent of the after-tax old age pension in 1945 (Thomson, 1991a, p.108). Education funding in New Zealand, as in most countries, has also been mainly universal in character. Pension policy has experienced many changes during the twentieth century, being at various times heavily means-tested, partially means-tested, and universally provided. Similarly, other forms of social assistance have included both universal elements (for example, family benefit, maternity care, home care, assistance for foster parents and the disabled) and targeted elements (for example, family rebate, family support, the domestic purposes benefit, the widow's benefit, the invalid's benefit, the sickness benefit and most forms of housing assistance) (see Koopman-Boyden and Scott, 1984). Importantly, during the first half of the twentieth century, policymakers gave considerable emphasis to ensuring that families—and particularly the male heads of households—received an adequate wage income (see Castles, 1985). A similar pattern was evident in Australia. Since the 1970s, there has been a greater reliance on using the tax system rather than wages policy to assist low-income families.

By the early 1980s, the bulk of social expenditure, including education, health care and some forms of income maintenance (such as national superannuation and student allowances), was largely non-means-tested. This policy regime was undergirded and made more affordable by a relatively low rate of unemployment. By 1981, however, registered unemployment had reached 3 per cent of the labour force, and by 1983 it was over 5 per cent. The rising level of unemployment, coupled with a protracted period of low economic growth, generated mounting fiscal pressures for significant changes to the character of the welfare state. Such pressures were matched by growing ideological pressures from certain policy advisers and interest groups. In particular, the Treasury (1987a and 1990) and the New Zealand Business Roundtable (1987 and 1988) argued for a substantial policy shift away from a rights-based approach towards a much more targeted or residualist social policy regime.

In response to these pressures the fourth Labour government (1984-90) decided, albeit reluctantly in some cases, to embrace a greater degree of targeting. For example, a tax surcharge on National Superannuation was introduced in 1985, greater assistance was provided to low-income families through the family support and youth support programmes, and part of the student allowance for 18- and 19-year-olds was means-tested from 1989 (see Koopman-Boyden, 1990; Stephens, 1987). Nevertheless, Labour rejected Treasury proposals for substantial cuts in welfare expenditure and the rigorous means-testing of most forms of social assistance, including health care.

Also important in this context was Labour's substantial flattening of the tax rate scale and its greater reliance on indirect taxes (see Stephens, 1990). This had three major consequences that are relevant here. First, it reduced the progressivity of the tax system, thereby increasing income inequality. Second, it put in place a top marginal tax rate of 33 cents in the dollar, one of the lowest such rates within the OECD. By so doing, the Labour government reduced the potential revenue available to the state, and arguably made a greater reliance on targeting necessary for fiscal reasons (particularly during a period of low growth). Third, the new tax regime made it easier politically to defend a greater degree of targeting. For one thing, it was possible to argue that, as a result of the lower tax rates, those on higher incomes could more readily afford to pay for their social services. For another, the equity arguments for targeting became more difficult to refute. Without doubt, therefore, the flattening of tax rates in the late 1980s influenced the direction of social policy during the 1990s.

Social Policy Developments in the 1990s

Since the general election in October 1990, New Zealand has had a series of centre-right administrations: a majority National government between late 1990 and September 1994; a series of mainly minority governments (including two short-lived coalitions) between September 1994 and December 1996; and a majority National/New Zealand First coalition government after December 1996. Following Labour's resounding defeat in October 1990, there was some expectation that the newly elected National government would continue the previous administration's largely incrementalist approach to the reform of the welfare state. For instance, National had committed itself during the election campaign to abolishing the surtax on superannuation, maintaining the existing level of public expenditure on health care, and abolishing the standard tertiary fee of $1,300 per annum. Against this, however, senior members of the party had talked of undertaking a significant restructuring of welfare benefits, reducing overall public expenditure, and eliminating the fiscal deficit. In the event, the policy decisions announced in late 1990 and in the 1991 Budget were anything but incremental. On the contrary, National embarked upon a major transformation of most aspects of New Zealand's welfare state. This included large cuts in the value of most welfare benefits, a significant increase in the degree of targeting in education, health care and income maintenance, and major changes to the means by which social assistance is delivered, especially in health care and housing. Since these changes were announced, developments in the social policy arena have been characterised by the following features:

- a protracted, and often controversial, period during which the major policy proposals, especially in relation to ACC, health care and housing, were gradually implemented;
- the non-implementation of some key proposals as a result of unforeseen administrative complexities and political opposition;
- the gradual, and in some cases significant, modification of the major policy changes in areas like ACC, health care and housing in response to evidence of unsatisfactory or undesirable impacts, together with continuing popular protest;
- the implementation over a two-year period (mid-1996 to mid-1998) of a substantial tax reduction and social policy programme, ostensibly designed 'to assist, strengthen, and empower low- and middle-income families' (Birch, 1996a, p.8);

- a modest return to universal coverage in several areas of social policy and an increase in public expenditure on certain social services following the formation of the National/New Zealand First Coalition in late 1996;
- an overwhelming public rejection, in a referendum in late September 1997, of the Coalition government's proposal for a compulsory retirement savings scheme; and
- the commencement of a further series of reviews during 1997 of various aspects of social assistance with the aim of reducing so-called 'welfare dependency', establishing work for the dole schemes, introducing a code of social responsibility and developing the 'Strengthening Families Strategy' (see Peters, 1998a; Preston, 1997; Sowry, 1997; St John, 1997a).

The details of these and related policy changes during the 1990s are outlined elsewhere in this volume. The intention here, therefore, is to provide a brief overview of the key changes, and comment briefly on their main objectives and impact.

The Rationale for National's Social Policy Revolution in the Early 1990s

National's initial social policy decisions in the early 1990s were based on a range of ideological, philosophical and economic considerations. Fundamentally, there was a perception, certainly on the part of the market liberals within National's caucus and among many of the government's senior public service advisers, that the public sector was too large and that the state absorbed too great a percentage of GDP. For example, Minister of Finance Ruth Richardson maintained that New Zealand had experienced 'decades of chronic overspending by the state' (1991, p.7), and that the heart of the country's problems was 'the crushing burden of government spending' (1990, p.17). Interestingly, at that particular time the level of public expenditure as a proportion of GDP was around 40 per cent, which was broadly in line with the average within the OECD, and substantially less than that of some of the small, yet successful, European states (for example, Denmark and Norway). Nor was there any conclusive empirical evidence at the time that the size of the public sector was a major contributor to New Zealand's economic woes (see Castles and Dowrick, 1990).

A more compelling short-term influence on National's decision to cut social expenditure in 1991 was the size of the Budget deficit (see Dalziel, 1992a). When Labour introduced its 1990 Budget, the Treasury expected a deficit of around 2.8 per cent of GDP during the 1990/91 financial year, falling to 1.9 per cent in the following year. Three months later, however, when the Treasury prepared its post-election briefing papers for the incoming government, the deficit forecast had widened to 4.8 per cent for 1991/92 and 5.7 per cent for 1992/93. This rapid deterioration reflected both a slackening in economic growth and a rise in expenditure. But whatever their immediate cause, deficits of this magnitude were regarded by the government's economic advisers as unacceptably large and likely to impact negatively on the country's medium-term growth. Since any increase in taxes to reduce the deficit was deemed to be undesirable (because the public sector was already too large), there was no option—given the relevant forecasts and economic assumptions —but to reduce government expenditure. Moreover, with almost two-thirds of total public expenditure devoted to income transfers, health, housing and education, cuts in these areas were unavoidable.

A further argument for reform was the claim that social assistance was poorly targeted. It was claimed, for instance, that many of those who received state assistance in the form of subsidised health care or education could readily pay for it themselves, and that a disproportionate amount of assistance went to those in least need. This was seen as being both inequitable and inefficient (see Chapter 6). The solution, in Richardson's view, was to introduce a much more rigorous system of means-testing:

> This Government believes that, in general, those individuals and families with reasonable means should attend to their own needs. As a broad principle, the top third of all income earners can be expected to meet most of the cost of their social services (1990, p.20).

Although this broad principle was never fully implemented, the opposition of senior National politicians to universal forms of social assistance played a pivotal role in determining the direction of social policy during the 1990s.

Another concern on the part of the government and its advisers related to the perverse incentives generated by the level and structure of welfare benefits (see Chapter 13). For instance, it was argued that the margin between benefit rates and (post-tax) wages (or the so-called 'replacement rate') was too small, so that many of those on benefits had little incentive to find employment. Since any increase in wages was likely to generate additional inefficiencies and exacerbate unemployment, the only solution, it was claimed, was to reduce benefit rates. Equally, it was argued that the existing state providers in areas like housing and health care were seriously deficient. According to the critics, the public organisations responsible for the delivery of social services were bureaucratic, wasteful, inefficient and inadequately accountable. What was required was greater competition among providers, enhanced opportunities for private provision, and stronger political and managerial accountability on the part of public providers.

Finally, underpinning National's social policy changes in the early 1990s was a rejection of the long-accepted proposition that the welfare state should be designed to ensure that all citizens, irrespective of their socio-economic background, were 'able to feel a sense of participation in and belonging to the community' (Royal Commission on Social Security, 1972, p.65). Instead, it was contended that the state should provide no more than a 'modest safety net' for those unable to meet their own needs (see Shipley, 1991, p.13).

In announcing the first major programme of social policy changes in December 1990, Prime Minister Jim Bolger claimed that National's social philosophy was based on four key principles: fairness, self-reliance, efficiency, and greater personal choice (see Bolger, 1990, pp.11-12). He defined 'fairness' as ensuring that those in 'genuine need' have 'adequate access to government assistance', and that 'those who can make greater provision for their own needs should be encouraged to do so' (p.11). 'Self-reliance' was taken to mean that policies should be designed to 'increase the ability and incentives to [sic] individuals to take care of themselves' (p.12). 'Efficiency' was defined in terms of achieving the 'highest possible value from each tax dollar spent', while 'greater personal choice' was about encouraging 'alternative providers of health, education, housing, and welfare services' (p.12).

However well intentioned, these principles—at least as defined in Bolger's policy statement—were unsatisfactory and incomplete. Nor were they applied appropriately or consistently by his government. For example, it soon became apparent—from the huge growth in the demand for food parcels from voluntary agencies in the aftermath of the benefit cuts in April 1991—that the new structure of welfare benefits did not provide 'adequate' assistance (see Chapter 13). Similarly, the definition of efficiency as simply getting the 'highest possible value from each tax dollar spent' is a very narrow one. If the pursuit of this objective results in a substantial shifting of costs to the private sector or the household sector, then overall efficiency may well be undermined. Nor does a greater reliance on private provision necessarily increase consumer choice and preserve equal access to good-quality services for those of limited means (see Chapters 8 and 12).

Specific Measures

National's objective of reshaping the welfare state in the early 1990s included the following specific measures (see also Easton, 1997a; Kelsey, 1997a):

Benefits: There were substantial cuts in the nominal value of most welfare benefits (with the exception of the invalid's benefit), effective from 1 April 1991; much stricter eligibility criteria for all benefits; the abolition of the universal family benefit; new rules governing the stand-down periods before unemployed people are entitled to receive a benefit (up to six months in some cases); and an increase in the age at which youth rates no longer apply, from 20 to 25 (see Richardson, 1990). Overall, these changes substantially reduced the disposable incomes of most beneficiaries, in some cases by up to 30 per cent (see Chapter 13; Waldegrave and Frater, 1991).

Pensions: The 1991 Budget heralded major changes to the Guaranteed Retirement Income (GRI) (see Shipley, 1991; Chapter 15). But rather than abolishing the unpopular surtax, as had been promised, the government outlined plans for a much more tightly targeted regime. In the event, its proposed changes proved to be neither politically nor economically sustainable. Hence, a new package of changes was announced in early November 1991. As a result, the surtax was increased to 25 cents in the dollar (up 5 cents) from 1 April 1992; the 'free zone' of earnings before the surtax applied was substantially reduced; the value of the GRI was reduced in real terms with no inflation adjustment for two years; and the age of eligibility for superannuation was to be gradually increased over ten years from 60 to 65, with those between the ages of 60 and 64 without work or other income having to live on the unemployment benefit.

Health Care: A radical overhaul of the health care system was another central feature of the 1991 Budget (see Upton, 1991). As will be discussed in Chapter 8, the major changes included the replacement of the fourteen area health boards with 23 semi-commercial Crown health enterprises (CHEs); the separation of funding, purchasing and provision; the introduction of part-charges for hospital services from 1 February 1992; and a tighter targeting of health care assistance. As part of the new targeting regime, the population was initially divided into three groups, with a community services card being introduced for identification purposes. Also foreshadowed in the 1991 Budget was the introduction of compulsory private health insurance, with the premiums of low-income individuals and families being subsidised by the state. This proposal, however, received very little public support and was quickly abandoned.

Housing: In July 1993, a targeted cash subsidy known as the accommodation supplement was introduced to replace the previous mix of cash and in-kind assistance, which had included subsidised rental accommodation and housing loans from the Housing Corporation and accommodation supplements for beneficiaries from the Department of Social Welfare (see Luxton, 1991). In addition, the Housing Corporation (a non-profit social service agency) was replaced by Housing New Zealand (a Crown-owned company with a legislative mandate and governance structure not unlike a state-owned enterprise). As a result of the new policy, most Housing Corporation tenants experienced significant rental increases as their rents were adjusted to market rates.

Education: The most significant changes in education policy in the early 1990s were those affecting tertiary education (see L. Smith, 1991). As will be outlined in Chapter 11, National introduced a much more targeted system of student allowances in 1992, with all students aged between 16 and 24 having their allowances means-tested on the basis of parental income. Equally important, significant changes were made to the funding of tuition costs. Under a new Study Right scheme, some students received subsidies of 95 per cent of their course costs, while others had their subsidies cut to 75 per cent over a period of three years. In order to assist access to tertiary institutions under the new policy regime, a government-funded, income-contingent loans scheme was introduced.

Accident Compensation: While retaining the no-fault concept introduced in the mid-1970s, National made changes to most of the key features of the accident compensation scheme (see Birch, 1991; Chapter 9). In so doing, it undermined most of the principles on which previous arrangements had been based, such as community responsibility, comprehensive entitlement, complete rehabilitation, and real compensation. For instance, the responsibility for funding non-work accidents was shifted from employers to employees, with the costs of motor vehicle accidents being funded through licence fees and a special levy on petrol. Lump-sum payments for permanent disability were replaced by a disability allowance, and lump-sum payments for pain, suffering and loss of enjoyment of life were abolished.

Integrated Targeting Regime: One of the more radical policy initiatives foreshadowed in the 1991 Budget was a proposal to introduce a more comprehensive and integrated system of targeting, with the 'core family', as it was termed, as the unit of assessment (see Prebble et al., 1991; Shipley, 1991, pp.43-53; Chapter 6). Under the proposed system, a single, uniform abatement rate of perhaps 50 cents in the dollar would be applied to most forms of social assistance, excluding housing and compulsory education. The preferred approach was for each form of assistance to abate sequentially, starting with benefits and family support, moving next to health premiums and finally to student allowances. In order to implement a sophisticated targeting regime of this kind, consideration was given to the introduction of so-called 'smart cards' and family accounts (see Prebble et al., 1991; Shipley, 1991, pp.81-5). National quickly rejected the idea of smart cards, but officials worked on the concept of family accounts for several years before it was finally abandoned for reasons of administrative complexity and political unacceptability (Boston, 1994).

Policy Outcomes

The overall impacts—political, economic, distributional and social—of National's changes to the welfare state in the early 1990s were significant and enduring, and in many cases sobering and distressing. While more detailed accounts of these impacts are provided in subsequent chapters, some brief comments are in order here.

In political terms, most of the measures proved to be very unpopular, and were largely responsible for the dramatic fall in support for National at the

1993 general election. They also contributed to a loss of confidence in the political system, and were an important factor in the demise of the first-past-the-post electoral system and its replacement by a system of proportional representation following the electoral referendum in late 1993 (see Vowles et al., 1995).

The economic effects of the changes, especially the benefit cuts, have been the subject of some controversy (see Dalziel, 1992a; Chapter 13). Some economists have claimed that the cuts exacerbated the recession in the early 1990s, while others have pointed to their positive longer-term impact on fiscal balances and labour market incentives. But whatever the final verdict, the short-term impact of the various changes on the fiscal deficit was much less favourable than had been anticipated by the government's advisers. Among the many reasons for this was the fact that some of the key measures proved to be politically unsustainable, while others, most notably the health reforms, failed to deliver their expected efficiency savings (see Chapter 8).

As to their distributional and social consequences, the evidence is clear-cut: the social policy changes, combined with the impact of the Employment Contracts Act (see Chapter 7), accentuated income inequalities, intensified the incidence and severity of poverty, and contributed to a greater sense of social exclusion and alienation (Easton, 1997a; Kelsey, 1997a; Moore, 1996; Stephens, 1992; Waldegrave and Frater, 1991; Whale, 1993; Chapter 13). Voluntary agencies reported a huge increase in demand for food and clothing during the early 1990s, with growing numbers of people unable to meet rental and mortgage payments. Furthermore, it was not only beneficiaries and their families who found themselves unable to make ends meet, but also many of those on low wages in full-time employment. To compound matters, National's social policy changes failed to achieve one of their key objectives, namely to reduce the number of people of working age receiving welfare benefits. As will be explained in Chapter 13, the number of recipients of various categories of benefit (including the domestic purposes and invalid's benefits) has continued to increase during the 1990s. For the government, therefore, the problem of 'welfare dependency' remains unresolved.

Subsequent Policy Developments

Since the comprehensive social policy changes of the early 1990s, policy developments have been much more ad hoc and incrementalist in nature. Throughout the decade there has been continuing political rhetoric from the various centre-right administrations, and market-liberal parties such as ACT, about the need to reduce welfare expenditure, overcome welfare dependency, target resources more effectively and enhance economic incentives. Yet it was evident by 1993/94 that much of the revolutionary zeal of the early 1990s had dissipated. It was not that the advocates of market liberalism had been forced to recant or had abandoned their quest for a genuinely residualist model of the welfare state, but rather that they had lost the political initiative. This was reflected in a gradual rejection of virtually all the major reform proposals, including the idea of an integrated system of targeting, the development of family accounts, the establishment of competing private health care purchasers, and a substantial privatisation of health care funding. Another sign of the resurgence of political pragmatism was the quest for multi-party agreements on some key policy issues, in the interests of securing greater policy stability and de-politicising controversial matters. The best example was in the case of superannuation, where a short-lived Accord was eventually hammered out between National, Labour and the Alliance in the run-up to the 1993 general election (see Chapter 15).

Governments during the mid-to-late 1990s also demonstrated a willingness to modify some of the policies introduced in the early 1990s in order to stem political opposition and mitigate some of their worst (and often unintended) consequences. For instance:

- the hospital part-charges were gradually withdrawn;
- the eligibility criteria for the special needs benefit were relaxed;
- frequent modifications were made to the regulations affecting ACC;
- there was a gradual easing of targeting in a number of policy areas (for example, primary health care for young children and long-stay geriatric care);
- the structure and level of the accommodation supplement were altered in response to clear evidence of acute housing needs;
- the attempt to apply a competitive, commercial model to the secondary health care sector has been all but abandoned; and
- there has been a substantial increase in health expenditure towards the end of the decade.

Such modifications should not be interpreted as a fundamental rejection of the residualist model or a major step back towards a social citizenship model. Rather they reflect the enormous administrative and political difficulties associated with changes of the scale and complexity of those initiated in the early 1990s, not to mention the serious social costs they generated, the institutional inertia, the failure to win substantial mass support for a radical transformation of the welfare state (especially with respect to health care and education), the political effectiveness of a number of powerful lobby groups such as Grey Power and the Coalition for Public Health, and the restraining influence of electoral reform on the power of the executive (see Boston, Levine, McLeay and Roberts, 1996). Yet if the ambitions of the more radical reformers in the early 1990s were thwarted, there can be no denying that the welfare state in New Zealand in the late 1990s is significantly different from that of a decade earlier. The state's role as a provider of services has been reduced, and this trend is continuing. More forms of social assistance are targeted. There are significant costs for those wishing to study at the tertiary level. And the assistance provided to most of those who experience temporary or permanent loss of income (for example, through unemployment, illness, disability, accident or retirement) is less generous than previously, and often more difficult to obtain.

Moreover, despite a period of relatively robust economic growth and the achievement of significant fiscal surpluses, recent governments have firmly resisted calls to restore welfare benefits to their pre-1991 levels. Indeed, they have made a virtue of keeping a tight rein on public expenditure while using the fiscal surpluses to repay public debt and reduce taxes for those on middle to high incomes (see Peters, 1998a). Yet such an approach will not only accentuate existing inequalities (see Dalziel, 1996; Chapter 4), but also constrain the capacity of future governments to address the problems of poverty and social exclusion (unless, of course, they are prepared to reverse some of the tax cuts or are blessed with sustained economic growth).

Whither the Welfare State?

As the twentieth century draws to a close, the debate over the welfare state in New Zealand remains very much alive. At opposite ends of the spectrum are two radically divergent views. The first is of a welfare state that is largely residualist in nature. Under this model, the functions of the state would be reduced to 'an essential core' (Menzies, 1991, p.5). Accordingly, the funding of health care and education (especially at the tertiary level) would be transferred increasingly to the private sector, and all forms of social assistance, including superannuation, would be stringently means-tested. The eligibility criteria for welfare benefits would be tightened even further, with private welfare agencies expected to carry an ever-increasing burden of caring for those unable to provide for their own needs. Under this model, even compulsory education would no longer be free. As a report published by the Business Roundtable argued in the early 1990s:

> [T]he government has a responsibility to raise taxes and finance those who genuinely could not otherwise send their children to school ... It would be perfectly possible, and probably much more desirable, for the state to take less in taxes and only assist those in need (Sexton, 1991, p.6).

The alternative vision is of a welfare state similar to that found in Scandinavia and other parts of northern Europe. Under this model, education and health care would be (more or less) fully funded by the state; most forms of social assistance would be provided on a universal basis; and those who experience a temporary or permanent loss of income would be guaranteed a reasonable standard of living. Full employment and high labour-market participation rates would be key policy objectives. However, they would not be pursued through efforts to increase the margin between welfare benefits and post-tax wages, as in the residualist model, but rather through heavy public investment in training and research, and the provision of high-quality childcare facilities.

Plainly, both models have their strengths and their weaknesses. Nonetheless, as will be argued in subsequent chapters, there is a strong case to be made, based on a wide range of ethical and empirical considerations, for New Zealand adopting a model closer to the latter than the former. In the spirit of academic inquiry which guided the contributors to this volume, readers are encouraged to explore the evidence and reach their own conclusions.

CHAPTER TWO

SOCIAL JUSTICE AND THE WELFARE STATE

JONATHAN BOSTON

The comprehensive welfare states that emerged in most industrialised societies during the first half of the twentieth century were the product of multiple forces and pressures. Arguably the most important of these was the quest for greater justice or fairness, and in particular for greater social or distributive justice. Of course there has never been any agreement about what social justice means, let alone what moral weight it should receive (relative to other notions of justice, for example, or to other values altogether). Rather, there are widely divergent conceptions of what constitutes a just social order (see Barrett, 1988; Cheyne et al., 1997; Commission on Social Justice, 1993 and 1994; Lebacqz, 1986). This is readily apparent from any cursory analysis of the views of contemporary political philosophers (for example, Barry, 1973 and 1989; Dworkin, 1989; Miller, 1976 and 1992; Rawls, 1972) and the various principles of justice advanced by the major ideological traditions of the twentieth century.

In New Zealand, as in most other OECD countries, the main influences on conceptions of a just society have been the social-democratic tradition and various strands of liberalism (most recently, market liberalism). While social democrats and market liberals differ on many issues, for the most part they share a commitment to a number of basic principles:

- human life is precious and human beings are of equal moral worth; they are thus entitled to equal consideration and respect;
- the institutions of a liberal representative democracy not only give expression to many intrinsically desirable values, but are also the proper vehicle for the pursuit of economic and social reform;
- individual autonomy, freedom and the protection of property rights are highly important, and the state (which is the legitimate repository of a society's collective responsibilities) should guarantee an extensive range of civil and political rights; and
- the state should seek to ensure that citizens are able to satisfy their basic needs.

Of course, the adequacy, meaning and policy implications of these principles remain the focus of much debate. Among the many areas of continuing disagreement are:

- the nature and scope of basic human needs, and the proper role of the state in meeting such needs;
- the proper balance between individual and collective responsibility (and the sharing of risk), especially in areas such as health care and income support;
- whether the state is obliged to provide only a 'modest safety net' for those unable to meet their own needs, or a standard of living more comparable to that of the average citizen;
- the relative priority that should be given to the principle of need compared with other principles of justice, such as rewarding people for their contribution, merit or effort;
- the nature of the rights that should be guaranteed by the state, and in particular whether they should extend beyond the sphere of 'negative' rights (that is, rights not to be interfered with) to embrace a full range of 'positive' rights (that is, rights to be treated in certain ways), including welfare rights; and
- whether the principle of equality should apply solely to political and civil rights, or whether it should be extended to embrace opportunities, social status or condition, and outcomes; in other words, what kinds of inequality should be regarded as unjust, and what efforts should be made to reduce or eliminate them?

Until the early 1980s, social-democratic approaches generally held sway, both in New Zealand and in many other OECD countries (Boston, 1993; Easton, 1980). Accordingly, there was a reasonably strong commitment to progressive taxes, universal forms of social assistance, and an active role for the state as a provider, as well as a funder, of various social services. Moreover, while one of the objectives of such policies was to achieve greater social justice via *interpersonal* redistribution (that is, from better-off individuals to less well-off individuals), an equally important objective was to transfer resources on an *intrapersonal* basis (that is, from one part of a person's lifetime to another), thereby reducing the 'alternating cycles of want and plenty' that were a feature of social life before the introduction of comprehensive social assistance programmes (see Falkingham et al., 1993, p.44).

Since the 1980s, support for market liberalism, especially at the elite level, has gathered momentum. This has been reflected in significant policy changes, many of which are described elsewhere in this volume (for example, cuts in welfare benefits, greater targeting of social assistance, less emphasis on racial and gender equity, and a less progressive tax system). Leading advocates of market liberalism in this part of the world have included the New

Zealand Business Roundtable (for example, Green, 1996; Kerr, 1997; Robertson, 1997), the Australian-based Centre for Independent Studies (for example, Jones, 1997), the Treasury (1987a; 1990), various current and former politicians (for example, Sir Roger Douglas, Richard Prebble and Ruth Richardson), and a number of economic commentators (for example, Gareth Morgan).

The continuing debate over the welfare state has both empirical and ethical dimensions: it is simultaneously about facts and values, and in various ways the two are closely interrelated. At the empirical level, there are important issues such as the impact of taxes on work incentives, the relationship between public expenditure and economic growth, and the impact of particular forms of social assistance on human behaviour. Without denying the importance of such questions (some of which are dealt with elsewhere in this volume), the *primary* purpose of this chapter is to explore some of the conflicting conceptions of social justice, and their implications for public policy. In particular, the chapter examines and evaluates the philosophical challenge posed to the welfare state by market liberalism. While most of the issues addressed here are not country-specific in nature, New Zealand examples and authors have been deliberately included to illustrate the subjects under discussion. For reasons of space, no attempt has been made to examine the full range of justifications for, and challenges to, the welfare state (see Barr, 1994). Nor is consideration given to some of the recent philosophical debates between liberals and communitarians, and between neutralists and perfectionists, over the nature of 'the good society' and the proper role of the state.

The Market-Liberal Critique of the Welfare State

Market liberalism represents a relatively diverse body of thought, bounded on one side by libertarianism and on the other by various strands of reformist liberalism, communitarianism and Christian democracy. Whereas libertarians (for example, Nozick, 1974) maintain that only a minimal state dedicated to the protection of certain inviolable civil and political rights is morally justified, most market liberals accept that the state is morally justified in using its coercive powers to raise revenue for social purposes, including the satisfaction of basic human needs for those unable to provide for themselves. Likewise, whereas communitarians and Christian democrats place a high value on social solidarity, the fostering of communities and social institutions (especially the family), and the use of co-operative models of economic management, market liberals stress the importance of enhancing individual liberty, maximising choice and minimising state paternalism. They argue that individuals are generally the best judges of their own interests, and that in most cases socially optimal outcomes will be achieved by using economic incentives and allowing individuals to engage in voluntary contracting via relatively free, competitive markets (see Goodin, 1990).

Market liberals are by no means in agreement as to the nature of a just society. The late Austrian economist and market liberal, Friedrich von Hayek (1976), argued for example that social justice is a meaningless concept. This conclusion was based on his highly contentious claim that, since the results of allocating income, wealth and property via market processes can be neither foreseen nor intended, they cannot be meaningfully described as just or unjust. Thus, while Hayek defended the idea of the state providing a minimal welfare safety net to assist the poor, this stance was not based on considerations of justice but largely on prudence. In other words, he believed that a safety net was necessary in order to maintain political stability and protect a liberal constitutional order. Without it, he contended, there was a risk of revolution. Hayek's view of social justice has by no means been accepted by all market liberals, let alone those of a more social-democratic orientation (Plant, 1985). Nonetheless, market liberals have generally supported Hayek's opposition to the idea of a comprehensive welfare state, and the egalitarian principles with which it is commonly associated.

The starting point for most market liberals is the contention that freedom or liberty is the most important value. Accordingly, the state's first priority must be the protection and enforcement of political and civil rights. Beyond this, the state is justified in providing certain public goods (defence and recreational areas, for example) and ensuring that all citizens have their basic needs met. But while supporting a minimal safety net as a 'guarantee against the failure of personal effort and private welfare' (Kerr, 1997, p.311), market liberals tend to reject the idea that the state has a moral obligation to provide a standard of living beyond a bare minimum. In other words, the achievement of a higher threshold lies within the domain of charity, not justice. They are equally sceptical about the idea that the state should guarantee not only political and civil rights but also a wide range of economic and social rights, such as those outlined in the International Covenant on Economic, Social and Cultural Rights (1966). These include the right to work, the right to adequate housing, and the right to education. Such rights are criticised for being costly, vague, 'impracticable', 'internally self-contradictory' and 'hopelessly utopian' (Robertson, 1997, p.4).

Furthermore, market liberals generally reject egalitarian principles of social justice, including the equalisation of outcomes and social status, and equality of opportunity. At a philosophical level, such principles are challenged on numerous grounds. First, it is claimed that they represent a threat to liberty. This is because they justify the use of state coercion to reduce certain kinds of inequality, thus undermining individual property rights and the right for people to enjoy the fruits of their labour. The second and related claim is that egalitarian conceptions of a just society place too little weight on desert-based principles. Thus many people are denied their just rewards, while others receive undeserved benefits such as generous welfare payments, free education and heavily subsidised health care. Third, it is argued that most egalitarian principles are vague about the degree of inequality they sanction (Gray, 1992, p.33). They are thus of little practical use to policymakers, quite apart from being morally dubious.

Market liberals also object to the emphasis that egalitarian principles place on 'relational properties' or interpersonal comparisons (Gray, 1992, p.38). In particular, it is argued that where such principles constitute the *entire* foundation of morality, they imply that what matters is not a person's well-being *per se*, but their well-being in relation to other people. According to Raz (1986, p.235), they imply that:

> ... the happiness of a person does not matter except if there are other happy people. Nor is there any reason to avoid harming or hurting a person except on the ground that there are others who are unharmed and unhurt.

At the empirical level, market liberals reject comprehensive welfare states on the grounds that they are economically damaging, socially and morally corrosive and ultimately self-defeating (see Kerr, 1997). They are economically damaging because the high tax rates required undermine work incentives, thwart entrepreneurial activity and reduce investment. In turn, these outcomes slow the rate of economic growth and exacerbate unemployment. The net result is a lower overall standard of living and more limited employment opportunities. There is thus a stark choice to be made—between welfare and wealth, between egalitarianism and prosperity. The best way to help the poor, in short, is not through extensive income redistribution but through economic growth, which potentially makes everyone richer.

It is argued that comprehensive welfare states are socially and morally corrosive because they undermine notions of individual and family responsibility and damage the fabric of family life. They also threaten the richness and vitality of civil society by undercutting the role played by voluntary organisations such as charitable foundations, self-help groups and co-operative societies. Where too many risks are collectivised via the state, self-reliance and private charity are replaced by individual irresponsibility and welfare dependency. Thus the breakdown of the traditional family unit and the substantial growth in the number of sole parents in recent decades are largely blamed on the provision of social assistance by the state: Likewise, enforcing a minimum wage and providing unemployment benefits to school-leavers are blamed for the high rates of youth unemployment and the related problems of crime and violence in the community. It is argued that unless welfare benefits are cut and eligibility criteria significantly tightened, social cohesion and stability will be seriously undermined. Conversely, if individuals are to behave responsibly, if communities are to be rebuilt and if civil society is to flourish, there is a need to de-collectivise many risks, and to rely to a much greater extent on market mechanisms such as private insurance, and on voluntary support services.

Finally, it is claimed that comprehensive welfare states are ultimately self-defeating because they not only reduce efficiency and economic growth but also create new and serious inequalities. As a result, the very people for whom the assistance was intended are often left worse off in real terms, or at least worse off than they would have been under a less interventionist system. Moreover, it is argued that many interventions to relieve relative poverty may be unnecessary, because such conditions tend to be temporary and self-correcting (see Barker, 1996). A further criticism relates to the claimed tendency for the middle class to 'capture' a disproportionate share of the benefits arising from state provision, most notably in education and health care (see Chapter 6).

In short, market liberals view comprehensive welfare states as philosophi-cally flawed and counter-productive. As Richardson (1995, p.208) has said of the New Zealand welfare state:

> It set out to reduce poverty and ended up increasing poverty. It set out to reduce income inequality and ended up increasing inequality. It set out to allow people to live in dignity, and ended up creating ghettos where lawlessness and hopeless-ness are rife. If that is success, its ways must be mysterious indeed.

An Evaluation of the Market-Liberal Critique

How robust are these arguments against a comprehensive welfare state and the associated principles of social justice? While the concerns raised by market liberals deserve careful attention, many of their objections lack substance. Let us explore these objections, beginning with the satisfaction of basic human needs.

The Satisfaction of Basic Needs

Although most market liberals accept that the state ought to have a role in ensuring that citizens are able to satisfy their basic human needs, they are quick to point out the serious conceptual and practical problems posed by the concept of 'need'. Common objections to needs-based arguments include:

- the distinction between genuine (or objective) needs and mere wants is often unclear;
- many so-called needs appear to be culturally, economically or socially determined rather than universal in nature;

- some people have needs that cannot be fully satisfied (that is, they are insatiable) or are extremely expensive to satisfy (for example, certain health-related conditions);
- in a pluralistic society, it is difficult to arrive at an agreed schedule of needs or to determine their relative priority or urgency;
- there is considerable scope for disagreement about which needs the state has an obligation to meet and which are the responsibility of individuals and their families;
- some societies are so poor that it is difficult for their governments to meet even the most basic satiable needs of their citizens; and
- interest groups often exploit needs-based arguments as a convenient tool for pursuing sectional advantages.

Some critics have also suggested that to talk about needs (basic or otherwise) is to invoke paternalistic judgements about other people's well-being, and that such judgements do not provide a sound basis for governmental intervention. From this perspective, public policy should be concerned with satisfying individuals' preferences rather than their needs, and doing so via cash transfers rather than in-kind provision.

It must be readily admitted that some of these objections have force (see Cheyne et al., 1997; Culyer, 1980; Miller, 1976; Ware and Goodin, 1990). Determining the boundary between needs and wants, for instance, is undoubtedly a complex and controversial matter, and what constitutes a need will vary, at least in part, according to the economic, social and cultural context. This does not mean, however, that the concept of need should be abandoned or that the state should be relieved of any responsibility for meeting the needs of its citizens. Rather, what is required is for policymakers to seek relevant and agreed criteria for identifying needs and determining their relative importance. One plausible approach is to distinguish needs and wants on the basis of whether an individual is likely to be *harmed* in some clear and demonstrable manner if a particular good or service is unavailable—or unaffordable. Thus, being denied the opportunity, for financial reasons, to climb in the Himalayas or ski in the Rockies is unlikely to cause a person demonstrable harm. By contrast, if they are unable because of financial hardship to participate in any kind of sport or recreation, or enjoy any form of leisure, they may well suffer physically or mentally.

If needs and wants are distinguished on the basis of the harm principle, then a *basic* need is one where a significant, severe and potentially irreversible harm is highly likely to occur if the need in question is not met (see Feinberg, 1973, p.111). For example, if individuals are denied the opportunity to learn how to read and write they are likely to be harmed in a crucial manner, by being denied access to most forms of employment and being unable to participate fully in society. Hence, primary education can be regarded as a basic need.

Similarly, if people have no food for long periods of time they will be significantly harmed, and ultimately die. Thus food is also a basic need. Other basic needs are generally considered to include clothing, shelter and health care.

While basic needs are largely, if not wholly, independent of a person's economic, social and cultural context, the same is not true of other kinds of need. In New Zealand, having hot running water in one's home is deemed by most people to constitute a need, whereas in many developing countries it is considered a luxury. Much the same applies to having a phone or an internal flush toilet. Of course, it is perfectly understandable, and to some extent justifiable, for needs to be interpreted differently in different contexts. For example, having a phone is of much less economic and social value, and thus less necessary, when few people have one than when phones are an accepted and expected feature of every household and business. Thus, the fact that the concept of need is interpreted more broadly in advanced industrialised countries than in poor, developing ones is neither surprising nor improper.

In policy terms, the critical task is to identify as precisely as possible in each particular context the range of needs it is desirable for individuals to satisfy, in the interests of justice and human well-being. This is no easy matter, and conflicting views are inevitable. In New Zealand, for example, it might be readily agreed that the state should ensure that every individual and family has access to affordable housing (see Chapter 12). However, there may be disagreement about the minimum standard of housing that is deemed appropriate, as well as the amount of space that each person needs. Similar differences are likely in regard to the cost of adequately feeding and clothing various types of household, for example a retired couple compared to a sole parent with three young children, or a married couple with two teenagers (see Chapter 13). Nevertheless, if the satisfaction of human needs is regarded as an essential condition for a just society, then such issues must be grappled with. As Chapter 13 will argue, one of the current problems in New Zealand is that the setting of benefit levels since the early 1990s has been dominated by fiscal and efficiency imperatives rather than a careful needs assessment.

A Modest Safety Net or a Higher Standard?

As noted earlier, most market liberals generally accept that the satisfaction of basic needs is critical for building a just society, but reject any suggestion that the state is obliged to do more than provide a 'modest' or 'minimum' safety net (Shipley, 1991). But is a bare minimum standard of living an acceptable threshold, particularly in relatively affluent countries like New Zealand? Many would suggest not. Philosophers such as David Copp (1992), Ronald Dworkin (1989), John Rawls (1972) and Samuel Scheffler (1976) have advanced a range of principles of justice that involve more demanding thresholds. According to the so-called 'difference principle' advocated by Rawls, for example, inequalities in the distribution of desirable social and economic goods, such as income and wealth, are justifiable only to the extent that they protect or improve the position of the least advantaged in society. Hence, if social and economic inequalities are not to 'the greatest advantage of the least advantaged' (1972, p.302), they are unjustified.

In New Zealand, many people have been attracted to the principles espoused by the Royal Commission on Social Security in 1972. According to the Commission:

> The community is responsible for giving dependent people a standard of living consistent with human dignity and approaching that enjoyed by the majority, irrespective of the cause of dependency (p.65).

In a similar fashion, the Commission argued that one of the key aims of the social welfare system should be:

> to ensure, within limitations which may be imposed by physical or other disabilities, that everyone is able to enjoy a standard of living much like the rest of the community, and thus able to feel a sense of participation in and belonging to the community (p.65).

A broadly similar approach was advocated in the *Social Justice Statement* issued by the leaders of ten Christian denominations in New Zealand in July 1993. They argued that social justice requires, among other things, 'fairness in the distribution of income, wealth and power', and that citizens are able 'to be active and productive participants in the life of society' (see Boston and Cameron, 1994).

A number of arguments have been advanced for adopting a higher income threshold or standard of living than the mere satisfaction of basic needs. If those needs are defined narrowly, as suggested above, the provision of a minimal safety net will be consistent with people merely eking out an existence. They may have sufficient food, clothing, and a roof over their heads, and have access to basic health and education services, but that is all. They will be denied many of the social and cultural opportunities available to the average citizen in a country like New Zealand. They will have difficulty participating in associations, clubs and societies, buying presents, attending plays, films or concerts, socialising in the local pub or cafe, and paying for a phone. They will thus be more limited in their capacity to use their gifts and talents, to maintain their network of social contacts and to pursue employment opportunities. Those living on the margins of society are likely to feel excluded, and this can diminish their sense of well-being. Children brought up in such circumstances will also be deprived, and may experience significant disadvantages in later life. In short, living on the bread-line is socially debilitating and disabling; it contributes to cycles of dependency rather than fostering economic independence.

It is therefore argued that although the satisfaction of basic needs is a necessary condition for achieving a just society, it is by no means a sufficient one. In particular, the least advantaged or most vulnerable members of society must have incomes that:

- enable them to live in dignity;
- are close to the average (or that of the majority of citizens); and
- enable them to participate fully in the nation's social and political life.

This has implications not only for those who are unable to earn an income, perhaps because of sickness or disability, but also for those whose labour market incomes fall below an agreed minimum level.

Two other points are worth highlighting at this juncture. First, a degree of income equalisation (a levelling down as well as a levelling up) is inevitable if such principles are to be satisfied. Second, such principles are often defended not only on the grounds that they are just or fair, but also because of a range of other claimed benefits, including enhanced political and social stability, greater industrial harmony, improved social cohesion, and enhanced standards of health and education. These outcomes, it is contended, can be expected to provide a good environment for investment and growth. Accordingly, a just society may facilitate rather than undermine economic success.

As noted earlier, principles of this kind are typically rejected by market liberals. One reason has to do with their lack of precision. What does it mean, for example, to distribute resources 'fairly' or 'equitably', or to be 'active and productive'? But many principles, values and concepts are relatively vague, or at least are open to competing interpretations. This includes values such as individual autonomy and freedom, so cherished by market liberals. However, this is not a sufficient reason for rejecting them.

Another objection to the idea of thresholds above a bare minimum safety net is that they infringe on individuals' property rights and reduce their freedom. This is because higher thresholds require additional public expenditure, resulting in a loss of liberty for those required to pay more tax. However, as noted earlier, market liberals are prepared to countenance the use of state coercion and the violation of property rights in order to ensure that basic human needs are satisfied. They thus accept that liberty, in the sense of freedom from constraints, should not be accorded an absolute or unconditional priority. A critical issue, then, concerns the point at which further redistribution in the interests of assisting the least advantaged members of society is no longer justified because of the infringement of property rights required. Plainly, market liberals believe that this point is reached as soon as citizens have had their basic needs met, or met to a sufficient degree. But the issue cannot simply be reduced to a trade-off between liberty and certain principles of distributive justice (Goodin, 1982). There is also a trade-off in relation to liberty itself. While redistribution to the poor reduces the liberty of the wealthy, it also extends the opportunities, and thus the liberty (at least in the 'positive' sense of the word), of the disadvantaged. Moreover, the gain in liberty for the disadvantaged is likely to be greater, at least in relative terms, than the loss of liberty experienced by the better-off. From this standpoint, providing a higher threshold than a minimum safety net can be justified not simply on general equity grounds but as a means of enhancing the overall liberty within society.

Finally, it has been suggested that those advocating an income threshold beyond that required to satisfy basic human needs place an undue emphasis on relational states (that is, how one person's well-being compares with another's). Yet what matters, it is argued, is a person's *actual* well-being, not their well-being in relation to others. Such arguments can be readily addressed. First, in moral terms there can be little doubt that a person's actual well-being (for example, whether they are hungry or not) is more important than their relative position (how much more hungry they are than others). At the same time, of course, a person's actual well-being can be significantly influenced by their relative situation, and thus the two conditions cannot be treated in isolation. Second, a higher income threshold can be justified without reference to a person's relational state. The principal aim of thresholds above mere subsistence level is to ensure that all citizens have a reasonable opportunity to participate fully in society, rather than being excluded, marginalised or alienated by virtue of their financial circumstances.

What Kind of Equality: Opportunities, Social Status or Outcome?

Most modern philosophical traditions, including market liberalism and social democracy, have placed a high priority on the principle of equality (Franklin, 1997). However, the kind of equality they favour (that is, their views on what precisely should be equalised), and their reasons for supporting the ideal of equality, vary greatly. Political equality via democratic institutions, and equality before the law, are critical values for both market liberals and social democrats. But beyond this there is considerable debate. Social democrats have typically been committed to the principle of equality of opportunity, and to achieving a significant measure of economic and social equality. Some also believe that justice requires the equalisation of outcomes, such as income or wealth. Market liberals, by contrast, firmly reject attempts to equalise outcomes, and while supporting a weak notion of the principle of equality of opportunity, they generally give little weight to equality of social status or condition.

Let us briefly consider some of the reasons for these different views. Equalising outcomes, rather than opportunities, has been a cherished objective of many on the left of the political spectrum. Over the years various candidates for such equalisation have been suggested, including income, wealth, welfare, well-being, happiness and utility. Each suggestion, however, poses major conceptual and practical problems, and is open to serious philosophical objections (see D. Miller, 1997). For example, equalising income is likely to be incompatible with the principle of satisfying each person's needs (or, alternatively, equalising their utility). After all, a seriously disabled person is likely to need greater assistance than someone who is able-bodied. Moreover, it can be argued that some inequalities in income and wealth are deserved, and thus justified. Beyond a certain point, efforts to achieve economic equality will undermine incentives and reduce efficiency, thereby leaving society worse off overall. Likewise, any attempt to equalise utility or happiness would pose numerous difficulties relating to measurement, interpersonal comparisons and the cost of implementation. In short, a good case can be made for the view that many inequalities are justified, or at least must be tolerated in the interests of pursuing other values or because they are too difficult to correct.

Defenders of the principle of equality of opportunity fall into at least three camps. First, there are those who argue for a broad application of this principle to most, if not all, social and economic opportunities. Yet if this goal is taken to mean the attainment of absolute equality of opportunity at each and every point in time, it can never be achieved in a world characterised by constant change, diverse social circumstances and large differences in natural abilities. Furthermore, any serious attempt to reach such a goal would require a massive redistribution of resources which is bound to be both economically and socially damaging. Alternatively, if the goal is defined as equality of lifetime opportunities or enabling people to start the race of life on an equal footing, the difficulties and objections are likely to be no less great.

Second, there are those who believe that equality of opportunity requires no more than the absence or removal of external constraints or barriers which might prevent individuals from utilising their gifts and talents. This is a minimalist position. While favoured by some market liberals, it fails to address the unfairness arising from large inequalities in the distribution of natural attributes and economic resources, via either inheritance or sheer luck.

Third, there are those who believe that the equalisation of opportunities should be confined to a number of specific 'goods' which are important for ensuring human well-being, such as employment, health care and education. For example, the opportunity for people to participate in the labour market and use their talents and skills in a productive and satisfying manner is widely seen as being critical to building a just society:

> Work, both paid and unpaid, is central to well-being ... How work is distributed, the conditions under which it is performed and the significance attached to it have an impact on every other aspect of social policy ... The primary instrument for achieving a fair and just society must be economic and social policies designed to provide wide employment opportunities (Royal Commission on Social Policy, 1988b, pp.31-2).

From a social-democratic standpoint, there is merit in arguments of this nature—or what Tobin (1970) refers to as 'specific egalitarianism'. The critical problem, however, lies in determining the range of goods to which the principle of equality of opportunity or access should apply, the quantity and quality of the goods that should be provided, and the relative priority this objective should receive.

Finally, those of a social-democratic persuasion have often argued that another necessary condition for a just society is the equalisation of social status (Crosland, 1956; D. Miller, 1997). Such equality involves 'a society in which people regard and treat one another as equals, and together form a single community without divisions of social class' (D. Miller, 1997, p.83). The aim, in other words, is to eliminate privilege and minimise social differentiation or social distance between people, so that individuals do not feel stigmatised or have their self-respect undermined because of their 'station' in life. Related values include the idea of achieving fellowship, solidarity, social cohesion and a genuine sense of community, while overcoming social exclusion (see O'Higgins, 1987; Tawney, 1931; Titmuss, 1974). According to D. Miller (1997), the achievement of social equality requires the provision of equal citizenship rights, including civil, political and welfare rights; the absence of social segregation, especially in relation to public institutions such as schools and hospitals; the avoidance of very large income differences; and the pursuit of what Walzer (1983) calls 'complex equality'. This is the idea that social goods such as education, income and public recognition ought to be allocated in different, non-cumulative ways, so that 'having more of good X gives a person no particular advantage in the competition for good Y' (D. Miller, 1997, p.95). Where this condition does not hold (in other words, where social goods are interdependent and accrue in a cumulative manner to the same person or group of people), equality of status or condition will be difficult to achieve, for some people will be privileged and seen to be privileged.

Balancing Equality and Other Considerations

While a reasonable case can be mounted to defend certain egalitarian principles, important philosophical questions remain. For example, what overall weight should be given to egalitarian principles as opposed to desert-based principles of justice, such as merit, contribution and effort? Furthermore, are inequalities of rights (or access) to scarce resources justifiable if they serve the common good, for example by creating significant efficiency gains? At the policy level, such questions are highly relevant for matters such as inheritance taxes, wage differentials, pay equity and income tax rates.

There is only space here for a very brief response. First, in relation to considerations of desert, it seems unreasonable to suggest that people should be denied any kind of differential reward for their effort, creativity or productivity.

To do so would imply that an individual's contribution or effort is beyond their control, and hence something for which they can claim no recompense. Conversely, it seems equally indefensible to suggest that desert-based principles should have absolute priority over all other values. After all, any individual contribution to social and economic wealth is likely to be small, relative to the vast physical and social infrastructure provided by countless generations (Feinberg, 1973, pp.114-16). If these two extreme positions are removed from contention, the real debate is over the proper *balance* that should be struck between egalitarian and non-egalitarian principles. Reasonable people are always likely to differ over such matters, and accordingly there is bound to be ongoing disagreement over the extent to which individuals should be rewarded, financially and in other ways, for their contribution to the economy and to society.

Second, it can be argued that the overall weight given to non-egalitarian principles of justice should reflect a society's relative wealth. Thus, when a society is poor, the first priority of the government must be to satisfy the basic needs of its citizens. However, as production and prosperity increase, there is both more scope and more justification for rewarding individuals on the basis of their contribution and effort. In these circumstances, it would seem perfectly reasonable for those who work hard and those who use their gifts wisely and creatively to enjoy higher economic returns, for example in the form of better rates of pay.

Third, the argument that some inequalities are justified because they serve the common good is perfectly plausible. For example, unequal rewards in many instances may well contribute to greater productivity. However, efficiency and incentive-based arguments of this kind justify only certain kinds of inequality, require appropriate supporting evidence, and do not necessarily justify very large salary differentials. It is interesting to note that countries with relatively narrow post-tax earnings differentials, such as Japan, Norway and Sweden, do not appear to have performed less well economically than those with much larger differentials. Huge income inequalities are now a feature of many OECD countries, including New Zealand, with some senior business executives earning seven- or even eight-figure salaries. These sums appear to be disproportionate to the actual contribution being made by such individuals, and incompatible with the quest for social equality.

Negative and Positive Rights

It is accepted by most market liberals that a just social order entails a clear specification and defence of citizenship rights. The critical issue, however, is what rights the state should guarantee. In addressing this issue, two important distinctions are frequently made. The first is between civil and political rights on the one hand, such as freedom of thought, speech, religion and peaceful assembly, and economic and social rights on the other, such as the right to private property, work, food, education, and health care. The second distinction is between negative and positive rights. Negative rights are essentially rights not to be interfered with. They include freedom from arbitrary arrest, detention or imprisonment, the right to be secure against unreasonable search or seizure, and the right not be subjected to cruel or inhumane treatment. Positive rights, by contrast, are rights to be treated in certain ways. They include the right to life, the right to a fair trial, the right to vote, and the right to adequate housing and health care. As should be evident, some civil and political rights are negative while others are positive. This same distinction applies to economic and social rights.

Whereas market liberals have strongly supported most kinds of negative rights, they have been more equivocal about embracing positive rights, especially welfare rights (see Boston, 1993; Coote, 1992; Plant, 1990, 1992a and 1992b; Robertson, 1997). One reason for this is based on the claim that negative and positive rights differ with respect to the corresponding duties they place on citizens and the state. Negative rights primarily entail the duties of others, including the state, to abstain from action, and it is argued that these duties are relatively cheap to enforce. Positive rights, on the other hand, entail a commitment to act, for example to supply certain goods and services, which in turn requires resources and imposes costs.

There are various problems with this argument. Protecting negative rights, such as privacy or the security of a person's life and property, imposes significant and often costly obligations on the state, and not merely obligations of non-interference. Not only does it require the provision of police, courts and prisons, but also the maintenance of adequate armed forces. Such institutions come at a price. Indeed, in wartime, public expenditure on defence may well outstrip expenditure on education, health care and social welfare combined. Therefore, to suggest that negative rights do not involve a significant commitment of public resources, or that they do not encounter problems of scarcity, is simply incorrect. Conversely, while many positive rights impose large resource costs, some do not. Free and fair elections and the right to vote, for example, can be provided relatively cheaply—certainly when compared to the cost of providing a criminal justice system.

A related argument is that, whereas negative rights are limited in scope, positive rights are open-ended and potentially unlimited. The case of health care is especially relevant here, as new technological developments continue to expand the range of potentially beneficial medical interventions and thus the number of services that can be regarded as positive rights. But much the same argument applies to many negative rights, such as the rights to privacy and freedom from assault. As Plant (1992a, p.23) points out:

Physical security depends on all sorts of things from police forces to street lighting and there is always more that could be done. Also these needs change with technology ... the need for privacy changes in relation to information technology; the need for physical security, for example, in air travel has changed since the invention of plastic explosives and depends upon newly invented security devices.

A further argument is that because positive rights are sensitive to resource scarcity, they tend to conflict or compete with each other. But the same can be said for most negative rights (Feinberg, 1973). Not only do different kinds of negative rights conflict with each other (for example, freedom of speech with privacy or safety), but the same negative rights can also conflict between individuals (for example, a large group of people gathered for a meeting cannot exercise their freedom of speech simultaneously). Moreover, there is frequently competition between negative rights for scarce resources. As Plant (1992a, p.21) observes, the resources of the police in protecting and enforcing negative rights 'are subject to the same problems of scarcity as doctors and teachers'. Thus negative rights have to be traded off against each other in exactly the same way as positive rights.

Another argument is that negative and positive rights differ in the degree to which they are conditional. Whereas individuals continue to enjoy the full protection of the law against assault, theft, rape and so forth, irrespective of their character or criminal convictions, some positive rights are conditional on the completion of certain tasks or obligations (such as the right to a university education being made conditional on academic performance). But this comparison is flawed. In fact negative rights are not treated as unconditional in many countries. Prisoners, for example, often lose some of their rights, including the right to vote. The crucial point here is that neither negative nor positive rights are absolute. Not only do they have to be traded off against each other, but they also have to be balanced against other values and moral claims.

Finally, the question arises as to why negative rights are deemed important in the first place. Why, in other words, do we believe that people should be protected from coercion, assault, theft and other harmful forms of interference? Market liberals usually defend negative rights on the grounds that they are necessary for individual autonomy, self-determination and self-respect. But while the absence of interference is undoubtedly a necessary condition to achieving this goal, it is not a sufficient one—an individual also needs the ability, resources and opportunities to act autonomously. Hence, just as negative rights can be justified on the basis that they are needed to guarantee a reasonable degree of autonomy, so too can positive rights (including various welfare rights). In short, a concern for individual autonomy logically requires both negative *and* positive rights; it requires both the absence of interference *and* certain resources and opportunities to act. Put differently, if human life is highly valued, and if the state is deemed to have a duty to prevent murder, it is clear that the state has a similar duty to provide the means for maintaining human life.

In summary, there is little substance to the claim that negative and positive rights are fundamentally different in nature. This is not to suggest that there are no problems in determining the nature and scope of positive rights (especially welfare rights), meeting the costs of their provision, or dealing with competing rights claims. But such problems are not unique to positive rights: they can also apply to negative rights. Nor is it being suggested here that positive rights are absolute, unconditional or categorical, or that all such rights have equal moral weight. Some are clearly more important than others, because the interests they seek to protect are more fundamental. The same, of course, applies to negative rights. Furthermore, there is plainly scope for debate about whether certain suggested positive rights, such as the right to education or the right to work, should be made 'justiciable' (that is, legally enforceable), or whether they should be seen as ideal directives, aspirations or goals, which states ought to realise to the fullest extent possible, consistent with the availability of resources and other policy imperatives. (For contrasting views of New Zealand contributors to this debate see Hunt, 1993; Robertson, 1997.) As Marshall (1996, p.293) points out, it is rare for welfare rights, even in countries that embrace a social citizenship or rights-based model, to be given the same legal status as civil and political rights. In determining whether certain welfare rights should be legally binding, critical issues include the manner in which such rights are specified, and the nature of the justified limitations that ought to apply to their interpretation and enforcement. But if welfare entitlements are not treated in exactly the same way as civil and political rights, it is nonetheless vital for social programmes to be operated within a framework of clear legal rules, which bind public agencies to provide assistance to everyone who meets the requisite criteria (see Goodin, 1988, p.38). Only in this way can arbitrary decision-making be avoided and the demands of justice met.

Empirical Issues

Many of the empirical objections that have been levelled by market liberals against comprehensive welfare states are dealt with in other chapters, including the relationship between taxation and economic growth (Chapter 4), and the concern over middle-class capture (Chapter 6). One issue, however, deserves mention here. The welfare state has been increasingly attacked on the grounds that it is socially corrosive—encouraging dependency, undermining individual responsibility, destroying families, and reducing social capital. Evidence to support such claims, however, is very limited (Goodin, 1982). To be sure, virtually all policy interventions have certain unintended and negative consequences; abuse of income support arrangements cannot be denied and occurs in all jurisdictions. However, the main impact of the welfare state has been to broaden opportunities, foster independence, and reduce the risk of exploitation, not to cultivate long-term dependency or irresponsibility (see Chapters 13 and 14). Relatively few people, other than pensioners and those with long-term disabilities, spend extended periods wholly reliant on state support. Likewise, any suggestion that the provision of free or heavily subsidised education and health care has undermined individual responsibility for health status or educational performance is open to serious doubt. Furthermore, most welfare states have incorporated certain kinds of reciprocal obligations or conditions into their social assistance programmes. For example, the availability of income support for tertiary students frequently depends on evidence of adequate academic progress, and those receiving unemployment assistance are usually obliged to look for work or to undergo further training.

Finally, while it is true that the institution of marriage and the nature of family life have changed significantly in recent years, whether this is attributable to the welfare state (and if so, to what extent) is open to serious debate. For one thing, such changes have occurred in countries with sharply divergent policy regimes and forms of state assistance. For another, changing social values rather than public policies appear to be more important causal factors. Quite apart from this, the provision of financial support to families, via tax credits and child benefits, has greatly assisted the family unit, not undermined it.

Conclusion

The nature of a just society has been, and will doubtless remain, the subject of vigorous debate. The development of the welfare state during the twentieth century has represented an attempt to achieve a greater measure of social justice, at least as viewed from the perspective of reformist liberals and social democrats. Market liberals, however, have taken a different approach, and in recent decades have challenged the welfare state on a range of philosophical and empirical grounds. In particular, it has been argued that while the state should endeavour to ensure that its citizens are able to satisfy their basic needs, it is under no obligation to pursue a greater measure of economic and social equality or guarantee an extensive range of welfare rights. A minimum or modest safety net to address the worst forms of poverty is thus justified, but nothing more.

Such a position, however, is open to various objections, as outlined in this chapter. From a social-democratic standpoint, providing a safety net for society's least advantaged citizens is certainly desirable, but is not sufficient to achieve a just society, especially in a relatively affluent country like New Zealand. Social justice, it can be argued, requires not only that individuals and families are able to subsist, but also that they are able to live in dignity and participate in their society and culture. Additionally, it requires a commitment to specific egalitarianism and social equality, including gender and racial equity. This is not to suggest that all inequalities are unjustified; but those that are unjust should, wherever possible, be reduced, if not eliminated. The precise implications of such conclusions for public policy are beyond the scope of this chapter. Nevertheless, in the current New Zealand context there is a good case for significant increases in the real value of most welfare benefits (see Chapter 13).

Yet the practical constraints on building a just society cannot be ignored (see Glennerster, 1992). Globalisation and the increasing interdependence of national economies place limits on the extent to which economic and social policies in New Zealand can deviate from those of our major competitors. Thus, if social democrats are to recapture the moral high ground in the current policy debates, it will be necessary to combine vision and principle with hard-headed realism.

CHAPTER THREE

SUSTAINABLE SOCIAL POLICY

MĀNUKA HENARE

This chapter focuses on the importance of culture and values for sustainable government policy—economic, social and political—as it has developed in the 1990s. It follows an approach that emerged early in the decade, one that critiques the dominant policy of iwi development as a means of giving effect to the principles of Te Tiriti o Waitangi/the Treaty of Waitangi.[1]

In 1991 the late Revd Māori Marsden, recognised as a leading theologian and philosopher on tikanga Māori (Māori customs, ethics and values), spoke to a national conference organised by a commission of the Catholic Church, Te Rūnanga o Te Hāhi Katorika, on the theme 'Kia Māori tūturu, te iwi Māori i roto i te Hāhi—To be truly Māori in the Church' (p.8). The adjective 'tūturu' is a powerful generative word in contemporary Māori discourse, meaning 'authentic and real' as opposed to 'spurious'. Marsden argued that it is the task of the Māori communities of each generation to seek out those things that are authentic to the culture in the compositions, wise exhortations, proverbs, songs and ritual prayers that constitute the lore and corpus of knowledge in Māori custom and tradition, and to reproduce them in the present. Following this religious and humanistic theme, Dame Mira Szaszy, scholar and former leader of the Māori Women's Welfare League, has expressed concern about trends in Māori social ethics. Speaking to the 1993 Māori graduands' capping ceremony at Victoria University of Wellington, Dame Mira offered an ethical response for today's world, claiming that the essence of being Māori can be found in ancestral values:

> ... what we need in essence is a new Māori humanism, i.e., a humanism based on ancient values but versed in contemporary idiom. Our current humanism does not seem to have found its own balance—with the rich lurching forward, disposing of their cultural roots and becoming rootless, and the poor, particularly unemployed, becoming poorer without even the sustenance of cultural or spiritual strengths (Szaszy, 1993, p.7).

Consequently, the first part of this chapter aims to describe fundamental ethics and values that are 'tūturu' to Māori in the context of sustainable social development. The chapter then goes on to discuss the debate about the role of iwi in determining Māori identity and self-definition, one that has been at the core of many government initiatives in social policy and in policy concerning Te Tiriti o Waitangi/the Treaty of Waitangi in the 1990s.

Authentic Māori Development

Historical experience of Crown injustice under various settler governments points to Māori having been the recipients of policy initiatives and implementation. Māori have thus been objects of assimilation rather than subjects of authentic Māori development. As a consequence, social policy aimed at Māori has not been sustainable, and will not become sustainable until it is based on authentic Māori values. The idea of sustainable social policy is a useful criterion for testing policy initiatives and implementation. It requires that policies—social, political and economic—of both Māori and government can be sustained over a long period, and that the policies meet the needs of the present without compromising the ability of future generations to meet their own needs (see World Commission on the Environment and Development, 1987, p.87). Discovering what is 'tūturu' in this context is not an end in itself—it is a means towards revealing the truth of things in order to know what is to be done to maintain tradition and change reality. Living with the paradox of maintaining tradition and seeking change is a feature of being Māori and Polynesian (Schrempp, 1992). Like many other indigenous people, we concentrate on principles rather than techniques (see, for example, Beck et al., 1990).

The lessons of the past and the values imbued in cultural practices constitute a general corpus of Māori knowledge, particularly sacred knowledge, which serves as a guide for the future. It sets a distinctive and contextual framework for articulating spiritual and general principles that have been tried and tested over countless generations. This corpus of knowledge represents the corporate experience of communities, culturally transmitted from one generation to the next (Marsden, 1991, pp.5-6). Marsden argued that, historically and philosophically speaking, the process of adaptation changed the 'how' of things—how resources were to be utilised, for example, and how the challenges of new situations might best be met—but that the 'why' of things—the meaning and purpose of life—remained constant. These constants provide the absolutes of life. Accordingly, just as the laws of the universe do not change, similarly 'ture wairua' (or 'the laws of the spirit', as Marsden called them) do not change (see also Szaszy, 1993, p.7).

In this section, I focus on 'ture wairua'. My purpose is to seek a basis for a Māori ethical system in which morals and values make sense in the context of sustainable social development in Aotearoa New Zealand. I argue that the market place, efficient or otherwise, is not and should not be the sole universal arbiter, and that human communities need to be governed by ethical and moral considerations of consequences, as well as by legal controls (Arrow 1992, p.21). In Aotearoa New Zealand, the free market is not culture-free, and is therefore not values-neutral. Contemporary social and economic policies are imbued with ethical and moral codes, and their delivery involves forms of behaviour that are often at variance or in direct conflict with those of Māori and other Polynesian peoples (see Royal Commission on Social Policy, 1988a). The Pākehā settler society established after the signing of Te Tiriti o Waitangi/the Treaty of Waitangi was founded on three philosophical cornerstones: positivism, utilitarianism and secularism (see Henare, forthcoming, for a lengthier discussion). These represent a particular world-view— a Pākehā way of seeing and doing things. Yet Māori and other indigenous peoples offer an alternative worldview, a system of codes of ethics and moral standards by which the economy and the market can be evaluated. The ethics of indigenous peoples can be a 'kind of praxis which generates critical reflection on the value content and meaning of one's social action' (Goulet, 1995, p.26). This process allows priority to be assigned to essential needs, basic power relationships to be exposed, and criteria for determining levels of well-being to be established in promoting social change.

Sir James Henare (1987, p.i), a philosopher and expert on Māori culture, wrote that:

> Māori literature was for centuries preserved only by memory which naturally influenced the development of different forms of literary art, such as proverbs, poetic allusions, metaphor, epics and songs to name but a few. These were handed down from one generation to another in which wise sages embodied the results of their experiences and judicious observations.

According to Sir James (1987, p.i), these literary art forms exemplified in the oral traditions of Māori society are 'a veritable treasure house of genius, wit, condensed wisdom and silent telepathy in the storied souls of our ancestors calling across the ages to their descendants struggling towards the cultural light'. This 'condensed wisdom' of Māori people is illuminating, as the next section describes.

The Creation of Aotearoa Landscape and Identity—Atua Sources of Tapu and Mana

World-views, ethics and associated cultural practices are part and parcel of a people's ancestral legacy, which strengthens unity, preserves identity and ensures continuity with the past. They signify where a people are. They are welded together in the present to indicate directions for the future, based on tried and tested methods gleaned from the past. They are the general principles, the constants that need to be applied according to the demands of a particular situation.[2] Many indigenous peoples explain 'world-view' in similar ways. Alfonso Ortiz, for example, a Tewa man of the North American Indian people, has defined it as follows:

> The notion 'world-view' denotes a distinctive vision of reality, which not only interprets and orders the places and events in the experience of a people, but lends form, direction, and continuity to life as well. World-view provides people with a distinctive set of values, an identity, a feeling of rootedness, of belonging to a time and place, and a sense of continuity with a tradition which transcends the experience of a single lifetime, a tradition which may be said to transcend even time (cited in Beck et al., 1990, pp.5-6).

This approach, which has immediate application to any Māori discussion on social policy, can be illustrated by an extract from the recent *Muriwhenua Land Report* (Waitangi Tribunal, 1997, p.15):

> The people's accounts started before time began, at Matangireia, home of the first being, Io-matua-kore, and proceeded from there on a mental and spiritual journey through aeons. It told of an enterprising people, pragmatic but deeply religious, so intimately tied to land, sea, and space that in their cosmos all life forms, and phenomena like the sky, sun, wind, and rain, are bound to them by treasured links in ancient genealogy. Māori thus see themselves as descendants of gods [atua], and as partners with them in a physical and spiritual universe.

In Māori society, atua- or God-consciousness as expressed in this extract is regarded very highly, because atua are the primary source of all tikanga and ritenga (customs, ethics and values) that drive human behaviour. According to tribal traditions in North Auckland, for example, long after the creation of the world and universe by Rangi-nui and Papa-tua-nuku (Father Sky and Mother Earth) and their children, the land and surrounding region of Aotearoa were created by the actions of atua or taniwha (spirit beings). In another creation tradition, the taniwha Maungataniwha decided to travel to Aotearoa from Hawaiki to ensure there was sufficient food, the climate was kindly, and there were no dangers the people could not manage. When Maungataniwha arrived, chaos was apparent. Lesser taniwha had arrived earlier and were scrambling up the mountainsides, scratching deep indentations in the terrain. They had already gouged out the harbours of Hokianga, Kaipara, Kawhai, Mangonui and Whangaroa. Maungataniwha crushed the lesser taniwha. The final one to be dismissed was at Omapere, close to Kaikohe, where its death throes ripped the earth and caused a lake to appear.

His work completed, Maungataniwha decided to return to the northern Pacific islands of Te Moana Nui a Kiwa. While resting in the tropical sunshine, he heard the south wind whispering that serious trouble was disturbing the peace and calm of Whangaroa. Maungataniwha grew anxious because he had left behind Taratara, a beautiful woman in whose fidelity he had absolute confidence. However, the seeds of suspicion blown by the wind were already planted in his mind. He returned at speed to Whangaroa to see what evil had occurred. His fears were well founded—Taratara had been unfaithful. In a rage he spurned her with his foot, breaking her back and scattering her, together with her attendants, Kōkakohiria, Puketona and Tūrau. Her head now lies off the coast and is the island of Horo-iwi (the destroyer of bones), near the point of Otāwhiri. These names are all prominent landmarks along the western approaches to Whangaroa harbour, along with Uma-kūkupa (the pigeon's breast).

Maungataniwha then turned on Hotou, the lover of Taratara, slashing him on both sides of his head with his taiaha. In a last fit of rage, he kicked the dying Hotou as far as he could. Today, Hotou is a sharp conical mountain beyond Kaikohe on the way to Dargaville. Maungataniwha then took up his final observation post behind Mangapa, the highest mountain in the area. He now watches over the insignificant Hotou to the south and his unfaithful Taratara to the north (Sale, 1986, p.1; for further accounts, see Heta and Kira's interpretation of the Muriwhenua landscape, cited in Henare, 1997b).

These creation accounts of Whangaroa and outlying areas explain how the people used such accounts to identify themselves with the land, the surrounding coastlines, the rivers and forests, and all other forms of creation. In so doing, the people remind themselves and others of the primary sources of their tapu and mana.[3] Having settled and developed the area, the people gained an intimate knowledge of the physical landscape. Over time this became sacred knowledge, and an identity was forged between the people and their environment. Thus the people became the tangata whenua—the people of the land. By frequently re-asserting their mana tangata (power from people), mana whenua (power from land) and mana wairua (power from the spirit) in this way, they re-asserted their responsibilities and obligations to the region. In particular, the mana of Whangaroa is the tapu of a number of associated atua (spiritual powers). That tapu is the people's greatest possession (see Shirres, 1997, pp.53-60). The enhancement of the tapu and mana of the people and the physical environments in which they live must be identifiable outcomes of authentic and sustainable social policy

The relationship with the first being, Io-matua-kore, the creative parents Rangi and Papa and their atua children, and the recognition that the world and all created things have their source in primary spiritual powers, serve as the basis of Māori culture and law. The ethics and values embodied in the Māori worldview confirm a consistent understanding of the universe and its purpose. In the words of Māori Marsden (1991, pp.6-7):

The past and present are caught up together and commingle into an integrated whole where time and space, life, the universe [are] seen as the 'one'. The approach of Māoridom under this view is holistic. There is no disjunction between the sacred and secular, between the spiritual and material. All life is sacramental.

We see ourselves as holding a special relationship to Mother Earth and her resources; an integral part of the natural order, recipients of her bounty and therefore indebted to her largesse rather than controllers. She is to be treated reverently, not to be abused, misused, exploited, ravaged.

Māori Religious Values and Social Policy

Another encounter crucial to the elaboration of a Māori world-view was that between the ancestral religion and Christian theology, ethics and values. Māori religion before Christianity is best described as a belief in spiritual beings (see Tylor, 1873) and a system of motivating symbols. It conceives of an order of existence that to Māori is factual and uniquely realistic (Schrempp, 1992, p.4). Within the framework of Māori cosmology and religion in the Muriwhenua region, for example:

> Māori law (or the Māori world) was primarily concerned with human and divine relationships.... The fundamental purpose of Māori law was to maintain appropriate relationships of people to their environment, their history and each other (Waitangi Tribunal, 1997, p.22).

Māori religion (cf. Mbiti, 1975) is not found in a set of sacred books or dogma, as in the Christian Bible or the Muslim Koran. Nor does it have a founder prophet like Jesus Christ or Mohammed. Rather it is a religion that can be observed in the experience of living life as a Māori within the culture, namely in tikanga Māori and Māoritanga. In this sense, Māori religion *is* tikanga Māori and Māoritanga; the culture *is* the religion. The maintenance of the religion is dependent on the maintenance of the culture and its many practices and rituals. In developing the culture, the religion and philosophy are enhanced. In developing the religion and philosophy, the culture is enhanced. This does not imply that Māori religion and philosophy constitute a closed system of beliefs and rituals (Salmond, 1985, p.240). History points to the Māori religion being constantly open to evaluation and questioning in order to seek out that which is tika. Maintaining tika is the means whereby ethics and values can be identified. Māori religious values can best be described by studying the culture and its practices, as follows (Henare, 1997b and 1998):

- tikanga pure, whai kawa, hui, wānanga (rituals, ceremonies and hui of the people);
- wāhi tapu, urupā and taonga tapu (shrines, sacred places, religious objects);

- whakairo, kāwhaiwhai (art and art forms);
- waiata, haka (songs, dances);
- whakatauki, pepeha, panga (proverbs, wise sayings, riddles);
- whakaingoa, huaina (naming, names of people and places);
- pūrakau, kōrero tuku iho, pakiwaitara (myths and legends); and
- tikanga and ritenga (customs, beliefs, practices).

Christianity and Ngā Tikanga me Ngā Ritenga

The encounter with the foreign worldview, ethics and values contained in Christian theology, rituals and institutions was one of the most influential episodes in Māori history. Stories of the arrival and activities of Christian missionaries throughout Aotearoa have already been well recorded (Henare, 1990). The initial encounter with Christianity promised much, but was quickly entangled with Pākehā settler politics and economics. The encounter between the two religious traditions was thus somewhat obscured by the encounter between the two cultures.

The accounts of those early interactions between Māori and Christianity are often presented as adventure stories of the European missionaries and their adaptation to the world of Māori, rather than as Māori accounts of discovering the teachings of the Old Testament, the Christian God (Ihowa), and the person of Jesus Christ. Despite somewhat difficult beginnings, however, North Auckland can claim to be the cornerstone on which Māori Christianity was founded and built. The relative speed with which local rangatira utilised the new religion—its teachings, rituals, institutions and missionaries—for Māori purposes points to great powers of adaptation, acculturation and incorporation. The role played by many rangatira and tohunga in establishing a Māori nation state is a subject on which both Māori and Pākehā histories have hitherto been silent. However, many younger voices are rediscovering this history in assertions of mana Māori motuhake and tino rangatiratanga (self-determination, self-reliance and Māori sovereignty).

The European cultural mix of politics, economics and religion was not foreign to Māori, for whom it was the norm. That mix is aptly seen in the endeavours of North Auckland leaders to work closely with British whalers, traders, missionaries and government officials from 1800 to 1840. The first known official missionaries to visit Aotearoa were Revd Samuel Marsden, Thomas Kendall and party who, accompanied by Ruatara and Korokoro, landed in Matauri Bay in 1814. Encouraged to come to the new land by rangatira such as Hongi Hika, Marsden brought technology, new agricultural ideas and methods, and a theological world-view, all of which were welcomed by many Māori leaders. A number of rangatira such as Te Puhi, Hoori Te Ara and others closely associated with North Auckland travelled to Sydney and further afield. The visit of Hongi Hika and Waikato to England in 1820 led to many new economic and political ideas being fostered on their return. A letter in 1831 from some of the Northern rangatira to King William IV requested better and more trade. This was followed by the appointment of James Busby as the first British Resident in 1833. Acting on his advice, Northern leaders took the initiative and designed a distinctive Polynesian flag in 1834. This gave them a modicum of international respectability, and enabled whānau- and hapū-owned ships to sail the seas freely with exports and imports. It later became the flag of Māori independence, and flew throughout the country from the Far North to Ruapuke Island south of Bluff (Henare and Douglas, 1988, pp.88-9, 95).

In 1835, the Northern leaders were instrumental in drafting, with James Busby, Te Wakaputanga o Te Rangatiratanga o Nu Tireni—The Declaration of Independence. This established a confederation of hapū to be a new political and economic force, aimed at uniting Māori society around a parliamentary congress. It was the first formal statement of Māori desire for a 'whenua rangatira' or independent state, and included a request to Britain for assistance to establish a civil society based on notions of ture tangata and ture atua—the laws of humanity and the laws of God (Henare, 1996). These initiatives continued in 1840, when an even greater consensus was reached by many more rangatira who combined to sign Te Tiriti o Waitangi with the British Crown. This event, from a Māori historical perspective, consolidated initiatives by rangatira since Hongi Hika's handshake with King George IV in 1820. The Treaty was meant to gain British help in establishing a Māori nation state, and was seen by many Māori leaders as a 'kawenata hou' or sacred covenant (Orange, 1987). However, the British Crown and subsequent settlers developed a different economic and political agenda. Thus began the colonisation of Māori.

Colonisation and assimilation had a profound impact on the mindset developing within Māori Christian communities. They brought a dramatic change in circumstances for Māori, from the dominant population and culture before the 1850s, to an oppressed minority in their own land. Their minority status, experience of colonisation and the assault on their culture caused Māori to adjust their worldview, ethics and values to meet the changing circumstances.

With the subsequent demise of many of their customs and practices (Ward, 1978, p.36), Māori Christians identified with the sufferings of the children of Israel in the Old Testament. Māori prophets emerged who found biblical parallels to the condition of their own people. In the twentieth century, Ngata would write: 'The promised land was Aotearoa restored' (Ngata and Sutherland, 1940, p.351). Māori Marsden (1991, p.3) described the need to call 'Christianity back to a full, integrated, holistic Gospel in which mana, tapu, ihi, wehi, wana, ira tangata, ira atua can overcome powerlessness, impurity, degradation, rebellious pride, loss of identity and self-esteem, isolation from God; and thereby restore divinity lost by the first Adam (Tiki).' New Testament qualities of peace-making, humility, goodwill, charity, law-abidingness, obedience and faith seemed to provide a new concept of rangati-ratanga. While at first glance they may appear to conflict with the principles of the indigenous religion, their acceptance was eased by the fact that some of these qualities were also inherent in the traditional concept of rangatiratanga (Winiata, 1967, p.51, quoted in Henare, 1988, p.34).

In time, Māori communities claimed Christianity and its teachings as their own. Through the process of acculturation and adjustment, many of the Christian teachings and rituals became part of Māoritanga. Indeed, Christianity has assisted in the elaboration of a Māori world-view and the development of Māori ethics and values. These form the basis of any set of ethics and values that may be applied to sustainable social development.

Mana Māori and Ngā Pou Mana E Whā

The previous section mentioned the central importance of tapu and mana in the Māori worldview. Mana Māori has a part to play in almost every ceremony, ritual, and everyday activity. It is essential in maintaining the integrity of both the group and the individual. Mana involves the wholeness of social relationships and well-being, as well as continuity through time and space. It encompasses the social, economic and political well-being of the whole community. The promotion of the common good and of authentic Māori social policy thus requires structures and institutions that enhance mana Māori.

Mana is manifested through action, as is aroha (compassion and love). It is linked to the powers of spiritual ancestors as well as of ariki and rangatira. High-status genealogies suggest that ariki have divine beginnings. In older Māori society, religious ritual was used to influence parts of life where the atua influences were considered helpful. These attitudes and concomitant behaviour, while ancient, continue today.

Mana is also linked to generative power. Mana wahine—the integrity of women—connects to Papa-tua-nuku and her generative and nurturing power, while mana tane—the integrity of men—links to the power of Te Waiora a Tane, the source of life. The imparting of order (which enables life forces to avoid chaos, destruction and pollution) also contributes to mana Māori. The association of mana with form and order is the basis of Māori concern for ritual and convention. Mana is exhibited in its completeness when order and form are right. It is a religious quality and power, bestowed on individuals or groups by others, and not by oneself. An understanding of mana is essential for under-standing the world-view of Māori and Polynesians in general.

Four sets of concepts—Ngā Pou Mana E Whā—contribute to the development of tapu and mana, and therefore provide criteria for sustainable Māori social development (see Henare, 1988, pp.24-5). They are interdependent, interrelated and interacting. The following outline of Ngā Pou Mana E Whā is descriptive only. However, as we explore the concepts and their practices, it will become clear which concepts are likely to be the most important. As stated earlier, our task is to find the principles or the 'why' of tikanga and ritenga. These form the basis for further research and enquiry into sustainable social development in a restored Aotearoa.

1. Whanaungatanga—Whānau, Hapū, Iwi, Waka

Belonging and solidarity are implicit in the concept of whanaungatanga, where kinship rights and obligations underpin te whānau, te hapū, te iwi, te waka and te iwi Māori. Individuals, families and larger social groups are strengthened by these rights and obligations. The sense of belonging thus developed is deeply ingrained. Solidarity is a basic cultural value that must be felt by members of the group for it to operate effectively. Whanaungatanga includes the following values:

- tohatoha—the social responsibility principle of the fair distribution of material things;
- whakapapa—the linking principle, in which human beings and natural phenomena are genealogically connected;
- manaaki—the principle of caring, expressing mana, generosity;
- hau—the fundamental religious and philosophical principle for the obligatory reciprocal exchange of goods and services in a Māori mode of production;
- utu—the principle of exchange;
- mauri—the principle of the life essence, life force, life itself, imbued in all human, material and non-material things.

Pre-European Māori understood themselves as the norm, and were identified by their whānau-hapū kinship relationships, reinforced by local economic, social and political activities. From about the 1830s, as contacts with Europeans increased, along with competition for the control of land and other natural resources, Māori began to identify more strongly with the nascent iwi, which became established in about 1850. Waka—founding canoe associations—became another means by which tribal groups identified themselves. The notion of being a Māori people, te iwi Māori, had begun to emerge from the 1820s as the relationship with Europeans developed. Māori referred to the latter as te iwi Pākehā.

Te whānau was the smallest social group and the basis of the domestic economy in the early and mid-nineteenth century. Several generations of extended family lived together under the guidance of the kaumātua and kuia. This group was the basis of food-production and land-holding, and thus the fundamental social unit. Day-to-day decisions were made at te whānau level.

At the next level was the hapū, whose members traced their descent from a common ancestor. Most Māori people were connected to an extraordinary number of hapū. Headed by rangatira, each hapū had autonomy, but its primary purpose was to foster and support its member whānau. Larger cultivation, fishing, canoe-making and political matters were dealt with at hapu level. The larger group identity was reinforced in a range of activities and events. The social and political processes were dynamic, and land and other resources could be reapportioned as change occurred.

The notion of iwi is at the heart of discourse between Māori and Crown agencies in the 1990s. The meaning of 'iwi' is contestable. While the term is as old as the language itself, its primary meanings have changed and been elaborated over time. Its base meaning is glossed as 'human bones' (Williams, 1975, p.80). Historically it was used to refer to people connected to each other through a common ancestry. Later, as Māori communities reorganised themselves from the 1800s, and later still as colonisation developed, hapū groupings formed into iwi, which became more institutionalised from about the 1850s onwards. The process of colonisation was a significant factor in the emergence of the larger tribal configurations.

Williams (1975, p.80) thus glosses iwi as 'nation, people'. In this sense, an iwi is a larger grouping of hapū, over which it often exhibits some political and social control in opposition to other kinship groups and in dealings with the Crown. In many parts of the country, iwi acquired a territorial entity and became the basis for a wider group ideology. These iwi were alliances of hapū who remained together as interdependent political units, achieving self-sufficiency and self-government in economic and social matters. Prominent landmarks, significant ancestors and oral history all helped to establish iwi identity. Today, a tension remains between those who see the iwi as the fundamental social, political and economic unit of its members, and those who regard the hapū as the fundamental unit, served by the iwi (see below). Furthermore, urban Māori authorities such as Te Whānau o Waipareira in West Auckland (commonly known as the Waipareira Trust) have organised themselves like an iwi. They would argue that they represent and serve the diverse interests of iwi Māori, Māori people, who live in their part of the city.

Te Waka is defined as a group of people with a common territory and common links with members of a voyaging canoe. The term is used to identify larger groups than iwi or hapu. While very strong in some regions of Aotearoa, the identification with a single primary waka is not found in all Māori communities. For example, waka affiliation in Te Tai Tokerau (North Auckland) is extremely complex because most of the whānau and hapū are associated with many different waka which landed around the peninsula. Some voyagers initially settled but later moved south to other areas around the North and South Islands. The Northern peoples celebrate their multiplicity of waka associations as part of their identity. Other hapū and iwi groupings in other parts of the country are associated with a sole primary waka.

2. Taonga Tuku Iho—Tangible and Intangible 'Gifts' Handed to Generations

Taonga are treasures—both material and non-material—which are therefore considered valuable. 'Tuku iho' refers to taonga handed down from earlier generations. As will be discussed later, taonga are ultimately derived from spiritual powers or from God. It is the recognition of the primary source of taonga that establishes their value. Taonga tuku iho include the following values:

- kete mātauranga—the knowledge and the gift from Io-matua-kore (the primary source of all creation), the wisdom of past generations, the skills passed down (now includes continual learning);
- tikanga—the principles that determine ethics, values and behaviour, and the rights of the individual or group;
- ritenga—the philosophy of behaviour; the practices determined by tikanga.

3. Te Ao Tūroa—The Environment

Te ao tūroa refers to guardianship and stewardship over the visible and invisible worlds, where the well-being of the land is linked with mana Māori and personal well-being. The features of the land are often personified and used to link people to the land and to their ancestry. Some important concepts include:

- whenua—land linkages, usage and responsibility for the future, given by those of the past; the mauri (life force) is present and is respected through the ritenga of food production and gathering;
- ngahere—forests, including flora and fauna;
- moana—seas;
- awa, puna—lakes, water-ways;
- kaitiakitanga—guardianship.

4. Tūrangawaewae—To Stand is to Be

According to Bishop Manuhuia Bennett (see Sir James Henare, 1981), the concept of tūrangawaewae is essentially that land becomes an outward and visible sign of something that is deeply spiritual. It is a source of nourishment for the inner person, rather than for their physical needs. It is the origin of the person's identity—their awareness, their mana, indeed their very life. It includes the following values:

- kāinga—primary place of abode and living;
- papakāinga—earth on which the kainga stands, closely related to Rangi-nui and Papa-tua-nuku (Father Sky and Mother Earth);
- marae—the land on which the whare tupuna (ancestral meeting house) and the whare kai (eating house) stand, and the open space in front for oratory and debate; a place where one can stand tall and have a sense of belonging;
- rohe—a sense of place, a boundary;
- urupā—a sacred burial place where ancestors are interred; the idea that things have come to an end;
- koha—the gift or contribution towards another; reciprocity.

Māori Ethics and Sustainable Social Development

The *Muriwhenua Land Report* (Waitangi Tribunal, 1997, pp.26-7) identified a set of Māori values as being conceptual regulators associated with land rights and communal obligations to the environment. According to the Tribunal, they are also part of a general system for regulating Māori behaviour. These values include the following:
- whanaungatanga (kinship) stresses the primacy of kinship bonds in determining action, and the importance of whakapapa in establishing rights and status;
- arohatanga (compassion) is the basis for peaceful co-existence;
- manaakitanga (hospitality) is a desirable character trait that incorporates the qualities of generosity, caregiving and compassion, and is generally about establishing one's mana;
- utu (reciprocity) concerns the maintenance of harmony and balance, and of mana.

This list followed an earlier statement in the *Muriwhenua Fishing Report* (Waitangi Tribunal, 1988, p.179) that all resources were taonga, derived from spiritual powers. According to the Tribunal, the division of properties was less important to Māori than the rules that governed the user of the land. The following criteria underlie Māori thinking in this regard:
- a reverence for creation as a whole;
- a sense of kinship with other beings;
- a sacred regard for the whole of nature and its resources as being gifts from the spiritual powers or atua;
- a sense of responsibility as appointed stewards, guardians and rangatira for these taonga ;
- a distinctive economic ethic of reciprocity; and
- a commitment to safeguard all of nature's taonga for future generations.

To meet these responsibilities for nature's taonga, Māori required an effective form of control which ensured that both supply and demand were kept in proper balance, thus conserving resources for future needs.

The Tribunal accurately observed that although Māori customs were often portrayed as immutable, change was always happening. In this sense, values were not a rigid set of rules and did not prevent change; rather they were underlying principles that were to be maintained. Thus, 'by remaining true to its basic values, Māori culture was able to adopt and adapt while retaining its essential form' (Waitangi Tribunal, 1997, pp.26-7).

The Tribunal's identification of core values and criteria for holistic sustainable development is timely. However, the list may not yet be comprehensive enough to provide an ethical basis for sustainable Māori social development. It may be necessary to produce an expanded set of Māori values, world-view and customs. Such a set would be relevant not only for Māori but also for the common good, and could include the following fundamental principles (Henare 1997a, 1997b and 1998):

• an ethic of te ao mārama (wholeness, the cosmos);
• an ethic of mauri (life essences, vitalism);
• an ethic of tapu (being and potentiality);
• an ethic of mana (power, authority and the common good);
• an ethic of hau (spiritual source of obligatory reciprocity in relationships and in economics);
• an ethic of whānau (extended family as the foundation of society);
• an ethic of whanaungatanga (belonging);
• an ethic of te ao hurihuri (change and tradition);
• an ethic of tika (the right way, justice);
• an ethic of kotahitanga (solidarity);
• an ethic of kaitiakitanga (guardianship of creation); and
• an ethic of wairuatanga (spirituality).

This list does not represent a hierarchy of values, but rather a koru, a motif popular in Māori carving and scroll painting. In the proposed koru spiral, each ethic has its own unique nature, life and form (cf. Smith, cited in Salmond, 1985, p.247), yet each is part of a continuum that contains an identifiable core. Like a fern's frond, an inner core is revealed as it unfolds. Anne Salmond (1985, p.247) has described the spiral as 'a double dynamism that moves into and out from a primal centre'. The above set of ethics illustrates that we must understand the parts in order to understand the whole, as they are all integrated, interconnected and interdependent, both with each other and with clusters of other values significant to Māori.[4] Together they constitute a cosmic religious worldview and philosophy, a 'cosmology economics' from which emerges a Māori economy of affection and the utilisation of resources (taonga). This economy aims to provide for the people in Māori kinship systems (Henare, 1995a, pp.215-16), and operates within the wider national and international economy of production and consumption.

Government Policies in the 1990s

By the late 1980s, the quest for Māori development had emerged as one of the signs of the times, and was demanding economic, political, cultural and social responses in a nation still trying to come to terms with its history and the role of the Treaty of Waitangi. The National government of 1990–93 and subsequent Coalition governments inherited the fourth Labour government's policy initiatives in this area. Those policies were based on traditional iwi, loosely defined as 'tribes'. In releasing the policy statement *Te Urupare Rangapū—Partnership Response* in 1988, Minister of Māori Affairs Koro Wetere said 'there was no argument that Māori people themselves want a greater say in their own destiny' (p.1). The policy statement itself claimed that 'the success of the Government's proposals depend on strengthening the iwi and helping restore their independence' (p.5), and went on to articulate an idealised view of the structure of contemporary Māori society:

> The iwi is a group descended from a common founding ancestor. An iwi is made up of hapū (sub-tribes). Each hapū consists of related whānau (family) groups. Iwi have an identifiable historical and territorial base. The boundaries are known to the group and—on the whole—were identified by the Māori Land Court in the last century (p.9).

The statement identified three groups of people who made up an iwi: those who actively identified with their iwi and lived in their tribal territory; those who actively identified with their iwi but lived outside their tribal territory; and those who for residency, marriage or other reasons had become adopted members of another iwi. The statement announced a bold new policy initiative, founded on Te Tiriti o Waitangi/the Treaty of Waitangi, in which social organisations known as iwi authorities would be officially recognised and made central to the new system. The new authorities would 'deliver programmes that they and the Government have settled on as appropriate for their iwi— and they will deliver these programmes through various arrangements with government agencies' (p.13). It was assumed that the authorities would draw on the 'strength of the traditional iwi structure', and that such mechanisms would provide for 'practical partnership within the state sector' (pp.10, 12).

Midway through the 1990s, however, some Māori academics began to question the appropriateness of the tribe as the primary vehicle for Māori development. Roger Maaka, for example, claimed it was not a case of tribal versus pan-Māori development, 'but that political organisation must reflect social reality' (1994, p.311). He questioned the commonly held view that the 'tribe, as conventionally defined, is a social reality'.[5] Maaka identified 1978 as a decisive moment for Māori development, with the launching of the programme *Tū Tangata*, 'Stand Tall'. Led by a new group of Māori senior public servants, it had an underlying philosophy of self-determination and self-reliance, meaning Māori control of Māori programmes. There was then turmoil from 1984 to 1992, as successive governments tried to implement policies based on iwi development. 'Iwi' in this policy context was synonymous with 'tribe', meaning a specific group of people who shared a common ancestry, history and territory. In such tribes, membership is exclusive and each tribe operates according to its own particular social rules (Maaka, 1994, pp.312-15).

In 1995 Mason Durie, Professor of Māori Studies at Massey University and former member of the Royal Commission on Social Policy, reviewed the 1984-1994 Decade of Māori Development which had been launched at the Hui Taumata (the Māori Economic Summit) in 1984. From his examination of the formulation of Māori policies over the decade, six central themes emerged: the Treaty of Waitangi, tino rangatiratanga, iwi development, economic self-reliance, social equity and cultural advancement. According to Durie's analysis, by 1990 doubts had begun to emerge about the underlying intentions of the dominant political and economic agenda—beginning with the question of whether Māori development was primarily a Māori agenda, or whether it was part of the government's plan for privatisation, reduced state responsibility and user-pays.

Second, the focus on iwi development did not appeal to a significant group of Māori, for a range of reasons. There were those living in Auckland and other metropolitan centres who were alienated from tribal activities. Some saw traditional tribal structures as outdated, and believed that new structures were needed in the new environment. Others doubted that tribal sovereignty would make any difference to their daily struggle to provide adequate health, education and shelter for their children.

The third question related to the policy of devolution, which implied a transfer of decision-making and resources to Māori authorities. Often, what was transferred was a service-delivery role, devoid of policy functions, and with inadequate funding. For Māori, such devolution did not equate with rangatiratanga (being in charge).

Fourth, iwi authorities felt thwarted by the government's narrow, sectoral approach, which limited opportunities for integrated development. This approach created major obstacles for Māori at iwi and community levels, and contrasted with their preferences for holistic development—cultural, social and economic.

Finally, Māori planners were extremely frustrated by the short time-frames employed by successive governments. Māori leaders at the 1984 Hui Taumata aimed for ten-year development cycles. Instead, they were confronted by 'an ever changing policy environment within which changing directions became the rule' (Durie, 1995, p.7).

In the light of the experiences of the Development Decade, Professor Durie identified three principles for Māori development. In terms of the case for sustainable Māori policy, they are relevant today and for the coming millennium:

- Ngā Matatini Māori—Māori diversity;
- Ngā Tupunga Whakakotahi—integrated development; and
- Tino Rangatiratanga—self-determination.

Table 3.1 The Fourth Labour Government's Treaty Principles, 1989

Principle 1. The Principle of Government. The Kawanatanga Principle.
The Government has the right to govern and make laws.

Principle 2. The Principle of Self Management. The Rangatiratanga Principle.
The iwi have the right to organise as iwi and, under the law, to control the resources they own.

Principle 3. The Principle of Equality.
All New Zealanders are equal under the law.

Principle 4. The Principle of Reasonable Co-operation.
Both the Government and the iwi are obliged to accord each other reasonable co-operation on major issues of common concern.

Principle 5. The Principle of Redress
The Government is responsible for providing effective processes for the resolution of grievances in the expectation that reconciliation can occur.

Source: Lange (1989).

In late 1989, the Labour government articulated a set of Treaty principles to guide the Crown and its agencies in their response to Treaty claims and responsibilities (see Table 3.1). When National took over control of the Treaty settlement process in 1990, it did not necessarily endorse these principles. Rather, it attempted in 1995 to tighten its control of the process and the likely fiscal outcomes of Treaty claims. The Minister of Justice and Minister in Charge of Treaty of Waitangi Negotiations, Doug Graham, published *Crown Proposals for the Settlement of Treaty of Waitangi Claims* (1995). This document included a set of Cabinet-approved general principles for the settlement of historical claims, as well as a controversial proposal to limit total settlements to $1 billion over a ten-year period (the so-called 'fiscal envelope'). The amount was a political decision, and would not be open to negotiation. The government argued that the sum available for settlements had to be acceptable to the wider community, affordable to the government, viable to claimants, and provide durable settlements (Graham, 1995, p.24). Later, the Minister admitted that the $1 billion limit was not based on any serious costings, but rather on what politicians and bureaucrats thought was a useful figure.

Māori response was swift and decisive. In both government- and Māori-sponsored gatherings held throughout the country, the 'fiscal envelope' proposal was roundly rejected. Nonetheless, the financial constraints inherent in the proposal have endured, and appear to have succeeded in talking down the value of settlements. Recently, Graham has defended the process he was largely responsible for supervising on behalf of the Crown by providing a more developed set of principles (see Table 3.2).

In his set of principles, Graham states that the Treaty 'signifies a relationship like a partnership based on good faith and reasonable co-operation'. This phrase attempts to diffuse and thus weaken the effect of a very important decision in 1987 by the New Zealand Court of Appeal. In a unanimous decision, the Judges had defined some key principles. Sir Robin Cooke, President of the Court of Appeal, noted that the Treaty 'signified a partnership between races' and that 'utmost good faith … is the characteristic obligation of partnership' (Court of Appeal, 1987, pp.369-70). In contrast, Graham argues that the Treaty signifies a *relationship like a partnership*. This shift in understanding of the Treaty principle of partnership perhaps reflects the change in the mindset of the National/New Zealand First Coalition towards the partnership relations between Māori and the Crown, and may explain the growing gap between Māori and government in the 1990s. Yet Māori want to work as full and active partners in all areas of social policy.

It is interesting to note that Principles 2 and 4 of the Labour government's Treaty principles (Table 3.1) explicitly refer to 'iwi' as the counterpart of the government or Crown. Graham's list does not do this, although in practice negotiations over historical grievances under National have been carried out with iwi authorities. Indeed, it is reasonable to say that iwi authorities became an important administrative convenience for governments and the Crown during the late 1980s and throughout the 1990s. Consequently, the Crown has been instrumental in restricting the definition of 'iwi' to mean a traditional tribe, and hence in re-tribalising Māori—possibly even more instrumental than Māori themselves.

The Debate Over 'What is Iwi?'

This section has already noted Roger Maaka's (1994) questioning of the appropriateness of making the tribe the primary ·vehicle for Māori development, on the basis that it does not reflect social reality. This debate has intensified in recent years, involving Court action extending as high as the Privy Council. On one side of the debate is what may be called the 'tribal

Table 3.2 Doug Graham's Treaty Principles, 1997

The Crown is empowered to govern and to make laws in respect of the whole New Zealand community.

Māori have the right to exercise self-management within the law, to maintain Māori culture and to control their resources.

Māori are to enjoy equality before the law and are entitled to the protection of the Crown.

The Treaty involves the honour of the Crown.

The Treaty signifies a relationship like a partnership based on good faith and reasonable co-operation.

The Treaty relationship implies the implementation of the Treaty in a broad and generous spirit that takes account of cultural difference.

The Treaty contemplates evolution in the relationship and changes in factual circumstances relevant to Treaty interpretation.

The Treaty does not authorise 'unreasonable restrictions on the right of a duly elected government to follow its chosen policy' (See New Zealand Māori Council v Attorney General (the Lands case) [1987]).

There is a duty on the part of the Crown actively to promote the protection of Māori property and identify in accordance with Māori values to the fullest extent practicable.

There is a duty to consult with Māori when government policies may affect special Māori interests.

There is a right of redress to either party in case of breach with appropriate redress or compensation but not so as to create a new injustice.

Source: Graham (1997, pp.22-5).

essentialist' view, which looks for the culture behind the person (cf. Kernot, 1997, p.9), through the medium of the traditional iwi. According to this fundamentalist view, it is Māori culture that defines a person as Māori, so that one can be Māori only by belonging to a traditional iwi. The traditional iwi thus becomes both the means *and the end* of Māori development. This view, developed in the late 1980s, has dominated the discourse on Māori social policy throughout the 1990s. The process of Treaty settlements, the rise of New Right thinking and policies, and the emergence of a new elite of Māori bureaucrats and professionals are the forces behind this development. One consequence has been a movement towards an atomised Māori society, in contrast to the dynamics of Māori nationalism so prevalent since the 1890s.

On the other side of the debate is what can be termed the 'Māori humanist' view, which argues that it is Māori people who define Māori culture, and not the other way round. According to this view, the kinship and descent systems of whānau, hapū and iwi all engender a sense of belonging and solidarity. Iwi, while important, is not the sole source of identity and being. It is in tikanga and ritenga—worldview, customs, ethics and values—that identity and personhood are primarily defined. It is argued that 'iwi' can therefore refer to a group of Māori people who have formed a social organisation and called it an iwi, and that the evolution of this form of social organisation is appropriate to the modern age of Māori urbanisation and social mobility. Iwi is thus a means to an end, and the end is authentic Māori development. The Māori humanist view has been promoted in particular by Māori urban authorities, who claim that their organisation is an authentic form of iwi and deserves to be recognised as such.

At the time of writing (May 1998), this argument is being heard in the New Zealand Courts in the debate over whether Māori urban authorities should be included in the Crown's settlement of Treaty claims with respect to fishing assets. Whatever the outcome of that Court case, this is an issue that will not disappear. The number of Māori people involved in Māori urban authorities such as Te Whānau o Waipareira is simply too great for these modern-day iwi to be excluded from Māori development initiatives.

Conclusion

Generations ago, Te Aupōuri leader Meri Ngāroto reminded her people that te tangata (the human person) is more important than tribal ritual and custom (see Henare, 1995b, pp.15-16). During a time of crisis she told her people the following pepeha (proverb), which is often used in many different settings today:

> He aha te mea pai o te ao? He tangata, he tangata, he tangata! (Glossed as: What is the greatest good in the world? It is humanity, it is humanity, it is humanity!)

This pepeha captures the major theme of this chapter. I have argued that the set of ethics derived from the central concepts of tapu and mana provides guidance for social policy that will promote the authentic social development of individuals. In this context, 'individual' is not being used to mean an atomised being. Māori find their individual identity in belonging to a kinship group that is located in a particular time and place (represented here by the creation accounts of the Whangaroa region). To paraphrase Descartes, 'I belong, therefore I am' (Irwin, 1984, p.7; Maaka, 1994, p.314). He tangata (individuality) and aroha ki te tangata (altruism) are both strong ethics in Māori philosophy and religion, but individualism is not what drives Māori.

In my view, this concern for the common good of humanity should also determine the outcome of the debate over 'what is iwi?' in our generation. I have shown that one of the central components of policymaking in regard to Te Tiriti o Waitangi/the Treaty of Waitangi in the 1990s has been the 'iwi authority' model of Māori development. This narrowly focused approach is fiercely challenged by a significant sector of the Māori community as an inadequate response to people's essential needs and aspirations. Tribal development does not necessarily equate with Māori development. The Māori urban authorities that have arisen in particular areas are providing for the authentic social and economic development of their members. I have argued that this was, and is, the fundamental role of iwi. Although the form may change, the substance remains the same.

More generally, I have proposed that Māori well-being and integrity are the essence of te mana Māori, and that mana is essential both for the group and for the individual. In contrast, the relationship between Māori and the Crown has been one in which inequities in education, housing, health and employment have persisted from generation to generation (Ministerial Planning Group, 1991). This under-development is not simply an economic problem; it also points to a crisis in human values (Henare 1995b, p.20). In this context, sustainable social policy that promotes the common good will require diverse social, cultural, economic and political structures and institutions which can address people's essential needs in a holistic programme of change.

Endnotes

1 The phrase 'Te Tiriti o Waitangi/the Treaty of Waitangi' is used in order to recognise that there are two versions of the Treaty. The Māori version had some 500 signatories, and the English version only 40. The two versions say different things, as they are not exact translations of each other. The Waitangi Tribunal and the Courts follow the convention of addressing both versions in interpreting their meanings. Māori refer primarily to the Māori language text for interpretation of meaning (cf. Williams, 1989, pp.76-8).

2 Marsden (1991, p.6) proposed that this is the opposite to situational ethics, which deny absolutes, norms and standards. Situational ethics would seem to have been a characteristic of the dominant settler culture in Aotearoa New Zealand.

3 In their philosophical meanings, 'tapu' is glossed as 'being with potentiality for power', and 'mana' as 'power' (see Shirres, 1997, pp.33, 53).

4 Some of the other values are mentioned in this chapter to illustrate points about Māori ethics and values, but it is not claimed that the coverage here is complete.

5 One Māori Labour politician, Hon. Peter Tapsell, also questioned the re-tribalisation of Māori in a similar way (cited in Maaka, 1994, p.313).

CHAPTER FOUR

MACROECONOMIC
CONSTRAINTS

PAUL DALZIEL

Changes to New Zealand's welfare state during the last decade have been part of a broader programme of radical economic reform intended to address constraints on economic growth (see the recent surveys by Massey, 1995; Dalziel and Lattimore, 1996; Evans et al., 1996; Henderson, 1996; Scott, 1996; Silverstone, Bollard and Lattimore, 1996; and Kelsey, 1997a). The decision to initiate reform in 1984, for example, was based on a belief that poor economic management over many years had produced widespread inefficiencies and low growth, which could be reversed with more orthodox policies (Treasury, 1984, pp.103-4; ESC Secretariat, 1984, pp.37-8; Douglas, 1984, p.23). After the change of government in 1990, further reform was presented as a strategy 'to succeed in the battle for economic growth and a return to full employment' (Bolger, 1990, p.8), and 'to transform New Zealand from a declining debt-ridden country into a dynamic, enterprising and prosperous nation' (Richardson, 1991, p.6). More recently, the 1996 Coalition Agreement between National and New Zealand First contained a number of agreed principles including a commitment 'to ensure there is an economic climate conducive to sustainable development and growth' (p.6).

There is a paradox, however. Although the reform programme as a whole was directed towards promoting faster economic growth, virtually every policy change during this period involved restraint, retrenchment or redistribution towards the better-off, producing higher unemployment, increased poverty and a wider income distribution among households. Furthermore, these adverse effects were recognised by policy advisers in advance, but were discounted with the promise that higher output per person and higher economic growth *in the long run* would compensate for these current sacrifices. The 'short-term pain for long-term gain' argument continues to be used with persuasive effect—to justify, for example, the exclusion of social welfare beneficiaries from the government's 1996 tax cuts (Birch, 1996a, p.18), and to presage further reductions in taxation (Bolger, 1997).

The purpose of this chapter is to examine this argument in three parts. The first section looks backwards, and compares New Zealand's growth record before and after 1984 in order to measure the size of the sacrifice made during the transition phase of the reforms, and to consider whether there has been any sustained improvement in the growth indicator. The second section looks to the present, and examines recent research in New Zealand that has been used in support of proposals for reduced public expenditure on education, health and social security in order to finance further tax cuts. The third section looks to the future, with a discussion of an alternative approach to economic development that places greater emphasis on the role of the level and distribution of aggregate demand in generating economic strength than has been the case in the supply-side reforms since the mid-1980s.

Economic Growth During the Reforms

The primary indicator used by economists to measure macroeconomic performance is real per capita gross domestic product. Gross domestic product (GDP) is an estimate of the total value of economic activity in the marketplace or in the public sector. Real GDP is obtained by removing the impact of inflation on average prices, and thus measures the volume (rather than the nominal value) of economic activity. There are numerous conceptual and practical problems with this measure, associated with the activities that are counted as economic activity and those that are not (Waring, 1988), but real GDP remains for now the standard estimate of changes in a country's market income over time. Real per capita GDP is obtained by dividing real GDP by the country's population, which can be done in two ways. If total population is used, the result is an indicator of average market income. If working-age population is used, the result indicates average market productivity.

As the reform programme was implemented to improve productivity performance, Figure 4.1 uses working-age population as the denominator in presenting a graph of New Zealand's real per capita GDP. The data—which are for years ending March from 1960/61 to 1996/97—are calculated from Statistics New Zealand's historical series for real GDP (INFOS series SNBA. S2AZAT) and a working-age population series constructed from INFOS series DPEA.SBEC, scaled by official estimates of the proportion of the population aged 15-64 (Statistics New Zealand, 1996, updated). The graph shows a clear upward trend in aggregate productivity before the reform programme began in 1984/85. There was then a severe downturn during the transition phase of the reforms, followed by a strong recovery in 1993/94 and 1994/95.

Also shown in Figure 4.1 is a trend line calculated as the annual growth rate in real per capita GDP between 1966/67 and 1981/82. The construction of trend lines is notoriously controversial, because so much depends on the chosen endpoints. Figure 4.1 follows a method suggested by Solow (1997,

Figure 4.1 New Zealand's Real Per Capita GDP, 1960/61 to 1996/97

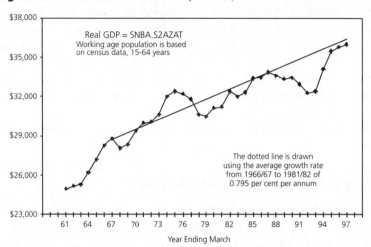

p.230) of using two peak years in the business cycle, which were also chosen to avoid the turbulent mid-1970s when New Zealand's terms of trade fluctuated wildly (see Dalziel and Lattimore, 1996, p.8).[1] The resulting calculation is that New Zealand's real per capita GDP increased at an average rate of just under 0.8 per cent per annum over the last two completed business cycles before the reform programme began.

Figure 4.1 reveals two important points affecting current economic and social policies. The first is the deep and extensive departure from trend that occurred between 1987/88 and 1993/94. The accumulated difference between the actual output path and the trend line during those seven years is $11,500 per working-age person (in 1991/92 dollars), which amounts to 32 per cent of annual GDP in 1996/97. The sacrifice of just under a third of a year's aggregate production during the transition phase of the reforms was undoubtedly a primary cause (along with the April 1991 benefit cuts) of the substantial rise in poverty and social exclusion apparent in the 1990s.

The second point to note from the graph is that although aggregate productivity bounced back strongly in 1993/94 and 1994/95, it returned only towards the pre-reform trend line. In other words, the data in Figure 4.1 do not suggest any clear-cut improvement in productivity growth that could compensate the large income sacrifices incurred during the reforms or provide extra resources to address the poverty created as part of their legacy. According to organisations such as the New Zealand Business Roundtable (1996), this implies that the reform programme must be accelerated, but I will argue later in this chapter that New Zealand's whole approach to reform must be re-examined in the light of this experience.

Taxation and Growth

Proponents of less government have concentrated on two major arguments. The first claims that there is a strong negative relationship between a country's tax burden and its rate of economic growth, at least beyond a certain level of taxation as a percentage of GDP (the tax ratio). The Inland Revenue Department has sponsored a number of studies exploring this relationship in New Zealand, all of which suggest that lower taxes could increase the trend rate of growth. The second argument adopts a welfare economics analysis to suggest that efficiency would be enhanced if the price distortion effects of taxes were reduced as a result of a smaller public sector. In particular, this analysis suggests that, leaving aside equity considerations, households should not be taxed to pay for public services that could have been purchased voluntarily in the private sector.

Both arguments will be examined in this section, but first it is useful to discuss where New Zealand stands in international comparisons. Cheyne et al. (1997, p.16) observe that 'Aotearoa/New Zealand is a unique society in the South Pacific, a neighbour of Asia, but with indigenous and European cultural heritages.' Table 4.1 reflects two of these elements by presenting a list of selected OECD countries on the left-hand side, and members of the Asia Pacific Economic Co-operation (APEC) forum (excluding Brunei Darussalam, Hong Kong and Taiwan, which are not included in IMF data sources) on the right-hand side. The distinction is required by the different coverage of the OECD and IMF sources, but it also reveals a divergence that is reflected in domestic debates about the optimal size of government. The left-hand side shows that taxation in New Zealand is relatively low compared to the comprehensive welfare states of Scandinavia and Western Europe (indeed, the list tends to overstate New Zealand's position, since European governments typically spend more than they receive in tax revenue). This has led Castles (1985, Chapter 1) and Stephens and Bradshaw (1995) to argue that New Zealand has fallen behind other high-income economies in providing social assistance. The right-hand side, however, shows that New Zealand's tax ratio is the highest in the Asia Pacific region. This has led Kerr (1994, p.6) and Brash (1997, p.313) to argue for a lower tax burden to avoid falling behind New Zealand's Pacific and Asian neighbours in economic performance.

Inter-country comparisons of this nature are fraught with difficulties. New Zealand, for example, provides income support gross of tax and has eliminated almost all personal tax exemptions that are common in other tax systems. These features increase New Zealand's recorded tax ratio, without necessarily implying a higher degree of government involvement in the economy than countries with lower ratios. As a further illustration, Kwon (1997) argues that

Table 4.1 Central and State Government Tax Ratios, circa 1994

Selected OECD Countries		Selected APEC Countries	
Country	% GDP	Country	% GDP
Denmark	51.6	New Zealand	34.6
Sweden	51.0	Canada	32.4
Finland	47.3	Australia	28.2
Belgium	46.6	United States	23.3
Netherlands	45.9	Malaysia	21.5
France	44.1	Papua New Guinea	19.4
Austria	42.8	Japan	18.0
Greece	42.5	Chile	17.8
Italy	41.7	Singapore	17.8
Norway	41.2	Korea	17.7
Germany	39.3	Thailand	16.8
Ireland	37.5	Philippines	16.0
New Zealand	37.0	Mexico	14.9
Spain	35.8	Indonesia	12.5
United Kingdom	34.1	China	6.1
Switzerland	33.9		

Sources: The OECD data come from *OECD Report on Government Revenue 1996*. The APEC data come from *IMF Government Finance Statistics Yearbook 1996* and *IMF International Financial Statistics Yearbook 1996*. Note that the different sources mean that there is a small discrepancy between the New Zealand data in the two columns.

although Japan and Korea have much lower public expenditure on welfare than the United Kingdom or Sweden, the role of the state is nonetheless comparable because private sector schemes for social security insurance and health care are compulsory in Japan and Korea and tightly regulated by government. Considerations such as these suggest that research might be more reliable if it focused on one country at a time. Several projects in recent years have sought to measure tax effects in New Zealand.

The Inland Revenue Research Programme

In 1995, Inland Revenue began a research programme examining the health of the tax system. This wide-ranging project has produced more than 35 working papers aimed at providing a better empirical foundation for assessing the efficiency, income dispersion and revenue consequences of New Zealand's tax system. Three of the papers (Caragata and Small, 1996; Scully, 1996a; Lovell and Branson, 1997) undertake an econometric analysis of the relationship between the ratio of tax receipts to nominal GDP (divided into direct and indirect taxes in Lovell and Branson's analysis) and the rate of change in real GDP. The papers derive or assume different mathematical forms for the relationship between the tax burden and growth, but in every case the data reveal a strong negative relationship, implying that lower taxes are associated with higher growth. Some of the mathematical forms allow an optimal tax rate to be calculated, which is found to be around 20 per cent in each case. Because New Zealand's tax receipts since World War II have ranged between 22 and 37 per cent of GDP, the authors argue that much higher income levels and growth rates could have been sustained by a lower average tax rate. Scully (1996a), for example, calculates that the income sacrificed between 1946 and 1994, due to taxes being higher than his estimated optimal rate, amounts to a staggering $1.17 trillion.

The manager of the research programme, Patrick Caragata, states that mainstream economic theory has ignored this negative relationship between taxes and growth, apart from a small number of journal articles and recent discussion papers (Caragata, 1997, p.14). Indeed, the consensus in the international literature does not support a general proposition that the size of government should be about 20 per cent of GDP. At the 1997 annual meeting of the American Economics Association, for example, Musgrave (1997, p.156) argued that 'downsizing [of government] as the ultimate policy goal makes no sense'; Tanzi and Schuknecht (1997, p.168) offered figures of between 30 and 40 per cent of GDP as the size of government at which 'much of the potential social gain from public spending has been obtained'; Hall and Jones (1997, p.176) explicitly excluded 'measures such as the size of the government inclusive of welfare spending' as capable of explaining differences in levels of long-term economic success across countries; and Sala-i-Martin (1997, p.182) concluded that 'no measure of government spending (including investment) appears to affect growth in a significant way'.

Within New Zealand, the debate has focused on the model and conclusions of Gerald Scully, after his visit to Wellington in May 1997. Chapple (1997), Jackson (1997), Lepper (1997) and Sieper (1997) have produced formal critiques of Scully's unorthodox use of economic theory to derive his relationship between taxation and growth.[2] Scully (1997a and 1997b; see also 1996b) has defended his models against these criticisms, as has Caragata (1997). This debate is likely to continue, but in the meantime some important observations can be made.

First, the negative relationship between taxation and growth reported in the research programme appears to be robust when applied to different specifications and time periods of New Zealand data. It is a mistake, however, to conclude from this that reducing the size of government would lead to higher growth, since a distinction must be made between the short-term impact of a lower tax rate on the business cycle and the long-term impact of lower taxes and lower public expenditure on the trend growth rate (which is the real research question). A reduction in the tax rate will typically give a short-term boost to aggregate demand (which is one of the reasons why monetary policy struggled to cope with the tax cuts of 1996, for example), and an increase in the tax rate will temporarily reduce aggregate demand. This is sufficient to produce a negative econometric relationship between taxation and growth using annual data, but *does not address the question* of whether a smaller public sector would produce higher or lower growth in the long run.

Second, the programme's models are described as 'parsimonious', meaning that they concentrate on only one factor that might affect economic growth—the tax burden. This means that the models do not explain the variation in growth well (in technical terms, their adjusted R^2 values are generally low). But it also means that claims such as the one that New Zealand could have produced an extra trillion dollars worth of output if it had had a lower tax rate are simply not credible, since they do not take into account the physical, environmental and social constraints on growth that create the fundamental economic problem of scarcity.

These points do not deny the general proposition that the public sector can get too large. Scully (1996a, pp.3-4) argues that some public services (for example, national defence, the justice system and economic infrastructure) increase the productivity of the country's resources, so that imposing taxes to fund these services is beneficial for economic growth. Once the government increases taxation further for redistributive purposes (for example, to finance public education, health and social assistance beyond minimal levels), this acts as a drain on private productivity, and economic growth will slow. These observations give rise to the hypothesis that there is an optimal level of taxation at which government expenditure is constrained to providing only public services that enhance productivity.

Notice that Scully's concern is with maximising growth. Yet the goal of policy is not to maximise growth in production *per se*, but to maximise growth in social well-being—and as every macroeconomic textbook explains, social well-being cannot be identified with gross domestic product. One of the reasons why governments become involved in redistributive policies is that the last dollar received in social assistance by someone with severely restricted opportunities to earn market income is likely to be worth considerably more to the recipient than it did to the taxpayer who paid it. This is based on the assumption that an extra dollar to a household at or below the poverty line has a larger impact on that household's well-being than would be the case for a higher-income household. If it is accepted that a market economy does not provide adequate opportunities for earning market income, a certain amount of income redistribution from high- to low-income citizens may be justified in the name of social justice. In this case, GDP is a particularly poor indicator of social well-being, since it ignores the benefits of a more equitable distribution.

Redistributive public expenditure also contributes to social well-being by building up 'social capital'—the social norms, community networks and levels of civic participation that encourage trust and co-operation among citizens. Economists are familiar with the role played by physical capital (factories, shops, houses, machinery, transport, roads, hospitals, schools and so on) and human capital (education and on-the-job training) in raising living standards. Putnam (1993a) argues that social capital also contributes to economic productivity. According to this theory, well-designed public expenditure that allows everyone 'to feel a sense of participation in and belonging to the community' (Royal Commission on Social Security, 1972, p.65) will produce social cohesion and civic responsibility in a way that enhances economic productivity, to the benefit of everyone (see Robinson, 1997, and Davis, 1998, for discussions of this concept in a New Zealand context).

Labour Responses and Welfare

A second line of argument in favour of a smaller public sector is based on an economic welfare analysis of the impact of lower income tax rates on labour supply responses. Let us suppose that the marginal tax rate on wages is reduced (for example, from 33 cents to 30 cents in the dollar). Economists distinguish two effects that might result from this change. First, the value to the worker of an extra hour of employment would be increased, since the after-tax wage rate would be higher. Under certain assumptions, this would increase the aggregate number of hours worked in the economy, since at least some workers could be expected to increase their level of employment at the expense of other activities (for example, family care, education, retirement or leisure), given the enhanced incentive for extra paid work. This is known as the substitution effect. Second, for any aggregate number of hours worked, the amount of take-home pay received by each worker will rise because of the lower tax rate. This might cause some workers to choose to work fewer hours and enjoy more leisure. This is known as the income effect.

The substitution and income effects move the labour supply in opposite directions, so that the impact of a change in income tax rates on hours of paid work can be very small. Measuring the net effect of such a change in New Zealand was the major focus of a study by Prebble and Rebstock (1992). Their computer simulation research suggested that a reduction in the tax rate which increased after-tax wages by one per cent (everything else staying the same) would lead to a rise in the labour supply of 0.38 per cent, with male employment being less responsive on average than female employment (Chiao and Walker, 1992, p.164). The introduction to the study describes this effect as 'weak' (Prebble, 1992, p.26), and argues that it would not by itself justify a policy of tax cuts.

However, Diewert and Lawrence (1994) and McKeown and Woodfield (1995) argue that there are large welfare gains to be obtained by lowering tax rates.[3] Diewert and Lawrence report that in 1991, 'a reduction in government spending financed by reduced labour taxes would have led to a real rate of return on this "investment" of 18.3 per cent' (1994, p.6; see also 1996, p.670);

in other words, the last dollar of tax collected cost $1.18 to the average taxpayer because of the disincentive effect of a higher tax rate. McKeown and Woodfield's study produces even higher estimates of between 24.6 and 65.4 per cent. These two studies, and their respective estimates, were cited in the government's *Budget and Fiscal Strategy Report 1996* (p.34, fn.1), and played an important part in supporting the policy of reducing the middle tax rate in 1996 and 1998.

The fundamental difference between these studies and Prebble and Rebstock's analysis concerns their treatment of the lower public expenditure that must accompany a tax cut. Prebble and Rebstock implicitly assume that lower government expenditure has no influence on employment choices, and that only after-tax earnings matter (see Fullerton, 1991, pp.304-5, and Ballard and Fullerton, 1992, pp.125-6 for further discussions). However, transfer payments and public services provide income-equivalent benefits to taxpayers, and lower taxes mean that these benefits will be reduced. It is plausible, therefore, to argue that this loss of income-equivalent benefits will offset the income effect of a lower tax rate.[4] Suppose, for example, that taxpayers with some choice about the hours they are in paid employment are working 40 hours per week. If these taxpayers were obliged to pay the full cost of their health and education services (previously subsidised from tax revenue), but faced a lower marginal tax rate, each might choose to work, say, 44 hours per week. This would be because the benefit of working one more hour is higher as a result of the lower tax rate (the substitution effect), while the cost of reducing their work effort is higher since they will no longer be able to afford health and education services if they do not earn sufficient income (offsetting the income effect of the lower tax rate). Not all taxpayers have a choice in the number of hours they work, of course, including those who are involuntarily unemployed or involved in the full-time care of children, or whose hours of employment are set by their employers. Even allowing for these groups, however, the income-offsetting effect of public transfers and services means that there is a larger labour supply response to a tax change than is measured by analysing the change in isolation.

The next step is to investigate whether individuals are better or worse off as a result of the lower tax rate and lower public expenditure. The first point to be made is that those who are involuntarily unemployed or involved in the full-time care of children are unambiguously worse off—they lose their entitlement to health and education services, but are not earning market income to take advantage of lower taxes. Similarly, because tax rate cuts typically favour high-income earners, lower-income households are disadvantaged by being less able to afford quality health and education services in the market-place to replace their previous entitlements. These are not trivial matters, but go to the heart of the role of a welfare state in fostering social cohesion and mitigating civil inequality, and in spreading the costs of raising the next generation across all workers, whether they have children or not (Hyman, 1994).

Within the economics literature, the tradition has been to overlook these issues by restricting attention to a 'representative taxpayer' who earns the average income and is assumed to be able to choose their hours of paid employment. Within this framework, it is possible to ask how much the last dollar of public expenditure must be worth to the representative taxpayer in order to justify levying taxes to pay for that expenditure. This is the question addressed by Diewert and Lawrence, and by McKeown and Woodfield. The 'marginal excess burden' estimates the extent to which the *value* of the last dollar of public expenditure (to taxpayers) must exceed its *cost* in order to justify the tax revenue needed to finance it. In other words, it represents the value that must be added to the resources employed in the public sector for the sector to be operating at an efficient level, given the representative taxpayer's preferences.[5]

For many market liberals, it is axiomatic that the state cannot add value, but can only transfer resources that have been created in the private sector. Kerr (1996a, p.22), for example, observes that New Zealand's liberalisation programme after 1984 'was grounded in the belief that it is private entrepreneurs—not governments—that create wealth' (see also Law, 1996). For most goods and services, it is reasonable to presume that economic efficiency is enhanced if consumers are able to purchase them voluntarily from competitive, privately-owned firms. There are, however, a number of important exceptions where the government is able to add considerable value to the taxpayer dollar by providing 'social goods and services'. These exceptions are examined in detail in Chapter 5. In each case, it is possible that public expenditure may be too high—or too low. Yet blanket statements such as that quoted earlier—'a reduction in government spending financed by reduced labour taxes would have led to a real rate of return on this "investment" of 18.3 per cent' (Diewert and Lawrence, 1994, p.6)—cannot be justified. It considers only one side of the equation, and neglects the marginal welfare benefits generated by the public spending that is being funded by the country's taxes.

Aggregate Demand

The economic reforms between 1984 and 1994 implicitly assumed that the major macroeconomic constraints faced by New Zealand lay on the supply side of the economy. Thus it was argued that policy should aim to increase producer efficiency through a number of initiatives: corporatising and privatising government trading departments; exposing private-sector firms to greater domestic and international competition; deregulating the financial sector; increasing incentives to seek and accept employment; targeting monetary policy to the single goal of price stability; targeting fiscal policy to lower public debt and tax rates; decentralising New Zealand's industrial relations system by basing it on individual contracts; and increasing the role of private-sector providers in health, education and other social services. These were radical and extensive changes, but as Figure 4.1 shows, they have not produced any clear-cut improvement in New Zealand's aggregate growth performance. Furthermore, Krishnan (1995), Stephens et al. (1995), Easton (1995b and 1996a) and Kelsey (1997a) have all recorded that there was a significant rise in poverty during the reform period (see also Chapter 13).[6]

One possible explanation is that the original diagnosis of New Zealand's macroeconomic constraints was wrong, or at least incomplete, because the focus on supply-side reforms ignored the role played by the level and distribution of aggregate demand in promoting economic development. There is a fundamental paradox in economics that while an individual household can improve its prosperity by increasing its income and reducing its expenditure, these actions cannot work at the macroeconomic level, since a person can earn income only if someone else is spending money or drawing on credit. Hence, aggregate income can be increased only if aggregate expenditure also increases. As a consequence, supply-side reforms may make producers increasingly efficient at supplying goods and services, but this will not lead to increased economic activity if aggregate demand does not rise at the same time.

The proposition that this justifies a role for the state in managing aggregate demand is associated with the theory of Keynes (1936), and its subsequent translation into policy in many countries after World War II. It appears to have played a part in allowing the growth in prosperity that took place in Western economies during the 1950s and 1960s, but is also blamed for the sustained inflation that occurred after the oil shocks of the 1970s. As a result, policymakers around the world now have more modest expectations of their ability to smooth fluctuations in aggregate demand, and are more careful to avoid inflationary impulses from budget deficits or accommodating monetary policy. In New Zealand, this reaction to the excesses of the 1970s has been taken to an extreme. No longer is there any conscious effort by the government to moderate the peaks and troughs in the economy's growth rate over time (Bryant, 1996); indeed, New Zealand policymakers have been more willing than most to disregard the effects of aggregate demand in implementing macroeconomic policy. Chapter 5 will discuss the 1991 benefit cuts and 1996 tax cuts as good examples of how fiscal policy in the 1990s has tended to amplify fluctuations in the *level* of aggregate demand, but there is also an issue of the way in which policy is tending to concentrate spending power in the hands of upper-income households rather than seeking to distribute it more widely.

This is well illustrated by the *Tax Reduction and Social Policy Programme* (Birch, 1996a). Researchers agree that the New Zealand households most vulnerable to poverty are those with children (Easton, 1995b, pp.205-6; Stephens et al., 1995, pp.103-4). A policy concerned with the distribution of aggregate demand would give priority to putting extra resources into such households, and this seems to have been recognised by the government when it signalled new steps 'to assist, strengthen, and empower low- and middle-income families in their efforts to achieve higher income and better quality of life', with the largest gains 'reserved for low- and middle-income working families'. (Birch, 1996a, p.8). Yet despite this rhetoric, the reality is very different (Dalziel, 1996), as can be analysed using Table 4.2.

Table 4.2 Estimated Gains in Weekly Net Income After the 1996 & 1998 Tax Reductions
Household Types by Quintile

Quintile		Non-Family	Over-59 Adult or Couple	Single Adult	Couple With No Children	Couple With Children	Sole Parent	Extended Families	All House-holds
	a	$3.52	$5.71	$0.58	$1.83	$37.85	$8.60	$16.81	$14.62
1	b	2.2%	2.9%	0.4%	0.9%	11.7%	3.1%	4.6%	6.2%
	c	0.05%	0.27%	0.07%	0.09%	5.43%	0.66%	0.87%	7.43%
	a	$8.06	$14.12	$3.92	$16.42	$57.90	$10.92	$16.79	$26.60
2	b	1.9%	4.6%	1.7%	4.3%	10.4%	3.0%	3.2%	6.2%
	c	0.11%	1.54%	0.13%	0.63%	8.97%	0.88%	1.12%	13.38%
	a	$16.33	$31.69	$15.48	$31.40	$46.37	$28.40	$41.29	$35.58
3	b	2.7%	7.5%	4.6%	5.9%	6.0%	4.9%	5.1%	5.8%
	c	0.41%	4.54%	0.30%	1.62%	7.27%	1.25%	2.37%	17.75%
	a	$47.83	$41.77	$33.87	$43.37	$60.88	$42.75	$62.13	$50.81
4	b	5.6%	7.0%	6.9%	5.9%	5.5%	4.9%	5.8%	5.8%
	c	1.10%	5.35%	0.71%	2.49%	11.87%	1.47%	2.38%	25.37%
	a	$87.40	$53.77	$44.85	$78.85	$83.63	$60.96	$95.37	$73.04
5	b	6.1%	3.7%	5.3%	5.7%	4.3%	5.8%	5.4%	4.8%
	c	2.01%	4.52%	2.74%	11.16%	12.63%	0.82%	2.19%	36.07%
	a	$37.62	$30.60	$16.87	$48.15	$57.98	$19.13	$36.62	$40.13
All	b	4.8%	5.3%	4.3%	5.7%	6.0%	4.1%	4.9%	5.5%
	c	3.66%	16.23%	3.95%	15.99%	46.17%	5.07%	8.92%	100%

Notes: 'a' is the average net income gain per week, after the 1996 and 1998 tax cuts.
'b' expresses 'a' as a percentage gain.
'c' is the share of the total gain going to each household type/income quintile.
Sources: Rows a and b come from Birch (1996a, Table 3.5, p.73). Row c is calculated from Birch (1996a, Figure 3.5, p.71, and Table 3.5, p.73), as described in Dalziel (1996).

The table is based on Treasury analysis using Household Economic Survey data to estimate the impact of the 1996 and 1998 tax reductions on households, classified by household type (columns) and income quintile (rows). The types are self-explanatory, except that the 'Non-Family' category refers to households in which there is an individual with no familial relationship with the person nominated as household head, and the 'Over-59' type refers to adults aged over 59 years living alone and to couples where the female is aged over 59 years. The income quintiles are derived by ranking households by their after-tax incomes, adjusted for the number of adults and children in the household. Quintile 1 contains the lowest-income 20 per cent of households, and Quintile 5 contains the highest-income 20 per cent of households.

The data are interpreted as follows. Each cell contains three statistics. The first (a) records the average net income gain per week after the full tax-reduction programme was implemented (that is, after both rounds of tax cuts, in 1996 and 1998); the second (b) expresses this as a percentage gain; and the third (c) records the share of the total gains going to the cell's household type and income quintile. Thus the first cell records that, between 1996 and 1998, non-family households in the lowest income quintile are gaining, on average, $3.52 per week, an increase of 2.2 per cent, representing just 0.05 per cent of the programme's total value (this last figure is very low because there are very few households in this category). The right-hand column records the average gains of households in each quintile, while the bottom row records the average gains of each household type.

At first glance, Table 4.2 suggests that the objective of targeting families is achieved. The largest gains in each quintile (except the top one) are going to couple households with children and to extended families, although sole-parent families receive considerably smaller gains in the lower quintiles. Note, however, that only 60.2 per cent of the total gains is going to families with children (the sum of the italicised figures in the final row for columns five, six and seven), while 39.8 per cent is going to other household types (non-families, over-59s, single adults and couples with no children). This 60-40 division is not too different from the proportions of the total adult population living in these two groups of household types. Thus the overall impact of the tax-reduction package in redistributing income from non-child households to households with children is minimal.

Furthermore, despite the programme's stated aim of directing assistance towards low- and middle-income families, only 7.4 per cent of the total gains is received by households in the lowest income quintile, and only 38.6 per cent is received by households in the bottom three quintiles. Well over one-third of the programme is going to the 20 per cent of households in New Zealand with the highest incomes. Similarly, of the gains to family households, just over half is going to families in the top two quintiles. Just under one half of 60 per cent of the gains will thus end up in the pockets of the programme's announced target group. That is, for every dollar of extra expenditure or forgone revenue in the programme, 40 cents is going to non-family households, 31 cents is going to families in the top two income quintiles, and only 29 cents is going to the target group of low- and middle-income families. Given the emphasis in recent years on tightly targeting government expenditure, this is a very poor outcome compared with alternatives such as restoring a universal family benefit to primary caregivers of children or increasing entitlements paid under the family support programme. The fiscal surpluses of the mid-1990s provided a unique opportunity to redistribute spending power through transfers or tax concessions to families whose needs could be supplied in New Zealand's market economy, but are not being met because the households do not have the means to translate their needs into effective demand. That opportunity has been lost.

Conclusion

The fundamental questions in economics arise from the problem of allocating scarce resources in the presence of unlimited demands for consumption and wealth. The political response in New Zealand for more than a decade has been to pursue supply-side policies that promise to increase the rate of growth in real GDP in the long run, even though in the short run they have involved retrenchment and many people being pushed to the margins of the economy. This chapter has presented evidence to suggest that there has been no clear-cut relaxation of macroeconomic constraints as a result of these policies. It has argued against the hypothesis that further reductions in tax rates would promote growth or social well-being. It has also put forward the proposition that policymakers need to be much more concerned about the level and distribution of aggregate demand in analysing future policy responses.

Endnotes

1 The starting point of 1966/67 was suggested by Evans et al. (1996, p.1872) and retained in my critique of their analysis (Dalziel, 1998a). This starting point also coincides with Easton's (1997a, pp.73-4) judgement that 1966/67 represents the major structural break in New Zealand's post-war economic history.

2 Lovell and Branson (1997) also adapt a well-known technique (frontier production function analysis) in an unorthodox way (by defining the ratios of direct and indirect taxation to GDP as two inputs producing the output of economic growth) to derive their relationship between taxation and growth. Caragata and Small (1996) present two mathematical forms—a quadratic function and a logistic function. The former produces non-significant parameter estimates, but the latter confirms the negative relationship (although this form does not allow an optimal tax rate to be calculated).

3 A third New Zealand paper, by Dods and McCann (1995), also provides an estimate of the dead-weight loss of taxation as part of a wider study. Their estimate, however, assumed that the tax burden imposed an output loss of either 30 per cent or 10 per cent in a base year (1980/81), and then constructed an efficiency index based on fluctuations over time. Thus the paper's conclusion, that for the June year 1994 the production loss was either about 26 per cent or about 5 per cent of reported GDP, simply reflected these alternate assumptions.

It provides information about the trend, but cannot be considered a genuine estimate of the actual dead-weight loss.

4 There is a more general point to be observed here. In discussions about tax cuts, it is often suggested that lower taxes will make people better off because they will have more money in their pocket to spend or save. This, of course, is just the income effect discussed in the text, but it misses the point that reductions in public spending on health care, education and income support to fund the tax cuts mean that households will be required to spend their extra money on health insurance, school fees and income protection insurance. Apart from the labour supply response considered here, whether people are better off depends on whether these services are more efficiently provided by the private or public sector. This is discussed in the following chapter.

5 It is perhaps worth emphasising that the 'representative taxpayer's preferences' is an artificial analytical device. There is no method to create an operational social choice mechanism based on this device, and indeed Arrow's (1950) famous 'impossibility theorem' indicates that it is not feasible to aggregate individual preferences into social preferences while maintaining certain minimum standards of efficiency and equity.

6 A poorly performing economy was, of course, the main justification for claims prior to the 1991 benefit cuts that New Zealand's traditional welfare state was unaffordable (a point taken up in more detail in Chapter 16). The point should be made, however, that a poorly performing economy also makes a high user-pays and low safety-net system unaffordable from a social point of view. If a lack of quality employment opportunities means that a large number of people cannot earn sufficient market income to support themselves and their families (including the need to save for retirement), then social welfare cutbacks simply transfer the costs from taxpayers in general to those least able to help themselves.

CHAPTER FIVE

THE ROLE OF GOVERNMENT

PAUL DALZIEL AND SUSAN ST JOHN

An often quoted epigram of the 1960s was 'we are all Keynesians now', so widespread was the view that there were fundamental tasks for the state in regulating and stabilising the economy, in providing the social and economic infrastructure to enhance development, and in undertaking income redistribution to promote social cohesion. Following 'stagflation' in the 1970s, however, widespread disillusionment with this consensus led to increased demands in many Western countries that the frontiers of the state be rolled back. Thatcherism in the United Kingdom and Reaganomics in the United States had their parallels in Rogernomics in New Zealand. So successful was the reversal in thinking that in 1990 a new Minister of Finance was able to justify her efforts to reduce public expenditure by referring to 'the crushing burden of state spending' which had 'sapped the initiative and the energy of New Zealand's wealth creators' (Richardson, 1990, p.17). The programme of privatising former state activity initiated by her two predecessors was continued, amid calls for its extension into health, education, housing and accident compensation. A rediscovery of the virtues of 'self-reliance' and the evils of 'state dependency' permeated policy discussions throughout the 1990s, and was reflected in radical changes to income support entitlements and industrial relations legislation. For some, the cuts and reforms have not gone far enough. Kerr (1997), for example, labels the growth of the state, 'collectivism' and the welfare state as among 'the seven deadly economic sins' that have inhibited economic growth and prosperity in New Zealand.

Against this background, it is timely to record the state's current activities, and some of the reasons for its involvement in certain types of economic activity.[1] Chapter 2 has discussed the broad concepts of social justice—including the protection of civil and political rights, and the pursuit of racial tolerance and cultural identity—that play an important part in guiding the work of public servants. The discussion in this chapter concentrates on six types of activity where state involvement is justified according to the narrower criterion of economic efficiency: natural monopolies; merit goods; externalities; public goods; poverty relief; and social insurance. In this context, the chapter addresses two important matters of principle still open to debate. The first concerns whether the government should intervene in the above activities directly by public provision, or whether it should purchase their provision by profit-motivated enterprises in either the public or private sector. Purchaser-provider splits have been attempted, for example, in secondary health care and in the bulk-funding of some schools. Such a split portends the privatisation of funding, whereby people are given tax cuts or cash subsidies to purchase their own social services. Proponents of this direction for further reform see the welfare state ultimately withering away, requiring only a small amount of taxes to fund little more than basic administration, defence, law and order. The second matter of principle concerns whether the government should attempt to use its revenue and expenditure decisions to stabilise fluctuations in economic growth around its long-term trend. This practice, perhaps more than any other, was associated with orthodox Keynesian economics for 40 years after World War II, but appears to have fallen into complete disfavour with current New Zealand policymakers.

The Government's Financial Statement

The New Zealand government's financial statement of revenue and expenditure for the year ending 30 June 1997 is presented in Table 5.1. The left-hand side describes government revenue, 90 per cent of which is tax. The rest is made up of non-tax public revenue and the investment income from government holdings of financial assets and its ownership of state-owned enterprises (SOEs) and Crown entities (CEs). The total revenue of $34,778 million is 36 per cent of gross domestic product (GDP). Because the government has moved to generally accepted accounting practice (GAAP), the left-hand side also records changes in the government's equity in its SOEs and CEs ($83 million for 1996/97), due to retained profits. The right-hand side of the statement records the government's expenditure and operating balance. The first expenditure group accounts for public services, classified here into eight functional categories.[2] The second group involves transfer payments, particularly for social assistance. The third expenditure group comprises the interest and other servicing costs associated with the Crown's public debt. The difference between total revenue (plus the increased equity in SOEs) and total expenditure is the Crown's operating surplus: $1,908 million for the year ending 30 June 1997 (which was 2.0 per cent of GDP for that fiscal year).

Figure 5.1 provides a good framework for discussing the current involvement of the government in economic activity. First, it is engaged in providing certain commercial goods and services, which it does through thirteen SOEs (fully corporatised under the State Owned Enterprises Act 1986) and approximately 2,900 CEs (a variety of agencies, authorities, boards, commissions, corporations, councils, foundations, institutes and trusts, including 2,664 school boards of trustees, 54 reserve boards, 39 tertiary education institutions, 23

Table 5.1 New Zealand Government Financial Statement for the Year
Ending 30 June 1997

REVENUE	$m	$m	EXPENDITURE	$m	$m
Taxation Revenue			Public Services		
Personal	15,324		Core Administration	1,483	
Company	3,233		Defence	946	
Withholding	1,932		Economic Services	1,859	
GST	7,725		Education	5,008	
Excise	1,796		Health	5,626	
Customs Duty	909		Law and Order	1,281	
Road User Charges	426		Social Welfare	1,475	
Other	571		Other Public Services	312	
		31,916			17,990
Non-Tax Public Revenue			Transfer Payments		
Fees and Fines	263		Superannuation	5,102	
Sales of Goods & Services	664		Domestic Purposes	1,447	
ARCIC Recoveries	130		Unemployment	1,327	
Petroleum Royalties	40		Family Support	785	
Other	217		Accommodation Supp.	662	
		1,314	Invalids	536	
Investment Revenue			Sickness	379	
Interest on Student Loans	142		Student Allowances	327	
Interest on SOE Loans	45		Other Social Assistance	1,118	
Interest on CE Loans	69		Official Development Aid	184	
Other Interest	361		Other Transfers	12	
SOE Dividends	892				11,879
CE Dividends	15		Debt Servicing Expenses		
Unrealised Losses	-48		Interest & Finance Costs	3,072	
Other	72		Currency Movements	12	
		1,548			3,084
Total Revenue		34,778	Total Expenditure		32,953
PLUS Increased Equity in SOEs and CEs		83	PLUS Operating Surplus		1,908
TOTAL		34,861	TOTAL		34,861

Source: *Budget Economic and Fiscal Update 1998*, Document B.3.

Crown health enterprises and 21 business development boards). The Crown's
equity in both types of trading organisation was valued at $18,483 million as at
30 June 1997. Interest and dividend payments from the SOEs and CEs are
recorded as part of investment revenue on the left-hand side of Table 5.1.[3]

Second, the government is involved in the provision and funding of what
are here termed 'public services', amounting to $17,990 million in 1996/97
and administered by 44 government departments. Education and health are
easily the largest items in this part of the government's budget. In most cases,
large portions of a department's budget are used to finance goods or services
purchased from appropriate Crown entities, which means that any distinction
between public services and commercial services has become blurred in

New Zealand. This has led to considerable controversy—for example, whether public hospitals (renamed 'Crown health enterprises' in 1991, but reverting to their traditional title in the 1998 Budget) should be motivated by profits. This is one of the key issues in the 'purchaser-provider split' model discussed below.

The third major area of government involvement is in the redistribution of income. Table 5.1 records that one third of total tax revenue is returned to households in the form of transfer payments, mostly as social assistance of some kind. Even without adjusting for different accounting treatments of tax expenditures,[4] transfer payments as a proportion of GDP (12.6 per cent) are low by OECD standards (especially when it is recalled that social assistance payments are taxed in New Zealand). Note also that transfers do not consume resources directly (although there are administration costs, included under public services). Nevertheless, as Chapter 4 has explained, there are efficiency costs associated with the taxation needed to fund any form of public expenditure, so this role of the government, like the others, needs to be properly justified.

Social Goods and Services

Because taxation reduces personal incentives for effort, economic efficiency suggests that individuals should not be taxed to provide goods and services that could have been purchased directly in the private sector. There are, however, a number of important cases where government intervention is justified, discussed here under six headings: natural monopolies; merit goods; goods with externalities; public goods; poverty relief; and social insurance. In each case, some special characteristic means that the extra costs of taxation can be outweighed by the benefits of public provision of what may be called *social* goods and services (to distinguish them from *private* goods and services).

Natural Monopolies

The fundamental theorems of welfare economics demonstrate that, under certain conditions, competitive markets are efficient in the sense that in a competitive market equilibrium, no one can be made better off without someone else being made worse off.[5] Some goods and services, however, are produced by technologies that allow only one supplier to be profitable, which means that the relevant market cannot be competitive. This occurs, for example, if a firm's average cost of production tends to fall as the quantity of its output increases. Increasing returns to scale (as this is called) mean that once a firm establishes dominance in the market, new firms cannot compete for market share since smaller firms must have higher average costs. Such a market is termed a 'natural monopoly', the best examples being network services such as the national electricity grid, the urban telephone lines of Telecom, the water supply piping system of a city council, and so on. It is not economic for any potential competitor to duplicate these networks in order to enter the market. Hence, in an unregulated market there is an opportunity for the incumbent to earn super-normal profits through monopoly pricing, thus imposing efficiency costs on the rest of the economy that may be considerable. Furthermore, a condition of economic efficiency is that the price of a service should equal its marginal cost (that is, the cost of the last unit of output produced). It is a mathematical property of increasing returns to scale that marginal cost is lower than average cost. Under these conditions, setting the price equal to marginal cost would create losses (since price would not cover the average cost of supply), thus posing further problems.

Policymakers have traditionally responded to this issue in one of two ways—state regulation or state ownership. Regulation is notoriously difficult. There is an obvious incentive for private-sector owners to exploit their firm's monopoly position, while regulators cannot impose a simple marginal cost rule since this would force the firm out of business. Instead, some compromise must be negotiated, in which regulators face the considerable problem of not having access to the same information that is available to the firm's managers, and the subsequent difficulty of monitoring compliance. Furthermore, if some other rule is adopted (for example, allowing a fair rate of return on capital), this can create other perverse incentives (for example, to over-invest in the firm's capital assets, or to overvalue them). An alternative approach is to place natural monopolies in state ownership, so that the lack of market control is compensated by political control. This approach removes the tension between private profits and the public interest, but leaves open the possibility that the government itself may abuse the firm's monopoly position, or that the firm might operate inefficiently, given inadequate commercial monitoring by its political owners.

Historically, the state in New Zealand came to acquire a large number and diverse range of commercial enterprises, including all of the important natural monopolies. Treasury (1984, Chapter 13) argued that these enterprises were inefficient for several reasons, and from 1986 the government began to corporatise and/or privatise them (Duncan and Bollard, 1992). These moves are generally considered to be sensible. While there may have been a sound rationale for the state's original involvement in providing purely commercial goods such as banking services, insurance, air travel, freight transport and so on, the efficient conduct of modern businesses in a competitive, free-trade environment is not compatible with state ownership. Thus, even among those of a social-democratic persuasion, it is rare to hear anyone suggest that the state should re-nationalise the enterprises privatised during the late 1980s and 1990s.

Critics have argued, however, that this reform did not properly address the problem of natural monopolies in either public or private ownership. The State Owned Enterprises Act 1986, for example, stated that 'the principal objective of every State enterprise shall be to operate as a successful business', which does not take into account the inherent conflict between profits and efficiency in a natural monopoly. Plans in 1998 to split the Electricity Corporation into three SOEs are very controversial for this reason, since the restructuring is complex, costly and unlikely to deliver efficiency gains through competition. Further-more, debate continues about whether some of the assets sold under the government's privatisation scheme effectively passed natural monopolies into private hands without sufficient provision for state regulation (the Natural Gas Corporation and Telecom's telephone network being two important examples).

Merit Goods

The term 'merit good' was coined by Richard Musgrave (1957) to describe cases 'where individuals, as members of the community, accept certain community values or preferences, even though their personal preferences might differ' (Musgrave, 1987, p.452). Musgrave himself gives as examples 'concern for maintenance of historical sites, respect for national holidays, regard for environment or for learning and the arts' (1987, p.452). In some cases, the accepted social norm is that the merit good should not be denied to anyone who wishes to have it, regardless of their income (tertiary education is discussed in these terms in Chapter 11 of this volume). In other cases, society's elected representatives decide that everyone must have the merit good for their own benefit, whether or not they can afford it and whether or not they would otherwise choose to purchase it. The most important example in current policy debates is primary and secondary education up to the school leaving age of sixteen.[6] Because a person's life opportunities are seriously curtailed without basic education, school attendance is compulsory. In both types of merit good, the principle of voluntary market exchange does not apply, and this opens up an essential role for the government.

Goods with Externalities

There are some goods and services that produce more social benefits or impose more social costs than are captured in the private benefits and costs of the market participants. Such goods and services are said to involve 'externalities', and economic theory shows that they tend to be under-supplied (in the case of positive externalities, where social benefits exceed private benefits) or over-supplied (in the case of negative externalities) compared to a socially efficient equilibrium.

An example of a good with a negative externality is tobacco. There are certain 'private costs' involved in the production of cigarettes, including the cost of growing and drying the tobacco leaves and manufacturing the final product, which are included in their retail price. Because smoking damages health, however, the government pays out large sums in providing health care to people who contract diseases as a result of their smoking. These 'externality costs' would not be included in the market price of a packet of cigarettes unless the government took some action—and indeed, there are large excise taxes on tobacco to bring the price of cigarettes closer to their full social cost. Non-market interventions, such as limiting the sale of cigarettes to those over a certain age and banning sports sponsorship by tobacco companies, are other tools the government may use.

Identifying positive externalities can be controversial. It is argued, for example, that health and post-compulsory education involve substantial social benefits beyond the private benefit to the patient or student, because there are advantages to the whole community if a person is healthy and well-educated. The controversy arises because it is impossible to measure these social benefits with any great confidence. There is thus scope for considerable debate about the size of the gap between the personal benefit (which typically is also considerable) and the social benefit (see, for example, Chapter 11 on tertiary education). However, if it is accepted that a good does have a positive externality, then there is a role for the government in encouraging a greater supply than would occur in markets based on private benefit alone, either by being involved in its production or by subsidising its market price. If not excessive, this intervention brings the volume of production closer to its socially optimal quantity.

Public Goods

Public goods are defined by economists as those goods or services for which use by one person does not affect the quantity available for use by another person, and for which it is impossible to exclude anybody from its benefits. The classic example is a lighthouse at the entrance to a harbour. The use of it by one ship for guidance does not prevent another ship benefiting from it at the same time. Nor can its benefits be denied to anyone who chooses to take advantage of them. (Compare these outcomes with the way in which a tug-boat can assist only one ship at a time, and will not be supplied to guide ships that do not pay the prescribed fee.) Public goods create unique difficulties in economic theory. There is little economic incentive for individuals to con-tribute towards their cost, since they cannot be denied access to them if they refuse to pay (the 'free-rider' problem). As a result, a public good will tend to be under-supplied, or perhaps not supplied at all (even though the sum of its benefits to its potential users may outweigh its cost by a considerable margin), unless the government or some other authority is able to impose compulsory levies or taxes on the relevant user population in order to pay for it.

There appears to be universal acceptance on both the left and the right of the political spectrum that national defence, an independent judiciary, a public police force and parliament itself all qualify as public goods in this tightly defined economic sense. Thus there is strong support for government to use tax revenue to finance expenditure on these items (listed in the public services category on the right-hand side of Table 5.1). Far more controversial is the proposition that spending on what has been termed 'social capital' might also be considered a public good justifying government involvement. This controversy reflects what Bertram (1997, p.40) has called 'the great intellectual divide underlying most modern economic thinking ... between communitarian and individualist views of society'.

Robinson (1997, p.1) records that recent interest in the concept of social capital in New Zealand was stimulated by the visit of Robert Putnam in August 1996. Putnam (1993a, 1993b, 1996) proposes the hypothesis, supported by empirical studies in Italy and the United States, that 'networks of repeated social interaction which reinforce social norms, especially trust' enable people to act together to meet shared objectives effectively (cited in Robinson, 1997, p.2). These networks he calls 'social capital'.[7] The term has been enthusiastically adopted by both left-of-centre and right-of-centre commentators, although it is apparent that it means different things to different people (compare, for example, the different perspectives of Riddell, 1997, and Barker, 1997).

According to one view, social capital is a resource created by the voluntary interactions of individuals which can be used by the state to deliver public services more effectively and at a lower cost than through government departments. Indeed, it is argued that if the state does attempt to provide these services, it will crowd out community initiatives and thus reduce social capital. The best developed discussion along these lines in a New Zealand context is by David Green (1996) from the United Kingdom, written after a visit sponsored by the New Zealand Business Roundtable (although he speaks of 'civil society' rather than 'social capital'). The alternative view warns that devolution of public services to voluntary organisations 'pushes community bodies into service delivery at the cost of community development, the very activity which they are best at and which is the strongest producer of social capital' (Onyx, 1996, cited in Riddell, 1997, p.28; see also Blakeley and Suggate, 1997, p.97; Higgins, 1997b; Nowland-Foreman, 1997). This view argues that there is a partnership between the state and voluntary organisations that needs to be kept in delicate balance if the goal of social well-being is to be achieved to its full potential.

A further step can be taken if it is recognised that social capital meets both parts of the economist's definition of a public good, stated above. First, social capital does not diminish for others when one citizen uses it. Indeed, Riddell

(1997, p.14, citing Putnam, 1993a, p.38) makes the point that because social capital is self-reinforcing and cumulative, the stock of social capital tends to be enhanced through use. Second, although any individual network, club or voluntary organisation may restrict membership to those who pay the required dues, it is not so easy to exclude individuals from the benefits of reinforced social norms and trust that such activities build up. Indeed, where attempts are made to exclude people on the basis of factors such as age, gender, race or sexual orientation, they are usually denounced as uncivilised and outlawed in human rights legislation.

Applying the economic theory of public goods thus reinforces the claim that the state has a role in partnership with voluntary groups in building up social capital. Without the state's ability to levy compulsory taxes to finance community activities, there is a classic free-rider problem, which economic theory predicts will lead to the under-provision of the public good of social capital. This does not imply that all community activities should be financed by the state, either in part or in total. Poorly designed community programmes are just as possible as poorly designed lighthouses. Rather, this argument suggests that state involvement in building social capital is essential, but judging the best ways for this to occur requires the same degree of professional expertise among social workers and community development officers as is expected of architects and engineers in designing physical capital.

Poverty Relief

This heading could be included under almost any of the others, but is sufficiently distinctive and widely supported to warrant its own discussion. Even those who advocate a very small role for the state, and support further cutbacks in New Zealand's public expenditure, accept that the state should provide a minimal safety net for those 'in genuine need' (Bolger, 1990, p.11; Richardson, 1991, p.8). There are, of course, arguments about what is an adequate income to meet genuine need (compare Brashares, 1993, and Easton, 1995a), but there is widespread acceptance that this minimal provision is demanded by fundamental principles of justice and compassion (see Chapter 2). There is far less agreement about whether the state should go beyond this position to provide social insurance for its citizens.

Social Insurance

Debates about the role of government frequently fail to recognise that the alternative to the public purchase of certain goods and services is not direct private purchase, but private insurance. Hospital surgery is a good example. If the New Zealand government did not provide hospital care for serious health conditions and accident emergencies, the typical response would not be for individuals to pay for their own hospital surgery if and when they needed it, but rather for those with sufficient means to take out private health insurance. A person who has paid the set premium in an insurance scheme is entitled to receive the services detailed in the insurance contract under certain predefined conditions of need, in much the same way as the current public health system entitles a citizen to hospital care under certain conditions. Thus health and some other types of public expenditure (most social welfare benefits, superannuation entitlements, accident compensation and perhaps post-compulsory education) are better treated as schemes of 'social insurance' when comparisons are made with the private sector.

A private insurance scheme begins with the identification of a population with a measurable probability distribution of some unpredictable event that is to be insured against (the probability of a car being involved in an accident and requiring a certain cost of repairs, for example). To be profitable, the scheme must attract a *representative* sample of the overall population willing to pay premiums that reflect their underlying risk probabilities, plus a margin to cover the insurance company's expenses (including a market rate of return on its capital). There are two important ways in which an insurance scheme can end up with a biased sample, with higher risks on average than the overall population used to calculate the probability distribution. First, customers might choose to enter the scheme only if they decide, on the basis of private information, that they are high-risk. The insurance premiums would then prove to be too low, but increasing them would make the scheme even less attractive to those who know they are low-risk. If an insurance company is unable to discriminate between risks, and charge different premiums accordingly, this process of *adverse selection* will leave the company with only bad-risk customers. To avoid this, there are strict rules about information disclosure (about a member's history of previous car accidents, for example) and incentives such as no-claims bonuses to encourage low-risk members to remain in a scheme.

Second, customers might take advantage of the presence of an insurance contract by engaging in reckless or fraudulent behaviour that increases their probability of a claim. They might, for example, take less care to lock up possessions securely if they know they will be fully compensated for any burglary loss. The propensity for the insured to change their behaviour as a consequence of having insurance is termed *moral hazard*. As far as possible, insurance companies try to identify and ban such behaviour in advance (a claim will be denied, for example, if a crashed car was being driven by someone under the influence of alcohol). Co-payments may also be used, with insurance companies meeting less than the full charge for visits to the doctor, for example, in order to limit unnecessary claims.

There are also issues arising from the customer's point of view. Once the premium has been paid, the customer must trust the company to honour its commitment to pay out on the agreed terms if the event insured against occurs. The company will not be able to do this, however, if it is made bankrupt by charging premiums that turn out to be too low for the risks being insured. Thus, a customer cannot assume that a new company charging lower premiums is offering a better product than an established company with a strong (and representative) client base, since there is a risk that the new company will not survive.[8] This feature of the insurance industry blunts the normal competitive pressures for efficiency found in other service industries.

Many commentators have argued that the principal role of the modern welfare state is to engage in social insurance schemes that would be too exclusive, or considerably more expensive, to operate in the private sector (Barr, 1994; Thomson, 1996). Social insurance schemes are underpinned by the power of the state to raise revenue through earmarked or general taxes. They may be 'funded' in the sense that future obligations to pay are backed by the accumulation of assets, but are generally pay-as-you-go schemes, funded by current taxpayers. While they may be restricted to those who pay the compulsory contributions (and their families), they are much broader in coverage and entail far less risk discrimination than do private insurance schemes. Social insurance typically involves special social security taxes, often separated from government finances. In New Zealand, ACC is the only pure example of a social insurance scheme, funded by its own payroll tax and other earmarked contributions (see Chapter 9). But public health, education and superannuation in New Zealand can also be considered forms of social insurance, although they are financed by compulsory general taxation and include the whole population. In these latter examples, entitlement is on the basis of residency or citizenship rather than previous contributions.

Social insurance schemes have many similarities with private insurance schemes—the conditions required for a claim must be clearly set out in advance, and care must be taken to minimise moral hazard. But the overwhelming advantage of social insurance schemes is that they involve broad populations, and so do not suffer the problems of sample bias or adverse selection. They are therefore generally cheaper to run than private insurance schemes provided by competing insurance companies. Further, there is little need for advertising and marketing, and large economies of scale are possible in administration. For example, bulk billing by doctors is possible in a national health scheme, and is cheaper than everyone claiming individually. Overall there may be considerable savings to the members of the scheme—in Chapter 9, for example, Susan St John reports that New Zealand's accident compensation scheme absorbs about 12 per cent of total expenditure in administration, compared to Wilson's (1994) estimate of about 40 per cent of each premium dollar in a similar scheme operated privately.

The main point of departure of the broad social insurance schemes in New Zealand from ACC or similar schemes in European countries is the source of funding. Under general taxation funding, citizens are entitled to the benefits of the scheme even if they are not current taxpayers (thus including people not in paid employment who would otherwise be excluded). Note also that the contribution of each taxpayer is based not on an assessment of individual risk but on their taxable income. Benefits likewise are 'flat rate' or uniform, rather than related to contributions as is the case for the earnings-related pension schemes in many other countries. Critics of tax-funded social insurance schemes point to the general efficiency costs of taxation, and also claim that it is unfair to require individual taxpayers to pay for benefits received by others (namely, the pay-outs to higher-risk individuals or to non-taxpayers, particularly in the case of some types of welfare benefit). These criticisms have some force, and place important limits on the role of such schemes.

From a social-democratic point of view, however, there are certain basic services—health care, retirement income, income support for workers suffering unemployment or illness, compensation for personal injury—that should be available to all citizens and are therefore well-suited to tax-funded social insurance schemes. In these cases, the weaknesses identified in the previous paragraph (the inclusion of citizens without market income, and contributions based on market incomes as a proxy for ability to pay) become strengths. Such schemes are a mechanism, for example, for reducing the economic sacrifices incurred by people involved in full-time family care. They provide access to services such as hospital care and superannuation that might otherwise be unaffordable or would increase economic dependency on income-earning partners. The experience in the United States provides a good illustration of the consequences of relying on private insurance for essential services such as health care. In that country, membership of a private health insurance scheme is usually a matter of being covered under a plan paid for by the individual's employer. Thus a very large number of people are not covered, and may also fail to qualify for restricted state Medicare and Medicaid insurance. Many Americans consequently fail to secure quality medical care, despite health expenditure being a larger share of gross domestic product than in New Zealand.

Provision or Funding

Even if it is accepted that there is a role for the state with respect to social goods and services, there remains the issue of whether the government should be involved in providing these goods and services, or whether it should restrict itself to purchasing (entirely or in part) their provision by private-sector firms or by Crown entities operating on a commercial basis. Traditionally, social goods and services were provided in New Zealand by government departments responsible to the relevant Minister. Following major reforms in the State Sector Act 1988 and the Public Finance Act 1989, this environment has changed (Boston, Martin, Pallot and Walsh, 1991 and 1996; Kelsey, 1993; Sharp, 1994; Boston, 1995). Departments now receive an annual budget which they use to purchase the goods and services they require, sometimes provided in-house (expert policy advice, for example), but very often provided by CEs or by firms in the private sector. This section will discuss the rationale for this purchaser-provider split, paying particular attention to problems that arise when there are significant transaction costs of contracting, or when the service is provided in a 'monopolistic competition' market rather than in 'perfect competition'. (The issue of whether the service should be funded on a universal or a targeted basis is left to Chapter 6.)

The purchaser-provider split rests on two economic models—principal-agent theory and the theory of competitive markets. Principal-agent theory explains how contracts written with an appropriate structure can be used to align an agent's incentives to perform certain tasks with the preferences of the principal who has the responsibility of determining the task's objectives (Evans et al., 1996; Scott, 1996). In particular, a contract that clearly defines the outputs to be provided, and defines a single performance indicator for each output, makes the agent more accountable than if they have discretion over how to pursue a set of loosely defined objectives. The theory of competitive markets indicates that firms in such a market will be forced to use resources efficiently (setting the marginal benefit of each resource equal to its marginal cost) in order to produce output at the lowest average cost and price allowed by technology. By combining these two theories, the reforms of the late 1980s appear to promise the achievement of social objectives, refocused in the form of precise outputs defined by the government, at the least possible cost and with the greatest economic efficiency.

Indeed, there are many areas where the restructuring of the government's activities into business-like CEs providing services under contract is likely to have produced strong gains in efficiency and accountability (Taggart, 1990; Duncan and Bollard, 1992). More controversial, however, has been the extension of this model to public institutions delivering services whose dimensions are many-faceted and whose impact on the social fabric is acute. The conversion of hospitals into Crown health enterprises (see Chapter 8), the corporatisation of Housing New Zealand (Chapter 12), the trialling of bulk-funding in schools (Chapter 10) and the proposals to restructure the governing councils of tertiary education institutions (Chapter 11) are good examples where critics argue that the costs and risks of a more business-like orientation outweigh the benefits.

Even within commercial settings, there are clearly recognised limits to the ability of contracts to resolve principal-agent problems efficiently, and indeed this is one of the core explanations given by economists for the existence of firms (Coase, 1937; Hart, 1995). The fundamental problem is that the negotiation, monitoring and enforcement of contracts involve 'transaction costs' that can be higher than the costs of other forms of economic co-operation. Hence it can be cheaper for a firm to employ a person to perform a series of tasks in-house than to contract with external agents to provide the required services. These contracting problems are exacerbated if the service in question is not easily defined in its entirety, or has beneficial aspects that are not clearly measurable in monetary terms—characteristics that are typical of social goods and services. Reducing the structural framework for state activity to one that fits with the structures of private business has meant that the 'social good' feature of state activity is often overlooked. While there are attempts to articulate an overall strategic direction via political flag-waving at election or Budget time, the relationship of 'outputs' to crucial social outcomes is largely left out of the picture. Thus the fragmentation or 'atomisation' of public sector activity results in the overall responsibility to the public being lost.

In many instances, the model of perfect competition is also unrealistic. If Crown health enterprises and tertiary education institutions are to be given a market category, they are more like monopolistic competitors than perfect competitors. That is, the output produced by each participant in the industry is similar but not identical to the product of other participants (education at Victoria University, for example, is similar to, but differentiable from, education at Auckland or Lincoln Universities). Theoretical predictions using the monopolistic competition model are just as strong—but not as favourable from an efficiency point of view—as those obtained from the model of perfect competition. First, each firm will engage in extensive self-promotion and advertising to differentiate its product and so build up brand loyalty among its clients. Second, the firms will charge a price that is greater than the minimum average cost possible, given current technology. Third, the industry will over-invest in spare capacity, imposing a social cost reflected in the higher-than-necessary prices. Fourth, as long as there is free entry into the industry, the firms do not earn monopoly profits, but the higher prices are fully balanced by the higher costs produced by this market structure. Translating these predictions into the health field, for example, economists would expect to see business-orientated institutions struggling to earn profits despite spending large amounts on management and public relations, with larger budgets that do not translate into shorter waiting lists, despite spare capacity in hospitals.

Given the presence of significant transaction costs and monopolistic competition in the relevant markets (these being empirical questions that cannot be wished away by assumption), the overall result is higher, not lower, government expenditure; fewer, not more, social goods; less public willingness to pay tax, in tandem with increased demand for the missing social services; and anger at the failures of state provision. In the mid to late 1990s, this scenario has been played out daily in New Zealand's core social services. The visibility of high salaries and generous bonuses paid to the managers of CEs accompanied by growing public disillusionment with actual outcomes, bodes ill for the future acceptability of higher taxes to pay for these services.

Macroeconomic Stabilisation

Chapter 4 contains a graph of New Zealand's real per capita gross domestic product from 1960/61 to 1996/97 (Figure 4.1). The graph shows a clear series of peaks and troughs tracing out what is termed the economy's business cycle (Kim et al., 1995; Hall, 1997). There is a widespread (though not universal) view that the cycle is generated by fluctuations in aggregate demand, which in turn are caused by changes in household confidence and consumption, business confidence and investment, the government's fiscal and monetary policies, and international trade patterns. If this is the case, there is a possible role for the government to use its fiscal and monetary policies with the objective of maintaining a steady growth path for aggregate demand. Attempting to moderate the peaks and troughs of the business cycle in this way is known as Keynesian demand management. There are two mechanisms for this—'automatic stabilisers' and 'discretionary policy'.

Automatic stabilisers refer to the way in which the government's tax revenue tends to fall, and its transfers expenditure tends to rise, if gross domestic product falls. Tax revenue falls because income taxes and expenditure taxes (GST) are positively related to production, and transfers rise because the number of people supported by the unemployment benefit will increase as the economy slows. These automatic stabilisers have the effect of reducing the Crown's operating surplus (perhaps moving it temporarily into deficit) when the economy is in the 'trough' phase of the business cycle. This maintains aggregate demand at a higher level than would otherwise occur if there were no unemployment benefits and if households faced a fixed tax liability every year. Section 4 of the Fiscal Responsibility Act 1994 allows for the operation of automatic stabilisers by permitting operating deficits as long as operating expenses do not exceed operating revenue 'on average, over a reasonable period of time'.

Discretionary policy refers to the ability of the government to adjust the main instruments of fiscal policy (tax rates and expenditure on transfers or public services) and monetary policy (interest rates and exchange rates) in an attempt to maintain a stable economic growth rate. During an economic downturn, for example, the government might reduce tax rates, increase its expenditure on road maintenance, and lower domestic interest rates through the Reserve Bank. There is a consensus in the economics profession that such discretionary policies are often ineffective (since business plans are based on long-term expectations rather than short-term manipulations of aggregate demand), and may be counter-productive (because of their ability to be used by the government for electoral purposes; see Dalziel and Lattimore, 1996, pp.42-43, 52). Thus the Fiscal Responsibility Act 1994 makes tax rate stability the objective for fiscal policy, and the Reserve Bank of New Zealand Act 1989 makes price stability the objective for monetary policy, but neither Act mentions economic growth stability as an explicit goal for policymakers.

In fact, New Zealand's discretionary fiscal policies since 1990 have been designed with no regard for the traditional role of output stabilisation. In the depths of New Zealand's worst recession since World War II, the government in 1991 cut social assistance entitlements by $1.3 billion in a full fiscal year (see Dalziel, 1992b, for a critique of this policy from an output stabilisation perspective). Then, after two years of very strong recovery and at the peak of the business cycle, the government announced in February 1996 its *Tax Reduction and Social Policy Programme* (Birch, 1996a), which was also valued at $1.3 billion in the first year (1996/97), rising to $2.7 billion in the second round of tax cuts (later postponed to 1998/99). Taking $1.3 billion out of the economy at the bottom of the business cycle and returning it in tax cuts at the top is the very opposite of responsible aggregate demand management. It necessitated a strong monetary response from the Reserve Bank in 1996 to maintain price stability, pushing up interest rates and the exchange rate to the considerable distress of New Zealand's tradable sector (Dalziel, 1997, 1998b).

In the second half of 1998, the second round of the tax cuts announced in February 1996 come through. Despite exhortations to the public to save, extra expenditure from these tax cuts is expected to cushion the downturn intensified by the financial crisis in Asia. Once again, unfortunately, there is little discussion about whether this is appropriate fiscal policy. In the light of the large and increasing balance of payments deficit, a consumption-led recovery is inappropriate. In the meantime, the state's infrastructure, the social welfare system and income distribution all continue to deteriorate.

Conclusion

Government does not create wealth, it merely transfers it at a cost so we need businesses to invest in people, jobs and ideas to add value. Good government does have a role to play in making the size of the cake bigger, but getting a bigger government doesn't give a big economy. (John Luxton, MP, *Independent*, 12 September 1997, p.30).

Among market liberals, it is hard to shake the firm conviction that the state itself cannot add value to the resources it uses. As a result, the recent trend in New Zealand has been to treat social goods and services increasingly as commercial commodities which may be provided in the private sector or in business-like CEs, even if funded by the state. The corporatisation and privatisation of provision, of course, leaves only a short step to a reduction in government funding that requires 'those individuals and families with reasonable means [to] attend to their own social needs', on the broad principle that 'the top third of all income earners can be expected to meet most of the cost of their social services' (Richardson, 1990, p.20). The following chapter will discuss the problems this principle creates as a result of the need to target expenditure towards low- to middle-income households.

This chapter has sought to explain that there are important cases where government expenditure can provide goods and services more efficiently and more effectively than profit-motivated firms in an unregulated market. In making this claim, we recognise that government failure is as possible as market failure, and that the latter does not always justify state intervention. It is also true that the public sector has increased in size during the past century (even allowing for serious problems in measurement and cross-country comparisons), in ways that have not always been beneficial. New technology and globalisation mean that the traditional roles of government must be re-evaluated in order for the state to remain focused on areas where it can out-perform the private sector (using an appropriate range of objectives and measures that do not focus exclusively on narrow efficiency criteria). An ageing population creates its own policy pressures that also need to be addressed. These questions cannot be assumed away by an ideological commitment to smaller government, or an uncritical confidence that the market is always superior to public provision. Instead, informed analysis and open-minded debate of each case will be required to promote the overall goal of improving New Zealand's social well-being.

Endnotes

1 In a participatory democracy, of course, the role of the government of the day is to carry out the mandate received from its constituency. The discussion in this chapter rests on the assumption that 'economic efficiency' is a key consideration, although not necessarily an exclusive one, of all the main political parties in New Zealand.

2 The individual amounts in this category are estimates only, since the published financial statements do not analyse transfer payments by functional classification. Note also that the public accounts record twelve functional classifications: transport and communications, economic and industrial services, and primary services have been grouped together here under the heading 'Economic Services', while heritage, culture and recreation, housing and community development, and other expenses, have been grouped under the heading 'Other Public Services'.

3 Retained profits increase the state's equity in SOEs, recorded as an adjustment on the revenue side of Table 5.1, and so contribute to the operating surplus.

4 In many countries, tax relief is given for certain types of expenditure (saving for retirement, for example) or for certain groups of taxpayers (those with children, for example). These tax breaks are equivalent to explicit cash payments, but are typically not recorded in the public accounts (being treated implicitly as uncollected tax revenue). New Zealand has no tax relief for retirement saving, and is transparent in its accounting of tax credits such as family support, which are recorded as explicit tax expenditures. The widespread use of hidden tax expenditures in other countries makes international comparisons with New Zealand very misleading.

5 This is termed 'Pareto efficiency' in the literature. The definition of competition normally requires a large number of suppliers, but a more recent theory suggests that a market with only a few suppliers can still be efficient if it remains 'contestable'—that is, if it is open to competition by potential new entrants. The natural monopoly example discussed in this section is neither competitive nor contestable.

6 The Coalition government's announced plans to penalise parents who fail to immunise their children would also make immunisation a compulsory merit good. It may also be possible to conceptualise access to health care and a reasonable standard of living in retirement as merit goods, but these will be considered below under the heading 'Social Insurance'.

7 Note that a public broadcasting service may build social capital by encouraging a unique national identity that 'provides an important force for cohesion in the face of the myriad differences among individuals and groups within society' (Blakeley and Suggate, 1997, p.93). The 'public good' character of public broadcasting has been long recognised. At present, Television New Zealand is an SOE and Radio New Zealand is a CE, with both corporations facing pressures for privatisation (see Easton, 1997b, pp.62-70).

8 There is a further risk if a client's insurance company goes bankrupt. At that time, the client may no longer be insurable under the same conditions (for example, having developed a disease which any new insurance company would label as a pre-existing condition not eligible for cover).

CHAPTER SIX

TARGETING VERSUS UNIVERSALITY: SOCIAL ASSISTANCE FOR ALL OR JUST FOR THE POOR?

JONATHAN BOSTON AND SUSAN ST JOHN

For much of the twentieth century, one of the critical philosophical debates in the broad social policy arena has been whether public assistance should be provided only to those in greatest need (that is, the least advantaged) or to all citizens irrespective of their financial means. Advocates of targeting claim that it is more fiscally prudent, efficient and equitable (Richardson, 1990). Accordingly, the provision of universal assistance, whether in the form of education, health care, legal aid or pensions, is seen as unjustified and damaging. To quote the former Prime Minister, Jim Bolger (1997, p.4): 'I am waiting for someone to provide moral justification, much less economic justification, to tax people on modest incomes so as to pay benefits to individuals or families who don't need them.' Advocates of universality, by contrast, believe that there are robust moral and economic justifications for universal programmes in certain situations. They also argue that targeting can often be both inefficient and inequitable, as well as generating numerous administrative problems, stigmatising the poor and undermining middle-class support for social programmes and income redistribution. To quote Bertram (1988, p.135): 'Universal provision ... improves resource allocation, minimises qualitative differentiation of service, is politically sustainable because of the wide spread of beneficiaries, and performs an important socially integrative function by underpinning rights of citizenship.'

This chapter outlines the nature of targeting, examines the key arguments for and against targeting, explores recent policy developments in New Zealand in relation to targeting, and assesses the current policy framework.

The Nature of Targeting

Policy analysts generally use the terms 'targeted', 'means-tested' and 'selective' interchangeably to refer to policies that provide social assistance (such as housing or health care) on the basis of the income, wealth or socio-economic status of an individual, couple or family. Thus, a person who enjoys an income above a particular threshold or benchmark may receive no assistance at all. Moreover, various other non-financial criteria may apply to restrict access further, and sometimes in order to achieve other goals. For example, the Independent Family Tax Credit (IFTC) introduced in 1996 is restricted to low-income families who are also deemed 'independent from the state'.[1]

In considering the nature and degree of targeting, the following criteria are important:

- the scope of targeting (that is, the range of social services and forms of income support that are means-tested);
- the level or generosity of the support provided to those who qualify for the full amount of assistance;
- the basis of the measure of economic circumstances (for example, income only or a combination of income and assets);
- the income threshold above which assistance is reduced, and the range of circumstances that are taken into account in determining the threshold (for example, the number of children);
- the abatement rate (that is, the rate at which assistance is reduced as income or wealth increases); and
- the unit of assessment (that is, whether the means test is applied to individuals, couples or families).

On this basis, a tightly targeted policy regime would be one in which most forms of social assistance (including health and education) are means-tested; the means test is based on income (and possibly assets as well); there is a low threshold and a high abatement rate; the unit of assessment is a couple or family where feasible; and the non-financial eligibility criteria are tightly drawn. Such a regime was proposed by the National government in the early 1990s in *Welfare that Works* (Shipley, 1991).[2] Many forms of social assistance were to be aggregated, and abated from a low threshold against family income, as outlined later in this chapter. Under such a policy regime (which for various reasons was not implemented), most middle- to high-income individuals and families would have received little social assistance, except in the area of education (Boston, 1994).

A 'universalist' approach, on the other hand, provides social assistance to people irrespective of their means. Hence, individuals with similar needs but different means would generally expect to receive the same *quantity* and *quality* of state assistance. Of course, universalist policies are all targeted or conditional in the sense that people are eligible for assistance only if they meet certain (non-financial) criteria. For example, only someone over a certain age would be entitled to a retirement income.[3]

During the past decade, the dominant philosophy in New Zealand has been to provide welfare 'only for the poor', and accordingly there has been a sharp shift towards a tightly targeted policy framework. In a more balanced social policy regime (as is common in Western Europe), many forms of social assistance are provided universally, alongside a limited range of special-purpose, targeted programmes. This means that even relatively high-income individuals and families are eligible for significant social assistance.

The Targeting Debate

It is frequently argued, especially by those of a market-liberal disposition, that targeting social assistance imposes lower fiscal costs, improves efficiency, enhances equity, and encourages altruism and private charity. How robust and convincing are these arguments?

Fiscal Costs

Targeting is often defended on the grounds that, in a world of resource scarcity and fiscal constraints, it is better that the limited public funds available should be directed to those in greatest need (see Shipley, 1991, pp.17-18, 44). A targeted social policy regime, in other words, provides the cheapest and most cost-effective way of eliminating poverty and providing a minimum standard of living for all. However, if the targeting regime is poorly designed (excessively tight, for example), it may not produce the hoped-for fiscal savings. The proposal in the 1991 Budget for a 93 cents in the dollar clawback for National Superannuation provides a good case in point (see Chapter 15). Had the proposal been implemented, it would in all likelihood have promoted a variety of avoidance strategies, resulting in significantly smaller fiscal savings than were initially estimated.

A strong argument often advanced for targeting is that a government can afford to give the recipients of assistance more generous levels of support. By contrast, universal programmes must spread a lower level of assistance across the whole population or relevant group. Thus, given a fixed quantum of public resources, those on low incomes may not receive enough, while those on high incomes will receive assistance they do not need.

On the whole, however, targeted welfare arrangements tend to be more vulnerable to government expenditure cuts than programmes that also benefit the middle class (Barry, 1990, p.74; Goodin and Le Grand, 1987, pp.203-4; Skocpol, 1991). Thus targeting in New Zealand, far from producing a more generous level of assistance, has been associated with benefit cuts and more restrictive criteria. Similarly, in both Britain and the United States, the evidence of recent decades points to means-tested social policies suffering greater cutbacks than those programmes (for example, health and education) with a high proportion of middle-class beneficiaries. To quote Goodin and Le Grand (1987, p.204): 'In the United States, social insurance programmes—non-means-tested and thus enjoying a broad base of both poor and non-poor beneficiaries—have continued to flourish under the Reagan administration's cutbacks, while the means test for social assistance programmes targeted tightly on the poor has grown progressively meaner.'

It might be concluded that a key reason why a targeted system is cheaper than a universal one is that it facilitates lower, not higher, levels of support for those most in need. From a political economy perspective, the explanation for this is not hard to fathom. People are often more willing to pay taxes to fund programmes that benefit them personally than those that assist only the poor. Politically, it is much more difficult to reduce expenditure on social programmes that benefit a large proportion of the population, particularly if the beneficiaries are well equipped to defend their interests. Well-educated, middle-class citizens are generally better at such tasks than the poor. Thus in New Zealand, the retired population succeeded in reversing the 1991 Budget proposal to cut the state pension for middle- and upper-income people, while the more severe cut-backs affecting other beneficiaries remained in place. Interestingly, opinion polls during the 1990s indicate that the majority of New Zealanders would prefer to have greater public expenditure in areas such as education and health care (services that tend to be provided on a universal basis), rather than tax cuts.[4]

Efficiency

Universal policies are frequently criticised for their presumed detrimental impact on economic efficiency. For example, the higher levels of public expenditure and taxation necessitated by universalism are claimed to have harmful effects on economic growth. One reason for this is that higher average and marginal tax rates are believed likely to reduce profitability, enterprise and innovation, undermine work incentives, lower private savings, and increase dependency on the state.

However, the efficiency arguments against universalism are by no means as compelling as is often thought. For example, the claim that higher levels of public expenditure and taxation lead to lower rates of economic growth is not unequivocally confirmed by the evidence, at least for the range of expenditure and taxation levels common within the OECD (see Chapter 4; Atkinson, 1995). Furthermore, there are powerful efficiency grounds, based on externalities or third-party effects, for substantial universal funding of certain forms of social assistance, most notably education and health care (see Chapter 5; Barr, 1994; Blaug, 1972; Peston, 1966).

Similarly, because of the various well-known problems with private insurance markets (for example, moral hazard, adverse selection, high transaction costs and uninsurable risks), there are good efficiency arguments, not to mention equity arguments, for comprehensive, state-funded health care and income support arrangements (see Chapter 5; Barr, 1989 and 1994). Reliance on private insurance would result in many people either missing out altogether or being under-insured at high cost. By contrast, compulsory insurance through the state provides an efficient way of ensuring that all those who suffer misfortune (for example, unemployment, sickness, or injury) secure adequate income support and social assistance. Moreover, as Rankin (1991, p.2) argues, paying for such benefits via the tax system minimises administration and collection costs, while at the same time enabling contributions to be varied according to a person's ability to pay.

Equally important, the greater the scope and tightness of targeting, the higher the effective marginal tax rates (EMTRs) faced by many low- to middle-income earners. An EMTR is calculated by adding the relevant income tax rate and the abatement rate(s) applying to targeted forms of social assistance, and indicates the proportion of an extra earned dollar that is unavailable. Thus an EMTR of 70 per cent results in only 30 cents of extra disposable income from the next dollar earned. High EMTRs tend to reduce the incentives for people to increase their hours of work, or to change their jobs for better-paid employment.[5]

Under joint income-testing, high EMTRs mainly affect the secondary-income earner in the family (usually a woman).[6] When allowance is made for the costs of childcare and work-related expenses such as transport, some two-income families may be better off without the second income. To the extent that high EMTRs keep women at home rather than participating in the workforce, negative effects on skill levels and labour productivity can be expected. Longer term, this may exacerbate family stress, increase gender inequality and affect the income prospects of women after divorce.

Clearly, the greater the proportion of means-tested services, the larger the number of people affected by high EMTRs and the more severe the incentive problems are likely to be. In New Zealand, the shift towards full targeting of most types of social provision has resulted in many people being affected by overlapping income tests which generate very high and often arbitrary EMTRs, as will be discussed later in this chapter.

The Change Team on Targeting Social Assistance, which reported to the National government prior to the 1991 Budget, suggested that the liability to pay for one's own family's education and health care is not a 'disincentive to work in the way that an increase in the tax rate would be' (Prebble, 1991, A, p.2). This may be true for those on high incomes outside the targeting range: more income is needed to cover user charges, and so, along with lower taxes, such a liability may favour increased work effort. However, this appealing scenario overlooks the *income* effect of lower taxes. Thus, the well-off, who tend to make their own social provision anyway, may well reduce rather than increase hours worked. But more significant in terms of work effort is the mistaken view that targeting can be confined to just a few. Many of those faced with high EMTRs as a result of targeting and user charges may decide to work less. While in the past many wage and salary earners had little control over their hours of work, with the increased casualisation of the workforce and the growth in part-time employment, these disincentive effects are likely to be very significant.

From an efficiency point of view, the real issue is not whether targeting generates incentive problems for those on low to middle incomes, for this is generally accepted, but whether targeting is more efficient overall than greater universality, which would mean higher taxes, and hence in all likelihood higher marginal tax rates for the better-off. Not surprisingly, this matter has provoked considerable debate. To date, no clear-cut answers have emerged. Nevertheless, the evidence suggests that universal arrangements are no less efficient than targeted ones, though much depends on the design of the policies in question (see Kesselman, 1980). If the disincentive effects of high marginal tax rates on high-income primary earners tend to be less than on secondary workers and other low-income people, the efficiency case for targeting is open to serious doubt.

Quite apart from this, even if the labour supply responses to high EMTRs among low-income earners were demonstrated to be only modest, there is still an issue of justice involved. Surely it is not equitable for people to lose most, if not all, of their additional income when they choose to work harder or longer (Atkinson, 1993, p.60). Thus, in the same way that many people question the fairness of high marginal tax rates on top-income earners, so too the fairness of high EMTRs on low-income earners can be challenged.

Equity

The problem with universality, or so the argument goes, is that middle- to high-income individuals and families generally benefit as much as—if not more than—the poor, so that the redistributive impact is regressive (see Le Grand, 1982; Gibson et al., 1985; Goodin and Le Grand, 1987). This is sometimes referred to as 'middle-class capture' (see Bertram, 1988; Treasury, 1984). As former Prime Minister Jim Bolger (1997, p.16) put it: 'Part of the reason for the very high cost of Government provided social services has been the well documented phenomenon of "middle class capture", whereby the benefits of programmes tend to be diverted in various ways away from the most needy and towards middle and higher income groups.' Likewise, to quote the Treasury (1984, p.258):

If services are provided free or at a uniform price to all, then it is probable that the wealthy will benefit most. This is because there will always be some costs associated with using services, even if there is no direct charge. Such costs could include the cost of travel involved in order to use the service, the income lost through the time involved in using the service, or the legal and administrative costs involved in complying with complex requirements. These costs invariably weigh more heavily on, and discourage, the poor rather than the rich.

For example, the non-poor tend to make greater use than the poor of the education system, especially at the senior high school and tertiary levels. A similar pattern is evident with respect to health services. For these reasons, Julian Le Grand (who has undertaken considerable research on the redistributive impact of social policies in Britain, where many forms of social assistance are universal) maintains that 'almost all public expenditure on the social services ... benefits the better off to a greater extent than the poor' (1982, p.3). He goes on to conclude that:

> the strategy of promoting equality through public expenditure in the social services has failed. It has failed to achieve full equality of whatever kind for most of the services reviewed. In those areas where data are available it has failed to achieve greater equality over time; and in some cases it is likely that there would be greater equality if there was no public expenditure on the service concerned (p.132).

Similarly, Goodin and Le Grand (1987, p.4) maintain that:

> In so far as the non-poor are themselves involved in the welfare state in such a way as to make them, along with the genuinely poor, beneficiaries of such transfers, then to that extent the redistributive effects of the transfers are thereby diminished. Welfare state programmes characterized by beneficial involvement of the non-poor thus defeat, or at least seriously compromise, one of their most central purposes.

If, then, the central aim of the welfare state is greater vertical equity, the argument for targeting appears to be convincing. But is it? There is not the space here to provide a detailed response to the so-called 'middle-class capture' argument (for a fuller account see Bertram, 1988; Stephens, 1991). There are, however, powerful reasons for questioning the argument.

First, much of Le Grand's 1982 analysis, and the conclusions he draws, are open to serious doubt (Bertram, 1988; O'Higgins, 1985a, 1985b). His evidence is often fragmentary, indirect, inconclusive or inaccurate, and some of his conclusions are inconsistent with the evidence used. Overall, the degree of middle-class capture in Britain appears to be considerably less than he suggests. This is partly because his study ignores income-maintenance provisions and tax credits, which are generally redistributive in their impact. Furthermore, the suggestion that income distribution would have been more equal if certain services had not been publicly funded (or at least not on a universal basis) depends on how the tax revenue would otherwise have been spent, or who would otherwise have paid less tax. Bear in mind, too, that redistribution is not just about the absolute amount of social assistance received, but the amount relative to income. Hence, although under universal policies people may be eligible for the same quantity and quality of assistance irrespective of their means, the assistance is worth more to the poor than to the rich as a proportion of income.

Second, the degree of vertical equity depends not only on the nature and level of public expenditure and the use of public services by different socio-economic groups, but also on the tax system and labour market arrangements. In general, there will be less inequality under circumstances of full employment and a solidaristic or egalitarian wages policy. Furthermore, as long as the tax system is not severely regressive, a degree of income redistribution will occur even if certain kinds of social assistance, such as education and health care, are not means-tested. Hence, as Mendelson (1980, p.187) points out, the issue is not whether universal programmes provide social assistance to the rich, but whether 'the rich are net beneficiaries'.

Table 6.1 provides an illustration of the impact of universal transfers in the context of a proportional tax system with a flat income tax rate of 33.3 per cent. Plainly, the table is highly simplified, and assumes that all households receive exactly the same level of transfers. Nevertheless, it highlights the fact that significant redistribution occurs under a universalist strategy, with the ratio between the incomes of the top and bottom quintiles falling from 5:1 to 2.66:1 after taxes and transfers have been included. Of course, with a genuinely progressive tax regime, the degree of redistribution would be even greater.

Table 6.1 The Redistributive Effects of Universal Provision

Household	Average Weekly Income	Average Tax (33.3%)	Transfers	Net 'Income'
A (20%)	1500	500	300	1300
B (20%)	1200	400	300	1100
C (20%)	900	300	300	900
D (20%)	600	200	300	700
E (20%)	300	100	300	500
Ratio (A:E)	5:1			2.66:1
Total		1500	1500	

Source: Based on Rothstein (1993, p.496).

Third, while redistribution from the non-poor to the poor and the alleviation of poverty is certainly a central aim of the welfare state, it is by no means the only objective, nor the only one with redistributive effects (Thomson, 1996). Other important redistributive goals include:

* redistribution over a person's life cycle (for example, between work and retirement);
* redistribution from those without children to those with children;
* redistribution from those in good health to those who are ill, disabled or incapacitated;
* redistribution from the employed to the unemployed;
* redistribution within families (for example, to poor members of non-poor families, such as women in the unpaid workforce); and
* redistribution between racial groups and geographic regions.

Thus, as eminent political theorist Brian Barry (1990, p.75) has argued: 'It would ... betray a gross misunderstanding of the rationale of the welfare state to think of it as no more than a cumbersome way of bringing about a minor transfer of resources between income strata.'

Fourth, and related to this, the demands of justice are not limited to equalising opportunities or life chances (see Chapter 2). Also at stake are other notions of justice, such as the principle that it is just to compensate those who have suffered an undeserved misfortune or who are undeservedly discriminated against. The principle of desert applies most clearly in New Zealand with respect to accident compensation, whereby individuals are compensated for their misfortune irrespective of who was at fault or their financial circumstances.

Finally, the goals of the welfare state also include the promotion of social cohesion and racial tolerance, the minimising of social differentiation and stratification, and the pursuit of various efficiency objectives (see Barr, 1990 and 1994; Mulgan, 1991). State funding of education, for example, is not justified solely on redistributive grounds, though such considerations are vitally important. Instead, state support for education is designed to fulfil a range of objectives: economic (for example, improving the stock of human capital and enhancing labour productivity); social (for example, encouraging racial tolerance and social cohesion); scientific (for example, the pursuit of knowledge); and cultural (for example, the preservation and enhancement of a nation's languages or cultures).

In short, the 'middle-class capture' argument has relatively little substance. Above all, it ignores the fact that the welfare state has both redistributive and non-redistributive objectives, and is concerned with both egalitarian and non-egalitarian principles of justice. It is because of these multiple objectives, of which vertical equity is but one, that governments throughout the OECD have chosen to make extensive use of universal social programmes, most notably in health and education, and in certain areas of income support such as child allowances.

But even if the sole (or at least the primary) goal of social assistance is to enhance vertical equity, and in particular to alleviate poverty, there are still good grounds for a degree of universality. Four considerations are worth mentioning in this regard.

First, in contrast to universal programmes, targeting frequently ends up excluding some of the very people most in need of assistance because of low take-up rates, thereby reducing its relative effectiveness as a policy instrument. Various factors can contribute to take-up rates being low:

- some people may be unaware of their entitlements;
- some people may want to avoid being stigmatised, or may want to protect their privacy;
- some people may have difficulty securing their entitlements because of ill-health or infirmity;
- some people may be entitled to only trivial amounts of assistance (which will inevitably be the case if the level of assistance abates out to zero at a particular income level); and
- there may be high transaction costs involved in securing the relevant benefit, such as time-consuming procedures, and complex forms to fill in (see Atkinson, 1993, pp.47-53; Barr, 1994).

As elsewhere, take-up rates for targeted programmes in New Zealand appear to be significantly lower than for previous or comparable universal programmes. For example, the take-up rate for family support among non-beneficiaries has been estimated at around 75-80 per cent; the overall take-up rate for the accommodation supplement is estimated at around 65 per cent (with the rate for non-beneficiaries being significantly lower); and the take-up rates for the guaranteed minimum family income and the independent family tax credit, at least to date, appear to be quite low.

Second, attempts to use targeting to assist the poor and *only* the poor, however well motivated, are invariably less successful than intended. For one thing, means-testing encourages those who find themselves ineligible for social assistance to alter their behaviour so that they enjoy at least some of the direct benefits of the targeted programmes. Well-off individuals and families, moreover, are often able to manipulate complex bureaucratic rules to their advantage or organise their financial affairs and domestic arrangements so that they appear poor and thus become eligible for assistance (Goodin and Le Grand, 1986). In New Zealand, for example, some wealthy people have community services cards (which entitle holders to health care subsidies), and some young people from well-off families receive full student allowances.

Third, under a tightly targeted regime the objective of alleviating poverty comes up against the major dilemma that the larger the amount of assistance, the longer the income range for abatement, even if the abatement rates are high. It is therefore hardly surprising that switching from a balance of universal and targeted provisions to full targeting could mean a *reduction* over time in assistance to the most needy, not an increase. The dilemma is nicely illustrated by the changes that have occurred in family assistance. The abolition of the universal component (family benefit) in 1991, for example, did not initially result in more assistance in total going to the poorest families; indeed, assistance fell in real terms (Shirley et al., 1997). During the 1994-97 period, in response to evident hardship and the desire to foster 'independence from the state', there have been significant increases in targeted family assistance for selected families, including the introduction of the IFTC. The price is that families with two or more children are affected by the abatement regime well into the $40,000s and even $50,000s of family income, with EMTRs of over 60 per cent being common over long income ranges.

Finally, the issue of vertical equity is concerned not only with the relative position of the poor versus the non-poor, but also with the relative position of middle-income earners versus the rich, and the relative position of various groups depending on their family circumstances. Assessing such distributional impacts is complex, because one must take into account not only the direct effects of the move to targeting on individuals and families in different circumstances, but also the way in which the fiscal savings from targeting are distributed across society. As a general rule, however, tightly targeted regimes tend to impact relatively more severely on people with modest incomes than on those with high incomes (see Mendelson, 1980), and on individuals or couples with children than on those without. Such effects will be all the greater if the fiscal savings are used primarily to reduce the tax burden on the rich (that is, by reducing the progressivity of the tax system). For example, the move to greater targeting in the areas of health care and student allowances in the early 1990s had a disproportionate impact (certainly in relative terms, and in some cases also in absolute terms) on couples with children as opposed to those without, and on middle-income earners as opposed to those on high incomes (see Waldegrave and Frater, 1991). Hence, the net result was an increase in the inequality of access to health care and tertiary education *among the non-poor*. By contrast, if the revenue savings from the targeting of health care and tertiary education had been secured instead via an increase in the top marginal tax rate (or at least a move to a more progressive income tax regime), both the relative and absolute financial impacts would have been greater for high-income earners than for middle-income earners. Furthermore, individuals and couples on high incomes and without children would have paid as much additional tax as those on similar incomes with children.

In summary, attempts to assist the poor via targeting may actually leave some poor individuals and families worse off, both in absolute and relative terms. Likewise, attempts to prevent the non-poor enjoying the benefits of targeted social assistance programmes are also likely to encounter problems. Equally important, the distributional consequences of targeting may impact most severely on the poorest of the non-poor rather than on the rich, though much will depend on the nature of the tax regime and the way in which the fiscal savings from targeting are distributed across society.

Altruism and Charity

A final argument sometimes used to defend tightly targeted and minimalist forms of social assistance is that they leave scope for private caring initiatives, whereas more generous and extensive welfare programmes may undermine altruistic behaviour, philanthropy, and charitable giving (see Obler, 1981; Ware, 1990). Furthermore, as Green (1996, p.xi) has argued: 'Historically, voluntary assistance through charities and mutual aid associations supplemented by a minimum safety net provided by the state offered superior protection because it attended not only to material needs but also to character.'

While private giving and voluntary agencies have much to commend them, the capacity of the informal, market and voluntary sectors to replace the state's current role in areas such as income support appears to be relatively limited. Many of New Zealand's voluntary organisations have struggled during the 1990s to fill gaps left by the state's reductions in levels of social assistance. To return to a minimalist welfare state of the kind found in the nineteenth century would almost certainly result in much greater inequality, suffering, hardship, and poverty. Certainly, the scope for charity in such circumstances would be all the greater, but the record of history makes it plain that, because of free riding and insufficient altruism, even the most compelling human needs would be inadequately met by philanthropic activity. Equally important, assistance is likely to be distributed in a highly arbitrary, selective and intrusive fashion.

Administrative Problems and Intrusiveness

Any attempt to means-test social assistance raises a plethora of complex administrative issues. These include determining the appropriate unit of assessment; whether there should be an assets test as well as an income test; the appropriate income threshold and abatement rate; the range of family circumstances that should be taken into account; the relationship between different targeted programmes; and the methods of implementation, monitoring, and enforcement. How these matters are resolved will have important implications for income distribution both within and between families, economic incentives, lifestyle choices, stigma, privacy, the exchange of information between government agencies, and the costs of administration (see Prebble, 1990; Mulgan, 1991). In broad terms, however, there is little doubt that targeted schemes are more intrusive and a greater threat to liberty than universal schemes, with individuals being required to supply much more information to state agencies about their financial and personal circumstances.

Furthermore, targeting invariably entails much higher transaction costs than universality for both the state and citizens—in the form of administration costs, compliance costs, monitoring costs and enforcement costs. For example, the regime of targeted part-charges for health services introduced in 1991 imposed additional costs on both providers and consumers, with hospitals being required to install completely new billing systems (Ashton, 1992b; Stocks, 1993). Also, there is evidence (Parks, 1996) that access to community services cards has proved difficult for many people because of the complicated application process.

Social Differentiation

In considering the relative merits of targeted versus universal social policies, it is important to assess their impact on the tone of society and the degree of social differentiation (see Mulgan, 1991; O'Higgins, 1987). In other words, what effect do alternative welfare arrangements have on the sense of community, belonging and social solidarity? Are they unifying or divisive? As Titmuss (1974, p.141) asks, do they 'widen or diminish the concept of "who is my neighbour"?' Such questions are clearly contentious. However, whereas targeted policies often create problems of stigma and loss of privacy, universal policies tend to reduce social differentiation, especially if they involve both public funding and provision. As the former British Labour politician, Anthony Crosland, once put it (quoted in O'Higgins, 1987, p.13):

> If the state provides schools and hospitals, teachers and doctors, on a generous scale of a really high quality, then the result will be, not indeed a greater equality of real incomes, but certainly a greater equality in manners and in the texture of social life ... [T]he fact that people of every class go to the same school and use the same hospital facilities ... is an immensely important influence in creating a sense of social equality and lack of privilege.

Another dimension to this issue is noted by Mulgan (1991, p.62):

> There is a danger that greater targeting, combined with political commitment to values of so-called 'self-reliance' and 'independence', could reduce the general level of social compassion. It could encourage the attitude that most people should be able to stand on their own feet ... It could also progressively reduce political consent for remaining levels of welfare as fewer people are eligible for welfare benefits and more people are encouraged to see dependence on state welfare as an indication of personal failure.

Any society concerned to build a strong sense of community, common identity and shared citizenship will need to ensure that there are at least some social institutions that are shared by the whole population. Common education and health-care facilities are arguably of particular importance in this regard. Similarly, methods of means-testing that stigmatise the poor and make them feel like second-class citizens should be avoided.

Summary

While targeting is currently fashionable among policymakers, certainly in New Zealand, the case against universality is not nearly as compelling as many assume. As Atkinson (1993, p.62) correctly observes, any evaluation of the relative merits of targeting versus universality depends in large measure on what one is seeking to achieve. If the sole policy objective is to alleviate or reduce poverty, then a fully targeted set of social assistance programmes may appear sensible, at least at first sight. Closer inspection, however, indicates that such an approach may not prove successful, given the need to limit the income range over which abatement occurs, the creation of adverse incentives, and the problems of imperfect information, low take-up rates, administrative complexity, intrusiveness and stigma. Moreover, if the aims of social assistance are broad and multiple—as has been the case in most OECD countries—then it is by no means self-evident that targeting is always the best or most efficient option.

Generally speaking, the greater the weight given to fostering social cohesion and building a just society (in all its multifarious dimensions—including equity between social classes, races and different age-groups, equity between and within families, equitable access to education and health care, and so on), the stronger the case for universalism. This is why, for example, there is such a commitment to universal coverage in Scandinavia. It is not that Scandinavians are uninterested in reducing poverty, but rather that they see the welfare state as having a wide range of political, social and moral objectives. Such objectives necessitate a heavy reliance on universal assistance and, as a product of this, the imposition of relatively high tax rates.

A Brief Evaluation of New Zealand's Current Targeting Regime

The increasing reliance on targeted social assistance in New Zealand since the mid-1980s has generated a range of policy issues. One of these is the problem of multiple and overlapping income tests, and the resultant high EMTRs affecting many of those on low to middle incomes. The Treasury noted this matter in its *Briefing to the Incoming Government* in 1990 (p.110):

As a general rule, the more people facing higher effective marginal tax rates over longer ranges of potential income, the greater the costs to society and the greater the probable loss of output ... Many beneficiaries face rates that approach 100% for a significant range of potential earnings. An indication of the effect of such scales is the fact that very few people are in jobs with an income at the level where the maximum rate of benefit abatement applies; instead they tend to have no job at all, rather than work for little gain. This is worrying since it discourages part-time work, which may be the most appropriate employment for some beneficiaries.

The Treasury identified high benefit levels as a major factor preventing a more realistic abatement system. In late December 1990, it was announced that benefits would be cut significantly, and the Change Team on Targeting Social Assistance (Prebble et al., 1991) was established to design a new system of targeted social assistance. The policy document that emerged was a key background paper for the wide-ranging reforms foreshadowed in the 1991 Budget.

Family Accounts

The 1991 Budget document *Welfare that Works* claimed that the problem of high EMTRs generated by multiple and overlapping income tests could be addressed through the introduction of an 'integrated approach to providing targeted assistance with access to social services' (Shipley, 1991, p.5):

> Although any targeting system involves a reduction of total support as family income rises, the system will be designed in such a way that people are better off earning additional income and moving from dependence to independence. The reduction in assistance will not be in sudden steps because that would mean some people might be discouraged from earning more if the final result is a drop in the total of earnings and income assistance. (This is sometimes known as a 'poverty trap'.) Instead, assistance will be phased out over a range of income so the effects of the drop in assistance on total earnings will be less severe. Support for different services will be phased out service by service (p.18).

Welfare that Works put forward a grand vision of a seamless, global system of abatement of all social assistance. The mechanisms were described in detail with the aid of three-dimensional diagrams which showed that a single family income test and a single phase-out rate were to apply across all forms of social assistance. An integrated approach was necessary and would be facilitated by the development of 'family accounts':

> It would be difficult to institute a system that is sensitive to family needs by merely looking at each service individually. For example, the ability to pay for health care depends on what the family must pay for other social services. It is impossible to gauge the impact each service has on a family's total circumstances without taking an integrated approach (p.44).

Table 6.2 Welfare Benefits and Targeted Payments Which May Affect a Family Comprising 1 or 2 Adults and 3 Children (2 Under 13 Years and 1 Tertiary Student) as at 1 July 1998 (Indicative Only)

Benefit	Net Amount Per Week (Excluding Family Support)	Income for Abatement (Payback)	Income Basis	Exempt Amount*	Range of Income Abatement Applies	Abatement/ Repayment Rates (%)
Unemployment, Training, 55Plus Sickness	$260.94 $279.08	joint	current weekly	$80 pw	> $80 pw	70
Invalids DPB/Widows	$306.92 $230.24	joint if applicable	current yearly	$80 pw	$80–$180 pw > $180 pw	30 70
Accomodation Supplement *(a) For Beneficiary*	Up to $75–$150 Max. depends on area	joint	current weekly (note: cash assets test also applies)	no lower limit	$0–$80 pw >$80 p.w	25
(b) For Employed	Max. depends on area	joint	current weekly (note: cash assets test also applies)	sole: $338.13 pw couple: $400.15 pw	sole: >$338.13 pw couple: >$400.15 pw	25 25
Family Support & Independent Family Tax	Max $109 (two children)	joint (parents)**	current annual	$20,000 pa	$20,000–$27,000 > $27,000	18 30
Child Support	Min $10 Max varies	individual (parent)	previous financial year†	(living allowance)	upper limit varies	1 2 – 3 0 †
Child Care Subsidy	$69.60 max	joint	current weekly	$640 per week	$640–$741 per week	69 (average)
Student Loans	varies	individual	current annual	$14,716 pa	> $14,716 pa	10
Student Allowances††	Up to $98.21 at home $122.78 away from home	joint (parents)	previous financial year	$27,872 pa	> $27,872 pa cut out is $42,538 pa††	25
Community Services Card	varies	joint	expected next 12 months	N/A	couple: entitlement lost if income > $42,538 pa sole: entitlement lost if income > $37,692 pa	N/A N/A

Notes:
* Same for sole parent and couple unless noted.
** Parents' income only for those who are living together and both supporting the child.
† Adjusted for inflation. Provision exists for reassessment if income in the current year falls to less than 85 per cent of the previous year.
†† Student allowances are higher for students over 25, and depending on area, there is an accommodation allowance of up to $38 per week. If the student lives away from home, the upper income limit for abatement is higher. If there are two students, a cumulative loss of student allowances of 50 per cent is possible, although the threshold for the income test is raised.

Full integration was to proceed slowly, as it was recognised that all existing provisions could not be placed on this new basis overnight. Nevertheless, with respect to family support and student allowances, the 1991 Budget indicated that the decision had already been taken to proceed:

> ... those two schemes now operate in isolation to one another. They cut in and out and abate at different rates. As a result, the impact of one or both schemes on the resources of some families may be contrary to what was intended in assisting those families with access to social services. The Government has decided the administrative rules of the global arrangement will apply to Family Support and tertiary allowances (p.46).

Later, childcare subsidies and health subsidies were to be included. The phase-out was to be in a well-defined order:

> An important issue is the order in which state support for targeted social services is phased out, or abated. The order is intended to be benefits first, followed by Family Support, assistance with the health premium, any other services to be included at a later date (such as early childhood education if targeting is introduced there) and, finally, the (tertiary) student allowance scheme (p.47).

There was little emphasis on the fact that the more programmes that were included for abatement, the longer the income range over which the abatement regime would apply, and hence the more people that would be affected. The government's advisers appear to have favoured a high abatement rate of around 50 per cent, since anything significantly lower than this would have prolonged the abatement range unrealistically. Yet a rate of 50 per cent, together with income tax rates of 28 or 33 per cent (as applied in the early 1990s), would have generated EMTRs of 78 or 83 per cent. Moreover, even with a 50 per cent abatement rate, the range of income over which a couple or an individual would have been affected would have been relatively long.

In the event, many aspects of *Welfare that Works*, including the notion of family accounts, proved to be unworkable, and ultimately unacceptable politically (Boston, 1994). Despite this, the move towards an ever more tightly targeted welfare state proceeded. But rather than introducing an integrated targeting regime, as proposed in *Welfare that Works*, the various policy changes made during the early to mid-1990s occurred in an ad hoc and unco-ordinated manner.

Overlaps and Inconsistencies

As a result, the current policy framework contains numerous inconsistencies. Different definitions of income, for example, apply for different targeting measures. Some rely on estimates of income taken from the previous financial year (for example, the community services card), while others require an estimate of expected income and a squaring-up at the end of the year (for example, family support). Others adjust past income for inflation (for example, child support). Some allow for adjustment in cases where current income is well below past income (for example, student allowances). Some require a broader definition of income than taxable income, but often the inclusion of additional so-called 'income items' lacks any obvious rationale. To add to the confusion, some benefits are reduced if other forms of assistance are received. Thus, the 'living costs' component of student loans is counted as income for the community services card, as is the value of any family tax credit; and the accommodation supplement formula takes into account any increase in family support payments for the first child. Likewise, any increase in the accommodation supplement reduces payments of the special benefit, dollar for dollar, thereby leaving individuals and families no better off (McGurk, 1997, p.3). With accommodation costs for many low-income families having soared under the market rents policy (see Chapter 12), many of those who have sought the special benefit to meet their basic needs have been denied any real relief (see Chapter 13).

Furthermore, some forms of targeting are based on joint incomes, while others use the income of the individual. Who is counted as 'married' for purposes of income aggregation varies.[7] The choice of the 'core family' as the unit of assessment for most forms of assistance has significant social and distributional implications, and potentially longer-term implications for the tax unit (St John, 1991; Ministry of Women's Affairs, 1991). For one thing, family income is often inequitably shared among family members. For another, joint income-testing is more intrusive and administratively cumbersome, is difficult to apply to 'reconstituted' families and in situations where children are living with relatives, creates incentives for people not to marry (or alternatively to divorce), and will tend to increase the dependence of women on their husbands. Rather than this approach strengthening the family unit, the reverse is likely. The income ranges over which social assistance abates also vary strangely, with some benefits cutting out abruptly over a certain income level (for example, the community services card and child care subsidies). Finally, targeted programmes are administered by a range of government departments, so that some families are not aware of their full entitlements.

High Effective Marginal Tax Rates

As a result of all these complexities, the consequences for individuals and families—in terms of the impact of earning an extra dollar on their net disposable income—are often masked and difficult to assess. Nevertheless, many low- and middle-income families are acutely aware that, despite working harder than before, they are no better off. Furthermore, different groups are affected by a different range of targeted social assistance in ways that can produce very high and arbitrary EMTRs even for those who are not beneficiaries. Table 6.2, for example, illustrates how a sole parent or a one-earner couple with three children could be affected under the current targeting regime. Notice that the cumulative effects of abated social assistance could give EMTRs of at least 70 per cent, and in some cases much higher. Hence, let us suppose the family in Table 6.2 earns $35,000, and that the principal income earner has the opportunity to earn an extra $1,000. The net result (using the tax rates applying from mid-1998) is as follows: earned income ($1,000), less tax and ACC ($222), less family support ($300), less student allowances ($250), less repayment of student loan ($100), giving a net gain of $128. A child support payment or a second student in the family could push this particular taxpayer's EMTR over 100 per cent and make the returns from earning the extra $1,000 negative. Moreover, this example ignores the eventual impact of the loss of the community services card when income exceeds the threshold for this family type.

In the case of a beneficiary family receiving an accommodation supplement, the first $80 earned in a week produces a net gain of $42.24 (or an EMTR of 47.2 per cent) after allowance is made for tax and the loss of the accommodation supplement. After that, the EMTR rises steeply: for an unemployed family it becomes a discouraging 92.2 per cent; and for a domestic purposes beneficiary it becomes 52.2 per cent, rising to 92.2 per cent for incomes above $180 per week. Once an income of $20,000 is exceeded, abatement of family support takes the rate to 110.2 per cent; if the individual in question is repaying a student loan, the rate could be 120.2 per cent. While only certain categories of people face EMTRs of this magnitude, the fact that they arise at all reflects New Zealand's heavy reliance on targeting and the poorly integrated nature of the current policy regime.

The Tax Reduction and Social Policy Programme

The data in Table 6.2 incorporate changes to tax rates and abatement rates announced in the government's *Tax Reduction and Social Policy Programme* (Birch, 1996a), which were partly designed to address the inherent disincentives in the welfare system. The three critical policy changes were lower statutory rates of income tax, the introduction of the IFTC, and an improved abatement regime for some beneficiaries. The first phase of both the tax cuts and the IFTC were introduced on 1 July 1996. The second phase of the IFTC commenced on 1 July 1997, but the second round of tax cuts was delayed until 1 July 1998 (Coalition Agreement, 1996, p.62). Unfortunately, some of these changes have introduced yet more muddle into the 'welfare mess', partly through their failure to apply agreed principles in a consistent fashion. Thus, in contrast to the previous policy regime which treated all children of low-income families the same, the IFTC discriminates against the children of parents defined as being 'dependent' on the state. Determining eligibility for families who are in and out of the benefit system is thus extremely complex. And, while the intention is to 'strengthen families', the new abatement procedures for those on benefits manage to discriminate against those in 'intact' marriages with children.[8]

The Coalition Agreement

Following the formation of the National/New Zealand First coalition government in late 1996 there was a move back towards universality in some policy areas. Free primary health care for all children under six was introduced in 1997, the surcharge on New Zealand superannuation was removed in 1998, and means-testing for some of those in long-stay geriatric care is to be eased. The Coalition Agreement also foreshadowed a move towards a universal system of student allowances, but announcements in the 1998 Budget signalled it would be a non-event. Whether the modest increase in universality since 1996 proves to be lasting is far from certain. Many within National and ACT strongly favour a significant increase in targeting, especially in areas such as health care and pensions. By contrast, the Alliance, and to a lesser extent Labour, favour a more universal approach. Which view will ultimately prevail over the medium to longer term remains to be seen.

Conclusion

In comparison with most other OECD countries, New Zealand is relatively extreme in the degree to which social assistance is targeted—most European countries, for example, still make extensive use of social insurance. To compound matters, the administration of targeted benefits since the early 1990s has become ever more complex and even less well co-ordinated. As a result, the problem of high EMTRs, including genuine 'poverty traps', has been accentuated rather than reduced. Nor have the policy changes in recent years alleviated the degree of poverty within the community (see Chapter 13). Indeed, despite constant political rhetoric to the contrary, greater targeting has not protected the relative position of the poor, nor delivered a fairer society.

The efficiency costs of the high EMTRs now faced by many low- to middle-income groups have tended to be ignored in the rush to proclaim the virtues of a policy regime based on tight targeting and low direct taxes. To date, the various tax reductions that have occurred have been concentrated on the middle tax bracket and have had only a modest impact on the problem of high EMTRs.[9] They have also created pressure for a reduction in the top rate of tax to flatten the tax scale once more. In the meantime, some policymakers have expressed surprise at the apparently large size of the black economy and the lost revenue to the state from 'cash jobs' (estimated for example in Giles, 1995 and 1997). The role played by high EMTRs in encouraging such activities has not, however, received much attention. Thus, rather than seeking solutions through better designed systems of targeting and a general reduction in the overall degree of targeting, the emphasis has been on reducing statutory tax rates, especially the top rate. Such an approach is neither efficient nor just.

Endnotes

1 Thus, the intent is not only to provide assistance where needed, but also to promote the value of self-reliance and improve the returns from being in the full-time workforce. However, the inclusion of additional criteria applying to those on low income can make for greater administrative complexity and poor take-up rates.

2 This Budget document was based on the report of the Change Team on Targeting Social Assistance set up by the National government following the announcement of benefit cuts in 1990 (see Prebble et al., 1991; Boston, 1994).

3 Raising the age of eligibility for the state pension becomes in itself a form of targeting, as the older a person is, the poorer they are likely to be.

4 As one manifestation of this feeling, in late 1997 a petition was mounted by the former Auditor-General, Brian Tyler, to hold a referendum on increasing government spending on health care to 7 per cent of GDP.

5 The classic poverty trap occurs where the EMTR exceeds 100 per cent, so that people lose more than a dollar via tax and lost social assistance for every extra dollar they earn.

6 The literature suggests that secondary earners are more affected by high marginal tax rates than are primary workers (Brown and Jackson, 1990).

7 A student couple under 25 who live together are regarded as unmarried for student allowances, but married if they are on a benefit such as the unemployment benefit. Student allowances are abated for the joint income of the parents even if they are divorced or separated, but only the income of the caregiver parent in such cases is counted for family support.

8 A person on the DPB can earn $180 a week before the punitive abatement of 70 per cent of the net benefit applies. If the same person were married to someone on the unemployment benefit, the joint income before such an abatement applies is only $80.

9 The middle effective rate was reduced from 28 per cent in 1996 to 21 per cent in July 1998. ACC levies were raised to 1.2 per cent from 0.7 per cent. EMTRs have accordingly come down by 6.5 per cent.

PART II

POLICY ISSUES
AND DEBATES

REDESIGNING INDUSTRIAL RELATIONS: THE EMPLOYMENT CONTRACTS ACT AND ITS CONSEQUENCES

PAT WALSH AND PETER BROSNAN

The National government elected in October 1990 believed it had received a mandate to redesign the welfare state (see, for example, Richardson, 1990, p.18). Two factors that had placed enormous pressure on the traditional welfare state (particularly in the area of income support) were slow productivity growth by international standards for at least two decades, and rising unemployment from the late 1970s. Since a large part of the blame for this situation was placed on New Zealand's system of industrial relations, the new government's welfare reforms were accompanied by 'the most fundamental change to industrial relations in New Zealand since the inception of the Industrial Conciliation and Arbitration Act of 1894' (Birch, 1990, p.40). The purpose of this chapter is to examine the background and policy advice that led to the Employment Contracts Act 1991 being introduced, and to analyse some of the consequences of the new system of industrial relations it created.

The Development of the Employment Contracts Act

At the change of government in 1990, industrial relations had been unstable since the 1960s. Successive governments had wrestled with the seemingly intractable problems caused by the gradual breakdown of the traditional arbitration system. Over time, that system was slowly being transformed from one based on statutory regulation into a bargaining system organised around market power (Brosnan et al., 1990, Chapter 9). The debate over industrial relations or labour market reform came to a head in the 1980s. The elimination of compulsory arbitration in 1984 seemed to herald further major changes. But a radical programme of labour market deregulation was firmly

117

rejected in the struggle that led to the Labour Relations Act 1987 (Walsh, 1989). However, within one month of its enactment, the Business Roundtable had begun a public campaign, soon supported by the Employers' Federation, to amend the legislation.

Critics of the Labour Relations Act argued that it impeded labour market flexibility. It preserved the exclusive jurisdiction of registered trade unions, the blanket coverage of awards across all workers and employers within its coverage clause, and the ability of unions to negotiate compulsory member-ship. They claimed that it had preserved statutory monopolies for unions in a period when most other markets had been deregulated. This was linked to claims that unions were increasingly unrepresentative of their members, who should no longer be coerced into a particular organisation but be given a genuine choice as to which, if any, union they joined. Frustration over bargaining structures was another source of pressure for change. A key policy objective of the Labour Relations Act was to enhance the flexibility of collec-tive bargaining structures and outcomes without sacrificing the historical role of the arbitration system as the protector of vulnerable groups. The Act tried to promote enterprise bargaining while retaining award protection for weaker groups of workers. However, unions proved reluctant to undermine the integrity of their awards by removing significant groups of their members from award coverage and negotiating enterprise agreements. The number of private-sector workers covered by single-employer agreements fell by 60 per cent between 1986 and 1990 (Harbridge and McCaw, 1992).

There were significant changes to bargaining structures under the Labour Relations Act, but most were at industry level as multiple awards were con-solidated into one industry award. This derived from the strategic unionism approach adopted by some unions, who sought to shed the traditional reactive posture of the union movement and to respond proactively to events. This approach stressed the need for unions to focus explicitly on wealth *creation* rather than being preoccupied with its distribution. This led to an emphasis on improvements in job and workplace design, the efficient utilisation of labour, the adoption of new technology, and integrated programmes of skill development, linked to co-ordinated pay structures and consultative management (New Zealand Engineering Union, 1991, Appendix 8). Awards embodying this approach, although they set an important trend, still covered only a relatively small number of workers by 1990, and tended to be confined to the manufacturing and public sectors (K. Roper, 1991).

These developments pointed to the possibilities for much more flexible approaches to bargaining under the Labour Relations Act, and were welcomed by many employers. However, opponents of the Act dismissed them as too little and too late. More importantly, they were industry-based rather than enterprise-based. The pressure for radical deregulation continued unabated. The Business Roundtable (1990) and the Employers' Federation (Clark, 1990) argued that an award system, still based to a significant degree on occupational wage relativities, generated outcomes that applied uniformly across industries and firms, regardless of their suitability. This made it difficult, if not impossible, to respond effectively to changing product-market conditions, the needs of new technology, new patterns of skill formation and new possibilities for labour deployment. They argued that the speed of change and the intensity of competition, both domestically and internationally, demanded an industrial relations system based on the needs of particular firms. Their demand for change in this area was also tied to new patterns of management, themselves the result of changing market circumstances. In large firms especially, a new approach to human resource management linked industrial relations and personnel considerations into wider corporate strategy. This approach required enterprise-based industrial relations.

As Brosnan and Rea (1991a) observe, the dominant policy diagnosis was that the chief impediment to growth lay in the structure and operation of the labour market itself, rather than in the wider economic policies that had generated a no-growth outcome. By 1990 it was clear that the National Party had accepted this diagnosis, which was reflected in its 1990 election manifesto. Out of this policy diagnosis and the new coalition of the Business Roundtable, the Employers' Federation and the National government, emerged the Employment Contracts Act.

The Employment Contracts Act 1991

Immediately following its victory in the 1990 election, the National government introduced what became the Employment Contracts Act 1991 (for more detailed accounts, see Brook-Cowen, 1993; Harbridge, 1994; Deeks et al., 1994; Dannin, 1997). The Act applies to all employment contracts, in contrast to the previous legislation which applied only to workers covered by a registered award or agreement. Part One of the Act deals with freedom of association, and provides that employees may choose whether or not to join an 'employee organisation'. (Under previous legislation, awards and agreements could require all employees to join the relevant union.) There can be no undue influence on employees to join or not join a union, and employees may not experience any advantage or disadvantage in their employment as a result of union membership or non-membership. The Act breaks the historical link between union membership and negotiating authority. Employees may choose whether to be represented in their employment negotiations, and if so, by whom. Unions no longer automatically have the right to negotiate on behalf of their members, but must seek negotiating authority from them.

There are two types of employment contract—individual and collective. There are no statutory procedures governing their negotiation. Employers and employees are able to decide by negotiation which kind of employment contract to have. Even where there is an applicable collective contract, an employee may negotiate an individual contract that is not 'inconsistent with' (that is, inferior to) the conditions prevailing in the collective contract. The individual contract may cover issues not included in the collective contract, or may improve on conditions already in that contract. In such circumstances, the employee remains bound by the remainder of the collective contract. When a collective employment contract expires, employees are deemed to be employed on an individual contract with the same conditions as the collective contract. Collective contracts covering more than one employer may be negotiated, but only if the employers are willing to do so. Unions cannot take industrial action to force employers to negotiate multi-employer agreements. This is one of the most important provisions in the Act, for it shifts the bargaining focus from traditional multi-employer agreements to enterprise negotiations.

Those parts of the Act dealing with bargaining and representation distort the principles of contract law in a manner that weakens the bargaining position of workers. The parties to employment contracts do not have the same remedies against exploitation available to them as do the parties to other types of contract. A criminal standard of proof—beyond reasonable doubt—is required before the Court can exercise its power to make an order cancelling or varying an employment contract. Hughes (1991, p.181) has described the application of this standard to civil cases as 'little short of bizarre'. Moreover, the Act specifically excludes application of the common law remedy of 'unconscionability' or 'unfairness', and installs instead a much higher standard of 'harsh and oppressive' to be met before the Court can vary or cancel an employment contract. Under the 'unconscionability' doctrine, civil courts are able to take account of issues such as 'relative bargaining power, "one-sided" contracts, unfair standard form contracts and lack of independent advice, all subsumed under the general question of whether the stronger party has taken advantage of the weaker' (Hughes, 1991, p.182). However, the Act denies these standard common law remedies to the parties to employment contracts.

It is the responsibility of the parties to resolve disputes over the interpretation or application of their employment contract. All employment contracts must contain effective procedures to settle disputes and personal grievances, and in the absence of contractual provisions the model procedures in the Act apply. A 'personal grievance' means any grievance arising out of a claim of unjustifiable dismissal, unjustifiable action by the employer to the employee's disadvantage, discrimination, sexual harassment, or duress in relation to membership or non-membership of an employee organisation. The Act provides for disputes and personal grievances to be settled if necessary by adjudication. The

Act permits strikes and lockouts, but only in certain circumstances. A strike or lockout is lawful only if it relates to the negotiation of an expired or new collective employment contract for the employees concerned, or if those involved have reasonable grounds for believing it to be justified on safety or health grounds. The Act established two specialist industrial relations institutions. The Employment Tribunal was set up to provide a low-level, informal, specialist tribunal to ensure the speedy, fair and just resolution of differences between the parties to employment contracts. The Employment Court was established to oversee the role of the tribunal and to deal with issues referred to it.

The government's response to concerns about the danger of exploitation under the Act was to point to a 'minimum code of employment'—a range of basic employment conditions enjoyed by all employees, and delivered through other, and for the most part already existing, legislation. These include minimum wage legislation, the Equal Pay Act, the Holidays Act, various legislation providing for parental and special leave, and the Human Rights Act, which prohibits discrimination in any matter relating to employment on the grounds of a person's sex, marital status, religious or ethical belief, colour, race, ethnic or national origin, disability, age, political opinion, employment status, family status or sexual orientation (Brosnan and Rea, 1991b). It is not possible for any employment contract to provide conditions inferior to these, although it is of course possible to improve on them.

The Employment Contracts Act and Policy Advice

From the above description, it can be seen that the Employment Contracts Act presents an obvious contradiction. On the one hand, it deregulates the process of contract negotiation and withdraws the state from its century-old involvement in the extensive prescription of bargaining and representation. On the other hand, the Act maintains and extends state involvement in the process of contract enforcement. It requires the inclusion of procedures for settling disputes and personal grievances in all employment contracts, and assigns jurisdiction over them and any legal matters arising out of the Act to specialist industrial relations institutions. The inclusion of all employees in the Act's jurisdiction constitutes a remarkable extension of the state's industrial relations role. So what was the process of policy advice that led to this seemingly contradictory result?

The National Party's 1990 election manifesto clearly set out what the new government intended to do in the areas of bargaining and representation (National Party, 1990). Within five working days of the election, Minister of Labour Bill Birch presented officials with drafting instructions for new legislation. These were based on a document prepared by a former employee of the Wellington Employers' Association, working on contract to the National

Party in the period leading up to the election (Walsh and Ryan, 1993). Although the bargaining and representation provisions were fiercely contested in public debate and in submissions to the select committee on the Bill, their early and clear presentation and the Minister's firm commitment to them meant that only fine-tuning was possible. There was never any likelihood of significant change to the broad principles governing contract negotiation and employee representation.

The key policy debate was over contract enforcement, and in particular whether there should be any specialist institutions and procedures governing employment contracts. Treasury (1991) advised the government unequivocally that there should be none. It argued that labour law should have no special status; rather, it should be embedded in the general law of contracts. In Treasury's view, the common law offered the best way of protecting individuals from exploitation and protecting the sanctity of contract, its only deficiency being the absence of any protection against discrimination or sexual harassment. Treasury dismissed any other need for personal grievance procedures. Eventually it did concede the need for a tribunal to settle low-level employment disputes, but with a much narrower jurisdiction than that finally established for the Employment Tribunal.

Although Treasury consistently pressed these views, they were rejected by the government. Instead, it adopted the advice received from officials of the Department of Labour and the State Services Commission (Department of Labour, 1991), which was that the common law was not an adequate basis for the employment relationship. They argued for the inclusion of mandatory dispute and personal grievance procedures in employment contracts, and for the retention of specialist industrial relations institutions. Their argument was based on the greater expertise of such institutions compared with that of ordinary courts, their greater flexibility, informality, ease of access and speed of resolution, and their capacity to implement Parliament's intentions by moderating the common law's lack of concern with equity and fair treatment. The officials rejected the Treasury assertion that employment contracts should be treated no differently from other contracts. In their view, not only were employment contracts different from standard commercial contracts, but special arrangements applied in many of the latter. The outcome of this debate was that the government decided in favour of retaining specialist institutions with jurisdiction over all legal matters arising from the operation of the Act.

Consequences of the Employment Contracts Act

It is not easy to disentangle the wider social and economic effects of the Employment Contracts Act from the impact of other policies. Other chapters assess changes in the distribution of income and other economic developments, which are to some degree influenced by the operation of the Act. It is possible, however, to identify the changes that have occurred in the structure of the workforce, and the consequences for industrial relations institutions and procedures.

The Changing Workforce

One of the principal policy objectives of the Employment Contracts Act was to enhance labour market flexibility, and to liberate employers from alleged rigidities and restrictions which, it was argued, were limiting their ability to shape the composition of their workforce. It was expected that this would lead to a significant reshaping of the labour force. The degree to which this has occurred can be assessed by comparing the results of workplace surveys undertaken in May 1991, the month in which the Act took effect, and May 1995. The surveys covered a range of questions relating to labour usage and employment forms within workplaces. The samples were drawn by Statistics New Zealand from their Business and Agricultural Directory, the sample size being 2,000 in 1991 and 5,200 in 1995. The response rates were 33 per cent and 38 per cent respectively.[1]

Table 7.1 compares the structure of the New Zealand workforce in 1991 and 1995, and shows that the patterns were quite similar. The great majority of workers are still permanent full-time employees, with the percentage scarcely changing between 1991 and 1995. By far the largest category of non-standard employment in both 1991 and 1995 was permanent part-time work, which also showed little variation. The two forms of non-standard employment to show the greatest change were 'fixed term' and 'casual'. Fixed-term employment almost trebled, from 1.1 per cent to 3.0 per cent of the workforce. In 1991, fixed-term employment was almost entirely confined to the public sector, reflecting the new public management model imposed by the radical public sector restructuring of the mid to late 1980s (Anderson et al., 1996). By 1995, fixed-term employment had risen to 2 per cent of the private-sector workforce, and had doubled again in the public sector.

Table 7.1 Workforce Structure (%)

	1991			1995		
	Full-time	Part-time	Total	Full-time	Part-time	Total
Permanent	70.1	13.7	83.8	68.7	14.8	83.5
Fixed term	0.6	0.5	1.1	2.1	0.9	3.0
Apprentices	1.5	0.0	1.5	1.2	0.1	1.3
Temporary	1.0	0.7	1.7	1.3	1.3	2.6
Casual	1.6	6.7	8.4	1.4	4.0	5.4
Contractor/ Consultant	2.3	1.1	3.4	2.5	0.8	3.4

Source: Brosnan et al. (1997).

Much of the policy debate over the impact of the Employment Contracts Act on the composition of the labour force has focused on temporary and casual employment. These have often been identified as the two most precarious forms of non-standard employment, and the most likely to rise under the new Act with its conscious policy objective of a more flexible labour market. Indeed, common to both advocates and opponents of the Act was the belief that it would increase the casualisation of the workforce. However, the big change in casual employment has been in the reverse direction from that predicted by both camps. The survey data show that between 1991 and 1995, casual employment declined from 8.4 per cent of the workforce to 5.4 per cent. It is especially noteworthy that the fall in part-time casual employment accounted for most of this decline, while full-time casual employment fell only slightly. Temporary employment, on the other hand, rose from 1.7 per cent of the workforce in 1991 to 2.6 per cent in 1995. Most of that increase was in part-time temporary employment, which virtually doubled in that period.

One possible explanation for the fall in casual employment is that the impact of the Employment Contracts Act on the composition of the labour force has been overstated, and that the economic cycle is the chief determinant of labour force composition. The period between 1991 and 1995 was one of job growth (about 10 per cent) and, at least later in the period, of economic recovery. An alternative explanation is that under the Employment Contracts Act, with the widespread elimination of (or substantial reduction in) penal and overtime rates, it became cheaper to employ full-time permanent workers for longer hours, and this was preferred to employing a casualised workforce with its attendant management difficulties.

Table 7.2 shows the distribution of the workforce in 1991 and 1995 by gender. Although women were much more likely throughout this period to be in non-standard employment than men, the period of the Employment Contracts Act is not associated with an increase in non-standard female employment. In particular, claims that the Act has casualised the female labour force cannot be sustained by the data. Indeed the stability of the permanent female workforce is striking. Identical proportions of women were employed on a permanent full-time and permanent part-time basis in 1991 and 1995. For men, on the other hand, the permanent full-time workforce fell slightly between 1991 and 1995 and the permanent part-time workforce rose by more than half, albeit from a low level of 4 per cent to 6.5 per cent.

The proportion of women in temporary and fixed-term employment has increased, and at a faster rate than for men. In 1991, males held a slight advantage over females in fixed-term employment. By 1995, however, even though male fixed-term employment had doubled to 2.7 per cent of the male workforce, for women it had trebled to 3.4 per cent of employed females.

Table 7.2 Structure of Workforce by Gender (%)

1991	Male			Female		
	Full-time	Part-time	Total	Full-time	Part-time	Total
Permanent	80.4	4.0	84.4	57.5	25.5	83.0
Fixed term	0.8	0.4	1.2	0.4	0.7	1.1
Apprentices	2.1	0.0	2.1	0.6	0.0	0.6
Temporary	1.1	0.6	1.7	0.9	0.9	1.8
Casual	1.3	4.0	5.3	2.0	10.0	12.1
Contractor/ Consultant	3.8	1.3	5.1	0.5	0.8	1.3

1995	Male			Female		
	Full-time	Part-time	Total	Full-time	Part-time	Total
Permanent	77.7	6.5	84.2	57.5	25.3	82.7
Fixed term	2.3	0.4	2.7	1.9	1.5	3.4
Apprentices	1.7	0.1	1.8	0.6	0.1	0.6
Temporary	1.3	0.9	2.3	1.3	1.7	3.0
Casual	1.2	2.2	3.4	1.6	6.3	8.0
Contractor/ Consultant	4.1	1.0	5.2	0.6	0.6	1.2

Source: Brosnan et al. (1997).

Males and females were employed on a temporary basis in virtually the same proportions in 1991. By 1995, however, although male temporary employment had risen from 1.7 per cent to 2.3 per cent, female temporary employment had increased from 1.8 per cent to 3.0 per cent. Women were more than twice as likely as men to be casual workers in both 1991 and 1995, although the size of the casual labour force declined markedly, and at a similar rate for both genders, during the period. Thus it cannot be argued that the Employment Contracts Act has led to a more flexible workforce, at least as measured by the proportion of the workforce in non-standard employment, and nor can it be argued that women have been worse affected than men in this regard.

Trade Unions

Trade union membership has fallen dramatically since the enactment of the Employment Contracts Act. Many unions relied heavily on compulsory unionism to secure their membership, and on other legislative props to operate effectively. The membership of such unions went steeply into decline following the Act's prohibition of compulsory membership and removal of legislative supports. Official statistics of union membership are no longer maintained. The most widely cited figures, however, are those from the trade union membership database maintained at Victoria University's Industrial Relations Centre (Crawford et al., 1997). These figures, derived from union reports (as official statistics were previously), show that trade union density fell by 69 per cent in the first eighteen months of the Act (May 1991 to December 1992). Since then it has continued to decline, although at a slower rate, falling by 71 per cent between December 1992 and December 1996. By 1996, the database showed union density at 20 per cent. An alternative estimate by the Department of Labour was that union membership had held at 33 per cent (Armitage, 1996).

A third measure of union density comes from the 1995 workplace survey referred to earlier, in which employers were asked what percentage of their labour force were union members. (The requirement in the Act that unions submit to employers authorisations to bargain from each union member means that employers are much more likely than previously to have a very accurate idea of the level of union membership at their workplace.) The advantage of workplace survey data is that they allow a more detailed picture than aggregate workforce data of the spread and depth of union membership.

Table 7.3 Trade Union Membership (%) by Workplace, May 1995

Workplaces	All	Public Sector	Private Sector	2 to 9 Employees	10 to 49 Employees	50+ Employees
Union Membership	27	65	18	8	23	43
Unionised Workplaces	19	92	13	11	39	74
Density at Unionised Workplaces	57	74	47	· 64	52	51

Source: Brosnan et al. (1997).

The workplace survey's estimate of union density for May 1995, relying on employer estimates, is 27 per cent (Brosnan and Walsh, 1997). This does not differ greatly from the Victoria University database figure for December 1994 of 23.4 per cent (Crawford et al., 1997). The survey data also show that only 19 per cent of workplaces have any union members at all. Although such data are not available for earlier periods, there can be no doubt that this is a dramatic fall. It also means that more than 80 per cent of employers operate without the constraint of a union at their workplace. However, the data show that at unionised workplaces, 57 per cent of workers are union members. Thus, although unions are spread narrowly across the economy, their depth is considerable where they are present. The data also show that union represen-tation at the workplace rises with workplace size. As Table 7.3 shows, almost three-quarters of workplaces with more than 50 employees are unionised, compared with only 11 per cent of workplaces with 2-9 employees. Similarly, union density overall is much higher at large workplaces. Only 8 per cent of employees in the smallest workplaces are union members, compared with 43 per cent in workplaces with more than 50 workers. Interestingly, however, where small workplaces are unionised they have a higher density than larger workplaces.

Table 7.3 also shows that unions have retained a much stronger presence in the public sector than in the private sector. Just on two-thirds of public sector employees are union members, compared with 18 per cent in the private sector. The great majority (92 per cent) of public sector workplaces are unionised, but only one-eighth of workplaces in the private sector. Density at unionised workplaces is 74 per cent in the public sector and 47 per cent in the private sector. The survey results by industry sector show that union membership is highest in public services, manufacturing, and transport, and lowest in mining and construction, and trade and food. These results reveal that the new pattern of union membership is one in which unions are present in only a small minority of workplaces, and these tend to be large workplaces in the public sector, manufacturing, and transport. However, these workplaces have very high levels of union membership.

Table 7.4 Role of Trade Unions in Workplace Change Decisions

Role of Unions	Per Cent
Ignored	36
Informed	20
Consulted	22
Jointly involved	3
Bargained	18

Source: Brosnan et al. (1997).

Unions have struggled in this new environment. They negotiate many times more separate contracts on behalf of fewer members, and with fewer resources. In many cases they negotiate with employers who are emboldened by the new legislative regime and by the still depressed labour market to seek harsh changes to employment conditions. Nonetheless, they are still the predominant bargaining agent for workers. Non-union bargaining agents are of negligible importance, although in an increasing number of contracts workers are now representing themselves (Harbridge et al., 1997). Some unions have adopted new organising models which give them some prospect of adapting successfully (Oxenbridge, 1997; Boxall and Haynes, 1997), although Oxenbridge concludes that they are in a minority. According to the workplace survey, employers in the majority of unionised workplaces report that unions have no effective role in their decisions on workplace change (Table 7.4). While it is possible that employers under-report the significance of the union role, it is noteworthy that in only 21 per cent of unionised workplaces did employers report either bargaining with or jointly involving unions in such decision-making.

Some unions have failed completely, most notably the Communication and Energy Workers Union, which collapsed and was dissolved in December 1995. A small number of new unions have emerged, some of which have challenged existing unions, especially in the public sector. Industrial activity, one barometer of union vitality, appears to have been largely unaffected by the Act. The number of industrial stoppages had begun to fall during the latter half of the 1980s and continued to do so until 1992, when it began to rise again. This pattern seems to be more closely related to economic downturn and recovery than to any specific impact of the Employment Contracts Act, although the collapse in union membership immediately after the Act came into effect would have discouraged industrial action (Henning, 1995).

Bargaining

The structure of bargaining has changed dramatically since 1991. Unlike Australia and the United Kingdom, New Zealand does not conduct a national workplace industrial relations survey, which would provide a widely accepted estimate of the extent of collective bargaining coverage. Oxenbridge (1998) reviews a number of studies whose estimates range from 21 percent to 49 percent of the workforce. Her conclusion is that collective bargaining coverage is probably between 20 and 30 percent of employees, a substantial decline from about 60 percent in 1991 (Oxenbridge, 1998, pp. 7–10). However, the degree of uncertainty attached to this is very worrying from a public policy perspective.

The major change to collective bargaining has been the abandonment of the multi-employer bargaining that typified the arbitration system for almost a century. This is a direct consequence of the provision in the Employment Contracts Act that allows employers to choose between enterprise and multi-employer bargaining, and prohibits unions from undertaking any industrial action to achieve a multi-employer contract. Employers have exercised this option decisively in favour of enterprise bargaining. Just on one-third of the workforce are employed on single-employer collective contracts, and only 7 per cent on multi-employer contracts.

The shift to single-employer contracts has given employers and employees the opportunity to realise one of the Act's major objectives—the development of employment conditions appropriate to their circumstances. However, it is difficult to assess the degree to which this has been achieved, as employment contracts are private documents and are not published. It is clear from the studies of collective contracts that some significant changes have been made to employment conditions, although the wholesale changes that some predicted have not occurred. The proportion of the workforce eligible for overtime and penal payments has declined considerably, although more than half remain eligible for penal rates and more than three-quarters for overtime rates (Harbridge et al., 1997). Less than half the workforce are employed under a contract that specifies the traditional Monday-to-Friday working week, but 97 per cent have a specified working week of 40 hours or less (Harbridge et al., 1997).

The debate over whether the Act has achieved its macroeconomic policy objectives continues without any clear resolution, and is outside the scope of this chapter. It is noteworthy that labour productivity growth has fallen since the Act came into effect (OECD, 1996). Unemployment has declined substantially, from 10.6 per cent in December 1991 to 6.7 per cent in June 1997, although much of the associated job growth has been in part-time employment, which increased by 13.5 per cent between June 1994 and June 1997 compared with an 8.2 per cent growth in full-time jobs (Statistics New Zealand, 1997a, pp.32-3). Traditional wage relativities have been broken, and there is a much wider dispersion of wage settlements under the Act (Harbridge, 1994, pp.14-15). Real wages have continued to fall during the 1990s, although this continues a trend that began in the 1980s (Income Distribution Group, 1990; Statistics New Zealand, 1997b, p.102). A survey by the New Zealand Institute for Economic Research in December 1995 found that 85 per cent of employers had reduced or frozen overtime rates since 1991, and 83 per cent had reduced or frozen penal rates (Yeabsley and Savage, 1996).

The impact of the Employment Contracts Act on women is difficult to assess. Hammond and Harbridge (1993) argue that women have fared worse than men, but Ryan, on the basis of her analysis of the 1993 employee survey, concludes that gender has been less important as an explanatory factor than location in the labour market (Ryan, 1994, p.21). There has been no assessment of the effects of the Act on Māori and Pacific Islanders, but, as expected, their poverty levels remain much higher than those of Pākehā (Stephens et al., 1995).

Specialist Institutions

The contentious issue of specialist institutions has continued to be the main focus of policy debate since the Employment Contracts Act took effect in 1991. In December 1992, the Employers' Federation and the Business Roundtable jointly published a highly critical analysis of decisions by the Employment Court, and called for substantial amendments to the specialist jurisdiction (New Zealand Business Roundtable/New Zealand Employers' Federation, 1992). Since then, the two organisations have continued to press for changes to the structure and operation of the specialist institutions (Kerr, 1993a and 1993b; Marshall, 1993). They claimed that the Court set 'almost impossible standards' in its requirements for procedural fairness by employers, that compensation levels were too high, and that the Court was too quick to reinstate sacked workers. Another major joint report in 1996 reiterated these views, and argued that the Court's decisions were an unjust employment tax that went against the interests of all workers, and especially the low-paid (New Zealand Business Roundtable/New Zealand Employers' Federation, 1996).

In response to these claims, it can be argued that the Court establishes ordinary standards of natural justice; it very infrequently reinstates a sacked worker; its compensation levels for wrongful dismissal are very low (the average is about $7,500); and in only about half the cases where it finds the dismissal unjustified does it order reimbursement (Boon, 1992a and 1992b; Thomson, 1992). Nonetheless, it is true that the Court has refused to condone any shift towards making the dismissal and replacement of workers easier in a depressed labour market, and it insists that employers meet both procedural and substantive standards for dismissal. Freyer (1997, p.155) argues that the Court has placed too much emphasis on the former, at the expense of fairness to the employer. In cases dealing with representation and negotiation rights, after an initial series of decisions that placed major obstacles in the way of unions, the Court has issued a number of decisions that provide some measure of support for effective union organisation and activity (Harbridge and Kiely, 1995).

At first, the government was unsympathetic to the claims made by critics of the Employment Court and Tribunal. In 1993 Max Bradford, then chairperson of the Labour Select Committee, reiterated the reasons for establishing the Court and Tribunal. The government had wanted institutions that would resolve disputes as quickly as possible; were flexible and able to take into account what actually happened in the workplace; could provide expertise in employment law and industrial relations practice; were accessible in terms of cost and availability; and would provide procedures and outcomes that were considered fair and reasonable by society as a whole (Bradford, 1993, pp.6-7). He concluded that: 'Nearly two years after the introduction of the Act, I believe that the reasons for establishing specialist institutions are still valid. The government has yet to be convinced that the factors I mentioned earlier would be adequately dealt with in some other jurisdiction' (p.11).

In 1996, however, the Coalition Agreement included a commitment to review the operation of the Employment Court. By 1997 Bradford, now Minister of Labour, was no longer sure about the future of the specialist institutions. He argued that:

> There are signs the combined effect of the Employment Tribunal and the Employment Court decisions—as well as business practices flowing from those decisions—may be adversely affecting employment prospects and flexibility in

our labour market. Some Employment Court decisions are clearly inconsistent with the principles of the Act and have caused considerable debate over the role of the Court (1997, p.7).

Bradford suggested that by 1997 there was 'undoubtedly more currency' than in 1991 (and presumably in 1993) for the view that there should not be a specialist employment court. At the time of writing, the review of the Employment Court has not been released. The government did issue a discussion paper reviewing the Holidays Act 1981, in which comment was invited on the possibility of workers being able to trade either their eleven public holidays or one week's annual leave or both for cash (New Zealand Government, 1997a). Strong opposition from the public and from New Zealand First led to this idea being shelved. However, since the dissolution of the Coalition government, Bradford has indicated that he may revive the proposal.

There are other concerns about the operation of the specialist institutions, particularly about whether the government's policy objective of a speedy and accessible dispute resolution process is being achieved. The costs of access to the institutions, especially filing fees, adjudication fees and legal fees for non-union members, are massive for people on lower incomes (Hughes, 1992, p.46). It is clear that these costs put access to the Employment Tribunal and Court beyond the reach of a large proportion of the non-unionised workforce and thus defeat the stated purposes of the legislation. There are very considerable delays in the system, with the parties having to wait months for a Tribunal hearing. If they opt for mediation but do not resolve the dispute, they face another lengthy wait for an adjudication. By June 1996, there were 2,985 outstanding applications before the Employment Tribunal, almost three times the number at June 1992 (Department of Labour, 1997a). This backlog was not due to any lack of activity by the Tribunal, which during the June year 1995/96 disposed of 3,218 applications—more than four times the number dealt with in the first year of the Act. The key reason for the huge backlog is that the Tribunal is receiving more than twice as many applications (5,144 in 1996) as when the Act came into effect. More than three-quarters of these are personal grievances, most of which relate to claims of unjustifiable dismissal. There is no doubt that by 1996, thousands more employees were claiming they had been unfairly dismissed than was the case in the first year of the Act. One reason is obviously the Act's extension of the jurisdiction to all employees. The Minister has suggested that another reason for this staggering increase is that employees are capitalising on the provision that a dismissed employee who lodges a personal grievance claim can avoid the stand-down period for qualifying for the unemployment benefit (Bradford, 1997, p.9). It may also be that employers, emboldened by the Act and without the constraint of strong union coverage, are behaving more capriciously than before. Further delays ensue if a case is appealed to the Employment Court, and even further to the Court of Appeal. The Chief Judge of the Employment Court estimated this process as taking two years (Goddard, 1993, p.10).[2]

Conclusions

The provisions and operation of the Employment Contracts Act show both continuities and change. The Act retains specialist institutions which have, in one form or another, marked the industrial relations landscape since 1894. The character of these institutions reflects a process of change that began in the 1960s, as the Court of Arbitration lost its historical role as a wage-fixing body. The transformation of the Court into the present-day Employment Court, a body concerned wholly with the adjudication of disputes and personal grievances, underlines the continuity of the Employment Contracts Act. Indeed, the Act considerably extends the role of the state in industrial relations by extending the jurisdiction of the specialist institutions to all employees rather than just those covered by a collective contract. In this respect, the Act is consistent with the expansion of other forms of state regulation of the employment relationship, such as the Human Rights Act 1994, the Privacy Act 1993 and the Health and Safety in Employment Act 1992. Common to all these regulatory arrangements is the state's desire to guarantee certain standards for its citizens in their capacity as individual employees.

However, the state accepts no responsibility for promoting the collective representation of those citizens at the workplace. Accordingly, the Act withdraws the state from its historical role in regulating the collective representation of workers, and indeed places some important obstacles in the path of traditional forms of collective action. The result has been profound change. Trade union membership has plummeted. The character of trade unionism has changed. Trade unions have yielded the vast majority of workplaces to the unchecked authority of employers. The union movement is concentrated in large workplaces, in the public sector, and in manufacturing and transport. In unionised workplaces, union membership is high, but in only 43 per cent of these workplaces do unions play a significant role in decision-making on workplace change. The level of collective bargaining has fallen, but not by as much as might be expected. The opportunities offered by the Employment Contracts Act for free-riding have been eagerly accepted, and many more workers are covered by collective contracts than are union members.

However, this has not led to a reshaping of the workforce in the direction of more flexible forms of employment. The proportion of the workforce employed in non-standard forms of employment has not altered greatly since 1991. Indeed, casual employment, particularly part-time casual employment, has declined, although the significance of this is not clear. Some other forms of precarious employment (notably temporary employment) have risen, but not greatly. There is no evidence that women have been drawn into more vulnerable forms of employment under the Act. However, there has clearly been a progressive down-grading of many employment conditions since 1991, particularly in areas such as penal and overtime rates. While these rates have by no means been eliminated, the proportion of the workforce entitled to them has fallen considerably. The employment conditions of workers on individual contracts is difficult to assess. Many examples of exploitation can be cited, and there can be no doubt that a vulnerable underclass has developed. The debate on the macroeconomic effects of the Act continues. Certainly, labour productivity growth and real wages have fallen, although the drop in real wages continues a trend already well established prior to the Act.

It is clear that the government is resolved to continue with the Act. The only significant change under consideration concerns the future of the specialist institutions. Their fate will become clearer when the government announces the results of its review of their operation. However, the institutions have lost the firm backing of the Department of Labour, its saviour in times past, and the prospects of the Court continuing as before must be considered remote. The government was not in the least embarrassed by the highly critical report issued by the International Labour Organisation (ILO), which found the Act to be in breach of key ILO conventions (International Labour Organisation, 1995). Indeed, it used the report to criticise the ILO as being in need of major reform itself. The government is firmly set on its industrial relations path, and it will not easily be diverted.

Endnotes

1 In order to check on the sampling and weighting process used in analysing these survey data, they were compared with corresponding official statistics. The Household Labour Force Survey does not collect data for most of the employment categories used in the survey. However, where comparison was possible, the survey data correspond closely with official figures from the Household Labour Force Surveys for June 1991 and June 1995. For a fuller explanation of the survey methodology, see Brosnan et al. (1997).

2 It should be noted that these delays are not new, nor are they peculiar to the current jurisdiction. Similar delays were observed in the legislative review that preceded the Labour Relations Act 1987 (New Zealand Government, 1985).

CHAPTER EIGHT

THE HEALTH REFORMS:
TO MARKET AND BACK?

TONI ASHTON

In July 1993 the New Zealand public health system was radically restructured. The main objectives of these 'health reforms' (as the changes soon became known) were to encourage efficiency and to improve access to an effective and affordable health system. However, the widespread perception has been that the performance of the public health system has, if anything, declined since the introduction of the reforms. In the lead-up to the October 1996 election, health policy was the number one election issue (Coney, 1996a). Common concerns included:

- the cutting of local services, including the closure of some hospitals;
- ongoing debate about the adequacy of government health funding;
- lengthening waiting lists and other problems of access;
- some well-publicised resignations by chief executives and chairpersons of Crown health enterprises (CHEs);
- continued CHE deficits;
- objection to the 'profit-driven' model for health (Crown Company Monitoring Advisory Unit, 1996).

Public dissatisfaction intensified throughout 1997.[1] In October of that year, a national petition was launched in support of a referendum for the government to increase its annual spending on health services to at least 7 per cent of gross domestic product (Public Health Referendum, 1997). By the end of 1997, many thousands of people throughout the country had expressed their dissatisfaction with the government's management of the public health system by marching through the streets in public protests.

This chapter examines the validity of the common perception that the health reforms have failed. It begins with a brief review of the 1993 reforms, together with a summary of the proposals for change made in the Coalition government's health policy. A number of indicators of health sector performance in the 1990s are then examined. The chapter concludes with some comments about the future direction of health policy.

Health Policy in the 1990s

The central feature of the health reforms introduced in July 1993 was the splitting of the roles of purchaser and provider, which had previously been carried out by fourteen area health boards. Four regional health authorities (RHAs) were established as purchasing agents, to be responsible for purchasing all personal health and disability services. This required the integration into a single budget of funds for primary, secondary and disability support services, all of which had previously been funded via different funding streams. A separate agency, the Public Health Commission, was established to purchase public health (that is, population-based) services. Hospital and community services previously provided by the area health boards were reconfigured into 23 CHEs, which would operate along commercial lines. The new structure, which was originally proposed in what became known as 'the Green and White Paper' (Upton, 1991), is illustrated in Figure 8.1.

The Green and White Paper also outlined proposals for changes to subsidies and user charges for health services, and these were introduced in February 1992. The main feature of these changes—which included the imposition of part-charges for public hospital services for the first time since 1938—was a shift to tighter targeting of subsidies towards lower-income groups (Ashton, 1992a). Access to these higher subsidies was made available through a community services card (CSC).

The general direction of the reforms was towards a more market-oriented structure in which providers would compete with each other for contracts with purchasers to provide services. This reflected the direction of the health reforms taking place in other countries (especially the United Kingdom, the Netherlands and Sweden), where competition between providers was seen as the mechanism for improving efficiency in publicly funded health systems. The move towards a more market-oriented structure also followed the direction of economic reform that had prevailed in New Zealand since 1984.

The stated objectives of the health reforms (Upton, 1991, p.3) were to:
- improve access for all New Zealanders to a health system that is effective, fair and affordable;
- encourage efficiency, flexibility and innovation in service delivery;
- reduce waiting times;
- widen consumer choice of services;
- enhance the working environment for health professionals;
- recognise the importance of the public health effort in preventing illness and injury and in promoting health; and
- increase the sensitivity of the health system to the changing needs of the population.

In Figure 8.1 it can be seen that there were effectively four tiers in the

Figure 8.1 The Structure of the Reformed Public Health System, 1993-1996

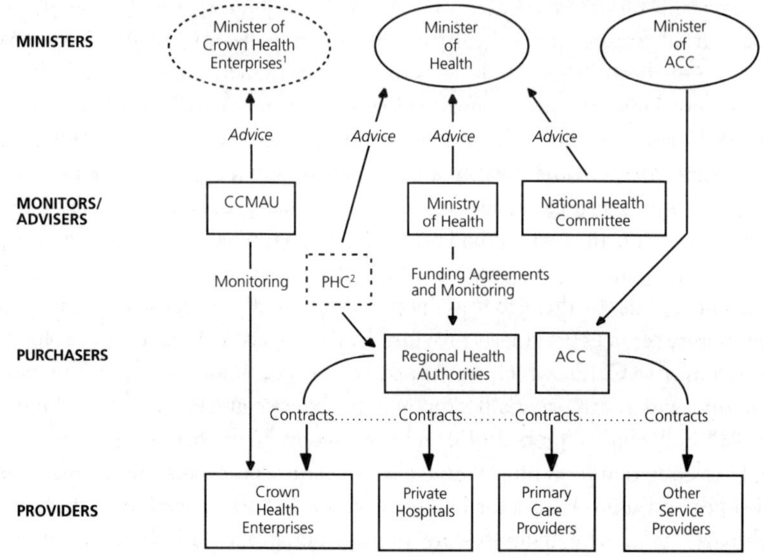

Notes:
1. The position of Minister of Crown Health Enterprises was abolished by the new Coalition government in December 1996. The Minister of Health took over the position's responsibilities.
2. The Public Health Commission, which had been both an adviser and a purchaser, was disestablished in July 1995.

reformed health system: ministers, monitors and advisers, purchasers, and providers. At the ministerial level, the Minister of Crown Health Enterprises was responsible for services provided through these newly established, publicly owned organisations, while the Minister of Health became responsible for the purchasing function undertaken by the RHAs. Advising the two ministers were the Crown Company Monitoring Advisory Unit (CCMAU) and the Ministry of Health. A range of other bodies also advised the Minister of Health, including the National Advisory Committee on Health and Disability (known as the National Health Committee), the Public Health Commission (until July 1995) and the RHAs.

The role of the RHAs was to monitor the health service requirements of their populations and to purchase services accordingly. They negotiated contracts with a range of public and private providers, including CHEs, private hospitals, general practitioners (GPs) and voluntary organisations. CHEs own and operate public hospitals and provide a range of community-based services. They are constituted as shareholding enterprises under the Companies Act 1993, and have statutory objectives (under the Health and Disability Services Act 1993) to exhibit a sense of social responsibility and also to operate as successful and efficient businesses.

Changes to the Original Proposals

Problems during the implementation phase led to a number of changes being made to the proposed structure. First, the government's intention had been to give people the choice of obtaining their health care through RHAs or through other, non-government, health care plans. The idea of this was to introduce competition between purchasers, thereby encouraging them to respond to community preferences. However, the proposal required that some assessment be made of the risk levels of individuals, and that a formula be developed to calculate the amount of public funds they would be entitled to take to an alternative purchasing agent. In spite of much research, health policy analysts world-wide have failed to come up with an ideal solution to this problem. There were also concerns that health care plans could lead to a system in which people with poor health status, particularly Māori, were grouped into a single plan which might not be financially viable (Scott, 1994). In the light of these problems, the proposal to introduce competing purchasers was eventually shelved. This left the RHAs with regional monopolies, even though they had been structured and geared to compete.

Attempts to introduce a separate market for public health services (that is, health protection, disease prevention and health promotion) were also problematic. In the original blueprint a single agency, the Public Health Commission (PHC), was to purchase these services from three regional providers called Public Health Agencies. In the event, these agencies were never established. Instead the PHC, which was established according to plan in July 1993, was required to purchase services either directly from providers or indirectly through RHAs. However, the PHC was abolished in July 1995 after just two years in operation, and its tasks were taken over by the Ministry of Health. The reasons given for this change were overlapping responsibilities and lines of accountability between the Ministry and the PHC, and problems of service co-ordination (Ashton, 1996). However, Beaglehole and Bonita (1997, p.185) suggest that while much emphasis had been placed on the need for contestable advice in the public sector generally, 'it is hard to escape the impression that a major reason that the Commission was abolished was its tendency to provide the government with advice contrary to the interests of the powerful health damaging interests in New Zealand, for example the alcohol and tobacco industries.'

Another part of the reform package that has not been achieved is the definition of an explicit core of health services to which all New Zealanders must have access. A National Advisory Committee on Core Health and Disability Services was appointed in 1992 to 'recommend annually to the Minister of Health which core health and disability support services should be purchased, how they should be distributed and the terms of access on which they should be available' (National Advisory Committee on Core Health and

Disability Services, 1992, p.5). Initial deliberations revolved around the need to develop a defined list of those services to which the RHAs should ensure access. However, by 1994 the committee had decided that: 'A "simple list" approach, with services "in" or "out" of the core, is not an appropriate way to describe people's eligibility or access to publicly funded disability support and health services' (National Advisory Committee on Core Health and Disability Services, 1994, p.13).

The notion of a defined 'core' was eventually abandoned entirely. Attention turned instead towards the benefits of particular services for individuals in particular circumstances through, for example, the development of clinical protocols, guidelines, and other strategies for encouraging evidence-based practice. In line with this reorientation of activities, and with the extension of the committee's jurisdiction to include public health services, the name of the committee was changed to the National Advisory Committee on Health and Disability (the National Health Committee) in 1995.

Problems also arose in integrating the funding for accident-related care into RHA budgets. The original intention had been to transfer responsibility for purchasing these services from the Accident Rehabilitation and Compensation Insurance Corporation (that is, ACC) to RHAs gradually over a number of years (Ministry of Health, 1992). However, after some delay it was finally announced in October 1995 that the RHAs would retain responsibility for purchasing acute care for accident victims, together with laboratory services which had already been transferred, while ACC would continue to be responsible for purchasing elective surgery, primary care and community services. Thus, the objective of establishing a single agent to purchase a total package of personal health services on behalf of individuals and their families has not been achieved.

Finally, various ad hoc adjustments have been made to the new regime of user charges in an effort to reduce financial barriers to care. The charges for inpatient hospital services were removed just thirteen months after they were introduced, following widespread public opposition and administrative problems. Other changes included the extension of the highest subsidies (that is, for Group 1) to recipients of partly abated family support (Group 2), a reduction in the level of user charges for pharmaceuticals, and the raising of the qualifying income levels (from 1 July 1996).

The existence of obstacles to implementation and the failure to implement reforms as originally designed have been common features of market-oriented health reforms internationally (Saltman and von Otter, 1995). This fact in itself probably speaks volumes for the notion of applying a market model to the health sector. However, in spite of ongoing changes and adjustments to the original model proposed for New Zealand, the three central themes of the

1993 reforms—that is, the splitting of the functions of purchaser and provider, enabling competition between providers, and introducing business practices into public hospitals—remained firmly in place.

In the lead-up to the 1996 election, there was a widespread perception that the health reforms were not working as intended. Whichever party (or parties) was elected, it was clear that something would have to be done to recapture the public's confidence in the public health system.

Health Policy in the Coalition Agreement

After the Coalition government was formed in December 1996, its plans for changes to the health system were announced in the Coalition Agreement (1996, pp.34-8). The main features were:

- the replacement of the four RHAs with a single central funder;
- the Minister of Health to be responsible for the whole of the publicly funded sector, including the CHEs;
- the replacement of CHEs with not-for-profit Regional Hospital and Community Services;
- a shift away from contracting for services on a competitive price and volume basis towards longer-term contractual agreements based on historic funding information and levels, benchmarking information and other comparative data;
- an increase in health funding, including funding to reduce waiting times;
- the provision of free GP services and pharmaceuticals for children under six;
- the removal of income- and asset-testing for the elderly in long-stay public hospital care, and of asset-testing for those in long-stay private hospital care;
- the removal of outpatient and day-stay hospital part-charges;
- increased emphasis on Māori health, child health and mental health services.

By the end of 1997, some action had been taken on most of these proposals. On 1 July 1997, the RHAs were formally combined into the Health Funding Authority (HFA)—initially called the Transitional Health Authority (THA). The HFA is responsible for determining health care needs and for developing and managing contracts with providers. However, the four regional offices have been retained to manage local relationships with consumers and providers.

Some changes in funding arrangements were confirmed in the 1997 Budget. From 1 July 1997, for children under six, the subsidy for GP consultations was increased (to $32.50) and pharmaceutical part-charges were removed. These changes should secure free doctor visits and drugs for most children, at least for the time being. Part-charges for hospital outpatient and day-stay services were also removed on 1 July 1997. However, the removal of income- and asset-testing for long-stay care for the elderly was deferred until 1 October 1998. Funding for Vote: Health was increased in the 1997 Budget to cover these and other spending promises. The funding package comprised an additional $300 million between 1997 and 2000, plus the possibility of a further $180 million in 1998/99 and $450 million in 1999/00, subject to confirmation in future Budgets.

Health Sector Performance

This section examines the performance of the health sector following the introduction of the health reforms. Each sub-section is devoted to evidence relating to one or more of the originally stated objectives of the reforms (see above). Although cost containment was not included in these stated objectives, a desire to contain government expenditure appeared to underlie the reforms.[2] Therefore, it is useful to set the scene by considering briefly the shifts that have occurred in expenditure on health services in recent years.

Health Expenditure

Prior to the 1993 reforms, total per capita expenditure on health had been increasing slowly (see Figure 8.2). However, this was due entirely to increased private spending on health services (that is, personal expenditure, private health insurance, and charitable donations), which had doubled in real terms since 1987. In contrast, real per capita expenditure by the government had been declining steadily since 1989.

The reconfiguration of area health boards into CHEs revealed that there was 'a chronic revenue shortfall in the public health system, that has previously been addressed through unsustainable erosion of assets' (Minister of Health, 1994, p.18). In the light of this shortfall, the government agreed to increase funding levels to enable RHAs to pay CHEs appropriate prices for their services. RHAs were then to be placed on an indicative funding path in which funding would be increased in line with population changes but not with inflation.

In the event, pressures in various parts of the system resulted in the baseline funding being augmented by frequent ad hoc injections amounting to almost $1 billion in the three years from 1993 to 1996. This resulted in a turnaround in the trend of public health spending per capita, from an average annual decline of 1.7 per cent in the four years from 1989 to 1993 to average annual increases of 1.1 per cent in the three years following the reforms (Sector Analysis Section, undated). Even so, reported public health expenditure per

Figure 8.2 Real Health Expenditure Per Capita: 1987-1996

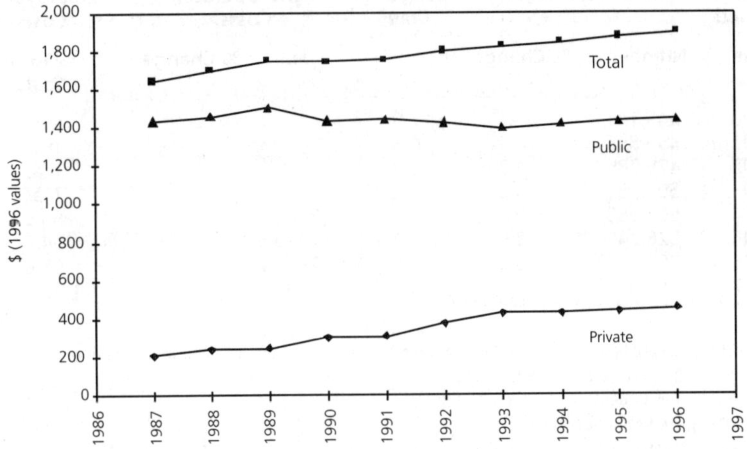

Source: Sector Analysis Section, Ministry of Health (undated).

capita—excluding CHE deficits—was still 4 per cent (or $60 in real terms) lower in 1996 than it had been in 1989.

Efficiency

One of the primary motivations for the health reforms was to achieve better value for money, especially in public hospitals. Unfortunately, efficiency in the health sector is notoriously difficult to measure. For example, the unit costs of procedures and other measures of output change in line with variables such as case mix and the degree of cost shifting to other providers, as well as with real changes in productive efficiency. The relevant data are often either not known, or not comparable across organisations or regions and/or over time. An added complication is that some data are regarded as commercially sensitive and so are not publicly available. The measures of efficiency presented in this section are therefore limited and should be interpreted with caution.

Some performance indicators for public hospitals are given in Table 8.1. While the number of discharges has increased since 1993, this was simply a continuation of an existing trend. Likewise, average length of inpatient stay has continued to decline steadily, as it did prior to the reforms. Although output has increased, so too have operating costs. CHE revenues have also increased steadily each year, but at a slower rate than operating costs. Thus 21 of the 23 CHEs have consistently failed to break even. Moreover, CHE deficits have grown relative to the former area health board deficits

Table 8.1 Some Public Hospital Performance Measures, 1990-1997

Year Ended	No. of discharges[1]		Length of Stay[2]	CHE Operating Costs[3]		Employee Costs
June	Number	% Change		$m	% Change	% Total Costs
1990	440,141	-	7.0	-	-	n.a.[4]
1991	459,855	4.4	6.6	-	-	n.a.
1992	479,289	4.2	6.2	-	-	n.a.
1993	504,781	5.3	5.8	-	-	n.a.
1994	507,988	0.6	5.6	2669.2	-	65.6
1995	526,245	3.6	4.3	2810.5	5.3	64.6
1996	552,607	5.0	4.1	2931.7[5]	4.3	63.6
1997	n.a.	n.a.	3.9	3099.4	5.7	63.5

Notes:
1. Includes day patient discharges. Inpatient discharge volumes are adjusted for the relative complexity of cases compared with the national average in 1989.
2. Includes day patients. Case mix adjusted.
3. Not adjusted for inflation.
4. Not available.
5. Revised.

Sources: Performance Monitoring and Review (undated); Contract Monitoring (1994/95);
Performance Management Unit (1995/96, 1996/97);
Ministry of Health (personal communication);
Statistics New Zealand (various editions).

(Figure 8.3). Reasons for operating losses include the provision of services above contracted levels, payment by RHAs at prices that are below the cost of provision, and a failure by CHEs to achieve the expected reductions in costs.

In its 1996 briefing to the incoming Minister of Health, CCMAU discussed a number of factors that might account for the failure of CHEs to achieve cost reductions. After 1993, inflationary pressures occurred in both wages and non-labour inputs.[3] Senior management processes were weakened by the entry of new managers who were unused to operating in an environment where information about costs and outputs was limited. Initial cost control efforts had focused on support services (such as the contracting out of cleaning and catering services) rather than on core clinical services, which account for the bulk of total costs. The reforms had also allowed cost pressures built up during the area health board era to be released (especially the costs of replacing equipment and maintaining facilities). Finally, any incentives for managers to achieve efficiency gains were weakened by the willingness of the government to provide deficit support, and by the political desire to minimise disruption during the change process. The incentive to perform was probably blunted also by the fact that some CHE boards paid their chief executives large personal bonuses despite the poor financial performance of their organisations. It also seems likely that expectations of efficiency gains by CHEs were overly optimistic.

Figure 8.3 Area Health Board (1990-93) and CHE (1994-97) Deficits[1]

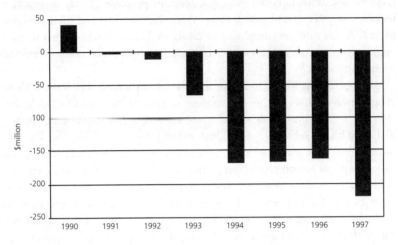

Note 1. Not adjusted for inflation.
Sources: Deloitte Touche Tohmatsu (1996); Statistics New Zealand (various editions).

It is possible that the failure to limit costs reflects improvements in quality. Innovations in treatments and medical practices are continually enhancing the quality of care given to patients. The complexity of cases treated in public hospitals—and hence the average cost per case—has also been increasing steadily in recent years. Some CHEs have recorded marked improvements in quality indicators such as levels of reported patient satisfaction and readmission rates. However, these measures are poor indicators of overall quality of care. In December 1996, Bill English (then caretaker Minister of Crown Health Enterprises) admitted that both clinical staff and the public had raised concerns about the quality of patient care and heavy workloads (Young, 1996).

Overall, these indicators suggest that the health reforms have not achieved greater efficiency in public hospitals. The situation was perhaps best summed up by CCMAU (1996, p.21) in its briefing to the incoming Minister of Crown Health Enterprises: 'The health reforms have yet to yield the original expectations. By a range of measures (e.g. average length of stay, personnel costs, bed numbers) the pace of performance seems, if anything, to have weakened since the advent of the reforms.'

In the primary sector, there are few cost or output measures available that provide reliable information about performance. Perhaps the most visible change resulting from the reforms has been the development of independent practitioner associations (IPAs), which represent groupings of GPs and/or other primary care providers. By 1997, around 70 per cent of GPs belonged to an IPA. In addition to negotiating with RHAs on behalf of their members, IPAs assist GPs to improve their management processes, to set up practice registers, and to collect basic statistics about their services and their patients. Most IPAs are now permitted to participate in 'budget-holding'; that is, they hold budgets for referred services such as pharmaceuticals, laboratory tests and community services.

Savings ranging from 8 to 23 per cent have been achieved by some of these organisations, primarily through changes in prescribing practices (Malcolm, 1997). These savings have been directed towards a diversity of programmes, including higher subsidies for children and other special groups, the development of patient registers, education programmes for doctors and patients, and various types of health promotion clinics. The difficulty is that, while budget-holding incorporates incentives to economise on the provision of services to patients, no information is available about the impact on patient outcomes. As might be expected, some commentators have expressed concern about the effects that budget-holding may have on patients in areas such as access and quality of care, consumer choice and patient autonomy (Coney, 1996b).

Another important development in the primary health care sector has been the establishment by the four RHAs of a jointly owned organisation, the Pharmaceutical Management Agency (Pharmac), to be responsible for managing the pharmaceutical schedule. Pharmac decides which medicines to include on the schedule and negotiates subsidy levels with pharmaceutical companies. Various initiatives have been taken by Pharmac in an attempt to contain costs at a time when new and more expensive drugs are becoming available and prescribing rates are increasing (Performance Management Unit, 1995/96).[4] Pharmac estimated that its decisions led to savings amounting to $47 million in the 1995/96 year (Pharmac, 1996).

However, these savings have been achieved at the expense of relations with the pharmaceutical industry. Negotiations between Pharmac and the industry have often been acrimonious, and a number of law suits have been filed by pharmaceutical companies against Pharmac. Towards the end of 1997, the Researched Medicines Industry (RMI) launched a hard-hitting public relations campaign against a range of new initiatives planned by Pharmac to contain drug costs. The RMI claimed that if these went ahead, consumers would lose access to some essential medicines. Although the advertising campaign was terminated prematurely (apparently after complaints about scare-mongering), its legacies included further damage to relations between the industry and Pharmac, and the exacerbation of public concerns about the sustainability of the public health system.

Finally, while no comprehensive figures are available on the costs of running the public health system either prior to or after 1993, there is a clear consensus among analysts that the costs of contracting between purchasers and providers for health services have been higher than expected (CCMAU, 1996: Ministry of Health, 1996a and 1996b). Because contracting involves negotiating, designing and monitoring contracts, any system of contracting will always have higher visible transaction costs than a system in which decisions are made internally, as was the case with area health boards. However, the costs of contracting in New Zealand seem to have been particularly high. Reasons for this include the additional layers of bureaucracy required to support the contracting process;[5] the poor state of information systems when contracting was first introduced; the legalistic approach to contracting, and hence the tendency towards complete specification of all obligations; the financial environment, with its gap between RHA revenues and the costs of service provision; and the adversarial relationship between purchasers and providers.

Access

For hospital services, surgical waiting lists and waiting times are the main indicators of access. Both increased steadily in the three years after 1993, until by 1996 there were almost 100,000 New Zealanders waiting for surgery (see Figure 8.4). In July of that year, the Minister of Health earmarked $130 million to be used over a three-year period to reduce waiting lists (Performance Management Unit, 1996/97). This sum was increased to $235 million in the 1997 Budget. The injection of funds resulted in a 3 per cent decline in the total number of people on waiting lists. While waiting times for the first specialist assessment also declined, the number of people having to wait longer than one year for surgery continued to increase.

One response to this situation has been the development of a points system to determine who is eligible for treatment, together with the replacement of waiting lists by a surgical booking system. The points system effectively means that approximately 30,000 people must be removed from waiting lists because they are not deemed sick enough to be eligible for publicly funded surgery (New Zealand Herald, 21 October 1997). While proponents argue that this system should ensure that the sickest patients are treated first, the points system has been widely interpreted as yet another way of cutting health spending.

The reduction in the amount of elective surgery performed in public hospitals has resulted in a growth in claims against private health insurance. This in turn has led to an increase in private insurance premiums, particularly for the elderly and other high-risk groups (Sheeran, 1997). Private insurance as an alternative to public provision is therefore becoming increasing inaccessible, especially for those most in need.

In the case of primary health care, overall GP consultation rates appear to have remained fairly stable in recent years, averaging around four consultations

Figure 8.4 Surgical Waiting Lists: 1990-1996

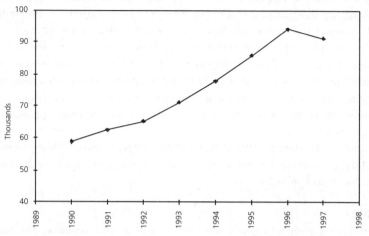

Sources: Contract Monitoring (1994/95) and Performance Management Unit (1995/96, 1996/97).

per person per year (Tilyard et al., 1991; Performance Management Unit, 1995/96). The rate of pharmaceutical prescribing increased from 5.6 scripts per person in 1993 to 6.2 in 1996. Immunisation rates have also increased significantly, from less than 60 per cent in 1992 to around 90 per cent in 1996 (Performance Management Unit, 1995/96).

It is not clear whether targeting subsidies to lower-income groups has improved their access to services. One major problem has been the poor take-up rate of the community services card. Parks (1996) reported that, of patients attending capitated primary health clinics, 28 per cent of those eligible for a card did not hold one.[6] Reasons for this included a lack of knowledge about the benefits of the card and its eligibility criteria, the complexity of its guidelines and forms, and difficulties in assessing gross family income. Two studies of the utilisation of GP services before and after the 1992 subsidy changes have produced conflicting results. O'Dea et al. (unpublished) reported results in line with expectations; that is, consultation rates increased for lower-income adults whose subsidy level had risen, but declined for children of higher-income families whose subsidy level had fallen. In contrast, Davis et al. (1994) found that GP consultation rates declined (by an average of 15 per cent) for all patient groups following the introduction of the targeted regime. For beneficiaries, whose subsidy level had increased marginally, the rate of decline was 30 per cent.[7]

No evidence is yet available on the effects of introducing free GP consultations and prescriptions for children under six. Child health is one of four health gain priority areas the government has identified as specifically needing improvement (Shipley, 1996). Primary care is usually the first point of contact with a health professional. Moreover, many preventive services for children are provided by GPs. Removing the financial barriers to primary care should therefore encourage earlier diagnosis and treatment, and wider use of preventive services. This in turn should reduce the potential for more serious problems—which usually require more costly treatment—at a later stage. The policy may be criticised on the grounds that higher-income families benefit most from the higher subsidies. However, given the low take-up rate of the CSC, a shift away from a targeted regime back to universal provision seems essential if the government is serious about its commitment to improving the health of children.

Accountability

One clear benefit of the purchaser-provider split has been improved accountability of providers to purchasers (Ashton, 1998). In the public hospitals, better information is now available about the mix, level, cost and quality of services being provided. In the primary health sector, while detailed information about service provision remains poor, some progress has been made in specifying more accurately the services that primary health professionals are expected to provide, and in developing information systems and patient registers. The IPAs have played an important role here. These organisations are also developing ways of improving the quality and efficiency of primary health services, for example through quality assurance programmes, peer review, and the development of clinical guidelines.

The question of whether the reforms have improved the accountability of purchasers and providers to consumers is less clear. Democratic accountability has declined because the partially elected area health boards were replaced by the government-appointed boards of CHEs and RHAs. Under the Health and Disability Services Act, RHAs are obliged to consult with consumers about their purchasing plans. There are, however, no guidelines as to what form any such consultation should take, or what might be considered a minimum acceptable level of consultation. Nor is there any requirement for RHAs to purchase the services that consumers prefer. The public thus have little right of come-back should their preferences not be met, as they neither hold shares in the RHAs nor elect the board members.

This lack of democratic accountability led the Coalition government to include in its proposed changes to the health system a review of elected community representation in the health sector. In the meantime, community representation should be enhanced by the government's decision, announced towards the end of 1997, to invite local authorities to recommend appointments to CHE boards.

The Working Environment

The working environment for health professionals seems to have deteriorated rather than improved since the reforms, and morale has been low. In a survey of hospital specialists in 1995, 54 per cent reported that their enthusiasm for work had decreased since 1990 (Perkins et al., 1997). As well as a lack of consultation by CHE managers and purchasers, reported problems include restrictions on resources and problems of access for patients, the introduction of new systems that may compromise patient safety, and feelings of alienation as a result of the shift from a co-operative to a competitive environment. In some CHEs there has been an antagonistic relationship between managers and clinicians, although there is 'some evidence that this is improving' (Ministry of Health, 1996b, p.21).

Relations between purchasers and providers have also been generally poor, and contract negotiations have often been contentious, stressful and protracted. RHAs face problems in making resource allocation decisions under tight budgets and without adequate information. CHE managers likewise face the difficult task of achieving a satisfactory bottom line at a time when the demand for acute care is increasing approximately twice as fast as the population. The result has been ongoing disagreements about both the price and volume of services. For the 1995/96 year, the Ministry of Health reported that: 'Provider relationships [with purchasers] improved in some areas but deteriorated in others' (Performance Management Unit, 1995/96, p.4).

A third area of concern with respect to the working environment has been the steady exit of CHE board members and chief executives since 1993. A central difficulty seems to be the conflict between the two statutory objectives of the CHEs—to be socially responsible and to operate as a successful business. As one departing chairman pointed out, if CHEs are to operate as successful businesses, they must be reimbursed at a price that reflects the real cost of production, and must be allowed to withhold services once the volumes specified in their contracts with RHAs have been reached. Apparently, government interference has sometimes prevented CHEs from acting as commercial enterprises.

Health Status

While the commercial orientation of the reformed system has encouraged a focus on financial indicators as measures of performance, the real bottom line is whether the reforms have improved the health of New Zealanders. One of the major initiatives of the Public Health Commission was the development of a strategic plan for improving the health of the population (Public Health Commission, 1994). This plan, which has subsequently been developed and

Table 8.2 Status of Public Health Targets in 1996

Public Health Goal[1] (n = number of targets)	Likely to be Achieved[2] %	Unlikely to be Achieved[2] %	No Recent Data %
To promote a **social and physical environment** which improves and protects the public health (n=18)	11	39	50
To improve and protect the health of **children** (n=19)	26	63	11
To improve and protect the health of **young people** (n=39)	41	41	18
To improve and protect the health of **adults** (n=12)[3]	58	17	25
To improve and protect the health of **older people** (n=1)[3]	100	0	—
All population groups (n=89)	35	42	24

Notes:
1. In addition to the five goals listed above, there is a sixth goal: To improve Māori health status so that future Māori will have the opportunity to enjoy at least the same level of health as non-Māori. Separate targets have been set for Māori within each of these five public health goals.

2. The assessments of whether the targets were likely to be achieved were made by the Public Health Group within the Ministry of Health.

3. The objectives and targets for adults and older people were still being developed at the time of this report.

Source: Ministry of Health (1996c, p.12).

refined by the Ministry of Health, comprises a set of public health goals, each of which has a range of different objectives. These objectives in turn have a number of specific and measurable outcome targets.

The status of these targets in 1996 is summarised in Table 8.2, which shows that, overall, only 35 per cent of the targets were likely to be achieved while 42 per cent were unlikely to be achieved. Almost a quarter could not yet be monitored, although data collection programmes are in place and these data will be monitored in future years. Of the five public health goals, those for young people and adults were more likely to be achieved than those for children. Of the sixteen targets that related specifically to Māori, only three (19 per cent) were likely to be achieved, eleven (69 per cent) were unlikely to be achieved, and two (13 per cent) had no recent data.

Overall, these figures suggest that progress towards the desired health outcomes has been poor. This may in part be due to the setting of inappropriate targets. It must also be noted that most of the targets are influenced by factors outside the health sector, such as poor housing, smoking, alcohol consumption, and road accidents. Even so, the health sector has an important role to play both directly, as a major purchaser and provider of health services, and indirectly, as an advocate for the health of New Zealanders.

Summary

In summary, the performance indicators reviewed here provide support for the public perception that the health reforms have failed to achieve their original objectives. While some of the evidence is equivocal or inconclusive, at the end of 1996 the Ministry of Health (1996b, p.16) summed up the situation as follows:

> Health sector performance over the last three years has been disappointing in a number of areas: costs have not been constrained in line with planned funding growth; both CHEs and RHAs have experienced deficits; although total output has increased, access to some services appears to have reduced; and only 35 percent of public health targets are expected to be achieved. There is widespread lack of confidence in the ability of the sector to meet performance expectations and in the credibility of policy settings.

The Way Forward

The challenge now is to find a way forward that addresses the problems of the current structure without reintroducing some of the weaknesses inherent in the system prior to 1993. At first glance, the proposals for change set out in the Coalition government's health policy seem to indicate a rejection of the market model for health services. This is in line with an emerging international trend away from the language and practice of competition and back towards a more patient-focused approach to health policy (for example, in the United Kingdom, the Netherlands and Sweden). The Coalition Agreement (1996, p.34) states that: 'The Coalition partners are committed to publicly funded health care that encourages co-operation and collaboration rather than competition.' The purchaser-provider split has been abandoned at the ministerial level, and the CHEs are to be reconstituted as not-for-profit organisations. The changes to funding arrangements also represent something of a policy U-turn, away from the tighter targeting of subsidies and back towards the universal provision of some services.

On the other hand, much of the structure and many of the incentives associated with the 1993 regime are to remain in place. The purchaser-provider split is to be retained at the operational level. Although the term 'purchasing' is being replaced by 'funding', the HFA, like the RHAs, will obtain health services by negotiating, managing and monitoring contracts for services with providers. Similarly, while CHEs will become not-for-profit enterprises, they will still be required to practise sound financial management and accountability and to cover all costs, including the cost of capital.

The replacement of the four RHAs by a central funding agency should reduce duplication, and enhance the process of allocating funds to providers by drawing on the best practices of the four RHAs and by improving national consistency in quality and access. On the other hand, the need for both central *and* regional offices could increase rather than reduce bureaucracy and its associated costs, and may lead to some confusion in the allocation of roles and responsibilities.

A steering group, appointed by the Minister of Health to advise on policy requirements and implementation issues raised by the proposals, has noted that much of the recommended change is to do with the culture of the health and disability system (Steering Group, 1997, p.33). A shift away from the jargon of economics and management is one essential prerequisite of any such cultural change. But changing the language is unlikely to be sufficient in itself to rekindle some of the values and practices that have been stifled by the market-oriented nature of the reforms. As well as collaboration and co-operation, these include trust, commitment, information sharing and openness. More tangible changes that would contribute to a better health system include:

- increased government spending on health services;
- a more democratic decision-making process, including the reintroduction of some elected members to HFA and CHE boards;
- longer-term contracts with providers, and hence a more certain planning environment;
- a co-operative and open planning process;
- the appointment to key positions of people with a good understanding of health systems and health policy;
- appropriate styles of management and strategic leadership.

Most importantly, real change will only be achieved if there is a willingness on the part of all those working within the health sector, especially those in decision-making positions, to work together to achieve the best possible outcomes for patients. The achievement of real change within the health sector also requires political determination. Unfortunately, the Minister of Health (Bill English from the National Party) and the former Associate Minister of Health (Neil Kirton from the New Zealand First Party) had a series of highly publicised disagreements about the direction of health policy during the first year of the Coalition government. While English continued to push the more-market approach favoured by National, Kirton remained a staunch supporter of a more co-operative, publicly funded and organised health system. Eventually Kirton was sacked by his party leader, Winston Peters, presumably in an effort to maintain some semblance of unity between the two coalition partners. This incident seriously undermined any political commitment to a more co-operative health system with a focus on health gain. The incident also highlighted the ideological differences between the two parties and the fragility of the Coalition Agreement.

Conclusion

The years following the introduction of a more market-oriented health system have been characterised by conflicting interests and cultures, a tendency towards secrecy, adversarial relationships, and constant change. Through all of this, the performance of the health sector has remained poor. Perhaps the most positive outcome of the reforms to date has been a halt in the steady decline in real per capita public spending on health, following a recognition that the cost of providing services exceeded the amount the government had been allocating to Vote: Health. Another benefit has been improved information about the cost and volume of services being provided. The Coalition government's proposed moves towards more co-operation and collaboration are to be welcomed. As yet, however, there is little evidence of any clear commitment to shift away from the business model, with its focus on financial indicators, towards a health system that focuses on patient outcomes.

Endnotes

1 For example, in a *New Zealand Herald* poll taken in October 1997, 81.3 per cent of those polled considered that the government was not spending enough on health services. Health was identified by more people (33.2 per cent) as 'the most important issue in the country at the moment' than any other single issue.

2 In the Green and White paper it was claimed that, between 1980 and 1991, the Department of Health's budget had increased by 'some 27 per cent more than the increase in consumer prices over that period' (Upton, 1991, pp.7-8). Although this statistic was incorrect, the clear implication was that the rate of increase in government spending on health had been too high.

3 For example, the average base salaries of medical specialists increased by 16.8 per cent between 30 June 1993 and 1 July 1996. This excludes any hours worked in excess of 40 hours per week, availability allowances, and any other salary enhancements (unpublished survey undertaken by the Association of Salaried Medical Specialists).

4 These initiatives include the introduction of statim dispensing arrangements, whereby pharmacists are required to dispense three-month prescriptions in monthly amounts; the use of reference pricing, where all drugs in a common therapeutic category are subsidised at the level of the cheapest drug in that category; and risk-sharing contracts, such as capped annual payments for a drug regardless of the volume prescribed.

5 These include RHAs as separate purchasing agents, a range of national advisory committees, CCMAU, and monitoring sections within the Ministry of Health. Any changes in employee numbers or administration costs are difficult to interpret because some changes simply reflect a shift in functions from one agency to another. In addition, some functions (especially advisory and development) previously undertaken by government departments are now contracted out to the private sector.

6 Capitated practices are paid according to the number of patients on their register. Because payments are higher for CSC holders, these practices have a financial incentive to encourage any patients who are eligible to apply for the card.

7 The authors of this study noted a number of methodological limitations, including a short time-frame, and the fact that the subsidy codes used for collecting the data overlapped only in part with the new subsidy categories.

CHAPTER NINE

ACCIDENT COMPENSATION IN NEW ZEALAND: A FAIRER SCHEME?

SUSAN ST JOHN

The New Zealand Accident Compensation scheme was set up in 1974 to replace an ad hoc, unfair, expensive, and litigious approach to accidents. The new approach involved comprehensive entitlement for all accident victims to compensation and rehabilitation without the need for recourse to the courts. The Accident Compensation Commission (ACC) became the Accident Compensation Corporation in 1981 and was again renamed the Accident Rehabilitation and Compensation Insurance Corporation (ARCIC) in 1992, although the scheme continues to be known as ACC. This chapter outlines how ACC has evolved from its bold beginnings, and explores the contentious issues surrounding its future.

ACC is a social insurance scheme with earmarked funding, predominantly from payroll taxes. By the late 1980s a lack of appreciation by many business people and politicians of the advantages of this unique approach had significantly undermined support for the scheme. In a supplement to the 1991 'Mother of all Budgets', entitled *Accident Compensation: A Fairer Scheme*, the National government signalled some far-reaching changes to New Zealand's unique arrangements. The Accident Rehabilitation and Compensation Insurance (ARCI) Act 1992 which followed these proposals fell far short of restoring faith in the ACC. Criticisms were widely articulated by various lobby groups such as the Coalition on Accident Compensation, the Council of Trade Unions, the New Zealand Engineers' Union, the Law Society, and the business-based Campaign for Choice in Accident Compensation. Workers complained that the scale of payments and the value of benefits had become so low that the social contract, in which they had given up the right to sue, had been seriously undermined. Women were upset to find that they were much less adequately covered than before in areas of particular concern to them. Employers complained about the high costs and inefficiencies, which they perceived to be a consequence of having a compulsory insurance scheme with monopoly status.

By the mid-1990s, serious allegations aimed at senior levels in ACC's administration had further undermined public confidence in the corporation. In 1997 a former chief executive of ACC was jailed for fraud; his replacement left under suspicion in May of that year and awaits trial for fraud. As well, there was a succession of alarming stories in the media about accident victims who had been badly treated by the system. Wilson (1994, p.18) cites the example of a worker who had lost an eye at work but was ineligible for compensation as he was deemed 'impaired' rather than disabled. In another case, a fit 73-year-old woman, seriously injured on a pedestrian crossing by a truck, was forced to sell her house to pay for 24-hour care, after being told by Minister of ACC Bill Birch that she had an 'age-related disability'. In yet another case, a tetraplegic teenager was described as 'trapped in hospital' because of the lack of ACC funding for home care. An incident at the other extreme brought the ACC into further disrepute. It involved a Court ruling in 1995 that a former mayor of Waitemata, who experienced mental trauma and depression after the bank refused him a loan of $1.5 million to finance a proposed marina, had suffered personal injury by accident under the 1982 Act. (See Campbell, 1996, pp.108-10, for a full discussion of work-related stress.)

Over this period, the insidious idea crept in that accident victims themselves were the cause of ACC's problems. It seemed that everyone in New Zealand had a story to tell of people abusing the system. By 1997 it had become usual for those on ACC for long periods to be referred to as 'welfare beneficiaries', rather than recipients of compensation for injury from whom the right to sue had been removed. A rather mean-spirited example of this attitude was the decision in 1996 to exclude those on ACC for over three months from the new independent family tax credit. The implication is that long-term ACC claimants, even if seriously disabled, can now be viewed as 'dependent on the state' and needing an incentive to get back to work.

Although many of ACC's problems were festering well before 1992, the ARCI Act marks a profound change in philosophical direction. This chapter discusses the significance of that change, as well as the pressures for further change in the mid to late 1990s. These raise the prospect of competition by private insurers, if not the full privatisation of ACC. Whether these and other proposed reforms are likely to destroy or restore the social insurance advantages New Zealand formerly enjoyed is also discussed.

The Nature of ACC

The scale of ACC's operations makes it of considerable significance in the overall welfare state. With a total expenditure in 1997 of around $1.6 billion (1.7 per cent of GDP), it ranks with the unemployment benefit or the domestic purposes benefit. ACC is a Crown entity, whose net assets are reflected in the Crown's Statement of Financial Position (Balance Sheet).[1] Most of its funding comes from levies on employers, motorists and employees. While these are not recorded as part of tax revenue, and can be used only by the corporation, any ACC surplus or deficit of income over expenses is included in the operating balance of the government's budget. Other things being equal, a rise in levy income thus has the same impact on the fiscal balance as a rise in taxes.

Table 9.1 provides a summary of revenue and expenditure for the year ending June 1997. Employer and employee premiums are levied on each employee's earned income up to $79,466 per annum (in 1997). This earnings ceiling, which is over twice the average wage, also determines the maximum weekly compensation of $1,222 (in 1997). Most accidents have short-term consequences, however, and do not involve earnings-related compensation. Of the registered 1.5 million claims for 1997, 92 per cent involved medical expenditure only, with just 8 per cent also making 'entitlement claims' for such things as rehabilitation expenses and home help, as well as earnings-related compensation. Around one half (52 per cent) of the entitlement claims paid in 1997 were ongoing claims, which absorbed 84 per cent of the costs of entitlements (ARCIC, 1997a and 1997b). This 'tail' of ongoing obligations to victims of accidents in past years has significance for the discussion of funding later in this chapter.

Background

Prior to the introduction of ACC, workers who were injured at the workplace—unless they were among the very few who succeeded with a negligence claim against their employer—were entitled to no-fault weekly compensation. However, the maximum amount was very low, and the maximum period was only six years even for the most seriously injured. In the case of non-work accidents, unless negligence could be proven, the only avenue for the seriously injured was the means-tested social welfare system. The Royal Commission of Inquiry into Workers' Compensation (known as the Woodhouse Commission after its chairman, distinguished jurist Sir Owen Woodhouse) described the system as 'fragmented and capricious', and the negligence action as a form of 'lottery' (1967, p.19).

In 1974, New Zealanders exchanged their right to sue for a no-fault, 24-hour, compulsory accident compensation scheme. The scheme reflected the five principles set out in the Woodhouse Report:
- community responsibility (that is, community-financed);
- comprehensive entitlement (that is, all are included, not just workers);
- complete rehabilitation (that is, to restore the injured as far as possible to their former position);

Table 9.1 ACC: Statement of Financial Performance For the Year Ended 30 June 1997

INCOME	*$000*
Employers' Account Premiums	1,189,370
Motor Vehicle Account Premiums	249,195
Non-Earners' Account Premiums	180,252
Earners' Account Premiums	282,165
Subsequent Work Injury Premiums	803
Medical Misadventure Account Premiums	9,953
Sundry Income	857
Investment Income	164,009
TOTAL INCOME	**2,076,604**
EXPENDITURE	*$000*
REHABILITATION BENEFITS	
Vocational Rehabilitation	13,292
Social Rehabilitation	106,979
Medical Treatment	198,273
Hospital Treatment	24,716
Public Health Care Costs	88,855
Dental Treatment	10,365
Conveyance for Treatment	31,622
Miscellaneous Benefits	8,943
COMPENSATION BENEFITS	
Income Maintenance	844,195
Independence Allowances	26,922
Lump Sums	4,751
Death Benefits	58,421
OPERATING COSTS and Other Payments	209,113
TOTAL EXPENDITURE	**1,626,447**
Net Backdated Attendant Care Expenditure	155,033
OPERATING SURPLUS	**295,124**

Source: ARCIC (1997a).

- real compensation (that is, compensation for monetary and other loss to be realistic, and not time-limited); and
- administrative efficiency (to minimise delays and costs).

The Woodhouse Commission stressed that the prime emphasis should be on prevention, followed by rehabilitation, then compensation for loss. 'No compensation procedure can ever be allowed to take charge of the efforts being made to restore a man [sic] to health and gainful employment' (1967, p.19). Although these principles were adopted in the Accident Compensation Act 1972, in many respects the legislation departed considerably from the scheme Woodhouse had originally envisaged.[2]

Under the Act as implemented in 1974, ACC was to provide comprehensive, no-fault insurance to all New Zealand citizens and visitors to New Zealand. Compensation included earnings-related payments for as long as necessary, full medical and rehabilitation costs, and lump-sum payments for loss of faculty, pain, suffering and loss of enjoyment of life. The social contract was a sophisticated package: workers no longer had the right to sue, but they would enjoy full coverage for work and non-work accidents; employers would be spared the costs of litigation and high administration costs, but the levies they paid were also to cover the non-work accidents of earners. In comparison with costs in other countries such as Australia, employers were leniently treated. It was estimated that under the old scheme, or in an equivalent scheme operated privately, administration costs and profits would absorb 40 per cent of each premium dollar (Wilson, 1994, p.18). In contrast, the administration costs of ACC were initially 6-8 per cent, although today they are around 12 per cent of total expenditure (ARCIC, 1997a).

The ACC scheme was a form of social insurance (see Chapter 5). Accordingly, the benefits were far more redistributive and comprehensive than private insurance alone could possibly provide. Also in contrast to private insurance, where coverage and scope must be clearly delineated, ACC was capable of evolving to reflect the increasingly complex nature of many injuries in a modern world.

From the beginning there was confusion about the funding of ACC. Initially it was partially funded. There were no long-term costs to be met, and income was expected to exceed costs until the scheme reached maturity in about twenty years. At this point the scheme could be self-supporting through levies collected each year and the income on the built-up reserves. Full funding in an actuarial sense (to align ACC with the principles of private provision) was neither necessary nor possible, given the very long-term and unpredictable nature of some of the compensation and other benefits involved.[3] Nevertheless, it was considered very important that the levies were set at a level that allowed contingency reserves to build up as the scheme reached full maturity (Woodhouse, 1996, pp.20-21).

The initial arrangements were based on three separate funds: earners, motor vehicle (for road accidents), and a supplementary scheme for non-earners. Each had a different source of revenue and an independent operation. A complex system of levies with differential rates derived from the old workers' compensation scheme was the source of funding for the earners' scheme (see St John, 1979; Campbell, 1996). A flat-rate amount was built into the levy structure to meet the costs of non-work accidents for earners, while the state's contribution from general revenue paid for the accidents of non-earners. Weekly earnings-related compensation was payable at 80 per cent of previous earnings after a pause period of one week. However, employers were obliged to meet 100 per cent of lost earnings for the first week of a work-related accident.

In the early days, ACC was subject to close international scrutiny (see Campbell, 1996, pp.49-50). It was unique in that it removed the litigious approach to compensation for work accidents while providing comprehensive coverage for earners and non-earners alike. In Australia, for example, a workers' compensation scheme was in place but only for work-related accidents, and the right to sue made the cost to employers significantly greater than in New Zealand. Outside the tort system, coverage for non-work, non-motor vehicle accidents in Australia and most other OECD countries depends on an individual's private insurance, backed up by a social welfare safety net.

Funding Issues

By 1985, ACC levies had been reduced markedly from an average of $1.07 to $0.74 per $100 of eligible earnings, following the Quigley Committee's ill-fated recommendation in 1980 that the scheme should become pay-as-you-go (see the Chronology of Major Events, at end of this chapter). In this period the corporation's expenditure was rising sharply (see Table 9.2), and would continue to do so as the ongoing expenditure for accidents that had occurred in past years accumulated. The removal in 1985 of a notional earnings test for weekly compensation (whereby ACC could take earnings capacity into account in setting weekly compensation amounts) also contributed to the rise in costs. Inevitably, the reserves were quickly run down. By 1987, after several years in which expenditure actually exceeded income, they were at an all-time low, sufficient to fund only two months' expenditure (Table 9.2). Woodhouse (1996, p.21) has reflected on the impact of the employers' demands for lower levies, and the 'inevitable roller coaster' of erratic levy increases that followed:

> It was never said: The scheme had some years to run before it reached maturity. [Nor that] an upgraded workers' compensation scheme would have been far more costly. Instead, the early confusion about the nature of the reserves as a painless side advantage of a still maturing scheme led directly to the remarkable political decision that they could be now eroded in order to supplement a reduction in the levies.

In 1987, following the 'funding crisis' which gave the impression of a worrying cost blow-out, levies were sharply increased by over 300 per cent. The employers' outrage at this necessary measure was palpable. In 1990, the incoming National government again bowed to employer pressure, and set levies below the level required to fund the employers' account. A major under-estimation of the cost of lump-sum compensation paid to people injured before 1992, under the transitional provisions of the ARCI Act, contributed to the problem. The result was another serious run-down in reserves over the next five years (see Table 9.2), creating the conditions once again for claims of a blow-out in costs, possible insolvency, and thus the need for sharp levy increases in the future. Wilson (1994, p.19), who claims that the scheme is now the 'meanest in the Western world', summed up the sense of frustration: 'The history of ACC has been punctuated by political concessions on employers' levies in response to special pleading by the Employers' Federation at the expense of: adequate compensation and rehabilitation assistance for the seriously injured workers; and the actuarial security of the ACC scheme.'

Accident Compensation Reviews

Over time, many changes have been made to ACC. To date there have been at least thirteen reviews (see Chronology of Major Events). The Act was rewritten in 1982, with some important changes being made to the level of compensation for the first week of an employment-related accident, and to lump-sum provision.[4] A comprehensive review of the scheme conducted by the Law Commission in 1988 suggested that ACC be extended to cover long-term illness, and that periodic payments were a more appropriate way to recognise pain and suffering than lump sums (New Zealand Law Society, 1988).

As foreshadowed by Woodhouse, there were difficulties and inconsistencies in a scheme that resulted in incapacity arising from an accident being treated much more favourably than an equal incapacity arising from illness. In 1989, following the Law Commission's report, the Labour government proposed that the scheme be extended to cover sickness, but this idea was later abandoned (see Chronology of Major Events). The argument that all sickness should be included was unconvincing, as this would have cost maybe four times as much as the existing scheme (Royal Commission on Social Policy, 1988a). But as accident compensation expert Ian Campbell (1996) comments, the failure to include those seriously incapacitated by sickness, coupled with the dramatic cuts to welfare benefits in 1991, has led to increasing public acceptance of the need to reduce the level of ACC payments. He notes that to a considerable extent this goal was achieved by the 1992 legislation.

The Law Commission also identified practical and conceptual problems in the differential levy scheme (see below), and suggested that flat-rate levies were the best way to give effect to the principle of community responsibility. In its view, more emphasis needed to be placed on prevention and rehabilitation, and less on meeting the costs of short-term accidents. The recommendation that the pause period be increased to two weeks was a reflection of this view.

Tensions became obvious between the goals of fully compensating all accidents and containing costs, with particular concerns also being expressed

Table 9.2 Financial Summary of the ACC Scheme, 1974 to 1997

Year	Income	Expenditure	Surplus	Reserves	
	$m	$m	$m	$m	Months
1974	4.0	1.1	2.9	2.9	
1975	81.3	31.6	49.7	52.6	20
1976	93.8	59.2	34.6	87.2	18
1977	110.4	81.3	29.0	116.2	17
1978	127.8	102.8	25.0	141.2	16
1979	141.9	114.7	27.3	169.0	18
1980	174.1	122.0	52.1	221.2	22
1981	200.5	148.7	51.8	273.3	22
1982	241.3	191.3	50.0	323.5	20
1983	282.4	252.0	30.4	354.1	17
1984	324.1	283.4	40.8	396.0	17
1985	299.0	338.8	-39.9	356.1	13
1986	342.5	454.5	-112.0	244.2	6
1987	423.4	578.3	-154.9	89.2	2
1988	970.9	694.2	276.7	366.0	6
1989	1,292.2	852.9	439.4	805.3	11
1990	1,340.9	1,024.0	316.8	1,122.1	13
1991	1,263.6	1,465.6	-202.0	920.1	8
1992	1,231.1	1,478.6	-247.5	672.7	5
1993	1,499.5	1,611.3	-111.0	560.8	4
1994	1,515.3	1,634.4	-119.1	441.7	3
1995	1,537.0	1,591.6	-61.6	384.3	3
1996	1,705.7	1,597.1	108.6	492.9	4
1997	2,076.6	1,626.4	295.1	788.6	6

Source: New Zealand Employers' Federation (1995) and ARCIC (1997a).

about incentives for a full return to work. Rising unemployment since the mid-1980s had meant that rehabilitated accident victims were often unable to find employment of an equivalent nature, or in some cases any employment at all. This raised the question of whether earnings-related payments, which might be far in excess of the unemployment benefit, should continue. The original notion of the social contract was beginning to fade in the minds of employers, if not the public. Employers were particularly resentful of the lengthy 'tail' of long-term claimants, and their obligation to fund the non-work accidents of their employees.

The Law Commission's report was largely ignored, and in 1991, amid mounting dissatisfaction, a ministerial working party chaired by Bernie Galvin began to think the unthinkable. It recommended that 'private sector insurers should be allowed to operate in the new injury compensation scheme in competition with the ACC (which will be operating as a SOE)', and that 'the ability to self-insure should be permitted in a market where premium rates are set without government interference, so long as the firm wanting to self insure meets a number of prudential requirements' (quoted in Campbell, 1996, p.84). This report preceded the 1991 Budget release, *Accident Compensation: A Fairer Scheme*, which in turn gave rise to the reforms of 1992.

The ACC Reforms of 1992

In 1991 the Minister of ACC, Bill Birch, claimed that some dramatic reforms were justified by the escalating costs of ACC, evidence of fraudulent claims, an inequitable sharing of costs, and the need for more individual responsibility. The focus was on changing individual behaviour as in other parts of the welfare state, reducing the costs for employers, and making the scheme more closely resemble private insurance, thus presaging privatisation at some future date.

The New Structure

Many of the changes introduced by the ARCI Act 1992 were designed to shift the costs away from employers. In particular, the new earners' premium made it clear that non-work accidents would no longer be the responsibility of employers. The scheme was restructured into six accounts, as follows:

- The earners' account for non-work accidents of workers, funded by a new levy on employees' wages—the earners' premium.
- The employers' account for work accidents, which was also to carry the ongoing costs of previous work and non-work accidents as a transitional measure. The account was to be funded by employers' premiums, levied on payroll, and by the self-employed. To-work and from-work motor vehicle accidents were excluded.
- The non-earners' account, which remained funded by the government.
- The motor vehicle account for all motor vehicle accidents, funded by a 2 cents per litre petrol tax, in addition to registration fees.
- The medical misadventure account (a minor account).[5]
- The subsequent work injury account (a minor account).

Campbell (1996, p.138) has described the implications of the Act in scathing terms: 'It would be difficult to conceive of a more savage attack on a system of compensation which, though not perfect, was serving many well.' For accident victims, compensation was much less generous than before. Lump-sum payments for pain, suffering and loss of enjoyment of life were abolished. An independence allowance was introduced to replace existing discretionary payments designed to meet additional costs of living with a disability. Whatever the intent, this new measure was perceived by the public (especially after the ARCI Amendment (No 2) Act 1996) as a replacement for the lump sums for loss of physical faculty, which had also been abolished. The allowance was of miserly proportions, with a maximum value (for 100 per cent incapacity) of $40 per week—far short of the type of periodic payment the

Law Commission had suggested. In 1996 the maximum value was increased to $60, with provision for CPI indexation, but this was still a derisory amount in comparison with victims' actual losses.[6]

These reductions were a severe blow for non-earners, especially for women, who tend to have broken earnings records, with time out of the workforce to care for dependants, and to have lower earnings on average than men when in employment. As well as losing any entitlement to a lump sum, non-earning women and their families were not compensated for the replacement of domestic services, and the care of long-term accident victims by family members was no longer paid for.[7] In rape and sexual abuse cases, the victims were no longer accorded lump sums for mental trauma (Coney, 1992). In addition, injured non-earners were not entitled to vocational rehabilitation, which was perhaps in breach of the spirit of equal opportunities legislation.

The definition of 'personal injury by accident' was narrowed and restricted in a number of ways (Campbell, 1996, pp.139-71; Duncan and Nimmo, 1993, p.295; Rennie, 1994, pp.16-18).[8] The specialist Accident Compensation Appeal Authority was made redundant with the transfer of its functions to the district courts (Campbell, 1996, pp.128-30). This move carried broad ramifications, and the prospect of a more adversarial review process. In addition, twelve months from the date of injury, earners were to become ineligible for earnings-related compensation once they had regained 85 per cent capacity for work.

In line with the view that ACC is analogous to (and ultimately replaceable by) private insurance, a complex system of experience rating was introduced for employers. Under the 'exempt employer scheme' (later known as the 'accredited employer scheme'), large employers have an opt-out provision, enabling them to self-insure for the first year's costs, in exchange for a modest reduction in premiums. It had been hinted that motorists and individuals would also be experience-rated, but this, unsurprisingly, proved difficult and has never eventuated. Nevertheless, experience rating, opt-outs for first-year costs, a name change to highlight the insurance nature of ACC, and more subtle changes such as the replacement of 'levies' by 'premiums', showed that the government was determined to reshape the scheme to make it more closely resemble private insurance.

Reactions to the 1992 Act

The rationale for this wholesale attack on the scheme was that costs were out of control. Yet the figures quoted in support of this claim have themselves been criticised (Campbell, 1996; Woodhouse, 1996) as overstating the case, by failing to:

• adjust for inflation;

- appreciate that business insurance costs in general had risen markedly over the same period;
- understand that claims must grow as the scheme matures; and
- appreciate the need to build up reserves.

The Employers' Federation was initially pleased with the direction of reform as it followed the 1991 Budget document, *A Fairer Scheme*, which was 'in general close to the Federation's policy decisions' (Poole, 1991, p.2). However, employer groups were generally disappointed by the implementation of the 1992 Act. The Business Roundtable had argued in a succession of documents since 1987 that the scheme was fundamentally unsound. It pointed out that New Zealand's path-breaking scheme, so lauded at its inception, had not been adopted anywhere else in the world in the twenty years since then (New Zealand Business Roundtable, 1991). It its view, the scheme's essential features of a monopoly insurer and no-fault liability were the problem. While the reforms were a step in the right direction, it claimed that they did not go far enough to unscramble the confusion between the two aims of insurance and welfare. The Employers' Federation (1995) argued that ACC should first be corporatised to reduce the risk of political interference, then opened up to competition, and ultimately be fully privatised as part of its overall vision of wider health-funding reforms.

The large unfunded liability that had resulted from the shift to pay-as-you-go financing was an obvious impediment to the goal of privatisation. The Act provided for a way to reduce this liability by making those judged more than 85 per cent fit for work no longer eligible for earnings-related compensation. However, the difficulty of distinguishing between the genuinely needy and others less 'deserving' were among the factors delaying the implementation of this provision.

The unions greeted the 1992 Act with dismay. While the right to sue was not to be reintroduced, it was clear that litigation could re-emerge for the expanding array of situations now excluded from ACC cover (Campbell, 1996, p.133). After the Act was passed, detailed regulations were promulgated for payments such as rehabilitation and home help, creating a raft of anomalies in cases that had formerly been treated on a more discretionary basis (Duncan, 1995, p.243). The origins of this move can be traced to the 1991 ministerial working party, which had made it clear that prescriptive regulations were a pre-condition for the introduction of competitive insurers.

Under public pressure in 1994, the Regulations Review Panel was set up to examine the regulations. The panel reported widespread dissatisfaction with the way ACC was operating, and was critical of the wide regulation-making powers of the Act and the loss of sensible discretion in its operation. ('Report of the ACC Regulations Review Panel to the Minister for Accident Rehabilitation and Compensation Insurance', 1994). Along with other pressure groups that arose to fight the 1992 Act, the Council of Trade Unions (1994, p.40) strongly condemned the changes to the scheme in its submission to the review panel:

> The CTU is absolutely committed to restoring the scheme, no matter how long it takes. It hopes that the Panel will recognise the disastrous mistake made with the 1992 Act, and will join with the CTU in further constructive dialogue which will rescue the Woodhouse vision and re-establish it as the basis of restored social insurance which will take us into the 21st century.

Woodhouse (1996) noted that, one year later, nothing had been done to implement the review panel's recommendations. The ARCI Amendment (No 2) Act 1996 failed to grapple with the major objections to the 1992 Act. It met neither the unions' demands for a complete overhaul and a return to first principles, nor the complaints of the business community that it did not go far enough towards privatisation. It did clarify some of the more obscure parts of the 1992 Act and modified the proposed work-capacity tests and the duration of vocational rehabilitation, but as Ross Wilson (1996, p.25) of the Council of Trade Unions has pointed out: 'The 1992 Act effected a substantial transfer of cost from the scheme to the injured person. The ARCI Amendment Bill (No 2) 1995 does little to redress the balance.'

Safety Incentives and the Levy System

There has always been confusion about whether differential levies (now called premiums), with or without their modification under experience rating, exist to promote fairness or safety (Campbell, 1996; St John, 1979 and 1981). Despite the reservations expressed in the Woodhouse Report, differential levies based on some assessment of class risk were initially thought to have something to do with safety and accident prevention. But one of the many difficulties has been that, under pay-as-you-go arrangements, the levies paid by everyone in a given class must fund the accident costs for that class in that year. Over time, some of the claimants will be from firms that no longer exist (this is especially true of the meat industry, where the levies on the remaining employers in a declining industry have risen sharply). Another problem is that multi-purpose firms pay a single rate for all employees, so that their premium is likely to be a poor reflection of actual risk.

Simply differentiating levies by class of risk is unlikely in itself to have any impact on safety, as one firm's behaviour is unlikely to influence the overall class rate (St John, 1981). Under the 1992 Act, small employers can get a no-claims bonus of 15 per cent of the work-related part of their premium, while larger employers can get a discount if their claims are low, or a loading if they are high. The intention was 'a fairer sharing of costs among employees with different accident claim costs; and a financial incentive for employers to reduce claim costs' (ARCIC, 1992).

A properly functioning experience rating scheme—one that rewards safe employers and penalises the unsafe within a given class—requires accurate data and a large experience pool. It is doubtful whether New Zealand firms are sufficiently big or homogeneous to provide a suitable statistical basis for these adjustments (Campbell, 1996, pp.200-13). In A *Fairer Scheme*, Birch (1991) acknowledged the lack of evidence, even in much larger countries, that experience rating is effective in preventing injury. Rather, he implied that the levy scheme is all about making each firm pay its rightful share. Taking this notion too far can, of course, destroy the pooling basis of insurance.

The operation of the levy or premium system has, at best, been erratic.[9] Frequent large adjustments have often served more to address funding issues than to reflect accident experience. The confusion engendered by an experience rating scheme that purports to relate to safety, yet operates more as a mechanism to correct inaccurate premium levels, suggests that differential premiums in New Zealand have so far had nothing to do with promoting safety.

Nor are the changes to the financing of the employers' account, as outlined in the 1992 Act, likely to see experience rating have a significant impact on injury prevention. The real reason for differential premiums and experience rating is more likely to be ideological, as they make the scheme appear to simulate private insurance more closely. Proponents of deregulation argue that 'correct levy rates' are most likely to be those set by the unfettered insurance market. But it can be surmised that the operation of experience rating—either within ACC as at present, or in a competitive environment—will be contentious and expensive.

The Health and Safety in Employment Act 1992

> The cost of maintaining the experience rating scheme is difficult to justify since it is obviously less effective than the Health and Safety in Employment Act in achieving workplace safety (Rennie, 1996).

Penalties for unsafe practices and negligence under the Health and Safety in Employment (HSE) Act 1992 were implemented in 1993 and are enforced by the Occupational Safety and Health Agency (OSH). These direct approaches appear to have merit, but rely on an expensive judicial process. In recent years, prosecutions have fallen dramatically (from 517 in 1994/5 to 174 in 1996/7), as it appears that OSH has been under-resourced. Concern at the apparent increase in the number of workplace fatalities in early 1998 rekindled controversy over the role ACC should play in prevention. Some commentators have sought an increase in the direct costs met by employers, such as the first week's compensation, and argued for stiff penalties to be levied on unsafe work practices, as in the system of administrative penalties, based on observed risk in the workplace, that operates in British Columbia. More generally, Wilson (1997, p.29) observes: 'Good models for effective injury prevention exist internationally. It merely requires political will and competence to ensure they are adopted in New Zealand.'

Recent Directions

The Principle of No-Fault

Some business lobby groups clearly see a return to the right to sue as a valuable deterrent (New Zealand Business Roundtable, 1991). It is not clear, however, that the threat of being sued necessarily enhances the incentives for injury prevention. Kerr (1996b, p.5), for example, recognises that it should not be the role of the tort system to provide compensation, and that the excesses of such systems, as exemplified in the United States, are to be avoided. Rather, Kerr argues that 'well-conceived liability rules' can be devised to take away the protection of negligence provided by the current rules. But legal actions, as discussed above, are already possible under existing laws.

However, the issue of separating compensation from prosecution is important, because penalties under the HSE Act have increasingly included compensatory payments to the victim. Clearly, these are awarded in some cases because of the perceived inadequacy of ACC payments. The abolition of lump-sum compensation has opened the door to this type of payment in the absence of the right to sue for personal injury. Duncan (1996, p.35) notes that 'with the HSE Act fines being increasingly used as awards to the injured workers and with the ACC experience rating leading to work injury disputes, we may wonder what happened to the idea of "no-fault" accident compensation'. Thus, once again, the extent to which an injured worker is compensated depends on fault being proved. Yet unless adequate compensation is restored under ACC, it is difficult to see this trend of 'top-ups', using other legislative means, diminishing. Thus, both the 1992 Act's abolition of lump sums and the principle of no-fault are being undermined, portending a return to the arbitrary, unjust and inadequate arrangements of the past.

The Accredited Employer Scheme

The concept of imposing direct costs on employers has been taken one step further under the accredited employer scheme. This scheme supplies an opt-out provision that enables an employer to carry the full costs of accidents for the first year (at the same level as ACC) in exchange for a corresponding rebate. In this manner, firms that believe they are cross-subsidising other industries or firms within their own risk classification are given some control over costs. The rationale for the scheme is that self-insuring and firm-level claim management give the employer greater incentives for safety and rehabilitation.

Unfortunately, there is also a perverse incentive to pass work accidents off as non-work accidents, and in general to minimise claims. The new compensatable but often vague condition of Occupational Overuse Syndrome (OOS), to say nothing of the many occupational diseases with long incubation periods and multiple causes, illustrate the grey areas that can arise. If employers are to treat employees fairly, there must be extensive regulatory control, which then negates the freedoms implied by the opt-out provision.

Employers would like the scheme's criteria to be considerably broadened (Golder, 1997, p.4), and in 1997 the government signalled an extension of the scheme to involve more employers, and a doubling of the time period to two years.[10] But opt-out provisions in insurance are dangerous, to the extent that self-insurance undermines the value of risk-pooling, reduces the security of injured employees, and encourages claims control rather than accident reduction.

The Coalition Agreement and ACC

The Coalition Agreement (1996, p.12) heralded a brave new direction, with the pledge to 'rebuild public confidence in ACC by restoring it to a world leading, 24 hour, comprehensive but affordable accident cover'. It signalled the retention of public ownership, and stated that 'harsh and unfair aspects of existing legislation and regulation' would be replaced. Ambiguously, there was a commitment to review periodically the level of compensation and the independence allowance. It was made clear, however, that savings would be made by expecting work-ready clients to undertake part-time community work or training, or to return to the full-time workforce.

On 5 November 1997, after a trial and public consultation, a work-capacity assessment procedure was introduced. Long-term claimants who are deemed fit for 30 hours of paid work a week are given three months' notice of their weekly ACC compensation being terminated (although they may retain an independence allowance, if entitled to it). Of the estimated 30,000 people on long-term compensation, about 9,000 were expected to be found fit and ready for work. Despite government reassurances that far fewer would be affected, there are real concerns that there will no longer be adequate earnings-related compensation under ACC for the seriously injured, just a welfare benefit or an unsuitable job. Ironically, as Wilson (1997) points out, these provisions will effectively limit earnings-related compensation to a maximum of two years for most injured people, making the scheme less generous than the pre-1974 regime. Nevertheless, there is a genuine equity issue here that has arisen as the economy changed—one perhaps not envisaged in the original provisions.

Full Funding for ACC

No one disputes the benefits of no fault universal coverage for accidents. There is growing concern which I share that once again a monopoly provider is not the best way to go. So I want to look at how, while retaining a state provider, fair competition may be brought into this $1.6 billion a year industry which annually deals with 1.4 million claims. I feel confident that we can improve the delivery of accident cover and give New Zealanders better service. Any move to introduce competition would almost certainly require full funding for future claim liability (Bolger, 1997).

Repeating history, ARCIC indicated in early 1997 the possibility of reducing average employers' premiums from $2.61 to $1.67 per $100 of employee covered earnings. This reflected emerging surpluses in the employers' account and better claims control, and was greatly welcomed by employers.[11] Unfortunately, because of the way ACC is treated in the government accounts (see above), the price of such a reduction in premiums would be a significant reduction in the government's operating surplus of around $1.5 billion over three years (*National Business Review*, 1997).

In December 1997, despite lobbying by employer groups, it was announced that employers' premiums were to fall by only 10 per cent. On average, they fell to $2.35, although those for professional sports players went up by the maximum 25 per cent to $3.74, reflecting the high cost of rugby accidents in particular. The earners' premium, on the other hand, would rise by 70 per cent, from 70 cents to $1.20 per $100, thus adding to the effective marginal tax rate and significantly offsetting the 1998 tax cuts. Increases in the levies on petrol to fund the motor vehicle account were expected to be announced in early 1998.

The changes were intended to increase reserves. Indeed, the government argued that there was a strong case for returning ACC to a fully funded basis over a fifteen-year period. The aim was to align ACC more closely with private insurance, thus allowing a greater degree of competition. This argument was somewhat convenient for a government worried about disappearing surpluses, and perhaps the inadvisability of the pending tax cuts. It also mollified business interests, who would otherwise have been upset at the small reduction in employers' premiums (*National Business Review*, 1997).

Privatisation of ACC?

As the quote from former Prime Minister Jim Bolger indicates, there is support for at least some of the original Woodhouse principles. Over time, however, they have been submerged by the theoretical insurance overlays to the scheme, and the views expressed by Green (1996, p.124) are heard more often:

> The ultimate objective should be to replace compulsory state provision by private provision. Existing commitments would need to be honoured, but notice should be given that from a future date no new sickness or invalids benefit payments will be made. As expenditure falls, taxes should be cut, thus assisting people to take out private insurance. The ACC should be abolished. Its services can be provided privately and any gap left [by] its demise would soon be filled.

Kerr (1998) argues that private no-fault accident compensation is perfectly feasible, just as it is for sickness. A fully privatised scheme, he claims, would have at least six advantages over ACC: the integration of sickness and accident insurance under one policy; a range of premium options and coverage; freedom of choice of insurer; the security of a binding contract; the removal of politics, allowing the market to meet consumer needs; and competition to reduce costs. Social assistance would be available for those who are uninsurable or who cannot afford insurance.

Yet under such a regime, many people would have no security at all, and it is difficult to see how a return to the fault principle and the right to sue could be avoided. Private insurance would also have high administrative costs, would generate injustices, and would entail numerous other disadvantages. It is not geared to administer the same kind of scheme, and clearly those insurance companies that have indicated an interest in offering private schemes have much narrower coverage in mind. For example, there are many aspects of ACC cover, such as domestic violence and crime, and high-risk occupational activities, that would not be insurable privately.

Equally damaging, however, are the 'privatisation by stealth' implications of the 1992 Act, stemming from the blueprint of the 1991 working party. The opting-out by the self-employed is one example, while the accredited employer scheme can be viewed as the Trojan horse of privatisation, since it allows the private insurance sector to provide cover for the opt-out period. If private insurance creams off the most profitable employers and individuals, leaving the unattractive bits of ACC to the public sector, the notion of spreading risks through *social* insurance will be destroyed. The 1998 Budget promised legislation to allow competition in the delivery of the employers' account and for the self-employed (Peters, 1998b, p.9). This appears to go much further than the accredited employer scheme, which is likely to be axed if the proposal goes ahead.

The need for private insurance firms to cover their advertising and marketing overheads and to make a profit has yet to be appreciated. It is certainly difficult to see how their administration costs would be contained.

Private insurance schemes control costs predominantly by limiting coverage and entitlements. The ACC, on the other hand, has begun to control costs through partnerships among medical practitioners, employers and care providers, in a case management approach. There are no marketing and advertising costs with a national scheme, and bulk-billing of various kinds is possible. Moreover, a national scheme allows for uniformity of coverage. In a privatised scheme, uniform coverage is possible only by surrounding private providers with a plethora of regulations. This would be costly and complex, and would defeat the goals of freedom and choice. It is also difficult to see how non-earners and high-risk people could purchase adequate cover without substantial state assistance, which again suggests the need for a high degree of supervision and control if outcomes are to be both efficient and just.

Conclusion

Is the unique scheme put in place in 1974 salvageable? In the 1970s, New Zealand led the world; in the 1990s, there is far less certainty. The most serious signal is the widespread conviction that workers have given up their right to sue in exchange for an inferior system of limited compensation. Far more of the direct costs (for example, for medical treatment, transport and funerals) have been shifted to the injured and their families. It is clear that in the drive to reduce costs, the needs of the seriously injured have been overlooked, to the point where some believe New Zealand can no longer claim to be meeting its international obligations under ILO conventions (Wilson, 1995, p.22). If these problems are not addressed, there will undoubtedly be more pressure for a return to the right to sue—not just for excluded matters (of which there are now many), but even for personal injury as currently covered under the Act.

It is also difficult not to conclude that the short-term financial interests of the employers are driving the reforms, to the detriment of society as a whole. It is, for example, the large employers who stand to gain the most from the cost control implied by the opt-out provisions. Of course there must be accountability and efficiency within ACC, as in any other social insurance scheme. However, the reference in the Coalition Agreement (1996, p.12) to 'modernising the administration and management of ACC' is a signal that these issues are being recognised, and there is evidence that they are being addressed.

ACC represents the only significant example of a pure social insurance scheme in New Zealand (see Chapter 5). While full funding is not always necessary or desirable for all social insurance schemes, its non-application to ACC in the past has obscured the true costs of accidents and passed them forward into the future. The result has been to undermine ACC in a way that has threatened the viability and integrity of the scheme. The changes announced in 1997 signal the return to a fully funded basis, but not for the pragmatic reasons put forward by Woodhouse. Rather, the idea of full funding is being promoted to make the insurance mechanisms of experience rating more viable, and to ensure that ACC can eventually be privatised. Both the theory and the practice of experience rating and opt-out provisions to date suggest that the former goal may be a forlorn hope. The pursuit of the latter goal may take New Zealand no nearer to any nirvana of private insurance, but could well destroy the hopes of many seriously injured citizens for a reasonable future.

ACC should be adequately funded, not in order to make it a good candidate for privatisation, but because this is the prudent and fair way to finance the scheme. International law requires that employers accept responsibility for the cost of work-related accidents. As long as such laws are not breached, there are some arguments in favour of reducing the funding for short-term accidents, for example by extending the pause period for non-work accidents, and by increasing the direct obligations of employers for the initial compensation payments for work accidents. Any such moves require great care, and the monitoring of outcomes from the perspective of the injured. Already, modest co-payments for medical treatments of minor accidents have reduced the extent of moral hazard. While there are some distributional issues to be faced, these moves have been tolerated well by the public and the medical profession.[12] But if the funding of the major provisions is privatised, as has been signalled, this may begin to unravel a scheme whose collectively provided sum will be shown in hindsight to be much greater than its individual parts. As Woodhouse (1996, p.22) himself has pointed out:

> ... our social responsibilities are not to be tested by clever equations or the latest economic dogma. They depend upon decent fellow feeling and the ideas and ideals which support it. That I am sure is the continuing attitude of New Zealanders. It is something which ought to be applied to the future of the Accident Compensation system.

As in other areas of social policy, New Zealanders need to understand why they have ACC, and the disadvantages of abandoning its unique approach. There must be wider appreciation of the issues of social justice, gender equity, international obligations, and how financial incentives for safety might or might not work. Accident prevention needs to take priority again as a major role of ACC, without relying on ineffective experience rating and opt-out provisions. The promotion of safety is a public service with widespread benefits, and should not be left largely to private initiatives. There needs to be public debate about the seriously injured, who now qualify for only meagre ACC payments, and a refusal to reduce their treatment still further to the level of a social welfare benefit. As well, the issue of today's minimal support of the seriously ill, and how they could fit into a comprehensive social insurance scheme, must be revisited.

New Zealand's ACC scheme has been so seriously weakened in the 1990s that a new social contract now needs to be struck, in which the focus is once again on the needs of the seriously injured. Like superannuation, it requires a multi-party approach. At the very least, the promise of the Coalition Agreement (1996, p.12) to provide 'greater flexibility to meet individual circumstances and expedite social and vocational rehabilitation' should be implemented without delay. It is hard to escape the conclusion that, as with the superannuation debate of 1997, the main way to prevent bad ACC policy is for New Zealanders to be well informed and politically active, and to remember why they adopted their unique model in the first place.

Endnotes

1 The unfunded liability ($8.1 billion in 1997), which represents the cost of meeting ongoing claims in the future, does not appear on the balance sheet of either ACC or the Crown. However, it will be brought onto the Crown's balance sheet in 1999, which will reduce the Crown's net worth by the outstanding amount.

2 For example, Woodhouse did not see that differential levies were necessary; instead he proposed a flat-rate levy that recognised the interdependence of all economic activity. He also believed that the scheme should not emphasise short-term compensation at the expense of long-term compensation, and thus proposed a much lower weekly payment for the first four weeks. Beyond that, 80 per cent earnings-related compensation would apply if necessary, without a time limit. Under the Act, however, the first week of a work-related accident was to be covered by the employer at 100 per cent of lost earnings, before ACC took over the compensation at 80 per cent.

3 Full funding requires that in any year the scheme's accumulated reserves are sufficient to meet all present and future liabilities arising out of accidents that have occurred up to that point in time.

4 Compensation for the first week was changed to 80 per cent of earnings, inclusive of overtime. The maximum lump sum for permanent functional loss was increased to $17,000, with a minimum disability of 5 per cent. Later, the sum of $10,000 for pain and suffering was reinstated.

5 The fund has been of minor significance to date, but there are enormous implications in this area that are too wide to canvass in this chapter (see Campbell, 1996, pp.128-30 for a full discussion).

6 The argument has been that the capitalised sum of the independence allowance is much greater for a claimant who has it for 40 years than the old maximum lump sum. However, it is not able to be capitalised, and for those who die young it provides little assistance.

7 An amendment in 1993 allowed for some retrospective payment of caregivers of long-term accident victims.

8 The definition of an accident was tightened to require the application of some physical force, thus excluding many mental injuries and others that may arise, say, from passive smoking (Campbell, 1996, pp.96-111).

9 Under the 1992 Act, employers were reclassified from 109 categories into 27 classes or

group activities, according to risk. These were replaced in April 1996 by 55 new risk-based categories, using 500 classification units. For some employers, the increase or decrease in premiums under the new system was large, and a maximum increase of 25 per cent per annum was specified. The historical pattern of volatility in levies was continued in late 1996, when new rates for employers were announced. While the average rate of $2.61 per $100 of liable earnings did not change, some industries had an increase of up to 25 per cent. The declining meat industry, suffering the effects of claims incurred in previous years, saw its rate go to $10.02, more than eight times the lowest rate of $1.21 for employers of clerical workers.

10 By April 1998, this scheme had been expanded to cover 89 employers and 180,000 employees. In the 1998 Budget, the government proposed legislation to open up workplace accident insurance to private companies in competition with ACC (Peters, 1998b, p.9). Under this proposal, private companies could offer accident insurance, subject to meeting certain standards of cover and entitlement set by government, from 1 July 1999. The Labour Opposition promised to repeal any such legislation if it won the election scheduled for 1999.

11 The six months of premium reserves required by statute were expected to be exceeded in 1998.

12 It is important, however, to meet international obligations, so the excess medical costs of work accidents should be met directly by the employer.

Chronology of Major Events

1967   *Report of the Royal Commission of Inquiry into Compensation for Personal Injury in New Zealand* (Chair: Sir Owen Woodhouse).

1969   White Paper: *Personal Injury. A Commentary on the Report of the Royal Commission of Inquiry into Compensation for Personal Injury in New Zealand* (Chair: Geoffrey Palmer).

1970   Select Committee endorses the White Paper's recommendation of differential levies (Chair: George Gair). Recommends compensation from first week of a work accident, and exclusion of non-earners.

1972   The Accident Compensation Act 1972.
   • Includes lump sums for pain and suffering.
   • First week compensation at 100 per cent for work accidents to be met by employer; 80 per cent of lost ordinary-time earnings after first week.

1973   Scheme extended to non-motor vehicle accidents for non-earners.

1974   1972 Act comes into force on 1 April.

1975   Levies increased by 50 per cent.

1978   Bonus system for large employers based on accident records.

1979   Government Cabinet-Caucus Committee to Review ACC (Chair: Derek Quigley).

1980   Report of the Cabinet-Caucus Committee, in which Quigley recommends change to pay-as-you-go. First two weeks' compensation to be 80 per cent of lost earnings; two-week pause period for non-work accidents; abolition of lump sums for minor injuries.

1981   The Accident Compensation Commission replaced by the Accident Compensation Corporation. Other recommendations of the Quigley Committee deferred.

Rebates introduced for 'safe' employers (abandoned in 1985).

1982   Court ruling allows exemplary damages to punish offender.
The Accident Compensation Act 1982 replaces the 1972 Act.
- Extends definition of 'accident' to include heart attacks and strokes.
- Reduces first week compensation for work accidents to 80 per cent including overtime.
- Maximum lump sum for permanent impairment of greater than 5 per cent disability increased to $17,000.
- Maximum lump sum for loss of enjoyment, pain and mental suffering set at $10,000.

1983   1982 Act comes into force.

1983–85   ACC levies reduced by 30 per cent

1986   Officials Committee Report (Chair: Jeff Chapman).

December: Levies increased by 300 per cent for the 1987/88 financial year.

1988   The Law Commission's report: *Personal Injury: Prevention and Recovery. Report on the Accident Compensation Scheme.*

Recommends: Flat-rate levies for employees and the self-employed; pause period of two weeks; lump sums abandoned in favour of periodic payments; extension to sickness.

1989   Budget announces ACC to be extended to all forms of incapacity from 1991.

1990   Extension to cover the sick delayed until 1992.

The Working Party on the Accident Compensation Corporation and Incapacity Scheme (Chair: Bernie Galvin).

1991   Working Party recommends that the scheme should cover accidents only. Suggests: Reduction in coverage; introduction of insurance-based principles; prescribed entitlements and regulations.

Regulation reduces subsidy for medical costs by 15 per cent.

Budget Document: *Accident Compensation: A Fairer Scheme.*

1992   The Accident Rehabilitation and Compensation Insurance Act.
- Experience rating to be introduced.
- Employer scheme covers only work accidents.
- New earners' premium for non-work accidents.
- Work-capacity assessment.
- New independence allowance.
- Lump sums abolished.
- Accident Compensation Appeal Authority abolished.

Exempt employer scheme begins.
Internal audit reveals unfunded liability of $4.8 - $5.5 billion.
December: premiums increased.

1994   Informal group set up to advise Minister of ACC.

Review Panel set up to review regulations.

Exempt employer scheme becomes accredited employer scheme.

1996   ARCI Amendment (No 2) Act 1996.

Coalition Agreement promises reform.

Premiums adjusted to reflect risk categories.

1997   Work-capacity testing begins.

Earners' premiums increased from 0.7 per cent to 1.2 per cent.

Employers' premium reduced by 10 per cent and readjusted.

Opt-out for the self-employed proposed.

Intention to return to full funding announced.

1998   Budget proposes that ACC be opened up to competition from private insurers for the employers' account and the self-employed. Legislation expected to be introduced in late 1998.

CHAPTER TEN

COMPULSORY
EDUCATION IN A
COMPETITION STATE

MICHAEL PETERS AND MARK OLSSEN

It can be argued that the development of education in New Zealand was shaped and maintained by two ideals central to the welfare state: the ideal of social welfare and the ideal of egalitarian democracy. In return, education contributed to the maintenance of the welfare state and of social integration (Garrett and Bates, 1977, p.61).

> The contribution of education to social welfare has been seen, first, as providing the means of promoting an increasingly better society in which individuals are able to realise and exercise their abilities ... The schools were also seen as providing a means of civilising those whose abilities were limited or perverse. In other words educators' tasks have been to promote social welfare, equality of opportunity and social control.

One of the hoped-for functions of schooling was that of social, religious and racial integration, with shared experiences providing the basis of community development. According to Sutch (1971, p.123):

> New Zealanders do not perhaps realise what an integrating effect free and universal education system has had in the country. State education has avoided becoming a low quality system and, most importantly, it is socially approved, that is, there is no stigma, no sense of inferiority, no loss of family or individual self-respect in attending the state primary or secondary school.

This chapter advances the argument that since the reform of the compulsory education system initiated in 1988 by the Picot Report and *Tomorrow's Schools*, the system has become increasingly consumer-driven. This has seriously eroded the notion of education as a welfare right, with the consequence that access to and provision of education have become increasingly unequal. The chapter begins with a brief examination of education within the context of crisis in the welfare state; second, it reviews the role of Treasury in the restructuring of education; third, it discusses the reforms to the compulsory education system initiated by the Picot Task Force; fourth, it reviews policy developments under the National government since 1990; fifth, it considers the effect of choice-oriented policies in education; and finally, it discusses the Coalition Agreement (1996) as it relates to education policy debates under the first MMP government.

Compulsory Education and the Welfare State

The introduction in 1877 of a 'universal, compulsory, and secular' primary education system reflected the egalitarian principles of early policymakers, and was based on a number of historically important rights and claims. The 'positive' rights associated with social-democratic liberalism asserted that a universal and free education was a prerequisite to the freedom of the individual. Such education was to be compulsory for a variety of reasons. First, children needed to be protected from the self-interest of settler parents, who often ranked a child's contribution to the family economy ahead of schooling. Second, it was considered that a basic education should be accessible to all children, irrespective of class, race or creed, because it was essential to the development of moral and personal autonomy. Such rights underpinned a democratic society to ensure its reproduction through a common set of values. Universal and compulsory education thus served the community by addressing social needs. By providing students with a common set of values, skills and knowledge, schools helped create the basis for citizenship and the democratic functioning of society. Schooling also contributed to scientific, economic and social progress, thus helping to create the conditions for full employment.

The public benefits of education were additional to the sum of individual private benefits. Early New Zealand educators claimed that in order to derive public benefits from schooling, all children should receive an education with common features, whether they lived in town or country. This safe-guarding of a universal schooling experience would not be possible in a private system, where some parents might not be able to afford schooling for their children, and others might seek schooling that reinforced sectarian values and beliefs. As a consequence, the regulation of such things as teacher training and the curriculum would not be possible. Universal and compulsory education established common features in order to guarantee skills such as universal literacy and numeracy as the basis for active citizenship and democratic participation.

By 1914, the principle of universality, already firmly established in the political culture, was extended to secondary schooling, provided the pupil had passed the proficiency examination at the end of primary school. While private and denominational schools continued to cater for pupils whose parents could afford to pay the required fees, future generations of New

Zealanders were thus guaranteed access to a secondary education (Olssen and Morris Matthews, 1997, p.8).

From 1936 the first Labour government introduced a comprehensive welfare state. As part of this reform agenda, the state's commitment to universal, free and compulsory education was extended. That commitment was expressed by Minister of Education Peter Fraser in his famous statement of 1939 (*AJHR*, 1939, E2, pp.2-3):

> The Government's objective, broadly expressed, is that every person, whatever the level of his academic ability, whether he be rich or poor, whether he live in town or country, has a right as a citizen to a free education of a kind for which he is best fitted and to the fullest extent of his powers.

Universal education would be provided by the state 'as a citizen's right, not as an act of charity', in a package of benefits and services that would be 'non-contributory, universal, comprehensive, and adequate' (Hanson, 1975, p.49). By the end of World War II, the Minister of Social Security could boast that 'we have the best social security system in the world: everything is done' (quoted in Sutch, 1966, p.341). The period 1945 to 1960 was a time of consolidation, without significant new action. The commitment to free, universal and compulsory education continued, and at the basis of all welfare policies was the accepted goal of full employment which, it was claimed, made possible the dignified self-help of every member of the community (Rosenberg, 1977, p.53).

The Treasury and the Restructuring of Education

There are several different accounts of the role played by the Treasury in the public sector reforms from 1984 (Dale and Jesson, 1992). The most widely held view, and the one adopted here, is that the Treasury was the most influential state department in the reform process (Easton, 1990; Boston and Cooper, 1989, p.123; Oliver, 1989, pp.11-12, 18-19; B. Roper, 1991, pp.11-13, and 1992, p.250; Kelsey, 1993, pp.64-5). The power and influence of the Treasury reflect the high ranking of the finance portfolio within the government, the priority given to maintaining economic stability and growth, and historical factors related to the development of state bureaucracy in New Zealand.

During the 1980s the Treasury exerted increasing influence over government policy. Its adoption of market-liberal principles resulted in the move to a market model for welfare in New Zealand, although its implementation in various reforms and legislation has taken some time and occurred across successive governments. In 1984, the Treasury supplied the incoming Labour government with briefing papers (later published as *Economic Management*). These documented Treasury thinking at the time, which was based on 'New Right' theory, and set out strategies for improving the New

Zealand economy. The implication of such theory for education was to become clearer in 1987, when the Treasury produced a two-volume brief for the re-elected Labour government, entitled *Government Management*. In the second volume, which was devoted to education issues, it was maintained that:

- Education shares the main characteristics of other commodities traded in the market-place, and cannot be analysed successfully as a 'public good' (p.33).
- New Zealanders are too optimistic about the ability of education to contribute to economic growth and equality of opportunity (p.8).
- Increased expenditure on education does not necessarily improve educational standards or equality of opportunity, nor lead to improved economic performance (pp.8, 18, 39, 130, 132, 141, 142).
- Not only has the education system failed to adjust to changed circum-stances, but it has performed badly despite increased funding (pp.6, 16, 18, 140).
- The reason the system has performed badly is that teachers and the education establishment have pursued their own self-interest rather than that of pupils and parents. In other words, they are not responsive enough to consumer interests and desires (pp.37-8).
- Specifically, the education system lacks a rigorous system of accountability. There are no national monitoring procedures, nor any satisfactory ways of comparing the effectiveness of schools in order to account for the public resources employed (p.108).
- Government intervention and control have interrupted the 'natural' free-market contract between producer and consumer, causing bureaucratic inflexibility, credential inflation, and hence educational inequality (pp.37-9, 41, 132, 137).

In short, the Treasury argued that state provision and control of education had led to poor performance, and would continue to do so unless radical changes were implemented. It sought to buttress its arguments by referring to 'falling standards' and 'rising mediocrity', and by discrediting the notion of education as a public good (see Chapter 5). The central issues under review were those of *efficiency* and *equity* in education. The key related themes on which its recommendations were based included:

- school governance, with implications for the administration, management and funding of schools;
- the role of the state in the provision, management and funding of education;
- the merits of market or quasi-market models in relation to issues such as consumer choice in education;
- the nature of education as a public or private good (that is, whether the benefits accrue to the community or to the individual), and the respective merits of public versus private provision in education;

- parental choice, including the issues of zoning and targeted individual entitlements.

In its critique of education, the Treasury drew on research that questioned the ability of the welfare state to adequately distribute resources. Influential here were studies in England by Julian Le Grand (1982 and 1987), which documented the distributional failures of the old welfare state. Le Grand claimed on the basis of empirical data that the welfare state was not redistributive across class lines, but that most redistribution was intra-class and over the course of the individual's lifetime. He also argued that the middle and upper classes secured a disproportionate share of state-provided resources and services.[1] Reflecting its new-found interest in neo-liberal theoretical models, the Treasury grounded its critique of the welfare state on the concept of 'capture' (see Bertram, 1988, and Chapter 6). This concept is used both to account for the deficiencies of existing welfare policies in terms of egalitarian objectives, and to advocate a shift to neo-liberal solutions based on the minimal state and individual choice.

The Picot Report and Tomorrow's Schools: From Participatory Democracy to Self-Management

Administering For Excellence: Effective Administration in Education (1988), known as the Picot Report, and the government's response in *Tomorrow's Schools*, are usually seen as the official policy documents that initiated the restructuring of education in New Zealand from the late 1980s. An analysis of these documents thus enables a better understanding of the changes that took place.

The Picot Report, the product of a task force set up to review education administration, echoed the Treasury's analysis and recommendations. Its terms of reference emphasised the concepts of consumer choice, individual competence, cultural sensitivity and good management practices. The report relied heavily on standard neo-liberal criticisms of the welfare state, claiming that the Department of Education was bureaucratic and over-centralised; decision-making processes were too complex; there was a huge lack of information in the system, and virtually no choice; and as a consequence of these factors, parents felt disempowered.

The policy solutions recommended by the Picot Task Force largely reflected the wider political economy of reform, emphasising in particular the principles devised by the Treasury to reform the core public sector: greater accountability; a clearer specification of responsibilities and goals; devolution of management control and a move towards self-management; the separation of policy advice from policy implementation; the disaggregation of large bureaucracies into autonomous agencies; a greater emphasis on management rather than policy; and the development of a performance management system. In general, it was held that policies that encouraged individuals to make choices for their own good are the best means of achieving welfare objectives; that the way to improve schools is to ensure that they are consumer-driven; that the user should pay; and that private schools should be encouraged. These principles and beliefs substantially reflected the theoretical underpinnings of public sector reform, including the new institutional economics, public choice theory, principal-agency analysis, transaction cost analysis, and contract theory (Scott and Gorringe, 1989; Boston, 1991).

The main elements of the Picot reform proposals can be summarised as follows:

- the transfer of responsibility for the control and co-ordination of education away from the state to elected boards, associations and councils;
- the transfer of responsibility for the employment of staff away from the state to elected local boards;
- the transfer of responsibility for the management of assets, property and money spent in education away from the state to institution based boards;
- increased emphasis on the market discipline of choice in the early childhood, primary and secondary sectors, and the introduction of user-pays in the tertiary sector;
- greater state control of standards through charters, national curriculum guidelines and assessment procedures.

From 1988, a large number of other reports and policy documents were produced by government and its various advisory bodies which were directly or indirectly relevant to the restructuring of education. (The most important of these are listed at the end of this chapter.) This plethora of policy resulted in dramatic changes in the administration of education at all levels. The very nature of education also changed. For the first time in New Zealand's history, the concept of education as a private good, partially subject to market conditions, became a reality. The central issue of equality of opportunity, which had dominated educational debate until the end of the Muldoon era, gave way to issues of efficiency, devolution, choice, competition and account-ability. Schooling would be reoriented in line with these new themes, and schools modelled on structures more commonly found in the private business sector.

In 1990, the old Department of Education was broken up into a number of autonomous agencies, including a new streamlined Ministry devoted solely to providing policy advice, the prototype of the New Zealand Qualifications Authority (NZQA), and the Education Review Office (ERO). Much of the administration of primary and secondary education was devolved to individual schools. Elected boards of trustees replaced the old boards of governors and school committees, and were given a range of new responsibilities including the employment of staff, the management of school property, and the design and implementation of a charter, which formed the basis of a contract between the school and the Ministry. While this new structure increased the responsibilities of the individual school and its local community, some commentators have questioned whether it increased their effective control of key aspects of education (see Gordon, 1992; Bates, 1990; Codd, 1990a and 1990b; G. Smith, 1991; Kelsey, 1993).

These changes were incorporated in the Education Act 1989, the Education Amendment Act 1990 and the Education Amendment Act 1991. These Acts also created the framework for the bulk-funding of teacher salaries and school operations, revoked compulsory teacher registration, and abolished school zoning. In addition, an element of 'user-pays' was introduced into tertiary education, thus laying the basis for the National government's subsequent reforms of the post-compulsory sector, including the introduction of student loans.

The reforms appeared to embody the twin notions of 'devolution' and 'community', with local representatives on school boards of trustees working in partnership with principals, teachers, parents and the wider community. Both the Picot Report and *Tomorrow's Schools* had made strong appeals to the notion of 'community', including the recommendation that community education forums be set up to represent a broad range of local interests. The Picot Report explains why:

> We cannot emphasise too strongly the importance of community education forums. In many submissions to us, we read that one particular sector of education or another did not have the opportunity of finding out the views of others locally and so could not present a community viewpoint to us. Similarly, we were told of syllabus committees and such groups that have had trouble in finding people to represent a broad-based community view. We believe the establishment of community education forums would help overcome that kind of difficulty (s.5.8.4, p.55).

This is a clear attempt to ensure genuine community representation—the essence of participatory democracy. The Picot Report also proposed an Education Policy Council (to provide independent policy advice to the Minister), and a Parent Advocacy Council (to represent parents' views and grievances to Parliament). These proposals for stronger community representation, together with greater emphasis on the Treaty of Waitangi and wider equity provisions in school charters, seemed to promise genuine devolution and participatory democracy. *Tomorrow's Schools* underlined this pledge by gracing its opening pages with the following quotation from Thomas Jefferson, in both Māori and English:

> I know of no safe depository of the ultimate power of the society but the people
> themselves and if we think them not enlightened enough to exercise their
> control with a wholesome direction, the remedy is not to take it from them, but
> to inform their discretion.

Tomorrow's Schools was released under the name of David Lange, then both
Prime Minister and Minister of Education. His opening statement reinforced
the appeal to the principles of participatory democracy and the importance of
investment in education. Yet despite the rhetoric, the community education
forums and the Parent Advocacy Council were later abolished, and many of
the original Treaty of Waitangi and equity requirements for charters have
been abandoned.

In hindsight, 'devolution' as originally envisaged by the Picot Report was
never a genuine option, given the political economy of reform established by
the Treasury. The promise of community representation and participatory
democracy was replaced by a form of 'delegation', developed according to
principal-agency theory and the concept of self-managing schools (see
Bushnell and Scott, 1988). Principal-agency theory describes how the costs of
economic transactions may be minimised by monitoring and enforcing a set
of contracts with agents whose interests may diverge from those of the
principal. Thus 'delegation' is a contract relationship between individuals that
is controlled by monitoring performance and applying incentives and
sanctions to encourage managers to meet agreed objectives rather than follow
their own goals.[2]

Against the original policy intention, the Treasury model of accountability
(reflecting principles of new public management) prevailed. The crucial
accountability mechanisms that were set in place consisted of a set of
contractual relationships between the government and the chief executives of
educational agencies and providers (that is, the councils of tertiary institutions, and school boards of trustees).[3] Charters set out intended outcomes
and performance indicators, and ERO audits measure performance against
charter objectives.

The National Government: Qualifications Reform and an Enterprise Curriculum

Qualifications Reform

In the 1990s, a number of key developments have occurred in education. The
New Zealand Qualifications Authority has had a major impact, as has the
development of the National Qualifications Framework (NQF), conceived as
a single comprehensive and integrated qualifications structure. The origins of
the framework can be traced to a series of reports in the late 1980s, especially

the *Report of the Working Group on Post-Compulsory Education and Training* (1988), known as the Hawke Report, and the government's response, *Learning for Life* (1989).

One of the major overarching policy developments has been the attempt to integrate traditional forms of education with workplace training. The notion of 'seamless education' was first articulated in 1993 by Minister of Education Lockwood Smith in his report, *Education for the 21st Century*, and was based on the absence of barriers between school and post-school education and training. The concept is also linked to the NQF, where all courses of study (to be structured into an eight-level hierarchy) will lead to national qualifications regardless of where they are studied. The institutions making up the 'seamless system' include universities, polytechnics, the senior classes of secondary schools, private training establishments (PTEs), wananga, and colleges of education. Also related are the key units of Skill New Zealand—the industry training organisations (ITOs), with their capacity for workplace training, assessment and certification (see Fitzsimons, 1997).

Skill New Zealand, an industrial modernising strategy initiated under the National government, co-ordinates skills training across all industries. Skill New Zealand is designed to give industry the major role in setting and monitoring skill standards, which are benchmarked to international best practice. It emphasises national competency-based workplace training, and aims to increase New Zealand's competitiveness by producing a highly skilled workforce. The two core components of Skill New Zealand are the Industry Training Strategy (ITS) and the NQF. The strategy component attempts to link all private and industry training as part of the tertiary system of education administered by NZQA. Industry training organisations will play a key role in implementing the strategy, according to the Ministry of Education (1994b, p.32).

The NQF component, as developed by NZQA, is part of the broader policy of developing a consistent approach to the recognition of qualifications in academic and vocational areas. Under section 253 of the Education Act 1989, the NZQA has several functions (Fitzsimons and Frater, 1996, p.9):

- to oversee the setting of standards for qualifications in secondary schools and in post-school education and training;
- to monitor Industry Training Organisations and regularly review, and advise the Minister on, the standards for qualifications in secondary schools and in post-school education and training, either generally or in relation to a particular institution or Private Training Establishment, or a particular course of study or training;
- to develop a framework for national qualifications in the post-compulsory area;

- to establish registration and accreditation procedures to design qualifications (including pre-vocational courses provided under the Access
  Training Scheme) that have a purpose and a relationship to each other;
- to design a flexible system for gaining qualifications with recognition of
  competencies already achieved (recognition of prior learning, or RPL),
  and;
- to develop mechanisms to ensure that national moderation processes can
  be achieved.

Based on the SCOTVEC system in Scotland, the National Qualifications
Framework has become an integral part of the government's vision for
education. Its purpose is to provide for the flexible transfer of skills and
learning, where standards are protected by a quality management system
maintained by NZQA in partnership with industry and training providers. In
addition, the NQF is intended to introduce an assessment system that
measures achievement against standards, and involves a shift from norm-
referenced to competency-based assessment. Once providers are accredited
by NZQA, they are deemed to have the capacity to offer 'unit standards'
from the NQF, leading to the same or equivalent qualifications. The seamless
nature of the system is evidenced by the uniform approach to attaining
qualifications, based on equivalent systems of assessment and the recognition
of prior learning across all learning institutions. This requires the reduction
of all subjects to a single set of standards. The resulting proliferation of
'unit standards' is intended to produce a uniform educational product,
whereby a person's units of learning from whatever source can be recognised
and registered on their record of learning. It also entails a quality
management system, whereby NZQA approves and monitors programmes;
administers individual records of student learning; issues national certificates and diplomas; and registers, monitors and reviews tertiary providers and
their students.

There have been strong criticisms of NZQA and NQF. John Codd (1997),
for example, argues that the NZQA is overly technocratic in its approach
to assessment and credentialism. Others have criticised the epistemological
and conceptual assumptions underlying standards-based assessment and
competency-based approaches (see Peddie and Tuck, 1995; Irwin, 1997).

Established at the same time as the NZQA, the Education Review
Office has had a particular impact on schools. Its task is to carry out
assurance audits and effectiveness reviews on individual schools, in order to
evaluate their overall performance. Increasingly, these evaluations have
emphasised school management, with the criteria of effectiveness and
efficiency being given priority over principles of education (see Robertson et
al., 1997).

The National Curriculum

In May 1991, Minister of Education Lockwood Smith launched *The National Curriculum of New Zealand: A Discussion Document* in a speech to the Post Primary Teachers' Association (PPTA) Curriculum Conference in which he emphasised the needs of the labour market and a functionalist core curriculum. The National Curriculum comprises five essential elements: the curriculum principles, the essential learning areas, the essential generic skills, and the National Curriculum objectives, underpinned by new assessment methods.

In conjunction, NZQA released its discussion document, *Designing the Framework* (1991), based on the National Certificate. This qualification is a co-ordinated set of units of learning, available to students in senior levels of secondary schools, polytechnics, colleges of education, universities, wananga, and private training establishments. The idea of units of learning assessed by standards-based criteria, together with the capacity to recognise prior and experiential learning, has been received very positively by some, who argue that it can only empower students (Capper, 1992). Others have criticised both the National Curriculum and the NZQA system of certification for their centralised control and their fragmentation of principles, skills, learning areas and assessment (Marshall, 1992).

In a speech entitled 'Achieving Excellence in a Competitive World', presented in August 1992 to the APEC Education Ministerial Conference in Washington DC, Lockwood Smith outlined policy developments in New Zealand since 1984, describing them as 'an all-encompassing economic reform programme'. In so doing, he tacitly approved and 'owned' the reforms undertaken by the fourth Labour government (1984-1990), based on the strategies of corporatisation, privatisation and deregulation. The theme of competition in education is one the Minister often emphasised:

> Over recent years the word 'competition' has disappeared from the vocabulary of educationalists. Yet, the world is a competitive place. Our standard of living as a nation now depends on our competing successfully in the international environment. We do our young people a grave disservice if we shield them from that reality and if the curriculum ignores it ... The imperatives of the modern world require a new culture of enterprise and competition in our curriculum (L. Smith, 1991, pp.15-16).

At the heart of this notion of an 'enterprise culture' is the need to reconstruct education so that it will deliver the research, skills and attitudes required for New Zealand to succeed in an increasingly competitive international economy.[4]

Underlying the government's enterprise strategy was the explicit assumption that New Zealand's education and welfare systems had failed, creating a 'culture of dependency' (Richardson, 1991, pp.20, 26). The solution was to develop an enterprise culture based on individualism and promoting choice and self-reliance. Education was seen as a 'key investment in our economic future', and the government was committed to providing 'an environment that enables businesses and individuals to develop internationally competitive and innovative skills' (p.20). As part of this commitment, the curriculum came under close critical scrutiny. In his education policy document, *Investing in People: Our Greatest Asset* (1991), Lockwood Smith claimed that: 'Studies like the Porter Project questioned the relevance of our current curriculum with its excessive focus on social issues and poor preparation for the competitive world. It confirmed other recent studies that show inadequate skilling in technology compared with other qualifications.' The Porter Project was used to legitimise the government's market-oriented macroeconomic policy framework.[5] It was also used as a buttress for the so-called 'achievement initiative', which included the National Curriculum. In particular, the Minister of Education invoked the Porter Project to justify a new culture of enterprise and competition in the curriculum, the need to give greater emphasis to core areas, including a new subject called 'technology', and an emphasis on skills development at the expense of a traditional concern for knowledge and understanding.

The notion of 'enterprise culture' also became an important part in the rhetoric of Prime Minister Jim Bolger, who set up the Enterprise Unit (within his own department) and the Enterprise Council, and held the Education for Enterprise Conference in February 1992 to consider how educational institutions could be made more responsive to the needs of enterprise, and the government's role in promoting better links between education and enterprise.

The Effect of 'Choice' Policies in Education

Prior to 1991, the country was divided into 'enrolment zones', centred on primary and secondary schools, and each school was required to enrol eligible pupils from the zone in which it was located. The neo-liberal argument was that removing these enrolment zones would create more choice for working-class and minority families, who have traditionally been disadvantaged in education. According to the Picot Report (p.11):

> Consumers need to be able to directly influence their learning institution by having a say in the running of it or by being able to turn to acceptable alternatives. Only if people are free to choose can a true co-operative partnership develop between the community and learning institutions. Choice will involve providing a wider range of options both for consumers and learning institutions.

Embedded within this quotation are the two senses of choice—*voice* ('having a say'), which is choice in relation to participation, and *exit* ('being able to turn to acceptable alternatives'), which is choice in determining 'selection', 'entry', or 'access'. The notion of 'choice', like that of 'enterprise', is premised on a neo-liberal conception of a

> ... deeply individualist approach to social policy. All state intervention, in this view, is especially bad, and all social goods are reduced to private goods that can be achieved only by individuals exercising rational choice within a free market... . 'society' or the 'public' has no definable features and therefore no existence beyond the cumulative actions of individuals (Codd, 1993, p.32).

Such a notion assumes that the quality of educational choice made by the consumer is superior to that offered to consumers by providers with expert knowledge (Marshall, 1995). The choices of individual consumers, for example about which school to attend, or what happens within a particular school, are considered more rational, and better both for the individual and for the community.

Those who oppose choice models based on quasi-market principles argue that any system of choice must ensure that resources and opportunities are equally available to, and are of equal educational value for, *all* citizens. They claim that choice schemes ignore the impact of structural social and economic circumstances on an individual's ability to choose. Although targeted assistance in the form of supplementary educational entitlements might counter or moderate some of these effects, others, it is claimed, are more difficult to offset. Because neo-liberal 'choice' is essentially a market strategy applied to education, it will tend to exacerbate educational inequalities, and to parallel economic inequalities.

Furthermore, choice policies will have social effects in that they undermine community integration, and increase sectarian divisions in terms of class (wealth), race and creed. Choice policies not only promote some private interests at the expense of others, but given the competitive context in which they operate, they also insulate community subgroups from each other and hinder communication between those who hold alternative views. Hence, critics of choice would argue against the 'interest group' politics of those who advocate choice (Chubb and Moe, 1990). Rather, they regard schooling as a mechanism for promoting shared goals for their children and for their community. In this context, they emphasise the need for public debate, inclusive community forums, and a more expansive relationship between the school and the community. Michael Walzer (1983), in emphasising these issues, argues that there are cases where children need protecting by the state against unsociable values being imposed by their parents and other adults. On this basis, choice policies, if pushed too far, undermine the process of democratic deliberation by permitting the wealthy to ignore the less well-off members of the community, thereby misrepresenting the diverse populations that make it up.

In Dewey's philosophical writings, these communal factors are integral to the possibility of democracy. For Dewey, the two central traits of a democratic community are the existence of shared interests among members of groups in common, and interaction with other groups (Dewey, 1916, p.100). These in turn generate two questions: first, how numerous and varied are the interests that are consciously shared?; and second, how full and free is the interplay with other forms of association? (ibid.). Joseph Kahne asks two further questions about the implications for education policy: first, will school choice proposals constrain or promote interaction among students of varied communities?; and second, will school choice proposals increase or decrease the number of interests that students consciously share? (Kahne, 1996, p.106). Kahne comments that from Dewey's point of view, school choice proposals would seem to *constrain* interaction among different groups and *decrease* the number of interests that students consciously share (ibid.). Hence the development of private interests exacerbates conflict and undermines the democratic functioning of the community. As Dewey (1916, p.99) puts it:

> The isolation and exclusiveness of a gang or clique brings its anti-social spirit into relief. But this same spirit is found wherever one group has interests 'of its own' which shut it out from full interaction with other groups, so that its prevailing purpose is the protection of what it has got, instead of reorganisation and progress through wider relationships. It marks nations in their isolation from one another; families that seclude their domestic concerns as if they had no connection with larger life; schools when separated from the interests of home and community; the division of rich and poor; learned and unlearned.

Supporters of the welfare state, or those like Dewey who subscribe to a notion of democracy, see choice proposals as having several undesirable effects: they protect privilege; they deny all students equal access to education; they deny all students exposure to alternative social experiences; they limit the progress of a democratic community; and they undermine the basis of its social and political integration. Such views seem to be supported by Moore and Davenport's research on schools in the United States, where 'school choice schemes have become a new form of segregation ... based on race, income level and previous school experience' (1990, p.189).

In New Zealand also, research attests to the negative impact of quasi-market choice policies on welfare issues within the community. Wylie (1994) has documented the broad effects of increasing competition under choice schemes, citing changes in the ethnic and socio-economic composition of schools, and deteriorating relations between schools. In her interviews with school principals, Wylie noted that 'deterioration in the school's relationship with other local schools since the start of *Tomorrow's Schools* reforms was more likely to be reported by principals at those schools whose socio-economic composition had altered, and whose own school promotion had been affected by other local schools' actions' (p.106).

The Smithfield Project (Lauder, 1994) also documents the negative social effects of choice policies.[6] The project was initiated in January 1992 under contract to the Ministry of Education, and was designed as a three-phase longitudinal study of the impact of government reforms on education. Phase One (1992-93) sought to answer the question: What are the consequences of the creation of educational quasi-markets for parental choice? Phase Two (1994-96) focused on the impact of choice regimes on school effectiveness, and sought an answer to the question: What is the impact of education markets on policies and performance of schools? Phase Three (1997-99) will focus on the relationship between a market system of primary and secondary education and the tertiary and labour market sectors.

The project's first report argued that the abolition of zoning in 1991 had markedly increased competition and had significantly affected the rolls and composition of the schools. The overall effect of 'choice' was to magnify existing trends. Hence, a school at the 'bottom of the heap' had almost halved its third-form intake since 1990, while the roll of a successful school serving able middle-class students was increasing rapidly. Ultimately, the latter adopted an enrolment scheme to cap its roll (Lauder, 1994, pp.50-51).

In an analysis of the Smithfield data, Waslander and Thrupp (1995, p.22) concluded that social class factors had impacted directly on school choice, with schools tending to be chosen for reasons directly relating to their social and ethnic climate.

> In general terms our study has found that the concerns of market critics are justified. The choice to travel out of what was defined as the local zone prior to 1991 *is* more likely to be made by those from the upper end of each social stratum, irrespective of the ethnic background of the parents. Socio-economic segregation between schools *has* been exacerbated more than would be predicted simply on the basis of residential segregation. (Emphasis in original)

One of the key findings to emerge from the Smithfield study was that structural social and economic conditions affect individual consumer choices in crucial ways, frequently rendering them completely inconsequential. Where a school experiences excess demand for attendance, for example, it is the school, and not the parents or students, that *effectively* makes the choice. In a more general sense, the Smithfield study also reinforces the point made earlier that socio-economic circumstances must be seen as effectively diminishing or enhancing consumer choices (whether 'voice' or 'exit').

Such conclusions are also supported by Liz Gordon's (1994) research into the effect of social class on school choice. Her studies concluded that the status of a neighbourhood was a powerful factor influencing school choice. While poorer parents frequently did not have the option of shifting their children from one school to another, more affluent parents did. One implication of this trend, says Gordon, 'is that within schools, there will be increasingly homogenous class groupings, while between schools differences will be enhanced' (p.15). Similar patterns of segregation operate in respect to ethnicity. The class exclusivity of a school's population is reinforced by the adoption of enrolment schemes that place limits on numbers, and effectively enable schools to determine which types of pupil they will accept. Hence, 'because patterns of residence are themselves linked closely to ethnicity, Māori and Pacific Island students tend to be maintained in schools at the lower end of the market hierarchy' (ibid.). The net consequence of this process is that 'schools at the bottom of the local market tend to lose pupils to neighbouring schools', which in turn promotes a 'spiral of decline' (pp.15-16):

> As a result of the loss of students, funding is reduced, although the costs of running the schools barely change ... Teaching positions are lost, and the number of classes taught and the diversity of subjects declines as a result ... .As social disadvantage becomes concentrated in schools it becomes increasingly more difficult to raise funds through school fees and community fund-raising, while the costs of social disadvantage are increased ... As Boards of Trustees in poorer schools tend to have fewer qualifications than those in wealthy schools, the decline in roll numbers and associated effects may easily be blamed on poor governance ... Further, the process of decline causes enormous insecurity among poor schools as the threat of decreasing resources prevents planning for the future.

School access is a very important issue. Under systems of consumer choice, it is clearly the school rather than the consumer that effectively chooses the intake. In fact, the 'freedom' presupposed in theories of consumer choice depends ultimately on economic criteria. In this sense, the freedom is illusory, as the promises it makes cannot be met for *all*. Within the zero-sum context in which competitive market choice is structured, the 'freedom' of the few is premised on the 'non-freedom' of the many (Jonathon, 1997).

Any attempt to address the issue in education comes inevitably to the suggestion that, in order to have just principles of selection, and to guarantee effective quality and universality of provision, it is necessary that the state, once again, set guidelines and broad limits for schools with regard to their selection criteria.

Education Policy Under MMP

The Treasury's *Briefing to the Incoming Government* (1996) began a discussion of education by emphasising the link between success at school and social and economic outcomes: 'The more formal education an individual acquires, and the more successful that education is, the more likely he or she is to be employed and earn more over time' (p.46). The briefing papers commented favourably on the reforms under *Tomorrow's Schools*, which had 'delivered greater freedom to local communities to make decisions about how their schools are organised and managed' (p.46). Yet 'in many respects this move is not complete' (p.47). The big issue for the Treasury was the fact that only a small number of schools had opted for the 'direct resourcing' model (previously 'bulk-funding'). This situation, together with the continuation of centralised pay-fixing, had reduced flexibility in the capacity of schools to reward their staff. The ultimate goal for the Treasury was 'to build a more flexible performance culture' (p.47). The recent introduction of a performance management system into schools, together with the creation of additional pay units, have been viewed as steps in this direction.

The briefing papers also commented on accountability arrangements in schools, which still required improvement despite having been strengthened over the last decade (the ERO's focus on effective teaching was singled out for praise here). National standardised tests were seen as making a valuable contribution to the measurement of school outcomes. In response to the expected increase in the number of students attending school over the coming decade, the Treasury indicated the possibility of introducing alternative ways of providing capital to schools. Non-state sources of schooling were seen as an important way of meeting these supply pressures, as well as providing additional benefits through increased competition.

In the Coalition Agreement (1996), education and health between them accounted for the greatest proportion of all extra spending. The Coalition government expected to spend an extra $1.8 billion in Vote: Education during its three-year term of office, with the greatest share (about $1 billion) going to the compulsory sector. The key policy initiatives in the compulsory sector focused primarily on issues of staffing (teacher supply, maintenance of the dual system between primary and secondary teachers, introduction of a unified pay system, staffing of rural schools); professional leadership and workload (piloting alternative forms of administration based on school clusters and regional structures); quality (review of ERO, ERO reviews of home schooling); continued government support for private or independent schools; and the establishment of a Māori Education Commission (funded from Vote: Māori Affairs). In addition, the Coalition government gave its support to the notions of priority for attendance at neighbourhood schools and the development of middle schools (for communities who want them), and promised to review procedures under which school closures are permitted.

These key initiatives did not represent a radical departure from previous government policy. Indeed, while education spending in the compulsory sector was estimated to be somewhat higher than it would have been under a National government, the key initiatives did not run counter to the general policy direction established during the last decade, nor did they obviously cut across the Treasury's ideological position. The estimated increase in real or per capita spending under the Coalition is debatable, given that National would have been forced to spend more on education to cover the expected increase in teacher salaries (agreed to before the 1996 election); teacher shortages, and the increase in spending on teacher training; and the expanding primary school roll, with the need for a large investment in new buildings and the establishment of new schools.

Conclusion

In terms of the twin liberal ideals of social welfare and egalitarian democracy, education policy since 1988 has been severely compromised. As the system has become increasingly privatised and consumer-driven, links between education and welfare have been broken, and access to and provision of education have become increasingly unequal. A number of commentators (for example, Boston, Levine, McLeay and Roberts, 1996; Miller, 1997) have argued that the policymaking process tends to be incremental under MMP, and to favour the centre-right rather than the centre-left. This analysis seems to have been borne out during the first term of the Coalition government.

Education policy has also experienced the effects of a deep-seated change of ethos in social policy generally—what we might call 'the individualisation of the social' (see Ferge, 1997; M. Peters, 1997). The result has been the establishment of a neo-liberal policy paradigm, which emphasises individual responsibility for social reproduction at the expense of collective responsibility; it accepts unchecked the burgeoning of inequalities in the name of individual freedom of choice, even in the face of increasing levels of unemployment and the institutionalisation of poverty; it champions productivity and efficiency in the name of national and international competitiveness, ignoring the principle of equal opportunity; it favours the institutions of the market and the quasi-market over the social-democratic constellation of the market, the state and civil society; and it encourages private insurance, targeted social assistance and private charity over traditional universal benefits.

Endnotes

1   The Treasury ignored criticisms of Le Grand's critique of the welfare state in relation to his interpretation of distributional data. O'Higgins (1985b, p.167), for example, disputes Le Grand's analysis, arguing that 'criticisms of the redistributive impact of social welfare … may be quite misleading and unnecessarily pessimistic'. O'Higgins's analysis suggests that distribution through welfare, while not in all cases effective, is 'markedly more egalitarian than distribution through the market', and that the market is 'still the major determinant of inequality' (p.174). Furthermore, 'a substantial reduction in inequality therefore requires either a reduction in the role of the market or a reduction of irregularities within it' (ibid.).

2   By contrast, Mason Durie (1988), a member of the Royal Commission on Social Policy, defines 'devolution' in terms of three principles: participation, partnership, and subsidiarity.

3   The neo-liberal 'corruption' of the promise of devolution is given its clearest account in Sexton (1991). Stuart Sexton, then Director of the Education Unit at the Institute of Economic Affairs in the United Kingdom, and one-time adviser to Margaret Thatcher, was contracted by the New Zealand Business Roundtable to review the education reforms in New Zealand and comment on future directions. Sexton approved of the Picot Report but thought it did not go far enough in making schools entirely self-managing. Any pretence that the reforms should be based on genuine devolution and principles of participatory democracy was quickly dispensed with. The new boards of trustees, Sexton maintained, should be modelled on the 'non-executive board of directors of a company', with 'fewer elected trustees and more co-opted ones'. Neither teachers nor students should be eligible for election to the board, and principals should be non-voting members. Sexton commented: 'it seems to me that too much weight has been given to representation and not enough to effective management'. In Sexton's view, schools were *enterprises* or businesses first and foremost. In the last section of his report, he outlined a set of reforms that were meant to establish a system of self-managing schools, 'real parental choice', 'competition within the system', and 'funding on a per pupil basis'. The final step he recommended was the distribution of vouchers. See Peters et al. (1991) for further discussion.

4   The notion of 'enterprise culture' was imported into New Zealand from Thatcher's Britain, where questions of national economic survival and competition in the world economy increasingly came to be seen as ones of cultural reconstruction. The task of constructing such a culture has involved remodelling social institutions along commercial lines and encouraging the acquisition and use of so-called 'enterprising qualities'. The ideological function of the political rhetoric of 'enterprise', according to Keat and Abercrombie (1991), is to make sense of the kind of economic and cultural changes that have been variously described as 'post-industrialism', 'the information society', and 'post-Fordism'.

5   The Porter Project (Crocombe et al., 1991) was a study of the New Zealand economy based on a framework developed by Michael Porter of Harvard University. From the beginning, the project was bedevilled by internal disagreements over the Porter methodology, its applicability to New Zealand, and the selection of industries to be incorporated in the study (see Edwards, 1991; Philpott, 1991; Peters, 1992). Porter maintained that national prosperity was not inherited but created. National economic success was not simply a matter of cheap land and labour, or even the rate of capital accumulation. As the project's report noted: 'The industries that support a high and rising standard of living today are knowledge intensive', and 'success in international trade has become more a function of the ability to develop and deploy technology and skills, than of proximity to low-cost inputs' (Crocombe et al., 1991, p.26). According to the Porter prescription, New Zealand had to

become more 'innovation-driven', rather than factor- or investment-driven. This required sustained investment in human resources, the development of new skills, and the reform of education.

6 The Smithfield Project was set up to examine the education market in New Zealand and to assess its impact on parental and school choice. It studies the market position of eleven state and integrated (Catholic) secondary schools, with a total cohort of 3,297 students, in two cities and one rural area.

Major Education Reports and Policy Documents

Early Childhood Education

Report of the Early Childhood Care and Education Working Group (Meade Report), 1988, Department of Education.

Before Five: Early Childhood Care and Education in New Zealand, 1988, Department of Education.

Primary and Secondary Education

Administering for Excellence: Effective Administration in Education (Picot Report), 1988, Department of Education.

Tomorrow's Schools: The Reform of Educational Administration in New Zealand, 1988, Department of Education.

Today's Schools: A Review of the Educational Implementation Process (Lough Report), 1990, Ministry of Education.

The National Curriculum of New Zealand, 1991, Ministry of Education.

The New Zealand Curriculum Framework, 1993, Ministry of Education.

Tertiary Education

New Zealand's Universities: Partners in National Development (Watts Report), 1987, New Zealand Vice-Chancellors' Committee.

Report of the Working Group on Post-Compulsory Education and Training (Hawke Report), 1988, Department of Education.

Reforming Tertiary Education in New Zealand, 1988, New Zealand Business Roundtable.

Learning for Life, Vols I & II, 1988, Department of Education.

The Report of the Ministerial Consultative Group (Todd Report), 1994, Ministry of Education.

The Tertiary Reviews, 1994, The New Zealand Treasury.

General Significance: Education and the Economy

Economic Management, 1984, The New Zealand Treasury.

Government Management, Vol. II: Education Issues, 1987, The New Zealand Treasury.

Bulk Funding: Wage Bargaining in the Education Sector, 1991, Ministry of Education.

Designing the Framework: A Discussion About Restructuring National Qualifications, 1991, New Zealand Qualifications Authority.

Upgrading New Zealand's Competitive Advantage (Porter Project), 1991, Crocombe et al.

Learning to Learn: An Introduction to the New National Qualifications Framework, 1992, New Zealand Qualifications Authority.

Education for the 21st Century, 1993, Ministry of Education.

Economic Surveys, 1992-1993, OECD, Paris.

Towards an Enterprise Culture, 1993, New Zealand Business Roundtable.

CHAPTER ELEVEN

THE FUNDING OF TERTIARY EDUCATION: ENDURING ISSUES AND DILEMMAS

JONATHAN BOSTON

The question of how tertiary education should be funded has been the subject of continuing and often vigorous debate in many, if not most, OECD countries. New Zealand is no exception. Since the mid-1980s there have been no fewer than five significant governmental reviews of aspects of tertiary funding: the Labour government's Tertiary Review in 1987/88; the Hawke Report in 1988; the National government's Tertiary Review in 1991; the Todd Taskforce in 1994; and the Coalition government's Review in 1997/98. During that time, New Zealand has moved from a policy of more or less free tertiary education and relatively universal student allowances to a situation where substantial fees are charged for most courses and student allowances are highly targeted. Significant policy changes have also occurred in many other jurisdictions. In the United Kingdom, for example, as a result of the Dearing Committee's report in 1997, the Labour government introduced a targeted tertiary fee of £1,000 and abolished maintenance grants, while in Australia recent governments have carried out substantial funding reforms, with more changes likely following the final report of the West Committee on the financing of higher education.

Throughout the years of debate in New Zealand over the funding of tertiary education, policymakers have been relatively united in their commitment to building a successful, knowledge-intensive economy and highly skilled workforce. An efficient, responsive and internationally competitive tertiary sector, with equitable access and high rates of participation, has been seen as a necessary condition for achieving this objective. Yet there has been no consensus on how such outcomes might best be secured. Nor has there been agreement on how to reconcile the often conflicting roles and purposes—cultural, educational, economic, moral, scientific and social

—of the tertiary sector, especially the universities (see OECD, 1997; M. Peters, 1997).

At the policy level, debate has focused on a wide range of issues, including funding, governance, institutional diversity, quality assurance and ownership monitoring. With respect to funding, the key questions have been:

- What proportion of the costs of tertiary education should be borne by the state on the one hand, and by individuals and their families (or other funders) on the other? More specifically, should fees be charged for tertiary courses, and if so, of what magnitude?
- What priority should be given to tertiary education in the budgetary process, and what should be the overall level of funding per student?
- Should the state provide funds directly to tertiary institutions (and if so, on what basis), or should it fund individual students, perhaps via vouchers?
- Should public subsidies for tertiary education be differentiated on the basis of course costs (or perhaps other criteria), or should all tertiary students be entitled to more or less the same quantum of public funds?
- Should the ownership or governance of tertiary providers have any bearing on their eligibility to receive public subsidies?

This chapter examines these and related issues against the backdrop of the Green Paper on tertiary education issued by the Coalition government in September 1997. In addition, the chapter explores some of the issues surrounding the current loans scheme and student allowances. For reasons of space, no consideration is given here to a number of other important policy matters that have also been under review in recent years, including the funding of research; the governance and accountability of tertiary institutions; the proper framework for the regulation of the tertiary sector; and the issues of quality thresholds and quality assurance. Some of these matters have been dealt with elsewhere (for example, Boston, 1997; Scott and Smelt, 1995; University of Auckland, 1997; and Victoria University of Wellington, 1997a and 1997b).

The Policy Context

The tertiary sector is in the process of rapid change, both nationally and internationally (OECD, 1997; *The Economist*, 4 October 1997). This is the product of an increasingly competitive market-place in tertiary education and training; major technological changes, including the development of the Internet; economic pressures for institutional takeovers, mergers and amalgamations (exemplified by the moves by Massey University in 1997 to amalgamate with Wellington Polytechnic and the Auckland College of Education); and the changing structure of the economy, and its impact on the level and pattern of student demand. These changes pose important and unavoidable challenges for policymakers, not merely with respect to issues of public funding, but also in regard to questions of regulation, governance and ownership.

In early 1998, New Zealand's tertiary sector comprised a diverse range of tertiary education institutions (TEIs) (including seven universities, 25 polytechnics, four colleges of education, and three whare wānanga), and over 800 private training establishments (PTEs). During a typical year, these institutions cater for more than 300,000 full-time and part-time students. Of the approximately 244,000 students enrolled on 31 July 1996, around 43 per cent were in universities, 39 per cent in polytechnics, 12 per cent in PTEs, 5 per cent in colleges of education, and 0.3 per cent in whare wānanga (Ministry of Education, 1997b, p.72).

Prior to the late 1980s, the cost of attending a TEI was heavily subsidised by the state. As a result, course fees were generally low. Most full-time students were also eligible for allowances to cover living costs (Maani, 1997; Patterson, 1991; Tertiary Review Group, 1991). Entry to TEIs was relatively open, with policy being based on the principles of universal eligibility (that is, most tertiary courses were open to students of all ages who satisfied general admission and residency requirements) and unlimited entitlement (that is, there was no limit on the number of years someone could spend at a TEI primarily at the state's expense, although student allowances could not be drawn for more than five years).

In the late 1980s, the fourth Labour government abandoned the long-standing policy of free tertiary education and introduced a standard tertiary fee of $1,250 per annum for the 1990 academic year (Butterworth and Tarling, 1994). This was subsequently increased to $1,300 for 1991. At the same time, a fees subsidy was provided to students from low-income backgrounds, with the effect that the average fee paid by full-time students in 1991 was around $850. As part of Labour's tertiary reforms, a uniform funding regime was applied to all TEIs. Under the new regime, TEIs received an annual bulk grant based on the number of equivalent full-time students (EFTS) and adjusted by weightings for different course costs. Unlike the previous arrangements, the bulk grant covers capital expenditure in addition to normal operating costs. The EFTS-funding formula was originally designed to take into account both tuition and research costs. However, the precise balance between these two components has never been made transparent, and the 'base rates' for the various funding categories have not been systematically reassessed for almost a decade. In 1998, for example, there were ten funding categories, with subsidies (for Study Right students) ranging from around $6,000 for cheap courses (for example, arts, social sciences, commerce and law) to $26,000 for the most expensive post-graduate programmes.

The National government, elected in late 1990, retained Labour's new bulk-funding system but made significant changes to many other aspects of tertiary education funding (Boston, 1992b; Maani, 1997). The standard tertiary fee and the means-tested fees subsidy were abolished and replaced by the so-called 'Study Right' policy; the universal component of student allowances for those under the age of 25 was discontinued (as were the targeted transport allowances of up to $20 a week for 16- to 19-year-olds and the transport supplement of $11 a week for 16- to 17-year-olds); and a publicly funded, income-contingent loans scheme was established. Under the Study Right policy, those commencing their studies before the age of 22 are eligible for subsidies at a higher rate than other students for a maximum of three years. As it stands, TEIs receive 95 per cent of the base-funding category for Study Right students but only 75 per cent subsidies for non-Study Right students. The aim of this policy was to provide greater financial incentives for school-leavers to attend a TEI. In practice, however, a large number of institutions charge all their students the same fees irrespective of their Study Right status.

Since 1992, maintenance allowances for 16- to 24-year-olds have been targeted on the basis of parental (and student) income. The allowance abates at the rate of 25 cents in the dollar above a combined parental taxable income of $27,872 per annum (in 1998). The threshold increases by $2,200 for each additional full-time student aged between 16 and 24 years in the family. Single students aged 25 years or over and living away from home receive the equivalent of the unemployment benefit for single adults ($146.13 a week in 1998). Students are eligible for an allowance for up to five years, and are also eligible for an accommodation benefit of up to $38 a week if studying in areas with high rentals, such as Auckland. Because of the tightly targeted nature of the policy regime, only about a third of enrolled students are eligible for these forms of assistance (OECD, 1997, p.32).

Under the income-contingent student loans scheme, students are able to borrow to cover their tuition fees, up to $1,000 for course-related expenses, and up to $150 per week to cover living expenses (less any student allowance received). Students are required to repay their loans once their income exceeds a particular threshold (equivalent to the unemployment benefit for a person with two children) at the rate of 10 cents for every dollar earned above this amount. On 1 April 1998, the threshold was $14,716 per annum. As with the Higher Education Contribution Scheme (HECS) in Australia, repayments are made through the tax system via the Department of Inland Revenue. However, unlike in Australia, a significant real interest rate applies to student loans in New Zealand.[1] By the end of 1997, when the loans scheme had been in place for six years, around 230,000 people had student loans, of whom 100,000 were still borrowing. The take-up rate for loans among eligible students is close to half, with the average amount borrowed being approximately $10,000.[2]

Although the number of tertiary students funded by the government has risen very significantly since the mid-1980s, real public expenditure per EFTS has fallen consistently for more than a decade (with a drop of almost 10 per cent between 1992 and 1997 alone). This is due first, to the growing proportion of students taking cheaper courses (a product, in part, of the rapid expansion of the polytechnic sector), and second, to a deliberate policy of reducing real funding levels per student. For example, whereas most domestic students in the late 1980s were fully funded by the state, by 1998 the proportion of the costs of tertiary courses borne by the state had fallen to an average of around 75 per cent. Furthermore, the removal of universal allowances for students under the age of 25 in the early 1990s yielded substantial fiscal savings. The net result is that, whereas public expenditure on tertiary education (including student allowances) was around 2.2 per cent of GDP in 1991, by the mid-1990s it had fallen to around 1.5 per cent (excluding the loans scheme), a level comparable to that of Australia, Denmark, Norway and Sweden (Ministry of Education, 1997b, p.74).

From a comparative perspective, the current policy framework contains a number of distinctive features (see OECD, 1990a and 1997):

- The funding regime is more strongly demand-driven than in many other countries, with student choice being the principal determinant of resource flows. For example, the system of bulk-funding ensures that public subsidies follow students (at least within the TEI sector), albeit with certain time lags. Thus, the more students a TEI enrols, the more funding it ultimately receives. Furthermore, recent governments have sought to provide subsidies for virtually all those seeking places in TEIs. Hence, although there is an absolute cap on student places (for example, 148,841 EFTS in 1998), only a small percentage of students—typically 2-3 per cent—are unfunded.

- EFTS funding levels are set annually rather than on a medium-term basis, thus increasing the degree of uncertainty faced by TEIs. In many other countries (for example, Belgium, the United Kingdom, Finland and France), various systems of multi-year (or rolling-cycle) funding are used.

- With average fees for undergraduate degree programmes approaching $3,000 per annum for full-time courses, the overall level of fees (as well as the proportion of tuition costs borne by students) is relatively high by international standards, certainly in comparison with the European Union, where tertiary education is still free in many countries.

- Unlike the situation in many other jurisdictions, there is no government control over the fees charged by TEIs or PTEs.

- There is now a much greater degree of fee differentiation at the under-graduate level than in most OECD countries, where fees (if charged) tend to be relatively flat across courses. In New Zealand, by contrast, many TEIs now have large fee differentials. For example, at the university level in 1998, fees at Otago ranged from $2,220 for arts and commerce students to $20,060 for dentistry students. Lincoln, Massey and Waikato also had differentiated fees, with only Auckland, Canterbury and Victoria retaining a standard fee. Interestingly, in 1998 Waikato was alone in making a distinction between Study Right and non-Study Right students in setting its course fees.

Participation Rates

There are considerable difficulties in comparing tertiary participation rates across countries because of significant differences in the institutional environment, the length of courses, and the age at which people commence tertiary study. Nonetheless, it can be said with reasonable confidence that up until the late 1980s, participation rates in post-compulsory education and training in New Zealand were relatively low by OECD standards, particularly among 18- to 24-year-olds (Pool, 1987; Tertiary Review Group, 1991; Watts et al., 1987). This was due, among other things, to the restrictive nature of the secondary school assessment system and relatively low levels of unemployment, at least until the early 1980s.

However, between 1990 and 1997 the number of EFTS places funded by the government increased by at least a third, and there was a large expansion in the number of students attending PTEs. As a result, by the late 1990s around 50 per cent of school-leavers continued in some form of tertiary education, and it is estimated that around 90 per cent of the population now attend either a TEI or a PTE before the age of 25 (Ministry of Education, 1997b, p.72). Of course, many of these people participate for only relatively brief periods of time (for example, via short courses under the Training Opportunities Programme). Also, the participation rates for Māori and Pacific Islands students in degree-level programmes are still much lower than those for Pākehā students. Nonetheless, the rapid expansion in participation rates means that New Zealand now compares favourably with most other OECD countries; in terms of the participation rate of 18- to 21-year-olds, for example, it ranks sixth out of 23 OECD countries (p.74). Numerous factors appear to have contributed to the large increase in student demand: demographic trends; changes in school curriculum and assessment methods; higher retention rates at the senior secondary level; weak labour-market conditions, especially for unskilled workers; changing social aspirations; and a greater appreciation within the wider community of the value of tertiary education.

Whether New Zealand should have specific participation targets, and if so, what they should be, remains contentious. In 1994 the National government agreed to fund an increase in EFTS places (including pipeline growth) of 2 per cent per annum until the year 2000 (Ministry of Education, 1994a). On the whole, however, recent governments have not favoured explicit targets, preferring instead to focus on the need to remove barriers to, and expand opportunities for, participation. Such an approach has merit. After all, ever-higher participation rates in tertiary education should not be seen as automatically or inevitably a good thing, as if a 100 per cent participation rate among school-leavers represents the optimal outcome for society. In considering participation rates, it is necessary to weigh up the quality of the courses being provided, their cost, duration and suitability, the nature of the marketable skills and information being acquired, the kinds of qualification received, and the opportunity costs involved. Moreover, at the university level there is unquestionably a trade-off between quantity and quality—not everyone has the capability or aptitude for undertaking degree-level courses, and at some stage higher participation rates are likely to undermine the pursuit of excellence. Arguably, New Zealand universities are at this point already.

Recent Reform Proposals

As noted earlier, there have been regular reviews of aspects of tertiary education funding in New Zealand since the mid-1980s. The most recent of these was the review undertaken by the Coalition government in 1997-98. In August 1997 a report by officials of the Ministry of Education was leaked which proposed some fairly radical changes in tertiary policy, with major implications for funding. The key elements of the package included:

- the introduction of a system of funding students directly via vouchers, entitlements or individual non-transferable 'learning accounts' to replace the current bulk-funding regime;
- supplementary state-funded scholarships to cover doctoral-level study and other high-cost courses;
- a separation of the funding of research and tuition, but with research funds following students, much as at present;
- a significant deregulation of the tertiary sector, with public and private providers competing for funding on a level playing-field;
- all public tertiary institutions being established by 2001 as Crown companies with shareholding Ministers (like CHEs or CRIs);
- the replacement of the current semi-representative model of governance with wholly government-appointed boards of directors; and
- a requirement for tertiary institutions to generate a return on their capital.

The subsequent Green Paper, published a month or so later, took a more equivocal stance than some of these proposals. Nevertheless, it is evident that the government's policy advisers believe that the policy framework created during the late 1980s and early 1990s is seriously flawed. Particular concerns include:

- the lack of transparency with respect to resource flows;
- the relatively arbitrary nature of the EFTS cost categories;
- the poor monitoring of institutional performance;
- the unfair treatment of private providers;
- the lack of incentives for improving efficiency; and
- inadequate responsiveness to changing student preferences.

Underpinning some of these criticisms is a broader philosophical challenge to the state's continuing role as the principal funder and provider of tertiary education. The aim here is not so much to address the merits of the specific proposals outlined in the Green Paper, but rather to explore the more enduring issues at the heart of the debate over tertiary funding.

The Overall Level of Public Funding

The first major policy question is what proportion (if any) of the costs of tuition should be borne by the state. Answering this question poses two major difficulties. First, there is no agreement on the appropriate philosophical or analytical framework for determining such matters (Boston, 1988; Ministerial Consultative Group, 1994; Stephens and Boston, 1995). Many economists take the view that the proper role of the state in relation to tertiary funding can be properly and adequately assessed using the assumptions, concepts and techniques of standard economic analysis, in particular those of welfare economics. From this standpoint, if it can be demonstrated that there are significant market failures—perhaps because tertiary education is a public good, or because it produces substantial positive externalities, or because of problems in the functioning of capital markets—then there may well be a good case for public subsidies. If, however, no market failures can be identified, then public subsidies are unlikely to be justified.

Against this, other scholars maintain that access to educational services, including tertiary education, should be regarded as a human right or, alternatively, that education should be treated as a 'merit good'—that is, a good that people ought to consume, or at least ought not be denied the opportunity to consume because of inadequate means (Brennan and Walsh, 1990; Culyer, 1971; Head, 1974; Musgrave and Musgrave, 1980). Either way, it is argued that the state's role as a funder cannot be analysed *solely* from a traditional economic perspective. One reason for this is the significant divergence there is likely to be between individuals' market preferences (as expressed through their consumption behaviour) and their social or political preferences (as expressed, for example, through their voting behaviour), a divergence that is not captured adequately in concepts such as market failure, public goods or externalities. The fact that we make education compulsory for many years of a person's life signals something of this divergence. A related factor is that if tertiary education is a merit good, then equitable access becomes a critical consideration.

The second major difficulty is that, even among those who believe that welfare economics provides an adequate analytical framework for determining the state's proper funding role, there are radically different views about the appropriate level and structure of public subsidies (Industry Commission, 1997). Some maintain that large subsidies are justified, whereas others believe that there is no case for subsidies at all. Such differences of view reflect, among other things, the difficulty of identifying and placing a value on the social benefits or externalities generated by tertiary education. As the interim report of the West Committee (1997, p.143) in Australia put it:

> ... the amount of public funding provided to individuals should reflect the value of the benefits that are received by the community rather than the individual. In practice, determining the level of public funding is a matter for judgement. While the existence of the extra benefits that accrue to society is recognised by most (although by no means all) higher education policy commentators, measurement of their size is accepted as being virtually impossible. Even if the size of the benefits were quantifiable, the level of public funding required to induce them is unknown.

In New Zealand, as in many other countries, there has been vigorous debate over what proportion of the costs of tertiary education should be borne by the state. The Treasury (1987a, p.143), for example, has argued that 'for the generality of students, only limited government subsidy to reflect general social benefits not captured by the individuals concerned can be justified as possibly effective and not grossly inequitable'. By contrast, many others— including the Association of University Staff and the New Zealand University Students Association—have argued consistently that most, if not all, tertiary tuition costs should be subsidised by the state. Similarly, both the Watts Committee (1987) and the Hawke Report (1988) recommended that students should pay no more than 20 per cent of course costs.

In 1993, the National government established a ten-person Ministerial Consultative Group (MCG), known as the Todd Taskforce, to recommend an appropriate balance between public and private contributions for tertiary education. However, the MCG failed to reach a consensus (Stephens and Boston, 1995). Four members recommended that public subsidies should be reduced to 50 per cent of course costs, another four members recommended a figure of 75 per cent, while the remaining two members preferred a still higher contribution from the state. The National government decided in favour of 75 per cent. Unfortunately, no agreement was reached on the size of the total quantum (that is, the 100 per cent). More specifically, there was no consensus on how to set the base-rate levels and differentials for each course category, and how these rates should be adjusted over time to reflect changing cost structures. As a result, there has been considerable uncertainty over the meaning of the policy, and continuing controversy over the adequacy of the state's contribution.

At a conceptual or philosophical level, there is a sound case for the state funding the greater proportion of tuition costs. First, education at all levels is the kind of good, or more accurately service, that society ought to encourage individuals to consume and enjoy to the full extent of their powers and abilities. This is because of the critical role that education plays in the development of rationality and autonomy, in the acquisition of knowledge and marketable skills, and in the facilitation of democratic citizenship. Substantial state subsidies give proper recognition to the value that the community, through the political system, places on education, while at the same time encouraging high levels of participation.

Second, tertiary education represents a good investment for the state. Research, both in New Zealand and elsewhere, demonstrates that the public or social rates of return, excluding externalities, from most courses are positive, in many cases significantly so (Maani, 1997; Stephens, 1994). When the third-party benefits of tertiary education are also taken into account, there can be little doubt that the overall societal benefits more than justify the state being the dominant funder of tuition costs. For those who reject this kind of argument, it is possible to put the case a little differently. Under a largely tax-funded system for tertiary education, most individuals do in fact pay for their own education, but after the event. In other words (assuming the human capital model has some validity), tertiary studies generate higher incomes, which in turn result in the beneficiaries of education paying higher taxes. From this standpoint, a tax-funded system is also a user-pays system, but with an inter-temporal dimension.

Third, for many decades the principle of equality of opportunity has been a critical ethical value underpinning public policy on tertiary education internationally. This principle means, in short, that individuals of similar ability or aptitude ought to have equal opportunities to participate in education at *all* levels and across *all* courses, irrespective of gender, ethnicity or socio-economic background. If this principle is taken seriously, it is incompatible with both high fees and high fee differentials, even in the context of an income-contingent loans scheme. After all, it seems implausible to suggest that people from poor backgrounds will not be deterred from expensive courses such as medicine if they are required to pay the bulk of the costs involved.

Fourth, the New Zealand government has ratified the International Covenant on Economic, Social and Cultural Rights. Article 13.2 of this

Covenant provides that: 'Higher education shall be made equally accessible to all on the basis of capacity, by every appropriate means, and in particular by the progressive introduction of free education.' The wording of this article is absolutely clear. Yet rather than progressively introducing free tertiary education, New Zealand has been moving in the opposite direction for almost a decade. Accordingly, it is breaching its international treaty obligations.

Finally, high fees for tertiary courses are likely to have a range of undesirable consequences:

- They can have a negative impact on participation rates, especially among lower-income groups. The empirical evidence for this is consistent across a range of countries, although demand elasticities are influenced by a number of factors, including the nature of the loans schemes in operation (Maani, 1996 and 1997).
- They can have a negative impact on the environment in which tertiary study is conducted, with students working longer hours in paid employment to the detriment of their studies, campus life, and the early completion of their courses. For example, a survey conducted at Canterbury University in 1997 found that 65 per cent of students undertook paid work during the academic year, and 55 per cent worked across the full year, including term time (*New Zealand Education Review*, 10 December 1997).
- They can encourage people to choose courses of study for the wrong reasons (for example, on the basis of the perceived private rates of return rather than on the basis of the student's aptitude, interests and the academic merits of the course in question.
- They can generate high levels of indebtedness, with regressive impacts, especially for women.

Two objections to this line of reasoning are worth noting at this juncture. Some reject the idea of significant public subsidies on the grounds that students derive large private benefits from tertiary education. Accordingly, they argue, students should pay most, if not all, of their tuition costs. Admittedly, many tertiary courses do yield substantial private benefits, but that doesn't automatically justify a predominantly user-pays approach. After all, most young people derive significant private benefits from education at the sub-tertiary level, but few would conclude that public subsidies should therefore be removed (or at least sharply reduced). From a policy point of view there are a variety of factors to take into account in determining the level of student contributions (if any), including the respective public and private rates of return, and the impact of fee increases on private returns, equity of access and participation rates.

Another common objection to high subsidies is the claim that the middle class captures a disproportionate share of the benefits. Consequently, such subsidies are regressive in their distributional impact. Since the broad contours of this argument are dealt with elsewhere in this volume (see Chapter 6), there is no need to rehearse it in detail here. However, a number of brief observations are in order. First, given the relatively high participation rates that now prevail in New Zealand, the 'middle-class capture' argument has much less force than it may once have had. Second, the fact that a disproportionate number of students come from families on high incomes is at least partly the result of life-cycle effects (Stephens, 1994). That is to say, by the time most young people enter a TEI or a PTE, both their parents are in the workforce and are nearing the peak of their earnings potential. Finally, the evidence suggests that, rather than redistributing from the poor to the rich, tertiary subsidies take the form of 'revenue recycling' (Industry Commission, 1997, p.83). In other words, they entail a 'redistribution of tax receipts from middle and upper income families to the children of middle and upper income families' (ibid). Accordingly, significant subsidies are not nearly as regressive as is frequently claimed.

Bulk-funding versus Vouchers

Assuming that state subsidies for tertiary education are justified, the next question that arises concerns the best system for funding the costs of tuition. There are various broad options here: competitive tendering; bulk-funding; vouchers; and performance-based funding—for example, varying subsidy levels according to student progress rates or completion rates (Industry Commission, 1997). Internationally, many different funding models are used. For example, in both Denmark and Sweden (where tuition costs are fully subsidised by the state), a significant proportion of the revenue received by tertiary institutions is dependent on satisfactory completion rates by students. Such a system, of course, requires external examination systems (or at least external moderation) in order to avoid institutions manipulating their academic standards and examination results to meet the centrally designated completion targets.

As mentioned earlier, New Zealand has had a largely demand-driven system of bulk-funding since the late 1980s. This creates a good deal of competition between tertiary providers, certainly in the TEI sector. Despite its relatively market-oriented nature, the system has nonetheless been criticised for being too blunt, unresponsive and bureaucratic, and for facilitating 'game playing' by TEIs during each bidding round, enabling excessive cross-subsidisation between courses, and providing insufficient incentives to contain course costs and reduce course length. By comparison, some critics maintain that vouchers or entitlements offer the prospect of greater efficiency as well as equity. According to the Ministry of Education (1997a, p.6), for example, an entitlement scheme is likely to 'promote further participation, improvements in responsiveness of providers to students, greater innovation and flexibility, and more diversity'.

Assessing such claims poses a number of conceptual, methodological and empirical problems. To begin with, there is the problem of terminology. New Zealand's current bulk-funding regime is already voucher-like, in the sense that public funds follow students to the institutions of their choice, albeit with certain time lags and in the context of an overall funding cap. Similarly, the current funding regime meets many of the conditions normally associated with an entitlement system. For example, most courses are open to all those who satisfy general admission and residency requirements. Nor is there any limit on the number of years a person who meets the requisite performance standards can attend a TEI, largely at the state's expense. The main contrast with a normal voucher scheme is that students are unable at present to access PTEs on the same basis as TEIs (see below).

But if bulk-funding and vouchers have important elements in common, a number of conceptual differences can also be identified. First, bulk-funding systems provide resources directly to institutions rather than to students. Accordingly, students face fee levels that represent, in broad terms, the gap between the public resources received by institutions and the costs of providing the courses in question. This means that, at least in most cases, fees bear little relationship to true costs, and the relevant market signals are muted and distorted. By contrast, a genuine voucher system would provide resources directly to students, perhaps via individual, non-transferable 'learning accounts'. Institutions would then charge fees on a full cost-recovery basis, with students using their learning accounts to subsidise the fees for the courses they decide to take. Overall, this provides a sharper and more explicit relationship between prices and costs, and facilitates a greater reliance on market forces to influence the pattern, structure and level of student demand. Whether this is desirable is, of course, entirely another matter.

Second, bulk-funding schemes tend to be relatively blunt policy instruments, and generally involve time lags between the movement of students between institutions (or between courses) and the movement of public funds. They also entail the centralised determination of cost categories, thus providing opportunities for political interference and arbitrary changes in subsidy levels. By contrast, a genuine voucher scheme would enable funding to flow more directly between students and providers (although, of course, the nature and value of the vouchers provided would still be the subject of political decisions).

Third, bulk-funding provides the potential for multi-year allocations, and thus greater funding stability across institutions. This in turn is likely to increase the capacity of institutions to cross-subsidise various courses, disciplines and faculties, thereby enhancing their autonomy. By contrast, a genuine voucher scheme provides no scope for multi-year institutional funding.

In most other respects, bulk-funding and vouchers can be adjusted or manipulated in broadly similar ways to achieve various policy objectives. For example, under both regimes the resources provided to, say, full-time students could be exactly the same per annum in dollar terms or could vary according to the cost of the courses being taken. Likewise, under both regimes it is possible to fund public and private institutions differently or on exactly the same basis. Both funding mechanisms also permit the operation of various kinds of rationing mechanisms.

Because of the extent to which both voucher and bulk-funding schemes can be varied, it is difficult to assess their relative merits at a purely conceptual level. Furthermore, while bulk-funding is a tried and tested regime, there are no fully-fledged, comprehensive voucher schemes operating at the tertiary level anywhere in the world. Most funding arrangements that are sometimes referred to as 'vouchers' or 'entitlements', such as the one operating in Chile, are of a limited nature (for example, in terms of their funding levels and/or scope of application) and do not involve individuals receiving learning accounts or coupons (Education Directions, 1997). Accordingly, there is insufficient empirical evidence as yet concerning the impact of vouchers on tertiary education systems, especially on the level and pattern of student demand, institutional stability, information flows, and transaction costs.

Given these caveats, bulk-funding can be seen to have three potential advantages (see also University of Auckland, 1997, pp.72-5). First, it provides greater funding certainty for institutions, especially in the context of multi-year allocations. This in turn can be expected to promote greater institutional stability, and lower ownership risks for the Crown. It should also make it easier for providers to sustain programme quality and diversity, and to protect high-quality courses which experience significant fluctuations in demand. Second, bulk-funding avoids some of the problems generated by full-cost fees (which would be a feature of many voucher systems based on learning accounts). Such problems include the threat to equality of educational opportunity, and the increased tendency for students to select courses on the basis of price rather than considerations of aptitude, interest and academic merit. Third, bulk-funding probably gives governments greater flexibility in changing their funding priorities. This is because a learning account system will require governments to be reasonably explicit about how much money each person is entitled to (according to the various allocative criteria under which such a scheme might operate). Quite apart from these factors, the introduction of a completely new funding system would impose significant transitional costs, and could be destabilising for certain TEIs.

This is not to suggest, of course, that the existing funding regime is ideal or that it cannot be improved. There are plainly various options for modifying the current EFTS system in the interests of greater equity, efficiency and effectiveness (see OECD, 1997, pp.34-5; New Zealand Vice-Chancellors' Committee, 1997). These include the abolition of the Study Right/Non-Study Right distinction; the introduction of multi-year funding allocations (for example, a rolling triennium) and/or larger base grants; the removal of the EFTS funding cap; a realignment of base rates and course differentials to reflect the real costs of provision, and to ensure that public subsidies are maintained, if not enhanced, in real terms; the introduction of new incentives for inter-institutional co-operation, where greater collaboration is likely to produce efficiencies; and a different approach to the funding of PTEs (see below).

Equal versus Differential Entitlements

Irrespective of whether state subsidies take the form of bulk grants or vouchers, another crucial issue is whether the subsidies should reflect course costs or whether they should be of the same annual (or perhaps lifetime) value for each (potential) student. In most OECD countries, subsidies are usually proportional to the costs of each course (or course category), and thus vary significantly in their value (for example, engineering and science students receive a higher real level of public assistance than commerce or arts students). Some have argued that differentiated subsidies of this nature give disproportionate benefits to those with the greatest ability, and are thus unjust. To rectify this problem, it has been suggested that school-leavers could receive an entitlement to a fixed sum of money, which they could then draw on to fund their tertiary studies.

For example, a Ministry of Education report (1997a) proposed that each student might receive an entitlement equivalent to around five years of full-time study. On starting an approved course, students would be able to draw on this entitlement to fund up to 75 per cent of their course costs until the credit had been exhausted. The remaining 25 per cent would have to be funded from private sources or the current loan scheme. In effect, all students would thus have individual learning accounts. At the start of their studies they might have a credit of, say, $25,000 (that is, $5,000 for each year of full-time study). This could be drawn down over a period of time until exhausted (in the case of medical training, for example, the credit would be expended in little over a year). Under the proposed scheme, those who had not undertaken tertiary courses during the previous ten years would be entitled to another three years of full-time study. Merit-based scholarships and direct purchasing could be used to supplement such a scheme in the interests of making post-graduate courses more affordable.

Such a proposal is open to serious objections. First, giving a flat-rate subsidy for tertiary education to all school-leavers is incompatible with well-established principles of comparative justice. For example, it is frequently argued that people should be treated equally only when they are alike in all relevant respects (Feinberg, 1973, p.100). Such cases might include people having identical needs or being equally deserving. Conversely, where people are not alike in all relevant respects, it would be unjust to treat them exactly the same. At the tertiary level, it is plainly the case that students are not equal in all relevant respects. Some undoubtedly have a greater capacity than others to benefit from lengthy courses. Moreover, only a certain proportion of the population is suited to, or has the capacity for, university-level education. Hence, any tertiary funding regime that seeks to meet the requirements of comparative justice—in the sense that it takes into account the relevant differences between individuals in the allocation of resources—cannot start from the presumption that everyone should be entitled, as of right, to an equal call on the public purse. On the contrary, some people will need more public funds than others; or to put it differently, some people will be more deserving than others. A just tertiary funding regime must therefore recognise the relevant differences that exist between individuals (for example, in terms of their capacity to benefit, their socio-economic background, and the differences in course costs). In particular, it must ensure that people are able to access the kind of education or training that is best suited to their needs, aptitudes and interests, and ensure that individuals of similar ability enjoy equal educational opportunities irrespective of their socio-economic backgrounds. Flat-rate monetary entitlements, and the highly differentiated fees they would generate, are not consistent with such principles. They are therefore unjust.

Second, irrespective of the fairness of flat-rate subsidies, their efficiency is also open to doubt. Broadly speaking, it is likely to be more efficient for governments to invest in those who have the greatest capacity to benefit, rather than assuming that all students have exactly the same potential. To put it differently, flat-rate entitlements are likely to encourage over-consumption by some students and under-consumption by others.

Third, if flat-rate subsidies were provided via learning accounts of the kind outlined above, it would be much more difficult for the government to cap expenditure on an annual basis. This is because it would be impossible to determine accurately in advance how many people were going to access tertiary education in any given year, and how much of their monetary entitlement they were likely to use. Thus, the existing variations in expenditure generated by the fluctuating take-up of student allowances and loans would be exacerbated, with consequent implications for budgetary management.

Finally, the provision of supplementary scholarships for expensive courses and post-graduate degree programmes would be essential under a flat-rate entitlement scheme if equitable access and existing levels of demand were to be retained. However, there is a risk that such scholarships could be complex and costly to administer, as well as less culturally appropriate than the existing policy framework (for example, Māori students might be unwilling to apply because of a reluctance to promote their own achievements).

The Public Funding of Private Providers

The public funding of private providers of education has been a controversial subject in many countries during the twentieth century, New Zealand being no exception. At the tertiary level it has been relatively rare, certainly within the OECD, for public and private institutions to be funded on the same basis by the state. In some countries, private providers—whether PTEs or TEIs—are not eligible for public funds; in others, PTEs receive significant public subsidies but private universities do not. Only in a few instances are providers treated more or less equally, irrespective of the nature of their ownership or governance. In most countries, of course, the state provides indirect assistance to private, non-profit providers via tax concessions (that is, individuals and corporates can reduce their tax liability by making gifts to approved charities). There are at least three reasons why private providers, particularly private academic institutions, have been treated differently from public providers: constitutional requirements for a clear separation of church and state (as applies in the United States); public opposition to the state supporting educational institutions with particular ideological or religious commitments; and the difficulties of establishing a genuinely fair funding regime in a context where many private institutions have large endowments.

In New Zealand, there has been a dramatic expansion in the number of PTEs at the tertiary level since the mid-1980s. In 1982 there were only 50 or so PTEs; by the late 1990s there were over 800. Altogether, they provide programmes of various kinds, from certificates to post-graduate degrees, to well over 100,000 students (representing more than 30,000 EFTS). Over the years, the policy framework with respect to the funding of public and private tertiary providers has become increasingly inconsistent and arbitrary, and almost certainly requires a major reappraisal.

As it stands, there are major differences in the policy approach adopted at the compulsory and post-compulsory levels of education. At the compulsory level many, if not most, private schools have become 'integrated' into the state system, and although they remain in private ownership are funded on much the same basis as public schools (except in relation to capital expenditure and maintenance). By contrast, private providers of tertiary education receive only a fraction of the funding per student that is allocated to public TEIs. Whereas the EFTS funding pool for public TEIs exceeded $1.14 billion in 1998, the pool available for PTEs was a mere $7 million (Ministry of Education, 1997b, p.75). Furthermore, even when PTEs receive EFTS subsidies, they are funded at a lower rate than TEIs for identical programmes, and must comply with much more exacting requirements about minimum contact hours, course length, and so on (Finnigan, 1997). To compound matters, whereas basic training courses offered by PTEs are eligible for large state subsidies via the Training Opportunities Programme, more advanced (and usually more costly) programmes are funded less generously. Also, student support and loan arrangements for those taking courses at PTEs are less generous than for those attending TEIs. The net result is that TEIs (and their students) have significant advantages over their private-sector counterparts, certainly in relation to degree programmes.

If it is accepted that the funding of tertiary education should be largely, though not exclusively, student-driven, then the nature of the ownership of the provider is presumably less important than the quality and suitability of the programmes being offered. Likewise, in most cases the nature or quantity of the social benefits arising from tertiary education is not likely to be significantly influenced by the ownership of the provider. Accordingly, there is at least a *prima facie* case for funding public and private providers on a more equitable basis than has hitherto been the case in New Zealand. Having said this, there are significant policy matters that must be addressed before additional public funds are provided to PTEs. Among these are issues relating to competitive neutrality, fiscal risk, quality assurance, governance, the right of students to cross-credit programmes between institutions, the extent to which the funding formula should take endowments into account, and how any erosion of the distinction between public and private providers may affect the application of the General Agreement on Trade in Services (Kelsey, 1997b; New Zealand Vice-Chancellors' Committee, 1997). For example, there are various legal constraints and obligations that apply to TEIs but not to PTEs (such as those relating to equity considerations and the Treaty of Waitangi). If PTEs were funded much the same as TEIs, regulatory changes would be needed to ensure competitive neutrality. Also, any decision to fund private providers to a greater extent would have implications for public institutions. For one thing, the competition for students would be intensified, particularly within the non-university sector. For another, in the absence of additional public funds, any increase in subsidies to private providers would necessarily reduce the public resources flowing into TEIs. This could threaten the financial viability of some providers, especially the smaller polytechnics.

Rather than giving identical funding allocations to public and private providers for the same course categories, it might be more equitable and more efficacious to vary subsidy levels according to a set of clearly established criteria. Institutions that satisfied all the relevant criteria (such as those relating to governance, accountability, quality assurance, equitable access, and not-for-profit status) would be eligible for higher subsidies than those that met only some of the criteria. Of course, such a proposal raises significant admin-istrative issues, but in principle it is not so different from the system that applies already at the compulsory level of education.

Rationing

All systems of tertiary education employ rationing devices of some kind. These take various forms, including the allocation of places in tertiary programmes on the basis of academic ability, citizenship or residency require-ments, and the use of the price mechanism (with fees being employed to structure the level and pattern of demand). The Coalition government's Green Paper (1997, pp.16-18) outlined seven possible rationing options:

- reducing government subsidy levels as participation rates increase;
- allocating a fixed amount of tertiary education to each student;
- allocating resources on the basis of age;
- capping the number of student places;
- resourcing priority subject areas first;
- rationing on efficiency or quality measures; and
- targeting students on the basis of prior achievement.

None of these options is ideal, with each having advantages and disadvan-tages. Generally speaking, the aim of public policy should be to minimise the degree of rationing required by adjusting the level of public funding (and related taxes) to accommodate changes in the level and pattern of demand. To the extent that rationing remains necessary, particularly with respect to expensive courses such as medicine, a good case can be made for allocating places (particular at the degree level) *primarily* on the basis of demonstrated ability, rather than on other criteria such as age, gender, ethnicity, experience, or the willingness or capacity to pay. For example, rationing predominantly via the price mechanism is likely to be neither efficient nor equitable, for the reasons discussed earlier. Similarly, as argued above, there is no justification for giving everyone—irrespective of ability or academic progress—an equal cash entitlement or for allocating an equivalent amount of tertiary education to all school-leavers. Whether there should be a limit on the number of years for which a student is eligible to receive public subsidies is more debatable. On the one hand, it may seem overly generous to give people unlimited access to subsidised tertiary courses. On the other hand, few people, other than those undertaking doctoral studies, spend more than six years in full-time study, and rigid time limits are likely to reduce opportunities for retraining, thereby undermining labour market flexibility. Finally, any funding system that attempts to increase the number of places for the same real level of resourcing is bound, over time, to have a negative impact on the quality of the services provided. This is probably already occurring in New Zealand—although it is difficult to prove because of the lack of robust quality measures.

Allowances and Loans

With the removal of universal maintenance allowances in 1992 and the sharp increases in tertiary fees during the 1990s, there has been a rapid expansion in the level of student indebtedness. Total student debt under the publicly funded, income-contingent loan scheme (excluding private loans) is forecast to increase from over $1.8 billion in 1997 to more than $3.4 billion in the year 2000, and possibly to as much as $20 billion by 2024 (*New Zealand Education Review*, 10 December 1997; New Zealand Vice-Chancellors' Committee, 1997, p.5). Over time, an increasing number of borrowers, especially women, are likely to face a situation where their repayments (at the standard rate of 10 cents in the dollar) will not cover the interest payments on their debt. Indeed, it is possible that total student debt will continue growing because loan repayments in aggregate will be insufficient to cover interest payments and new borrowing. While the income-contingent nature of the loan scheme has doubtless mitigated the most adverse consequences of reduced state support and large student debt, at some point the level of indebtedness is bound to affect participation rates, course selection and equity of access. It also raises broader policy issues concerning intra-family transfers, income distribution, effective marginal tax rates, household consumption and savings, and investment behaviour (OECD, 1997, p.33).

If student indebtedness over the longer term is to be curbed, a number of policy options are available, the most obvious being for the state to increase real expenditure per EFTS and to reintroduce a more universal system of student allowances—perhaps by reducing the age at which allowances are no longer means-tested on the basis of parent income from 25 to 20. There are other issues that also require attention, such as the interest rates on student loans, the threshold for repayments, and the efficiency with which loan repayments are administered by the Inland Revenue Department. The Coalition Agreement committed the government to work 'towards a universal system of living allowances for tertiary students as part of a comprehensive system of youth income support that gives comparability between unemployed job seekers and students'. It appeared from the announcements made at the time of the 1998 Budget that the government would not be fulfilling this commitment, preferring instead to direct any additional funds available to providing more tuition subsidies.

Conclusion

In the late 1980s, tertiary education in New Zealand was moderately well funded by international standards, certainly if expenditure on student allowances is included. A decade later, this is no longer the case. Moreover, as the new millennium approaches, public expenditure in real terms per EFTS continues to fall, thereby ensuring further increases in tertiary fees and student indebtedness. This of course reflects a deliberate strategy to shift the burden of funding tertiary education from taxpayers to direct users, and to fund much of the expansion of the sector via fees. At the same time, there is continuing pressure for an even more market-oriented system of funding, possibly including the development of individualised, non-transferable learning accounts with fixed-sum subsidies, the removal of bulk-funding, and the abolition of targeted allowances. Were such a funding regime to be introduced, especially in the context of a less arbitrary approach to the funding of PTEs, the consequences for the tertiary sector could be profound.

It has been argued in this chapter that there remains a robust case for the state to continue as the principal funder of tertiary education, for the existing system of bulk-funding to be retained (albeit with significant modifications), and for subsidies to be differentiated according to real course costs. The fiscal costs of such a regime are undeniably substantial, but much the same applies to other major public services. Moreover, if New Zealand is to retain a relatively high-quality tertiary sector, together with equitable access and participation rates at least comparable to those of its major competitors, significant additional state investment in the tertiary sector will be essential. The budgetary implications of this are obvious and inescapable, and need to be addressed by policymakers—sooner rather than later.

Endnotes

1 The rate of interest is based on three components: the CPI; the cost of borrowing to the government (determined from a combination of past and projected ten-year base rates); and a risk-sharing margin of 0.9 per cent. The latter two components represent the 'base rate'. In April 1998, the base rate was 6.2 per cent and the CPI adjustment was 1.8 per cent, giving a total interest rate of 8.0 per cent. Students who are continuing to borrow face the full rate of interest on the amount already borrowed. Those who are no longer borrowing but who earn less than the threshold level ($14,716 in early 1998) are required to pay only the CPI component. The aim in this instance is to maintain the real value of the loan. Those earning insufficient to cover the full rate of interest are able to have part of the base rate written off, as long as they are resident in New Zealand and file a tax return. Nonetheless, their loan will be adjusted in line with the CPI component, thus leaving it constant in real terms. Hence, under the present scheme there is the potential for many borrowers on modest incomes to make substantial interest payments but never reduce their debt in real terms.

2 Note that the student loans scheme represents a major asset on the Crown balance sheet. However, the long-term fiscal savings from such a scheme are likely to be substantially less than might appear at first sight, because of the amount of the debt that will be written off.

CHAPTER TWELVE

HOUSING POLICY

LAURENCE MURPHY

The housing reforms of 1991 were designed to alter radically the nature of the state's involvement in housing. In line with neo-liberal approaches to social welfare and international trends in housing policy (Smith and Oxley, 1997), direct provision of state housing was increasingly supplanted by direct income supplementation. The reforms were designed to remove the state from its traditional role in the housing market as a provider of accommodation and finance, and to replace this system with a policy regime that purported to empower consumers to meet their own housing needs via income support.

This chapter sets out the details, and underlying rationale, of the housing reforms. In particular, it reviews the fiscal cost of the new regime, examines the capacity of the new system to assist low-income households to access affordable housing, and identifies the impact of the reforms on state tenants. Finally, the chapter sets out, and assesses, the policy initiatives that have been implemented by the first MMP government.[1]

The Housing Reforms of 1991

Housing policy in industrialised countries assumed a more residual character throughout the 1980s as a number of governments reduced supply subsidies or direct provision in favour of demand or income subsidies (Harloe, 1995; Smith and Oxley, 1997). Several factors contributed to this general trend. In countries such as the United Kingdom, Germany and the Netherlands, where considerable investment in social rented housing had taken place after 1945, it was believed that housing shortages had been eliminated. In addition, governments became increasingly weary of investing taxpayers' money in new public housing programmes, as the legacy of earlier such initiatives included poorly designed peripheral housing estates that housed the economically and socially marginalised poor. Fiscal retrenchment, in conjunction with welfare state restructuring, led many governments to pursue policies that favoured market provision (Priemus, 1997). The political and economic processes underpinning these international trends began to take effect in New Zealand in the 1980s, as the fourth Labour government restructured the state's role in both the mortgage and rental markets (Davidson, 1994; Ferguson, 1994).

The housing assistance regime that prevailed until 1991 encompassed a policy mix of subsidised rents and interest rates, cash payments and the direct provision of housing. Administration of these policies was spread across a range of state agencies, including the Housing Corporation, the Department of Social Welfare and the Iwi Transition Agency. The single most important agent operating in the housing market was the Housing Corporation. Established in 1974, the Corporation was a significant provider of mortgage finance for home ownership, managed the majority of state rentals, was responsible for implementing the Residential Tenancies Act (1986), and provided policy advice to the government. Its multi-functional character, and its position as the largest rental provider in the country, made it increasingly a target for reform. The post-1984 Labour governments engaged in a set of reforms that resulted in the Corporation playing a more focused role in the market, restricted to assisting those who had 'serious housing needs' (McLeay, 1992). Yet by 1991 it managed almost 70,000 rental properties, had annual revenue in excess of $700 million, and owned assets valued at $8,581 million (Murphy and Kearns, 1994).

The advent in late 1990 of a National government determined to implement significant welfare reforms prompted a review of the state's role in the housing market. The existing housing policies were viewed as failing to 'encourage fairness, self-reliance, efficiency or personal choice' (Luxton, 1991, p.ii). To remedy these perceived deficiencies, and to ensure value for tax-payers' money, the government proposed the creation of a Crown entity to manage state rentals on a commercial basis, the sale of the Housing Corporation's prime-rate mortgages, and the introduction of an accommodation supplement to assist all low-income households with their housing costs.

The government moved quickly to implement these policies. The Housing Corporation began a phased programme of rent increases almost immediately, and a transition board was appointed to guide the organisation through the process of restructuring. In August 1992 the Housing Restructuring Act transferred state rental properties to a Crown-owned entity, Housing New Zealand Ltd (HNZ), which was charged with operating in a commercial manner while assisting the government to meet certain unspecified social objectives. The accommodation supplement was introduced in July 1993 and replaced all existing housing benefits. Meanwhile, the Housing Corporation was restructured and became responsible for administering the privatisation of the state's residential mortgage portfolio.

The Reforms in Context

The reforms were justified on a number of grounds. It was argued that the existing system was inherently unfair, given that people in similar economic circumstances received different levels of assistance depending on whether they were state tenants or not. The reforms, based on market rents and a single income supplement, were designed to ensure equality of treatment across tenures. However, it was acknowledged that under the new system, state tenants would be required to pay more for their accommodation than under the income-related rents of the Housing Corporation. Embedded in the government's analysis of housing assistance was the belief that state tenants were an over-subsidised, and thus privileged, sector of the population of low-income households. This inequality of treatment was to be remedied by bringing the subsidies to state tenants into line with the assistance available to other low-income groups. While the new system was viewed as having the potential to assist a wider range of low-income groups, it also offered a number of benefits to the government. The accommodation supplement constituted a more simplified subsidy regime, while a commercially oriented, Crown-owned rental company enabled the state to distance itself from the bureaucracy of housing allocation.

The logic of the government's position was challenged by those who argued that the identified inequality reflected the low level of assistance given to non-state tenants via the accommodation benefit, rather than any over-subsidisation of state tenants. Moreover, by choosing to base its comparisons on the average level of subsidy, the government failed to take account of the degree to which the Housing Corporation's allocation policies had targeted people who were generally 'poorer and also suffer[ed] greater social deprivation and hardship than other tenants' (McLeay, 1992 p.125). Māori, Pacific Islands, elderly and sole-parent households were particularly assisted by the Corporation's allocation policies. Moving to a system that promoted equality of treatment would not ensure that those most in need would receive adequate assistance.

The existing system was deemed inefficient in that income-related rentals hid the true level of subsidy from individual state tenants, and provided no incentive for the rational consumption of space by individual households. Since tenants did not bear the costs of over-consumption (that is, households consuming more space than was necessary for their immediate needs), and were unaware of these costs, inefficient use of resources ensued. A policy that encouraged accommodation matching (where a single person, for example, lives in a one-bedroom property) would be more efficient. This matching was to be promoted by the introduction of market rents in the state sector. The early formulation of this policy failed to take into account the fact that New Zealand's housing stock has a distinct lack of single-bedroom properties. Hence, those households requiring smaller properties were disadvantaged. The policy also under-estimated the economic and social costs associated with households seeking matched accommodation. To the financial costs of moving, one should add the social costs of disrupting existing communities, the displacement of disadvantaged groups, and the removal of state tenants' sense of security of tenure. This latter cost is particularly significant for those who suffer discrimination (for example, ethnic minorities and the mentally ill) and may have to move on a regular basis in the private sector (Morgan-Thomas, 1997). Critics argued that despite the rhetoric of choice underpinning the reforms, the most likely reality would be 'coerced exchange', whereby those households in serious housing need would have few viable options, and would be forced to take whatever was available (Murphy and Kearns, 1994). With respect to the issue of affordability, it was argued that, in the absence of rent control, the introduction of an accommodation supplement was likely to encourage rent increases, and thus the supplement was susceptible to 'landlord capture' (Murphy and Kearns, 1994; Roberts, 1992).

At a more general level, the reforms were criticised for not taking account of the wider implications of relying solely on a market model of housing assistance. In particular, it was argued that the move to market rents was likely to result in an increased spatial segregation of low-income households, and in rents incorporating a location premium (Morrison, 1995). This could lead to households being priced out of their existing accommodation, or to part of HNZ's stock becoming 'unsuitable' for low-income tenants because of rental costs rather than physical conditions. Reliance on a market allocation process, it was argued, would result in the concentration of the non-working poor and other marginalised groups on the urban periphery (Morrison and Murphy, 1996). This would impose costs on these groups in terms of access to social, cultural and economic resources, and would carry considerable costs for society.

The Accommodation Supplement

The accommodation supplement was introduced in 1993, replacing the accommodation benefit and the Housing Corporation's subsidised rents and mortgages. It thus became the primary mechanism by which the state assists low-income renters, both public and private, and home-owners. The major parameters of the accommodation supplement are set out in Table 12.1. An individual's entitlement depends on whether their housing costs exceed the entry threshold, while the actual supplement obtained is determined by the level of regional maxima payments, the individual's income and cash abatements. The income abatement of 25 cents in the dollar means that the effective marginal tax rate on additional income for most tenants amounts to 46 per cent (excluding all other targeted benefits). Table 12.1 highlights the complexity of calculating an individual benefit, and identifies some key problems associated with this form of subsidy. Income and cash asset abatements create a potential poverty trap, as they act as a disincentive to individuals to

Table 12.1 The Structure of the Accommodation Supplement

1) Entry Thresholds

Beneficiaries and Superannuitants

Rent or board (no children)	>25% of net adult parent (main) benefit
Rent or board (with children)	>25% of net adult parent (main) benefit plus family support payment for first child
Home-owner	>30% of net adult parent (main) benefit plus family support payment for first child

Low-income earners

Rent or board	>25% of the net invalid's benefit
Home-owner	>30% of the net invalid's benefit

2) Co-Payment Rate

1993 - June 1997	65% of housing costs above entry threshold
From July 1997	70% of housing costs above entry threshold

3) Maximum Payments

Region	Household Type	1 July 1996	1 July 1997
Auckland	1 person	$80	$100
	2 person	$100	$115
	3 person	$125	$150
High Cost Area	1 person	$60	$65
	2 person	$75	$75
	3 person	$95	$100
Rest of New Zealand	1 person	$45	$45
	2 person	$55	$55
	3 person	$75	$75

4) Income Abatement

Beneficiaries

No other weekly income	Full Entitlement
$0-$80 per week in other income	AS reduces by 25 cents for every $1 of income

Low-income earners

Gross income in excess of the net invalid's benefit	Abatement at 25 cents for every additional dollar until AS is completely abated

5) Cash Assets Abatement

Single people

Cash assets < $2,700	Full Entitlement
Cash assets > $2,700	AS reduces by 25c for every $100 above $2,700
Cash assets > $9,100	AS fully abated

Sole parent/married couple

Cash assets < $5,400	Full Entitlement
Cash assets > $5,400	AS reduces by 25c for every $100 above $2,700
Cash assets > $18,200	AS fully abated

Sources: Ministry of Housing (1996); St John (1996b).

seek employment or to save (see Chapter 6). Perversely, given the government's long-standing policy commitment to home ownership (Thorns, 1986), the disincentive to save may adversely influence the capacity of households to buy their own home. This could have long-term negative consequences, as home ownership among the elderly has been shown to be a critical factor in maintaining an adequate lifestyle (Stephens, 1996a; Chapter 13).

The Ministry of Housing acknowledges the complexity of the accommodation supplement (AS) formula, but maintains that 'it is relatively easy for most recipients to estimate how much their AS will change with a change in housing costs' (Ministry of Housing, 1996, p.41). Clearly this is a moot point, but the complexity of the system is likely to deter non-beneficiaries from even applying for the supplement.

Two dimensions of the assistance regime are worthy of examination: the cost of the accommodation supplement, and who receives it. An analysis of the overall cost of the scheme, and emerging trends in those costs, provides insights into future policy directions, while an examination of the social profile of recipients offers insights into the effectiveness of the policy.

The Cost of the Accommodation Supplement

Figure 12.1 provides an overview of the actual and expected cost of the accommodation supplement from three Budgets, and highlights the rapid increase in the cost of the scheme since 1993.[2] When the supplement was introduced, it was envisaged that total costs would rise to $476 million by 1996 and stabilise thereafter (Birch, 1994, p.185). By 1996, the actual costs had risen to $561 million (18 per cent greater than originally estimated) and were projected to rise to $625 million in 1997 (Birch, 1996b). Under a revised structure announced in the first Budget under MMP, the cost of the accommodation supplement was projected to rise to $840 million by the fiscal year 1999/2000 (Peters, 1997b).

The upward revisions in the costs of the scheme reflect changes in the numbers receiving the supplement and also in the size of individual payments. These burgeoning costs suggest a process of 'fiscal blowout'. Indeed, the international experience highlights the difficulties that governments have faced in attempting to control the cost of housing benefits, especially within the context of static real incomes among recipients, rising rent-to-income ratios and increasing housing costs (Forrest and Murie, 1991; Kemp, 1994). The experience in the United Kingdom is particularly instructive in this context, as the scheme there has been characterised by a number of administrative restructurings aimed at reducing the relative size of housing benefits in the welfare budget (Kemp, 1990 and 1994). Yet despite these changes, expenditure on housing benefits in England alone exceeded £8.5 billion in 1994/95, and spending on rent allowances rose at an annual rate of nearly 26

Figure 12.1 Actual and Expected Cost of the Accommodation Supplement 1993/94-1999/2000

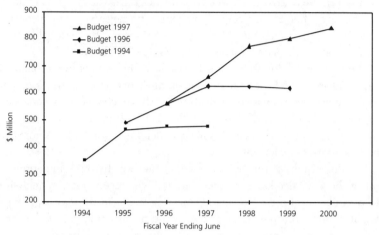

Note: Figures are expressed in current values.

Source: Budget Documents B6A (1994) and B3 (1996 and 1997).

per cent in real terms between 1988 and 1994 (Murie, 1997). Murie attributes these rising costs to the inadequacy of other welfare benefits, the shift in housing policy away from 'bricks and mortar' subsidies to benefit payments, and high rents in the Housing Association and private rental sectors.[3]

Two important questions arise as a consequence of the burgeoning costs of the accommodation supplement. First, if costs are to be controlled, what mechanisms are needed? In the absence of rent controls, the only options are to change the eligibility criteria, or to reduce the level of individual payments and increase the abatement rate. Moreover, given a policy environment that espouses fiscal responsibility, and a pressing political need to reduce welfare costs generally, the growing significance of the accommodation supplement (expected to be 7 per cent of total welfare payments in 1999/2000) is likely to be questioned. In this context, the imperative of fiscal responsibility may run counter to housing needs. Managing the welfare purse is likely to put pressure on the accommodation supplement regime in the long run.

Second, who benefits from the considerable injection of public money into the housing sector? It has been argued that the accommodation supplement is open to 'landlord capture' and is simply a subsidy to existing landlords. The logic underpinning the introduction of the supplement suggests that it will make the low-income rental sector more profitable and will, in the long run, induce a new supply of low-cost rental accommodation. However, this assumes a set of supply conditions that may not exist. A recent analysis of the low-cost rental sector in Australia (Industry Commission, 1993) questions the validity of this logic. Parker (1997, p.20) records that the Industry Commission

> ... found that most low-cost rental accommodation within the private sector filtered down from previous uses. It argued that this is a residual market, not generally attractive to private investors. Because supply responses in this segment of the market are restricted, governments wishing to attract more properties into private rental have to overcome this by outlaying additional amounts of rent assistance. Existing landlords are unavoidably paid more even though the additional payment is not needed to hold them in the rental market; and existing recipients of rent assistance come to require additional assistance.

If rents rise under the new welfare regime, then the effectiveness of the supplement as a mechanism for assisting households to meet their accommodation needs is undermined. In order to explore the issue of housing affordability, it is necessary to review the socio-economic characteristics of accommodation supplement recipients, and the changing nature of market rents.

Who Receives the Supplement?

Between September 1993 and June 1996, the number of people receiving accommodation supplements increased from 186,835 to 280,021. As beneficiaries accounted for 95 per cent of all supplements paid out in 1996 (see Table 12.2), it is clear that the supplement offers little assistance to low-income non-beneficiaries. This is significant, since the accommodation supplement replaced other forms of housing assistance such as subsidised mortgages, which helped low-income earners (Murphy, 1996).[4] Renters accounted for 59 per cent of all supplements, with the majority of these (67 per cent) being in the private rental sector. HNZ tenants accounted for 17 per cent of all recipients and 29 per cent of renters. Interestingly, boarders accounted for 25 per cent of all supplements. The significance of boarders raises issues concerning the manner in which low-income households may be altering their living arrangements in order to maximise their income and thus cover high housing costs.

Those on unemployment and domestic purposes benefits accounted for 69 per cent (183,671) of beneficiaries receiving the accommodation supplement (see Table 12.3). Average payments ranged from $23 a week for unemployed people to $49 a week for domestic purposes beneficiaries. While these figures disguise regional variations in levels of payment, they indicate that many people receive far less than the maximum payments available. Reflecting the increasing fiscal cost of the benefit, average payments have increased over time. In South Auckland, an area that accounts for 14 per cent of accommodation supplement expenditure, the average payment has increased by 93 per cent, from $33.19 in 1993 to $64.29 in 1997 (Friendship House, 1997).

Table 12.2 Accommodation Supplement by Type of Accommodation (21 June 1996)

Type of Accommodation	Beneficiaries & Pensioners	Low-income Earners	All
Renters			
Housing New Zealand	44,563	3,591	48,154
Te Puni Kokiri			17
Council	2,144	46	2,190
Residential Home	4,288	300	4,588
Housing Corporation	28	1	29
Other	105,444	6,020	111,464
All Renters	156,484*	9,958*	166,442
Boarders	70,046	399	70,445
Mortgagors			
Housing Corporation	7,522	343	7,865
Housing New Zealand			68
Te Puni Kokiri		1	1
Council			1
Residential Home	3,371	475	3,846
Other	27,768	3,577	31,345
All Mortgagors	38,730*	4,396	43,126
Not Classified	8		8
Total	**265,286**	**14,753**	**280,021**

Source: This table is taken from Department of Social Welfare (1996a, p.56). Some minor errors in summation are evident in this table, as indicated by an asterisk (*).

The effectiveness of the supplement, as a means of assisting beneficiaries with their housing costs, needs to be assessed within the context of recent changes to the social security system in New Zealand (see Chapter 13). As part of an attempt to reconfigure the welfare regime, the National government made significant cuts to the benefit rates in April 1991. As a consequence, the 'household income of beneficiaries fell from 72 percent of the mean equivalent disposable income before the benefit cuts to 58 percent in 1993' (Kelsey, 1997a, p.277), and domestic purposes beneficiaries with two children sustained an 8 per cent cut in nominal weekly payments.[5] Hence, it can be argued that the accommodation supplement, although directly linked to accommodation costs, represents a compensatory mechanism for deficiencies in the levels of primary benefits paid to the unemployed, the elderly, and sole parents, especially since these benefits are meant to cover normal living costs. Moreover, the reduction in beneficiaries' incomes in real terms, in conjunction with changes in housing policy and a booming housing market, exacerbates problems of housing affordability.

The inadequacy of welfare payments can be gauged by the extent to which the special benefit (paid to beneficiaries whose fixed costs leave them with

Table 12.3 Accommodation Supplement by Main Benefit Type (30 June 1996)

Main Benefit	Number	Average Weekly Value
Unemployment *	93,271	$23.17
Training	8,820	$33.25
Sickness	23,608	$37.84
Invalid's	21,774	$34.63
Domestic Purposes	90,400	$49.06
Widow's	3,334	$42.91
Transitional Retirement	1,707	$34.55
New Zealand Superannuation	22,012	$32.80
Veteran's Pension	342	$30.91
Low-income earners not receiving a main benefit	14,753	$40.84
Total	**280,021**	**$39.32**

* Includes 55-Plus benefit, job search allowance, and independent youth benefit.

Source: Department of Social Welfare (1996a, p.57).

insufficient residual income to meet their needs) has become an additional form of housing assistance. In 1996, 80 per cent of the 33,000 special benefit payments were due to high housing costs, and 9,000 of them were to HNZ tenants (Ministry of Housing, 1996). In addition, about 9 per cent (approximately 25,000) of all accommodation supplement recipients spent more than half their net income on housing costs (ibid.). While the Ministry argues that the composition of this group is constantly changing, with households moving in and out of the category, it remains a significant number of households, and highlights the problems faced by those seeking affordable housing. Surveys of users of foodbanks further attest to the rising incidence of housing-related poverty. A survey of 934 clients of Salvation Army foodbanks showed that 58 per cent of respondents were spending more than half their income on accommodation (Gunby, 1996).

Finally, it has been estimated that only 65 per cent of eligible households are actually receiving the supplement (Ministry of Housing, 1996). This low take-up rate is a common dimension of the international experience of means-tested programmes (Harloe, 1988; Chapter 6). It reflects a variety of factors, including ignorance of the scheme's existence, resistance to the stigma of receiving state assistance, and reluctance to face the bureaucracy associated with the scheme, especially given that for many the financial benefits are limited and transitory. The new regime has thus created a situation whereby low-income households who do not have a supplement, for whatever reason, are competing with those that do. If the introduction of the supplement has altered the rent-setting strategies of landlords generally, and helped sustain rent increases, then those who have not received a supplement have been disadvantaged.

Housing New Zealand

HNZ was established to manage the state's rental properties and is governed by its own legislation, the Housing Restructuring Act 1992. The principal objectives of the company, as set out in Part 1 of the Act, are to

> operate as a successful business that will assist the Crown's social objectives by providing housing and related services in accordance with its statement of corporate intent ... and to this end to be—
>
> (a) As profitable and efficient as comparable businesses that are not owned by the Crown.

Since its establishment, HNZ has implemented a staged programme of rent increases to bring rents to market levels, and has implemented a large and expensive maintenance programme. In addition, the company has set about 'reconfiguring' its stock through property sales and the development of a new rental agency operation whereby HNZ acts as a property manager for private landlords. As a result of these changes, HNZ had attracted private sector investment of $910 million by 1996 (Housing New Zealand, 1996). The creation of HNZ has fundamentally altered the relationship between 'state tenants' and the state, has prompted significant changes in the spatial charac-teristics of the housing stock, and has altered the 'community of interests' that will shape the future direction of state housing.

Building on the 1980s experience of corporatisation, the National government conceived of HNZ as an appropriate vehicle for promoting effi-ciencies in the provision of housing services. Within the wider policy context it had become almost axiomatic to consider bureaucratic structures such as the old Housing Corporation as inefficient, especially when compared to a system based on the principles of 'competitive markets'. Yet the creation of the company was not without problems, with senior National MPs questioning the capacity of a business entity to meet the social objectives of the state.

The imposition of market rents was a key feature in the strategic move to create a commercially responsive state-housing sector. HNZ's rent-setting procedure is described as 'market-referenced' (Housing New Zealand, 1996), meaning that the company is required to follow, rather than lead, the market. Rents are monitored on a regular basis and any increases are made on the anniversary of the tenancy. An elaborate structure for monitoring rentals has been introduced, based on 2,800 benchmark properties grouped into eight property types (according to bedroom configuration and other factors). Market rentals are formulated for the benchmark properties by collecting information on market characteristics from a variety of sources (Ernst and Young, 1996). While the structure is based on a lagged response to the market, it has resulted in significant increases in rents.

The impact of the move to market rents has been particularly noticeable in Auckland. In 1991, 91 per cent of tenants in public housing in Auckland paid rents of less than $150 per week, compared with 25 per cent of private tenants (Morrison and Murphy, 1996). By 1996, 30 per cent of HNZ tenants in Auckland were paying more than $200 per week; in Orakei, the figure was 51 per cent, compared with only 13 per cent in 1995 (Murphy, 1997). Table 12.4 shows HNZ market rents from a selection of the company's neighbourhood units for July 1997. Three important dimensions of the new structure are noticeable. First, there are significant regional differences in rental levels for comparably sized properties. Average rents for two- and three-bedroom properties in Auckland Central are considerably higher than in other parts of the country. And even within Auckland, a geographically peripheral, low-cost area such as Otara commands rents similar to those in central locations in other cities. Second, within Auckland there is considerable variation in rental costs at the neighbourhood level. Suburbs such as Auckland Central and Orakei are assuming rental characteristics that may make them 'unsuitable' (that is, unaffordable) locations for HNZ tenants. While the accommodation

Table 12.4 Average and Maximum Rents for Selected HNZ Neighbourhood Units and Property Types (1 July 1997)

Neighbourhood Unit	No. of Bedrooms	Average Rent	Maximum Rent
Auckland			
Auckland Central	2	$208	$290
	3	$249	$355
Glen Innes	2	$184	$255
	3	$228	$290
Mt Roskill	2	$187	$250
	3	$224	$335
Orakei	2	$217	$295
	3	$225	$315
Otara	2	$173	$215
	3	$198	$250
Other Centres			
Wellington	2	$162	$215
	3	$188	$265
Upper Hutt	2	$141	$175
	3	$164	$200
Lower Hutt	2	$150	$195
	3	$172	$210
Riccarton	2	$138	$175
	3	$166	$200
Dunedin	2	$121	$155
	3	$133	$170

Source: House of Representatives (1997b). Note that these rents refer to the period after the rent freeze of December 1996 – June 1997.

supplement takes some account of regional differences in market rents, it does not take account of differences at the sub-metropolitan level. Existing state tenants in these high-cost suburbs are feeling the effects of the move to market rents, while the logic of the new regime demands that these areas should eventually be 'cleared' of HNZ tenants.

Given that state tenants receiving the accommodation supplement have to bear a proportion of any rent increase, the move to market rents has adversely affected them. Significantly, housing costs in the state sector are undermining the capacity of households to meet their basic needs, as is evidenced by the number of HNZ tenants receiving special benefit payments. The potential impoverishment of state tenants was ignored in the rhetoric of 'consumer sovereignty' that surrounded the reform process. Yet the notion of consumer sovereignty assumes that tenants have sufficient information to make rational choices, and that the market does not discriminate against people. Both assumptions ignore the realities of the housing market. The capacity to make choices is constrained by the need to have shelter. Withdrawing from the market is not an option, especially for families. Moreover, once accommodation has been found, a form of location inertia can arise because of the substantial transaction costs involved in moving. Thus HNZ tenants may have little alternative in the short term but to bear the brunt of rent increases.

The reforms are likely to have significant socio-spatial implications. The policies of the Housing Corporation had created a stock of state housing with a distinctive geographical character. While the bulk of state housing was located on urban peripheries (Morrison, 1995; Morrison and Murphy, 1996), state housing was also to be found in the inner suburbs of Auckland and Wellington. The introduction of a profit motive, coupled with the imperative to house low-income households, has implications for the management of HNZ's stock of properties. Market rents incorporate a location premium, which reflects not only the physical character of the property (the number of bedrooms, quality of finish, and so on) but also its location and access to desired amenities. State housing in popular or attractive areas can command considerable rents. Since HNZ is required to meet housing 'needs' (low-cost rentals), rather than 'wants' (good housing accessible to jobs, etc.), there is a built-in mechanism which ensures that market signals can make properties 'surplus' to the company's requirements. Accordingly, HNZ has 'reconfigured' its stock, selling surplus (that is, unaffordable) properties while it still operates waiting lists (Murphy, 1997). The economic logic driving the process may seem impeccable, but the social implications are startling and are likely to reinforce a 'ghettoisation' of state tenants on the urban periphery. Between 1994 and 1997, HNZ sold 3,622 properties and acquired only 259 new ones (see Figure 12.2). Approximately one-third of these sales were to sitting tenants, while the remainder were part of the company's reconfiguration programme. In 1997 the company was in the process of completing 243 new properties, but the overall trend has been towards a residualisation of the stock. In Auckland, a region with significant demand, 677 properties were sold and only 145 were acquired. The reconfiguration programme has begun to erode the historical legacy of a geographically dispersed public housing stock, and potentially increases socio-spatial polarisation, with all its attendant social costs.

Figure 12.2 Housing New Zealand Sales and Acquisitions

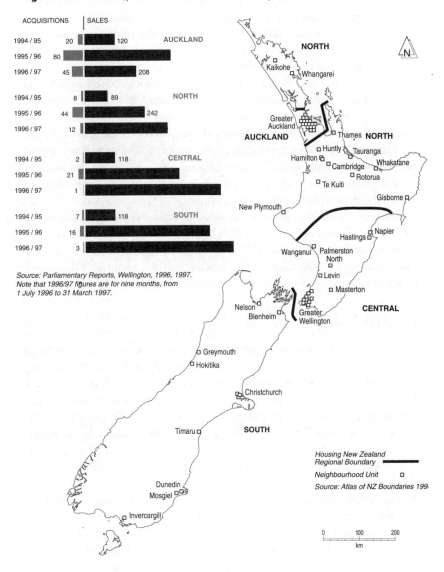

Source: Parliamentary Reports, Wellington, 1996, 1997.
Note that 1996/97 figures are for nine months, from
1 July 1996 to 31 March 1997.

A final element of the changing nature of state housing relates to the role of financial institutions. State housing, despite providing lucrative business for private construction companies in the past (Ferguson, 1994), has been characterised by a set of social relations centred on the state and its tenants. In establishing HNZ the government granted the company $847 million, primarily to fund a maintenance programme and to provide the necessary cash injection to allow the company to develop its competitive character. The maintenance programme, in conjunction with a booming housing market, provided the basis for HNZ to revalue its assets. In turn, the enhanced values of HNZ properties, combined with their new market rentals, allowed HNZ to raise capital from private financial institutions via the issuing of bonds. This enabled the company to repay $500 million to the state, but has introduced a new set of imperatives into the operation of the company.

The bond issue was designed to attract significant private funding, and required that the company not only provide an attractive rate of return but also insure against the possibility of default. Significantly, as part of the process of insuring returns to investors, the state has become responsible for the loans in the event of the trading conditions of the company being altered by the state. Thus, when the Coalition government introduced a rent freeze in December 1996, the company was quick to highlight the state's obligations to its bondholders, which amounted to $1 billion.

Reliance on international finance firmly entrenches market rents in the company's operations, but more subtly it alters the character of HNZ. Any government that seeks to direct HNZ to pursue social goals must be aware that interference with the commercial objective of the company will carry a financial penalty.

Housing Policy Under MMP

Despite the radical nature of the housing reforms, housing policy featured little in the public debate surrounding the first election under MMP. During the coalition negotiations, however, New Zealand First declared its interest in revisiting the reform process. The Coalition Agreement reaffirmed a long-standing policy goal of ensuring access to good quality and affordable housing for all New Zealanders. This goal was to be achieved by 'increased Income Support payments and improved participation in housing provision' (Coalition Agreement, 1996). The key policy initiatives stemming from this included:

- the introduction of an interim freeze on HNZ rents, pending an analysis of affordability issues and the accommodation supplement;
- acceptance in principle of the merger of the Housing Corporation, Community Housing and HNZ, while at the same time replacing the

profit focus of HNZ with a new emphasis on meeting the Crown's social objectives in a businesslike manner;

- a new 'right to buy' scheme for tenants;
- recognition of the housing problems of Auckland; and
- an increase in the accommodation supplement co-payment rate to 75 per cent and changes in the special benefit.

The Coalition Agreement identified the fiscal implications of the proposed changes. These included the increased costs of the accommodation supplement and special benefit, estimated at $110 million, and the state's potential liability for $1 billion of HNZ debt if the proposed reorganisation of HNZ was not in accordance with the contractual conditions governing the company's bond issue. As with other elements of the Coalition Agreement, the proposed changes were subject to agreed spending parameters designed to balance 'additional spending in priority areas' with prudent fiscal policy, including 'tax reduction and the repayment of debt' (Coalition Agreement, 1996, Budget Schedule B).

In advance of the Coalition government's first Budget, the Minister of Housing announced that the accommodation supplement co-payment rate would be raised from 65 to 70 per cent, effective from 1 July 1997. Resisting calls to increase the co-payment rate to 100 per cent, and moving away from the 75 per cent specified in the Coalition Agreement, the Minister reiterated the logic of the reforms as follows: 'fully compensating for housing costs would mean low income households would have no incentive to economise on their housing costs … A co-payment rate of 70 per cent will ensure low income households take into account the effect of actual housing costs' (House of Representatives, 1997a, p.1443).

The housing initiatives announced in the 1997 Budget included an increase in maximum payments of the accommodation supplement; changes in the treatment of board payments; and changes to the special benefit, making it more available to those in need. The Treasurer indicated that the cost of increasing the supplement amounted to $151 million, phased in over three years (Peters, 1997b).

With the announced changes to the accommodation supplement, the freeze on HNZ rents was lifted at the end of June 1997. Table 12.5 shows the average expected increases in HNZ rents for selected neighbourhood units. While the averages may be influenced by a few extreme cases, the table provides for some interesting reading. Once again, Auckland stands out in terms of both its differential rates of increase and the size of the increases. A high-cost area such as Auckland Central was expected to experience an average increase of $50 per week, while even in a low-cost suburb like Otara, rents were expected to rise by an average of $37 per week.

Given the level of rent increases expected in Auckland, it is unlikely that

Table 12.5 Average Expected Increase in HNZ Rentals for Selected Neighbourhood Unit Areas, Post-Rent Freeze (for all Properties)

Neighbourhood Unit	Average Rent Increase
Auckland	
Auckland Central	$50.25
Glen Innes	$51.42
Mt Roskill	$46.45
Orakei	$40.45
Otara	$37.24
Other Centres	
Wellington	$16.53
Upper Hutt	$6.08
Lower Hutt	$12.34
Riccarton	$7.39
Dunedin	$6.45

Source: House of Representatives (1997b).

the changes to the accommodation supplement announced in the Budget will do much to address issues of affordability. The government's decision to unfreeze HNZ rents reflects the power of fiscal prudence to constrain housing policy. The rent freeze became politically unacceptable, as it potentially burdened the government with new debt. Housing policy, once part of a Keynesian demand-management strategy, is now increasingly part of debt-management strategies. This is relevant in terms of HNZ debt, but also in regard to sales of Housing Corporation mortgages. HNZ has assisted the government in the wider programme of debt management by not only privatising its own debt but also enhancing the net worth of state assets. Market rents are significant in both these contexts. Moreover, since 1992 the state has privatised around $2.2 billion worth of Housing Corporation mortgages, which constitutes a significant element (13 per cent) of its privatisation programme. In effect, the Housing Corporation has become a 'cash cow'. Yet the revenue from selling mortgages is finite, while the costs of the accommodation supplement are ongoing.

Reflecting the need to respond to affordability issues, the Minister of Housing announced in October 1997 that HNZ's statement of corporate intent would include a stronger social mandate. The Minister, in negotiations with HNZ directors, set new performance targets for the company, including new procedures for identifying high-priority housing applicants, new rent structures (unspecified), target vacancy levels, and a reconfiguration of the company's housing stock (McCully, 1997a). With respect to Auckland's housing needs, the Minister announced that HNZ would provide an additional 2,000 rental units in the period 1997/98. These would include 'a mix of new properties in areas with strong Housing New Zealand presence, purchases from builders or developers, and head-leased properties which would be owned by private sector owners, but managed by Housing New Zealand' (McCully, 1997b). The Minister indicated that the company would take a flexible and commercially realistic view of what it should own, thus signalling that the head-leasing programme was likely to be an important element of the proposed expansion. In December it was announced that approximately 10,000 HNZ tenants in Auckland would receive an average rent reduction of $9 per week, following downward movement in private-sector rents in some areas of the city (McCully, 1997c).

Despite the Minister's announcements, the policy direction under the Coalition government continues to focus on income support and market rents. HNZ's 1997/98 statement of corporate intent continues to emphasise that the company's primary objective is to be a successful and profitable business. It is clear that the head-leasing policy will need to be based on market rents if it is to be attractive to private landlords, while the announced rent reductions, coming after a round of rent increases, reflect market conditions rather than any commitment to affordable rents. Yet the Coalition government has demonstrated a willingness to define more clearly the social objectives of the company, and this is to be welcomed. In particular, the statement of corporate intent now requires HNZ to 'assist tenants with special needs who may be facing hardship', and to 'recognise good tenancy records in the rent setting procedures' (Housing New Zealand, 1997, p.5). These requirements, in conjunction with the establishment of performance targets for HNZ, demonstrate that the government is willing to pursue housing policy objectives in a more direct manner.

Conclusions

Access to appropriate housing is a basic human right. Housing is more than a commodity; it is a site of socialisation, and provides a context from which individuals interact with the wider community. Expensive and/or poor quality housing dramatically affects the quality of life of low-income households, and contributes to the incidence of poverty. In this context, housing policy is not simply a 'consumer' issue but rather a 'community' issue. Appropriate, affordable and secure housing is a fundamental element of any 'decent society'. Moreover, while home-ownership is the norm in New Zealand, renters are not merely a transient group of aspiring home-owners. Renting accounted for 22 per cent of private dwellings in 1996, and includes many households/families who need secure, affordable and good-quality housing to rent on a long-term basis. The policies introduced in 1991 have impacted significantly on low-income housing in New Zealand.

The housing reforms were predicated on two assumptions: first, that affordability was the main housing problem facing low-income groups, and thus an accommodation supplement was an appropriate mechanism for assisting such households; and second, that market provision was always more efficient than bureaucratic allocative structures such as those operated by the Housing Corporation in the 1980s. These assumptions have underpinned housing reforms elsewhere, including in Europe and the United States. Yet both the New Zealand and international experience of income supplementation and market provision highlight the limitations of this model.

In the context of high housing costs combined with static real incomes among low-income groups, income supplementation provides the conditions for expanding welfare payments on housing, as the benefit follows housing costs upwards. The provision of an income supplement does not ensure housing affordability, as evidenced by the number of accommodation supplement recipients paying more than half their incomes on rent, and the extent to which the special benefit has become a form of housing benefit. Moreover, housing costs are contributing to increased poverty in New Zealand in the 1990s (see Chapter 13).

The creation of HNZ, with its requirement to be as profitable as other businesses not owned by the Crown, has altered the conditions under which current and future state tenants live. The commercial mandate of HNZ has promoted a significant 'reconfiguration' of its stock and altered the geography of the rental sector, resulting in socio-spatial polarisation in the main urban centres and a withdrawal of provision in rural areas of low demand. While the Coalition government has sought to emphasise the company's social mandate, the proposed changes represent only a modest, though welcome, modification of its commercial objectives.

The New Zealand and international experience suggests that there is no 'unambiguously best housing policy' (Galster, 1997, p.574). Yet despite the rhetoric surrounding the reforms, income-related rents have been shown to be a cost-effective mechanism for targeting assistance to low-income households (Stephens, 1996a). Similarly, large bureaucratic housing agencies offer potential economies of scale, and can apply resources in ways that make them more effective than small-scale, profit-driven housing providers (Murie, 1997). Future housing policy must take account of the variety of housing problems confronting low-income households. The provision of affordable housing, either directly or via production subsidies, in conjunction with targeted income supplementation and subsidies for low-income home-owners, would constitute a more responsive set of housing policies. Moreover, as Smith and Mallinson (1997) demonstrate, direct housing provision can offer governments the opportunity to develop strategic alliances between housing, health and social care agencies in implementing health and social care reforms. The community benefits accruing from the provision of good-quality affordable housing require that housing policy moves beyond its current focus on individual consumer rights, and comes to acknowledge that shelter is a basic right of citizenship.

Endnotes

1 While this chapter focuses on the housing policies of central government, metropolitan local governments such as those in Auckland, Wellington and Christchurch have been forced to reassess their role in the housing market in the light of the housing reforms. After considerable debate, Wellington and Christchurch councils have continued to provide subsidised housing, whereas Auckland City decided to sell its residential portfolio in June 1996 (see Austin et al., 1996).

2 In examining the fiscal costs of housing policy, it must be remembered that HNZ profits constitute a form of revenue to the government. HNZ made a loss of $81.3 million in 1995/96 and a profit of $111 million in 1996/97.

3 Housing Associations are non-profit, grant-aided and government-regulated organisations that provide rental accommodation for people who are unable to purchase their own home.

4 The Housing Corporation's role as a mortgage lender has declined significantly, with the value of new loans falling from $746 million in 1990 to $36 million in 1996.

5 This figure understates the full extent of the benefit cut, since it includes family support and does not take into account the fact that a promised 4.9 per cent adjustment for inflation was not implemented (see Kelsey, 1997a).

CHAPTER THIRTEEN

POVERTY, FAMILY FINANCES
AND SOCIAL SECURITY

ROBERT STEPHENS

In the 1990 election, the National Party campaigned on the slogan of a 'Decent Society'. The social security system has since been restructured, in two phases, to a more targeted and residualist system. The first stage in April 1991 cut social security benefits by an average of $25 per week.[1] Stricter entitlement rules were introduced, including work-tests for long-term unemployed, longer stand-down periods, and more rigid eligibility rules for each benefit category. The second stage came to the public's attention in March 1997 with the 'Beyond Dependency' conference, which resulted in further reviews of the benefit system. The objective was to transform benefit dependency into workforce contribution, with a code of social responsibility and work-for-the-dole schemes also on the policy agenda.

The National government argued that the 1991 benefit cuts would restore integrity to the benefit system and provide incentives for beneficiaries to become self-reliant through employment. Moreover, it claimed that the resulting fiscal savings would restore economic growth and thus provide new employment opportunities, as reduced government expenditure would permit cuts in interest rates, which in turn would stimulate private-sector activity. The focus of the benefit system shifted from a degree of universal provision, based on citizenship rights, to the targeting of 'vulnerable groups'. The standard of living deemed appropriate for beneficiaries changed from being 'much like that of the rest of the community' (Royal Commission on Social Security, 1972) to a minimum level of income with targeted supplements based on need (Cheyne et al., 1997). The provision of labour market incentives, by developing a margin between income from work and income from a benefit, became the major policy objective.

The immediate outcome of the benefit cuts was a substantial increase in the incidence and severity of poverty and hardship, with many beneficiaries having to supplement their family finances with food parcels from church-based foodbanks (Craig et al., 1992). Political denial that poverty existed continued until December 1994, when the government eased access to the highly targeted, means-tested special benefit and special needs grant. Nor did the anticipated economic growth occur immediately. Between 1990 and 1992 the economy was in recession, partly induced by the reduction in aggregate expenditure resulting from the benefit cuts. Any labour market incentives created by the cuts were swamped by the recession. When economic growth did occur from 1993, increased employment did not lead to a corresponding fall in the number of people on unemployment benefits, and the numbers receiving other income-tested benefits continued to grow.

The second stage in the restructuring was a consequence of this continued growth in benefit expenditure. It began with the strategy of 'from welfare to well-being', devised to encourage families to become self-reliant and contribute to society, with the benefit system providing a 'hand-up' rather than a 'handout' (Player, 1994). The new policy focus indicated that labour market incentives were not sufficient to ensure labour force participation by beneficiaries. They had to be complemented by active case-management and tighter conditions for receiving benefits, and enforced through work-for-the-dole schemes (see Chapter 14). The perception of why people were on a benefit also altered. Traditionally, being on a benefit was viewed as a consequence of adverse economic conditions or a rigid labour market. The new perception was that individuals were on benefits as a result of their own lack of motivation—a situation permitted by a benefit system that was poorly designed, structured and enforced (Preston, 1996). Moreover, while it was recognised that the future employability of beneficiaries would require investment in skills training and childcare, short-term fiscal constraints meant that insufficient funds were provided to implement the relevant programmes.

This chapter examines the two phases of the restructuring process in light of the opposing views on social security policy that were clearly expressed at two major conferences in Auckland in early 1997. The community-based 'Beyond Poverty' conference (O'Brien and Briar, 1997) identified poverty, stemming from lack of opportunity, as the major problem, while the 'Beyond Dependency' conference organised by the Department of Social Welfare (DSW) considered welfare dependency, resulting from deviant behaviour by individuals, to be the most pressing concern (*Social Policy Journal of New Zealand*, special issue, March 1997). The chapter begins by discussing the current system of social welfare payments, and analysing the reasons for the growth·in expenditure that led to the post-1990 changes in benefit levels and entitlement conditions. It then uses international comparisons to appraise the relative generosity of social assistance and entitlement in this country. This is followed by an examination of the impact of the benefit changes on poverty and family finances. The chapter concludes with an analysis of policy options to reduce poverty and the number of people on benefits.

The Social Security System in New Zealand

New Zealand's system of social security provides three tiers of assistance, all financed from general tax revenue. In addition to pensions for the elderly (see Chapter 15), the first tier provides benefits to categories of people who are likely to be in need—the unemployed, the sick, invalids, widows and sole parents. These benefits are flat-rate (although the rate varies between categories), and are adjusted for family size through the payment of the family support tax credit (FSTC—usually referred to simply as 'family support') on proof of dependent children. They are paid irrespective of past contributions or income, are selective in that they are based on an income-test, and are abated against any extra income received by the beneficiary (or their partner). Benefit levels are designed to cover 'normal' living costs, and are updated annually by Parliament according to movements in consumer prices. Including pensions, the first tier accounts for about 90 per cent of benefit expenditure (Department of Social Welfare, 1996b).

The second tier provides supplementary assistance, which recognises that different people have different unavoidable expenditures. The accommodation supplement, the child care subsidy, and allowances for disability, training and handicapped children are the main examples. Except for the handicapped child allowance, all are income-tested and provide a fixed rate of assistance up to a maximum, which is then abated against extra income. This second tier accounts for about 8 per cent of benefit expenditure (Department of Social Welfare, 1996b). In addition, there are other second-tier benefits that are not financed through the Department of Social Welfare. Family support is also available to low-income families in the workforce, while the guaranteed minimum family income (GMFI) and the new independent family tax credit (IFTC) are available only to low-income families in full-time work. These are paid by Inland Revenue. The community services card (which subsidises doctors' visits and prescriptions for beneficiaries and recipients of family support) is financed by the Ministry of Health.

The third tier provides 'safety net' assistance such as the special needs grant and the special benefit, which are designed to meet emergency and special needs. They are income- and asset-tested, and account for 3 per cent of benefit expenditure.

Saunders (1994) shows how the first tier of social security provision offsets a variety of contingencies. Pensions (and universal family payments) are designed to provide income support at stages in the life cycle when labour force participation is not expected. Invalid and sickness benefits relate to health contingencies that prevent labour market activity. Unemployment and domestic purposes benefits are designed to counter the effects of barriers to labour market activity, caused by a failure of the labour market itself or by a responsibility to care for children. This form of classification is recognised in the structure of benefit rates, work-tests and entitlement rules. In 1997, the net weekly rate for a couple was $321 on the pension, $304 on an invalid's benefit, $277 on a sickness benefit, and $244 on an unemployment benefit. The lower rate for the unemployed was designed to provide greater labour market incentives with the benefit rate designed to offset daily living expenses, based on the assumption that the unemployed are 'short-term' beneficiaries. The higher rates for the other benefit types include an allowance for asset replacement, and reflect less concern about labour market incentives. These distinctions are no longer clear-cut, with many sick, invalid and sole-parent beneficiaries being deemed eligible for work, while many unemployed are long-term beneficiaries.

Table 13.1 Social Security Expenditure as a Proportion of GDP

Benefit Type	1960	1970	1980	1990	1992	1994	1996
Unemployment	0.0	0.0	0.3	1.7	1.9	1.8	1.4
Domestic Purposes	—	—	0.9	1.6	1.5	1.5	1.6
Sickness/Invalid	0.3	0.2	0.4	0.7	0.8	0.9	1.0
Other[1]	1.4	1.4	1.0	1.8	2.0	2.1	2.1
Total Income-tested	1.7	1.6	2.6	5.8	6.2	6.3	6.1
Family[2]	2.4	1.4	1.1	1.0	0.5	0.8	0.8
Pensions[3]	3.3	3.0	6.7	6.7	7.4	6.5	5.9
Total	7.4	6.0	10.4	13.5	14.1	13.6	12.8

Notes:
1. Includes war pensions, widow's, orphan's, unsupported child, training, and miner's benefits and administration expenses.
2. The family benefit was abolished 1 April 1991. Family support was introduced in October 1986. Expenditure in 1990 covers both family benefit and family support. Family support to low-income workers is paid from Vote: Inland Revenue.
3. From 1976, superannuation and age benefits were replaced by National Superannuation, which in 1992 was renamed New Zealand Superannuation. Prior to 1994, expenditure includes a rest-home subsidy. Veteran's pensions are included from 1990, and the transitional retirement benefit from 1994.

Source: Department of Social Welfare (1996a).

The rate of benefit abatement with extra income differs between benefit categories. The unemployment benefit has a 'free area' of $80 of earnings per week before the benefit is abated at 70 cents in the dollar. As income tax at 21 per cent is paid on these earnings from July 1998, the effective marginal tax rate is 91 per cent. This structure is designed to encourage a small amount of part-time work and to provide maximum incentives to enter the full-time labour market. For sole parents, the free area is $80 per week before abatement at 30 per cent commences; once $180 of income is earned, abatement is at 70 per cent. This is designed to encourage part-time entry into the labour market.

The Growth of Social Security Expenditure

The motivating force behind the 1991 benefit cuts was the rapid growth in social security expenditure. Table 13.1 shows that gross social security expenditure rose from 6.0 per cent of GDP in 1970 to 13.5 per cent in 1990, and then fell to 12.8 per cent in 1996. Pensions represent both the highest level of expenditure and the greatest change. Support for families with dependent children has declined. The domestic purposes benefit (DPB) is now the most expensive income-tested programme. Expenditure on income-tested benefits has increased from 1.6 per cent of GDP in 1970 to 5.8 per cent in 1990 and 6.1 per cent in 1996. These changes are not merely due to more people receiving benefits, but can also be attributed to changes in accounting procedures, trends in real benefit levels and the introduction of new programmes.

Trends in Numbers of Income-Tested Benefits

The growth in the total number of people on income-tested benefits—from 28,000 in 1960 to 98,000 in 1980, 304,000 in 1990 and 354,000 in 1997 (see Figure 13.1)—indicates a greater reliance on benefits to provide income support. The rising level of unemployment, especially during the late 1980s, is the dominant feature.[2] The low rate of economic growth during the economic restructuring reduced labour demand, particularly for those with a high propensity to be unemployed such as the unskilled, youth and Māori.[3] There was also a significant increase in the potential labour supply as the number of people aged 15-19 grew by 17.5 per cent. During the economic recovery in 1993-96, full-time employment increased, with an extra 105,000 jobs for males and 62,000 for females, plus a further 44,000 part-time jobs. However, the number of unemployed fell by only 64,000 (Household Labour Force definition).

Maloney (1997) and Chiao and Walker (1992) argue that the benefit cuts had a significant effect on the unemployment rate. Maloney (p.65) has calculated that 'between 40 and 80% of the growth in employment after 1990 can be attributed to these reforms'.[4] Chiao and Walker estimated that beneficiaries' labour supply would increase by 2.2 per cent as a result of the benefit changes. By international standards, these estimates of labour supply elasticity are very high, and contradict earlier work which indicated that changing benefit rates would have a limited impact on unemployment levels (Brosnan et al., 1989).

The growth in the number of people on the DPB has been consistent since its introduction in 1973.[5] In the 1996 Census, sole-parent families accounted for 27 per cent of total families with dependent children, compared with 10 per cent in 1976.[6] Among OECD countries, only the United States has a

Figure 13.1 Trends in Numbers on Income-Tested Benefits: 1960-1997

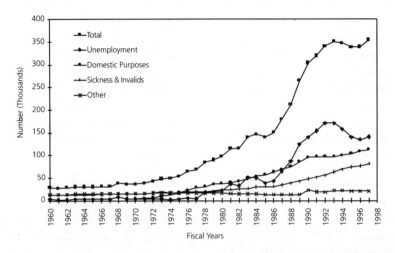

Source: Department of Social Welfare (1996a).

higher proportion of sole parents (Bradshaw et al., 1996). The estimated take-up rate of sole parents for the DPB and widow's benefit has risen from 60 per cent in 1976 to 89 per cent in 1991 (Rochford, 1993). Some of the post-1993 growth is the outcome of a police campaign against domestic violence, which led many women to leave violent relationships (Waldegrave, 1997). If Snively's (1995) estimate of the annual cost of family violence ($1.2 billion) is correct, then the campaign will have a socially desirable outcome, even if there is an immediate fiscal cost.

The proportion of sole parents in employment has declined. In 1976, 40 per cent of sole mothers and 83 per cent of sole fathers were employed, but by 1991 their employment rates were 27 and 48 per cent respectively. Internationally, these rates are low—in Australia and the United Kingdom, where childcare costs are high, 43 per cent of sole mothers are employed, compared with 60 per cent in the United States and Norway, 70 per cent in Sweden and 82 per cent in France, where childcare costs are low (Bradshaw et al., 1996). After New Zealand's economic recovery, the proportion of sole parents in work in 1996 had increased to 36 per cent for mothers and 55 per cent for fathers (Goodger, 1997).

Greater numbers on the sickness and invalid's benefits are partly a direct response to raising the qualifying age for New Zealand Superannuation. Some migration from the lower-paying unemployment benefit has also occurred, as many were unemployed because of their health or disability status. Their incorrect classification was unimportant when benefit levels were identical and work-tests were not enforced, but the distinction became crucial after the benefit cuts and the tightening of entitlement rules. This migration between benefits led to tighter administrative procedures in 1995. Regular medical reviews of sickness beneficiaries have curtailed growth in their numbers, but the restriction of the invalid's benefit to those who are almost totally blind or permanently and severely limited in their capacity to work has not as yet reduced growth in their numbers. In the mental health field, the active policy of deinstitutionalisation into the community has increased beneficiary numbers.[7] Moreover, tightening eligibility for accident compensation payments in 1992 forced some people to move to the invalid's or sickness benefit (Waldegrave, 1997).

Benefit Dependency

While this analysis questions some of the growth in benefit numbers, it is apparent there has been an increase in benefit reliance, but not necessarily in dependency. Policymakers exhibit considerable confusion over the definition of 'benefit dependency'. Their analysis often encompasses not only the total beneficiary population (excluding superannuitants) but also their families. For example: '(in) 1996, 400,000 (21%) of working age people are benefit dependent (including dependent spouses)—compared to 8% in 1985 … (and) 268,700 children (30%) live in benefit dependent families (only 12% in 1985)' (Department of Social Welfare, 1996b, p.5). But these numbers include people in full-time work receiving family support, and invalids who are not expected to work.

Discussions on benefit dependency also focus on long-term recipients of benefits, where 'the references are to the negative effects which long-term reliance on benefits can have for working-age people and their families. The Department does not consider that there are harmful effects from short-term access to the benefit safety net' (Department of Social Welfare, 1996b, p.7). The length of time on the benefit is an important consideration. The average time spent on the DPB is four years, but 40 per cent of recipients move off it within a year. The employment rates of sole mothers increase as the age of their youngest child rises, indicating that child-minding is a major reason for being on the DPB.[8]

The proportion of unemployed people who are long-term unemployed (that is, for more than six months) increased from 27.3 per cent in 1986 to 47.5 per cent in 1991, but fell back to 35.6 per cent in December 1996 (Labour Market Policy Group, 1997). Most spells of unemployment are short, with over half of all registered unemployed having left the register after six months, and three-quarters within a year. Nine per cent are still on the register after two years, however, and four per cent after three years. They tend to be male, middle-aged and Māori. Yet many of those with short spells of unemployment had repeat spells, with over two-thirds of a sample returning at least once (de Raad, 1997).

Benefit dependency, as opposed to benefit reliance, also requires pathological behaviour that prevents the acceptance of permanent employment. Drawing on work by Fergusson et al. (1993), the Department of Social Welfare (1996b, p.35) claimed that 'some 5 per cent of families (or some 25,000 in contemporary New Zealand) exhibit persistent, multiple and serious disadvantage, and may be described as being in a cycle of disadvantage', and a further 40 per cent of families are at risk if adverse circumstances prevail. Fergusson himself rejects any notion of a causal link between receiving welfare benefits and problem families. Families at risk of being trapped in a cycle of disadvantage, whereby 'social and psychological marginality is likely to be transmitted from one generation to the next' (Chapple and Yeabsley, 1994), tend to be long-term unemployed, sole-parented, highly mobile, and with low educational attainments.

Trends in Real Benefit Levels

Changes in social security expenditure are also influenced by the level of, and changes in, real benefits. Figure 13.2 charts the trends in real benefit levels between 1970 and 1997 (in 1996 dollars). While the results vary by benefit type and family circumstance, several phases can be shown. First, all benefit levels increased following the recommendation of the Royal Commission on

Figure 13.2 Trends in the Level of Real After-Tax Benefit Rates: 1970-1997 Selected Benefits and Family Types

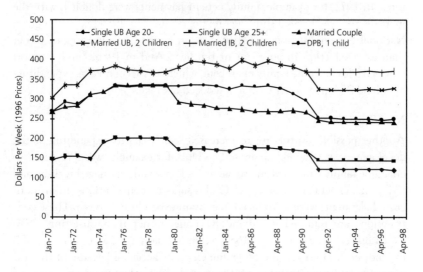

Source: Adapted from data supplied to the author by the Department of Social Welfare.

Social Security (1972) that benefits be set at a level that enabled beneficiaries to 'belong to and participate in the community'. Second, declines in the real value of the family benefit, and its periodic increases, account for the insignificant changes in real benefit levels through to 1988. The unemployment benefit for those without dependent children was taxed in 1979 without 'grossing-up' the amount of the benefit. Third, the substantial and different impacts of the benefit cuts in April 1991 are shown, with larger cuts for sole parents on the DPB, the unemployed with dependent children and the unemployed under 25, and smaller cuts for invalids and the unemployed without dependent children. Since 1991 real benefit levels have been maintained, and are now back to what the Royal Commission on Social Security (1972) described as a subsistence level.

Changes in Accounting Procedures

Some of the growth in social security expenditure is a mirage, being associated with no net use of resources. In 1986 all income-tested benefits became taxable, and the benefit was grossed-up by the amount of the tax liability. Only the net amount was paid out, but the change increased both recorded government expenditure and tax revenue by the amount of the tax imposition. Tax paid on New Zealand Superannuation also increases both expenditure and tax receipts. In 1992, taxation on benefits and pensions accounted for 19.5 per cent of social security payments, giving a net expenditure of 11.8 per cent of GDP compared with a gross expenditure of 14.1 per cent (Department of Social Welfare, 1992).

There has also been a switch from tax allowances to government expenditures. In 1972, for example, family benefit payments were doubled, with the increase financed by abolishing a child tax rebate. The 1985 tax surcharge on National Superannuation was treated as an increase in tax receipts, rather than as a reduction in government transfers. And in 1986, family support replaced a low-income family tax rebate, which was accounted as expenditure by Inland Revenue rather than as a reduced tax take.

New Programmes

Another possible contributor to increased social security expenditure is the development of new programmes. The DPB, for example, was a response to changing family structures and social attitudes towards marriage break-up and living in violent relationships. Child support contributions from non-custodial parents were introduced to contain expenditure growth. These contributions are retained by Inland Revenue, rather than offsetting DSW expenditure, and amount to $168 million annually (or 15 per cent of DPB expenditure). However, the programme is not successful because of the low minimum contribution rate of $10 per week, high administration costs, and the resentment of payers (because the money offsets state expenditure rather than assists the custodial parent).

Other programme initiatives have provided assistance to low-income parents in the workforce, although the abolition of the universal family benefit in 1991 has to be offset against this. That policy decision was motivated by fiscal savings, rather than poverty relief, as only 42 per cent of the savings from the removal of the universal family benefit went into family support. After the level of family support was raised, it cost $748 million in 1996. The GMFI has had a very low take-up. Expenditure in 1996 was only $7 million, the consequence of a failure to index it, the 100 per cent effective marginal tax rate on additional earnings, and a lack of publicity. The new IFTC, costing $144 million in 1997, is available only for people in full-time work, and will supplement family support. St John (1996a) describes this as a crude labour market policy, which 'will impact most unfairly on the lives of children and their caregivers when misfortune strikes'. She also points to the high administration costs of the policy and its discriminatory nature, being paid only when parents are independent of the state. The abatement of family support and IFTC with additional earnings produces high effective marginal tax rates and labour market disincentives. Dalziel (1996; see also Chapter 4) records that the tax cuts introduced at the same time as IFTC favour middle- and upper-income groups.

International Comparisons of Benefit Levels

A further motivating force behind the 1991 benefit cuts was the Treasury's claim that 'when minimum income levels are calculated using systems similar to those that are accepted as adequate in several other countries, New Zealand's current rates of assistance appear high' (1990, p.107). However, the Treasury's calculations are misleading. They made a comparison only with Australia, which has a similar flat-rate, non-contributory social security system. When adjustments are made for different definitions of average earnings, the introduction of GST in New Zealand and benefits-in-kind in Australia, and large as well as small families, New Zealand's benefit levels were not high, even before the benefit cuts (Stephens, 1996b). As the 1997/98 benefit review is apparently claiming that benefit levels in New Zealand are still high by international standards, it is worth reviewing recent comparative data.

'Model Families'

Comparisons of benefit levels in OECD countries have considered child assistance (Bradshaw et al., 1993), social assistance (Eardley et al., 1996), and the employment of sole parents (Bradshaw et al., 1996). Countries structure their assistance packages in different ways. Germany and the United States, for example, rely heavily on child tax allowances and child tax credits in their provision of assistance to families with dependent children. Belgium and Norway use universal family allowances, while Australia and New Zealand rely on income-tested family allowances (Stephens and Bradshaw, 1995). Restricting attention to the tax/benefit position of an average production worker—the approach adopted in an often-quoted OECD (1990b) study, for example—thus fails to capture the overall redistributive efforts of a country.

A more general study using a 'model family' methodology, with ten family types and eight earnings levels, shows that in 1993 New Zealand was sixteenth out of eighteen OECD countries in terms of the generosity of its family assistance package, relative to per capita earnings levels (Stephens and Bradshaw, 1995).[9] In this study, the amount of universal and targeted social security benefit payments, direct family assistance, tax credits and tax rates were calculated for each family type and income level, as well as the additional costs of housing, health care and education associated with dependent children. At very low earnings levels (half of average male earnings), the United States and Sweden made the most redistributive effort towards families with dependent children. New Zealand was the most generous country for the first child, reflecting the relatively high level of family support payment for that child.[10] For larger families, the degree of redistributive effort declined significantly. At higher income levels (one and a half times average male earnings) New Zealand, and five other countries, provided no assistance to offset the additional costs of children. Even at average earnings, New Zealand provided no such assistance except for families with four or more children. For long-term recipients of social assistance, New Zealand was only moderately generous, and this declined with the number of children. The study found that for families with young children, pre-school costs were a very important component of the child-benefit package. New Zealand had the third highest direct childcare costs, with limited state subsidies, and one of the least generous packages of support to low-income sole parents (Bradshaw et al., 1996).

The objective of New Zealand's family assistance package is one of poverty relief, or vertical redistribution to low-income families. The rationale behind the targeting of resources to those in need is that greater assistance can be provided to people on low incomes without imposing a high fiscal cost on society. However, the 'model family' study found that countries with universal provision of family assistance tended to be more generous at all income levels and for all family types. This supports Saunders' (1994) contention that universal provision increases the willingness of taxpayers to finance government activities, while selective programmes lack political support, thus eroding the real value of assistance to the poor (see also Chapter 6).

Table 13.2 uses the 'model family' methodology and looks at replacement rates for unemployed beneficiaries. The replacement rate has been calculated by comparing, for each family type, the unemployment benefit inclusive of family assistance but less any additional expenditure for health care and education, with the net income of the same family type on average earnings. Basing the comparison on net income, inclusive of targeted social assistance, gives a more realistic comparison of the impact on real disposable income of moving into the full-time workforce than comparisons based solely on earnings.

Table 13.2 Replacement Rates for Unemployed Beneficiaries (Per Cent) An 18 Country Comparison, by Family Type

Country	Single Adult	Couple	Single Parent	Single Parent	Couple	Couple
	No Children	No Children	One Child	Two Children	One Child	Three Children
Belgium	41	51	55	58	56	61
Denmark	54	71	61	66	73	95
France	16	34	34	36	41	46
Germany	17	28	26	37	36	48
Greece	0	0	1	3	0	5
Ireland	25	39	33	41	42	51
Italy	32	41	44	48	49	60
Luxembourg	43	52	46	55	58	75
Netherlands	45	61	55	57	62	66
Portugal	34	32	35	36	34	39
Spain	26	29	30	35	33	42
UK	21	31	32	39	42	54
Australia	31	54	43	51	60	73
Norway	55	72	54	64	63	80
USA	27	39	42	57	54	77
Japan	24	35	42	50	45	65
Sweden	62	93	69	77	97	100
New Zealand	27	46	48	53	58	65

Source: Bradshaw et al. (1993, Table 9.12).

While Australia and New Zealand have only income-tested social assistance schemes for the unemployed, all the other countries in Table 13.2 have an earnings-related unemployment insurance scheme that precedes the flat-rate unemployment assistance shown here. For these countries, such assistance represents a 'worst case' scenario, which the unemployed will move onto only after exhausting their eligibility for earnings-related benefits— which varies from six months in Austria and the United States to five years in France. Replacement rates for long-term unemployed in New Zealand are about average for OECD countries. Except for sole parents, they are lower than in Australia, above those in the United Kingdom and roughly similar to those in the United States, being higher for one-child families and lower for larger families. As the average social assistance benefit in the OECD is about 60 per cent of the social insurance benefit for a person on average earnings, New Zealand's social security benefit levels are relatively low. In most OECD countries there is one person on social assistance for every ten on social insurance, but in the United States the ratio is 4:10, while in the United Kingdom and Canada it is 3:10 and 2:10 respectively.

For sole parents, replacement rates do not appear to influence employment rates. New Zealand has one of the lowest proportions of sole mothers employed, and employed full time (27 per cent employed, of whom 63 per cent are employed full time). Japan, with roughly comparable replacement rates, has 87 per cent of sole mothers employed (Bradshaw et al., 1996); Sweden, with very high replacement rates, has 70 per cent; France has 82 per cent; and Germany, with comparable replacement rates, has only 40 per cent. Bradshaw et al. (1996, p.71) conclude that:

> ... the pattern of financial incentives is not a sufficient explanation for variations in the labour supply of lone mothers. There appears to be no simple relationship between replacement rates and the proportion of lone parents working outside the home; nor is there a relationship between marginal tax rates and the proportion working full-time.

Nor is there a direct relationship between the generosity of family assistance and the proportion of sole parents in the population.

Bradshaw et al. (1996, p.79) argue that 'the most important factor [in the employment of sole parents] is the availability of good quality, flexible and affordable child care'. The state of the labour market, the level of incomes and benefits, and cultural attitudes towards mothers in employment are all important, but changes in these factors prove irrelevant in the absence of sound and reliable childcare arrangements. People interviewed in New Zealand have stated that more accessible and affordable childcare would have allowed them to get into paid employment earlier (Levine et al., 1993). However, many of the jobs available to sole parents have non-regular hours, which makes organised childcare difficult. The experience of the Wisconsin Works programme, the Australian 'Jet' scheme and the Scandinavian case-management approach is that the re-employment of sole parents and beneficiaries requires subsidised training and childcare.

Poverty and Family Finances

The post-1991 benefit levels were an uneasy compromise between fiscal savings, labour market incentives and poverty relief (Stephens, 1992). The immediate outcome was a media portrayal of beneficiary hardship. Charitable and health organisations reported an increased incidence of stress, malnutrition, marital problems and poverty-related diseases such as tuberculosis, rheumatic fever, asthma and glue ear. Some of these problems were caused by the continuing high level of long-term unemployment. The move to market rents for state housing tenants exacerbated the impact of the benefit cuts, and caused overcrowding and substandard accommodation (see Chapter 12).

The relevant policy agencies seemed to do little to monitor and evaluate the effects of the benefit cuts on family finances until Whale (1993) published a systematic study of the growth of foodbank usage in the Auckland area, and the first results from the New Zealand Poverty Measurement Project were presented at a DSW seminar (Stephens, 1993).[11] Only then did the Social Policy Agency undertake studies of foodbank usage (Mackay, 1994) and income adequacy (Krishnan, 1995).

Foodbanks

Mackay's (1994) analysis showed that some 365 foodbanks were operating in 1994, providing over 40,000 food parcels each month at an annual cost of $25 million. The growth in usage was illustrated by the Salvation Army's experience of giving out 1,226 food parcels in the first quarter of 1990 and 14,906 in the corresponding period of 1994. Those who made greatest use of food banks were beneficiaries, sole parents, large families and Māori and Pacific Islanders. Most people applied for a food parcel when they had unexpected bills or were on a benefit stand-down. Many users were unaware of their new entitlements to special needs grants, but the way the Income Support system was administered meant that many people did not receive their full benefit entitlement.[12]

Mackay's (1994) report led to the criteria for receiving special needs grants being relaxed. In the five months to May 1995, grants increased by 75 per cent (to almost 200,000), and food grants by 142 per cent. Foodbank usage fell by 12 per cent over that period. In the year to June 1995, Income Support spent $9.8 million on food grants, compared with $3.4 million in the previous year (Mackay, 1995). The criteria for special benefits and special needs grants were again tightened, with a commensurate fall-off in the number of applications and in expenditure. As expected, foodbank usage increased once again.

The reliance on foodbanks and special needs grants indicates that the basic benefit level is too low. Applying for such emergency assistance is demeaning, with applicants having to declare need or prove that they have no cash assets. The take-up of the special needs grants is unknown. In Europe, take-up rates often fall to 20-30 per cent for programmes with this degree of targeting, complexity of rules, and vagueness of criteria for entitlement (van Oorschot, 1995). If the same applies in New Zealand, then a large number of people have an inadequate income. Determining how many requires some measurement of the incidence of poverty.

The Incidence and Severity of Poverty

Following the benefit cuts, the notion of poverty and its measurement became the focus of academic, political and media scrutiny. Community-based studies in 1991-92 were discredited by politicians because of their limited statistical basis, even though they were an accurate reflection of the living standards and conditions of a section of the population. When the New Zealand Poverty Measurement Project provided statistically based figures on the incidence and severity of poverty, Prime Minister Jim Bolger claimed that nobody in New Zealand was starving (*National Business Review*, 26 April 1996), thus implying a destitution-based poverty line. Minister of Health Jenny Shipley wanted a poverty line set at 50 per cent of median income, equivalent to the current unemployment benefit rate, to give a 'modest safety net' (*Evening Post*, 15 April 1996).

The Poverty Measurement Project used focus group methodology to establish a poverty line related to current economic conditions and social policies (Stephens et al., 1995). To achieve a 'minimum adequate household expenditure', the 1993 focus groups estimated that a family of two adults and three children, living in Lower Hutt, would require a disposable income of $471 per week. The itemised expenditure shows that the estimate was not generous—food expenditure for the family was $14 per day, housing costs $150 per week, clothing $20 per week, and power/heating $22 per week. Subsequent focus groups in Auckland, rural North Island and Wellington have given a wider range of estimates, reflecting local housing markets (Waldegrave et al., 1996).

Using the poverty threshold established by the focus groups, and adjusting it in line with consumer prices (to give an absolute poverty measure), Table 13.3 shows the increase in the incidence and severity of poverty between 1984 and 1993. In 1993, some 10.8 per cent of households (comprising 116,000 households and 393,000 people) were below the poverty line, compared with only 4.3 per cent in 1984 (42,000 households and 159,000 people). With the exception of households with three or more adults, all household types had a significant increase in their incidence of poverty, especially sole parents, whose incidence jumped from 11.8 per cent to 46.2 per cent as a result of the benefit cuts and reduced employment. The incidence is higher for house-holds with dependent children, and increases with the number of children, reflecting the low level of assistance given to families with dependent children.

The structure of poverty relates to the proportion of the total poor who are in each household type. In 1993, while single adults had a below-average incidence of poverty (9.1 per cent), they account for 17.4 per cent of the total poor (since they are a large proportion of the total population). Comparing the structure in 1984 and 1993, the most significant change is for sole parents, who now account for almost a quarter of the total poor. While there has been a reduction in the proportion of traditional 'nuclear family' households who are poor, the total number of children in poor households more than doubled from 82,000 in 1984 to 186,000 in 1993.

Table 13.3 Incidence and Severity of Poverty by Household Type, 1984 and 1993

Household Type	Incidence[1] (%)	Structure[2] (%)	PRE[3] (%)	Poverty Gap ($m)
1984				
1 adult	3.7	15.4	94.0	11.5
1 adult + children	11.8	10.1	85.4	6.5
2 adults	1.7	12.1	96.5	6.2
2 adults + 1 child	4.1	6.7	73.9	5.5
2 adults + 2 children	6.6	18.8	57.1	13.2
2 adults + 3 children	14.0	28.2	63.6	19.9
3+ adults	4.3	3.3	86.2	3.1
3+ adults + child	2.7	5.4	75.0	3.4
TOTAL	**4.3**	**100.0**	**88.7**	**69.3**
1993				
1 adult	9.1	17.4	83.4	55.7
1 adult + children	46.2	22.8	46.6	61.7
2 adults	3.7	10.7	88.6	35.8
2 adults + 1 child	14.0	8.1	54.1	18.1
2 adults + 2 children	12.4	11.2	49.8	33.3
2 adults + 3 children	24.1	15.7	27.2	55.8
3+ adults	4.2	4.5	77.1	14.6
3+ adults + child	13.3	9.6	55.1	33.5
TOTAL	**10.8**	**100.0**	**73.2**	**308.5**

Notes:
1. Incidence: Absolute poverty standard using income as the poverty measure, before adjusting for housing costs.
2. Structure: Number of poor in each household type as a percentage of total poor population.
3. PRE: Poverty Reduction Efficiency, or the extent to which social security transfers reduce the incidence of poverty. The formula is the number of poor before transfers less the number of poor after transfers, all divided by the number of poor before transfers.

Source: Stephens et al. (1995).

The efficiency of the social security system in reducing poverty (measured by PRE) has significantly diminished. In 1984 the system reduced the incidence of poverty by almost 90 per cent, but this had fallen to 73 per cent by 1993. The most noticeable drop was for sole parents and couples with dependent children. This can be attributed to a combination of the benefit cuts, the low level of assistance given to families with dependent children, and the increase in numbers in the most vulnerable groups, especially beneficiaries. The high PRE for single adults and couples with no dependent children is an indication of the success of New Zealand Superannuation in reducing poverty among the elderly.

The poverty gap indicates the severity of poverty, or how far below the poverty line the poor are living. It is an estimate of the cost to the government of alleviating poverty, assuming it could target its expenditure perfectly. The total cost has risen more than fourfold, from $69 million to $308 million, but this is still only 1.1 per cent of government expenditure, or 0.4 per cent of GDP. On average, the weekly income of the poor is $50 below the poverty line. Sole parents and couples with dependent children have the largest poverty gaps, although the gap for single people (mainly students and adults under 25 receiving the youth unemployment benefit rate) is also large.

Stephens et al. (1995) also report on trends in the incidence of poverty using a *relative* measure of poverty, based on 60 per cent of median equivalent household disposable income. Between 1984 and 1993, median income fell by 17.1 per cent, with similar declines for each of the bottom five deciles.[13] This dramatic fall in the benchmark poverty level meant that the incidence of poverty remained constant between 1984 and 1991, but then fell from 13.7 per cent to 10.8 per cent in 1993. This fall was due to the substantial reduction in poverty among single adults, from 25.9 per cent in 1991 to 9.1 per cent in 1993. The poverty line in this period went from marginally above to marginally below the level of New Zealand Superannuation. Yet most family groups actually had an increase in their incidence of poverty; for example, 35.8 per cent of sole parents were poor in 1991, compared with 46.2 per cent in 1993.

Initial analysis of the 1994-96 data, using the relative poverty measure, shows that the incidence of household poverty rose to 11.6 per cent in 1994, fell to 8.8 per cent in 1995 with the economic recovery, but rose again to 10.8 per cent in 1996. In real terms, the severity of poverty increased as the absolute poverty gap rose by over 10 per cent in 1996. In each year, over 20 per cent of all New Zealand children lived in poor households, while the poverty rate for adults was marginally under 10 per cent.

There is a substantial difference in the ethnic composition of those living above and below the poverty line in New Zealand. In 1993, using the relative measure of poverty, only 8.5 per cent of Pākehā were poor, compared with 27.3 per cent of Māori and 35.8 per cent of Pacific Islanders. Pākehā still constituted 63 per cent of the total poor, Māori 22 per cent and Pacific Islanders 11 per cent. The higher incidence of poverty for Māori and Pacific Islanders reflects their higher unemployment rates, lower work incomes and larger family sizes, where poverty reduction efficiency is lowest (see Table 13.3).

The relative poverty measure has also been adjusted for housing expenditures in order to calculate the impact of the introduction of market rents for state housing and the accommodation supplement. Housing New Zealand dwellings are targeted to low-income households, with two-fifths of residents being poor before adjusting for housing expenditures (Stephens, 1996b). After the first moves to market rents, and before the introduction of the accommodation supplement, almost two-thirds of state tenants were below the after-housing-costs poverty line. Home ownership, especially among the elderly, was shown as an excellent method of reducing after-housing-costs poverty.

Conclusions and Policy Options

The 1991 cuts in social security benefit levels substantially increased the incidence and severity of poverty among beneficiaries, but did not stop the growth in the numbers reliant on income-tested benefits. Although the incentive effect of lowering the benefit replacement rate may have increased the labour supply, the impact on beneficiary numbers was minor compared with the cumulative effects of the recession in 1991-92, changes in entitlement rules for ACC, the police campaign against domestic violence, the return of psychiatric patients to the community, and changes in social attitudes towards beneficiaries.

Policy development is driven by changes in social attitudes, as the 'Beyond Dependency' conference demonstrated. For some, a lifestyle on the benefit has become the norm. Those with few labour market skills or living in depressed rural areas have seen their employment opportunities diminish, but face substantially higher costs for housing, education and health care on a reduced income. They have had little positive encouragement to retrain or relocate to obtain employment. The state of the labour market is the major determinant of how long people remain on benefits. The post-1993 economic recovery raised employment rates among sole parents, and reduced the numbers and average time spent on the unemployment benefit.

Some policy initiatives provide positive support for people moving into work. Case-management, whereby DSW officers work directly with beneficiaries to overcome the barriers to re-entering the labour force, is a recognition that high effective marginal tax rates are difficult to eliminate, and that labour force incentive effects are small. But beneficiaries need more than just information on training and childcare: both have to be made affordable if case-management is to have a long-term impact on beneficiary numbers. Another positive move has been to extend the earnings threshold before benefits start to abate, although this will increase the number of part-time workers who are eligible for income support. Moreover, many of the part-time jobs that beneficiaries can get are marginal positions, providing little skill enhancement for those wishing to move into permanent, full-time primary employment.

Other policies have used negative incentives for labour force participation. Tightening up the rules for benefit entitlement ensures that the obligation to seek work is enforced, especially for the unemployed. But often child-minding or training may be superior options in the longer term for securing a return to work. Forcing beneficiaries into marginal jobs often results in a return to unemployment, whereas a higher level of benefit and encouragement to search for work may result in a primary job, and reduce the risk of recidivism (Wilson, 1996). Extending the stand-down period for 'voluntary' unemployment not only increases the likelihood of poverty but also results in expensive litigation over whether an employee left the job of their own accord (see Chapter 7). The Treasury's proposal, as part of the 'Strengthening Families' project, that benefit levels be reduced if parents do not comply with education and health requirements regarding their children, is likely to have serious consequences in terms of family stress, increased poverty and poor health. The positive approach would be to take the health professionals into the schools to carry out immunisation programmes, or to prevent truancy by making the education system more child-focused and responsive to their needs.

Current government policy seems rather confused about its objectives, resulting in contradictory policies. The major aim is reduced dependency on the state, but there is insufficient investment to achieve this goal. Instead, the onus is placed on the individual to pay for their childcare or training. Beneficiary parents are being held responsible for the behaviour of their children, but are not being given adequate resources to support them in their task. Much of the policy direction requires a parent (especially the mother) to be at home caring for the children; at the same time, sole mothers in particular are being exhorted to enter the labour market. This is not social responsibility (Boston, St John and Stephens, 1996), as the government claims, but individual responsibility. The government has abdicated from its own responsibilities in this area, except for its role as an enforcement agency.

Policy Options

Looking to the future, there are a number of inter-related and contradictory policy options available. They include:

- raising benefits to pre-1991 levels;
- increasing assistance to families with dependent children;
- having a generic benefit, and using work-ready/work-exempt categories;
- encouraging part-time work by increasing the income threshold before benefits abate;
- increasing the subsidies for training, education and childcare;
- introducing a time limit for benefits, especially the unemployment benefit;
- introducing tighter sanctions for non-compliance with work-tests and entitlement rules;
- encouraging the privatisation of welfare through greater reliance on charities;

- improving employment opportunities through macro-economic expansion;
- intensifying the case-management of beneficiaries; and
- expanding the coverage of work-for-the-dole (or 'workfare') schemes.

The last four options are developments of existing policies, and are considered elsewhere in this volume. The first two options would have an immediate fiscal cost, and could have a small disincentive effect on labour market participation. Raising benefit levels would not assist the 27 per cent of poor households who have at least one family member in the full-time workforce. Nor would increasing family support affect those who do not take up their entitlements, or the 35 per cent of poor households without dependent children. Given that the incidence of poverty increases with family size, combining the independent family tax credit with family support for beneficiary families as well as low-income workers would be a cost-effective way of reducing poverty without a policy reversal away from targeting. The combination would eliminate the discrimination between workers and non-workers with dependent children, and make for simpler administration as families move between the workforce and reliance on benefits. It would help to lessen the stigma attached to the working and non-working poor, but there would still be the problem of low take-up rates of family support among low-income workers.

The third option, which is the one preferred by Prime Minister Jenny Shipley (Laugesen, 1997), would be to return to the concept of a universal benefit, legislated for by Labour in 1989 but not implemented (Stephens, 1992). The benefit would probably be set at the same level as the current unemployment benefit, which would increase poverty. Invalids and sickness beneficiaries would have to apply for supplementary assistance related to their degree of disability. Administration and compliance costs would be high, and stigma would affect take-up rates. Work-testing would be tougher, and based on personal factors such as the age of children or the level of disability, rather than benefit category. The merger between the Income Support Services section of the Department of Social Welfare and the Employment Service section of the Department of Labour in October 1998 will facilitate the development of the single benefit, and provide a one-stop shop for the payment of benefits and the enforcement of entitlement conditions. The unemployment benefit is to be replaced by a community wage and training allowance.

The fourth option of extending the abatement thresholds will encourage part-time work, but not lead to full-time employment. Setting a time-limit for the dole would provide an incentive to find employment, but would lead to poverty in the absence of another safety-net benefit and a favourable rate of economic growth to provide sufficient employment opportunities (King, 1996). By international standards, New Zealand already has tight sanctions for non-compliance with work-tests for the unemployed (Eardley et al., 1996). Work-tests for sole parents were easier here than in most countries, not being applicable until the youngest child was fourteen, but the 1998 Budget lowered the age threshold to six years. In Sweden, people with children aged over one year are expected to enter the labour market, but the state provides fully subsidised and high-quality childcare. A similar investment is needed here to offset the cost of childcare, which is a major limiting factor in seeking employment. There is also the dilemma of whether mothers with young children should be forced out of full-time parenting and into the workforce.

A favourable macroeconomy is crucial to provide employment opportunities and satisfactory wage rates. Improved benefit levels and rates of family assistance, especially for larger families, are required to alleviate poverty. Case-management will allow entitlement rules to be enforced while providing information on training schemes and access to supplementary assistance.

Endnotes

1 Stephens (1992) analyses the process of cutting social security benefit levels, including the interplay between politicians and officials of various ministries. The impact of the cuts for each type of social security beneficiary is also shown.

2 In 1984 there were 50,000 people on temporary employment schemes. The recorded growth in unemployment during the late 1980s is thus exaggerated.

3 Between 1986 and 1992, over 120,000 full-time jobs for males were lost, and 30,000 for females. Part-time employment increased by 70,000.

4 Maloney also calculated that 16 per cent of the increase in employment was due to the introduction of the Employment Contracts Act 1991. By implication, the improvement in macroeconomic conditions has had a very small impact on the growth of employment!

5 Prior to the introduction of the DPB, sole parents were either placed on an emergency benefit or the widow's benefit. There has been some transference of sole parents between the widow's benefit and the DPB, as numbers on the widow's benefit have declined from a peak of 17,000 in 1973 to the current level of 9,000.

6 Only 4 per cent of sole parents in New Zealand are under 20 years. About 38 per cent are aged 25-35. In 1991, the age of eligibility for the DPB was raised to 18.

7 This problem has been exacerbated by changes in housing policy. A prime function of Housing New Zealand was to provide ready access to housing for those released from institutional care. This function was removed from Housing New Zealand with the shift to market rents and income-related accommodation assistance. Some short-term accommodation is now provided under contract to Housing New Zealand by voluntary organisations.

8 The 1996 Census shows that 78 per cent of sole mothers with children under 4 years are not in the workforce, compared with 60 per cent with children aged 5-9 and 47 per cent with children aged 10-17 (Goodger, 1997).

9 Since then, New Zealand has increased the level of family support payments, especially for older children, and introduced IFTC. At low income levels, New Zealand should have moved up the rankings, but it will still be below the OECD average at low income levels, and will still be last at average earnings and above.

10 This assumes a 100 per cent take-up rate of family support and GMFI. Estimates of the take-up rate for family support for low-income earners vary from 30 per cent to 70 per cent (Stephens and Bradshaw, 1995).

11 Team members of this FRST-funded project are Paul Frater (BERL), Charles Waldegrave (Lower Hutt Family Centre), and Robert Stephens. The statistical analysis for measuring poverty was undertaken by Statistics New Zealand, using the Household Economic Survey and the Jensen (1988) equivalence scales.

12 In 1997, the High Court overturned a decision by first a DSW desk officer and then the Social Security Appeal Authority concerning the eligibility of a beneficiary for an emergency food grant.

13 Only the top decile had an increase in its disposable income, with smaller declines for the next four deciles, which are dominated by full-time workers. This widening of the income distribution range resulted in New Zealand having the largest recorded increase in income inequality in the OECD (Hills, 1995). Since 1993, despite the economic recovery, there has been only a marginal reduction in inequality.

CHAPTER FOURTEEN

FROM WELFARE TO WORKFARE

JANE HIGGINS

There is a story, no doubt apocryphal, that in the immediate post-war years the Minister of Labour kept the names of the registered unemployed on a scrap of paper in his pocket (see, for example, Easton, 1996b, p.22). Apocryphal or not, the story is a sobering reminder that New Zealand has come a long way from the full (male) employment days of the 1950s and 1960s. The country's enviable employment record did not survive the shocks of the 1970s (the entry of Britain into the Common Market, and the oil price hikes). Ever since, policymakers here as elsewhere have struggled with the apparently intractable problem of unemployment.

The aim of this chapter is to explore one of the ways in which New Zealand's first MMP government has responded to this issue. In the 1996 Coalition Agreement, the National/New Zealand First government proposed the replacement of the unemployment benefit with a 'community wage' in a programme commonly known as 'workfare'. The programme would attempt to address two issues of concern to the government: employment, and the obligations of benefit recipients. With respect to the former, the chapter argues that workfare is based on a deceptively simple, and flawed, equation that assumes a ready match between an abundance of unemployed labour on the one hand, and a host of social and environmental tasks that require attention on the other. The chapter suggests that the resolution of this equation in a workfare programme is not as simple as it sounds, and consequently that the employment outcomes of such a programme may not be as positive as the government might hope. Some overseas experiences of workfare are discussed, together with suggestions for policy measures that may prove more fruitful for reducing unemployment. The second issue that workfare attempts to address goes to the heart of conservative (neo-liberal) thinking about welfare. This concerns the imperative that the unemployed should exercise some form of immediate reciprocal obligation for state assistance. As a work-for-the-dole programme, workfare offers a relatively straightforward way of enforcing direct reciprocal obligation on beneficiaries. In doing so, however, it conflicts in interesting ways with the employment objectives of the programme. The chapter closes with some reflections on the way in which workfare represents a rewriting of the social contract.

Moving From a 'Soft' to a 'Hard' Workfare Regime

In the 1996 Coalition Agreement (p.25), the new government agreed to:

> Introduce programmes over the term of the Parliament that require registered unemployed to undertake a prescribed level of work or training in return for the unemployment benefit by replacing the unemployment benefit with an equivalent community wage or training allowance. The first priority for the programme will be addressing long-term unemployment... .
>
> The main outcomes sought by this approach will be ... reducing the percentage of long-term unemployed, and maximising the involvement of jobseekers in suitable part time community work or training.

Eighteen months later, Minister of Employment Peter McCardle announced details of the 'community wage' to replace unemployment benefits from the following October:

> All job seekers receiving the Community Wage will have a contract which specifies their obligations, including being available for community work and actively seeking paid employment. There will be penalties for failing to comply (Ministerial Press Release, 22 April 1998).

This type of scheme has operated in the United States since the 1970s (Gueron and Pauly, 1991; Friedlander and Burtless, 1995; Rose, 1995) and, more recently, in the United Kingdom (Casey, 1986; King, 1992; Jones, 1996) and in Central and Eastern Europe (Standing, 1996). Because the nature of workfare varies across these diverse locations, some writers have chosen to classify workfare regimes as either 'hard' or 'soft' (Jones, 1996). The former is specifically concerned with individuals undertaking *work* in return for a benefit. The latter expands this to a range of activities including education, training and supervised job search, any of which may be required of claimants. What these two forms of workfare have in common is the mandatory nature of the requirements placed on those receiving state assistance. They must participate in approved activities in return for assistance, or else they will incur sanctions such as a reduction in, or cessation of, their benefit.

While the interests of semantic simplicity are better served by making work experience the defining feature of workfare, Jones's categories are useful in at least one respect: they allow us to observe that employment assistance policy in New Zealand has, for some years, been moving from a 'soft' to a 'hard' workfare regime. McKenzie (1997), mapping this movement, notes that in the 1970s and 1980s receipt of the unemployment benefit carried an expectation, often not formally tested, of active job-search behaviour.[1] In 1991, a more formal test of job-search activity was introduced in which sanctions were applied if the recipient turned down a second offer of 'suitable employment' or a second job interview. In 1997, work-test requirements became more stringent, with recipients failing to comply if they turned down any offer of suitable employment or training, or refused to participate in other activities if requested to do so. Included among the range of possible requirements was participation in a voluntary 'work-for-the-dole' scheme known as Community Task Force. At this time work-testing was also extended to a wider range of beneficiaries (McKenzie, 1997). With the introduction in 1998 of the community wage, New Zealand arrived at a 'hard' workfare regime. Under this scheme all recipients of an unemployment benefit became eligible to participate in work as a requirement of receiving a benefit.[2] For beneficiaries tested for full-time work, this meant being available for up to twenty hours' work per week, while those tested for part-time work could be required for up to ten hours per week.[3]

For a socially conservative government such as the National/New Zealand First coalition, the introduction of a mandatory 'work-for-the-dole' scheme was a logical extension of the trend towards increasingly stringent and immediate forms of reciprocal obligation. In some ways, however, workfare also represented a departure from forms of employment assistance practised since 1984. In particular, the scheme departs from a model, employed by the Treasury and other officials, specifying the appropriate nature of state involvement in employment assistance.

Shifting Patterns of Employment Assistance

When the fourth Labour government came to power in 1984, thousands of job-seekers were employed in a range of direct job-creation and wage-subsidy schemes operating in the public and private sectors. In 1985 the schemes were abolished, following trenchant criticism from officials about the way in which they interfered with the operation of the labour market (New Zealand Government, 1984; Treasury, 1984). Interestingly, although workfare differs in important ways from the earlier schemes, it bears considerable similarity to them at precisely these points of criticism, namely in its potential impact on the labour market.

Like workfare, many of the schemes of the late 1970s and early 1980s invited local bodies and community agencies to take on unemployed people for a limited period in return for a wage subsidy (generally at an award rate). Under workfare the 'wage subsidy' is simply the unemployment benefit paid in return for a certain number of hours worked per week. As with the earlier schemes, workfare thus promises an influx into the community sector (and possibly other sectors) of a large number of unemployed people at subsidised wage rates.

In light of the similarities between workfare and the schemes of the early 1980s, the fate of the latter is instructive. The schemes came under review following the 1984 election and were strongly criticised: 'It is important', remarked officials, 'that [wage] subsidies do not unduly interfere with the normal functioning of the economy, and in particular the labour market' (New Zealand Government, 1984, p.4). Criticisms focused on the multiple ways in which the schemes could distort the labour market, including their capacity to displace workers; encourage inefficient patterns of resource use by directing investment towards subsidised work; create an artificial competitive advantage for organisations using subsidised labour; and waste resources in assisting those who would have found work without a subsidy. In keeping with this intention of creating as little distortion as possible, officials recommended the replacement of the schemes with tightly targeted employment assistance directed towards those who were severely disadvantaged in the labour market. The new government concurred, and the schemes were replaced in 1987 by a single training scheme (Access), which became the primary form of active employment assistance (Higgins, 1997a).[4]

This is significant because the move to training signalled a shift in policy emphasis, indicative of a reassessment of the range of solutions to unemployment that were available to government. The scope of employment assistance policies narrowed to exclude direct intervention in the labour market, and their focus shifted from attempts to transform the market by creating jobs (however temporary) to attempts to transform the unemployed (through 'upskilling'). In keeping with this new model of appropriate state involvement, Access offered not a wage subsidy but a training allowance similar to the unemployment benefit, and was targeted at those demonstrating multiple labour market disadvantage. This change of focus towards the supply side of the labour market meant that a lack of job opportunities ceased to come within the ambit of social policy and, indeed, ceased to be addressed directly at all. Employment creation became an expected outcome of 'the right economic environment', itself a creation of economic policy. Attention within the employment assistance domain turned towards addressing barriers to individual employment, specifically the skill deficits of the unemployed. In this, as in programmes such as workfare, New Zealand tracked overseas developments closely (Finn, 1987; Gleeson, 1989; Higgins, 1995).

In the years following the introduction of Access, this official interpretation of the appropriate role of the state in addressing unemployment remained largely unchanged. The focus on reducing skill-based and behavioural barriers to employment meant that the main objective of most programmes during this time was the development and maintenance of labour discipline, broadly understood. Training schemes such as Access, and the Training Opportunities Programme that followed it, as well as job-search seminars of various types, have been concerned with developing and maintaining work skills and work habits (Department of Labour, 1996). Forerunners of workfare, such as Community Task Force and Job Link, have similarly been intended to 'improve job seekers' skills, experience and confidence' (p.164). The objectives of more passive employment policies, such as work-testing, are also consistent with this focus (McKenzie, 1997).[5]

In this policy environment, workfare presents the government with an interesting problem.[6] In many ways it is a descendant of the 'labour discipline' school of employment policy. By requiring beneficiaries to undertake work when receiving a benefit, it specifically addresses what is thought to be a lack of incentive to move into paid work (Mead, 1997). The scheme departs, however, from earlier training-focused programmes. Despite being introduced by a government that holds a strong neo-liberal line in economic policy, and therefore an anti-interventionist line in employment policy, workfare has the potential to significantly disrupt the labour market, as the following discussion will show.

Workfare and the Labour Market

Rejecting employment policy that risks intervention in, and distortion of, the labour market, governments since 1984 have pursued policies that target a relatively small percentage of the unemployed, specifically those regarded as disadvantaged in the labour market. In contrast, the community wage scheme has the potential to involve very large numbers of people indeed, thus raising the possibility of the scheme having a significant impact on the labour market.

Coalition documents on costings for the community wage indicate that the Minister of Employment considered two options for his workfare programme (State Services Commission, 1996a). The first involved only those who had been unemployed for 26 weeks or longer (Option One); the second assumed participation by all those receiving the unemployment benefit and other beneficiaries who were subject to a work-test (Option Two).

This report (from which, unfortunately, all costings were omitted when it was made public)[7] assumed that the programme would begin in mid-July 1997. Based on unemployment figures for that period, it estimated that the number of workfare participants would initially be over 68,000 for Option One and over 140,000 for Option Two. The estimated annual flow of partici-pants would be much greater: nearly 87,000 for Option One and over 220,000 for Option Two. These are substantial figures.[8] In 1985, when the programme of public sector wage-subsidy schemes was at its height (and about to be abolished), approximately 22,000 unemployed were involved in any single month (Department of Labour, 1985). No scheme since then has come close to dealing with more than a few thousand participants. The largest scheme in operation in 1997, the Training Opportunities Programme, involved approximately 17,000 trainees in any single month, while the main work-for-the-dole scheme, Community Task Force, seldom involved more than 3,000. In total, the variety of schemes in operation during 1997 dealt with about 30,000 placements in any month (*The Jobs Letter*, 1997).

Having chosen a version of Option Two the Minister was faced with some significant administrative hurdles, not least that of finding enough jobs for a scheme on this scale. The task was complicated by the refusal of key community organisations to participate (AUWRC, 1997; NZFVWO, 1997). Moving beyond administrative issues, a political-economic problem presents itself. Can a scheme of this size be implemented in a manner consistent with the view, dominant in employment assistance policy since 1985, that policy should not interfere in the operation of the labour market? In order to answer this question it is necessary to identify the type of work involved in the scheme.

The Work in Workfare

There are three broad categories of work that a workfare scheme may incorporate. First, it may involve genuinely productive work of the kind that a person would normally be employed to carry out—that is, work available through the labour market. Second, it may involve 'makework'—the 1990s equivalent of Depression-era work relief that had workers digging ditches and filling them in again. This is work for the sake of work, largely unconnected to the regular labour market. Finally, workfare may involve 'public good' work of the kind that Task Force Green, a wage-subsidy scheme of the early 1990s, was intended to provide. It commonly involves workers in environmental work such as cleaning beaches and making paths through the bush. It is work that is unlikely to be funded on a private basis because it benefits the whole of society. It is therefore work that properly pertains to the public sector (the state or local government) in terms of funding.

Of these three categories, makework has few connections to the labour market and is therefore unlikely to cause significant distortions. It is also unlikely to be politically acceptable, at least in any very obvious form, as an option for workfare. Apart from stimulating further outcry over the potentially punitive nature of a compulsory work-for-the-dole scheme (AUWRC, 1997; NZFVWO, 1997), using makework would provide ammunition for those who argue that by enforcing workfare New Zealand is in breach of ILO conventions (Department of Labour, 1997b).[9]

Public good work, on the other hand, appears to be the category favoured for workfare in the Coalition Agreement (1996, p.25), which referred to 'maximising the involvement of job seekers in suitable part time community work or training'. The April 1998 announcement of the scheme offered no further clarification, but earlier documentation mentions 'community work placements ... in the education sector, with local authorities and the voluntary sector in areas such as childcare, conservation projects, personal care and community welfare' (State Services Commission, 1996a, p.5).[10] By looking for placements in the non-profit sector, the scheme attempts to avoid problems of labour market intervention. However, this is only possible insofar as labour market vacancies for such jobs do not exist and are unlikely to do so in the foreseeable future.

But this is problematic. The boundary is porous between the kind of 'community work' mentioned in the official documents and work in the genuine labour market. The education sector, childcare, personal care and community welfare, all cited as potential areas for workfare placements, also engage workers through the labour market in both the public and private sectors. This means that distortions, particularly in the low-wage sector of the labour market, are inevitable. Displacement of waged workers by 'welfare workers' becomes likely, and the depression of (already low) wages a possibility.

Displacement

Relatively little research, either in New Zealand or internationally, has been done on the displacement effects of employment schemes (Gueron and Pauly, 1991). Nevertheless, official documentation on workfare does comment on this issue (State Services Commission, 1996a). Displacement in this context refers to the replacement of unsubsidised workers by subsidised workers. This can happen either directly or indirectly. Overseas experience of workfare programmes suggests that direct displacement (when employers take on workfare participants instead of employing wage workers) may be relatively common. Local government work is frequently mentioned as a site of direct displacement. In New York in 1996, for example, the City Municipal Transit Authority replaced 500 subway cleaning positions with workfare workers (Bacon, 1996), while the city's Department of General Services maintained 44 buildings with 40 per cent fewer waged workers by using workfare labour (Tilly, 1996). Drumbl (1994) likewise reports on a scheme in Saskatchewan, Canada, in which workfare participants built a golf course, a health spa and cleared ditches, at the same time as over half of the regular park maintenance workers were laid off because of an apparent lack of work.

Indirect displacement occurs if the employment of workfare labour allows an organisation in a competitive environment to lower labour costs, to the disadvantage of competitors who lose business, and jobs, as a result. This may appear to be a problem for the private sector alone, and not an issue for the community wage programme insofar as placements are sought mainly in the voluntary sector. In New Zealand in recent years, however, the state has restructured its funding relationship with the voluntary sector by introducing a quasi-market into the provision of health and social services (Higgins, 1997b). This has created the potential for competitive tendering for service provision by both not-for-profit and for-profit organisations. In this situation, indirect displacement may occur if groups who 'employ' welfare workers in place of wage labour become more competitive in tendering for contracts from state agencies than those who do not.

Displacement was a problem for the wage-subsidy schemes of the early 1980s (New Zealand Government, 1984). The major fully subsidised scheme, the Project Employment Programme, was calculated to have a displacement rate of 65 per cent, which appears to have been fairly standard for such a scheme, according to international comparisons at the time. In 1996, officials used a similar figure to calculate the likely displacement effects of the proposed workfare scheme (State Services Commission, 1996a). Their report offered best and worst case scenarios for displacement, arriving at a wide range of possibilities: 22 per cent for Option One, 33 per cent for Option Two (the 'best case'), and 66 per cent for either option (the 'worst case'). Because of the part-time nature of the programme, these figures were then pro-rated down to arrive at displacement effects ranging from 9 per cent for Option One, and from 13 per cent for Option Two, to 26 per cent for either option.

These calculations suggest that between 28,000 and 57,000 waged workers may be displaced by the scheme over the period of a year (given the likely annual flow of workers into the scheme, cited in the 1996 report). These displaced workers are likely to find themselves on the unemployment register, boosting unemployment figures and eligible for workfare—that is, eligible to receive the unemployment benefit for work they were once paid a wage to do.

Wage Distortion

This raises the possibility of another form of labour market distortion that may be introduced by any large-scale workfare programme. An influx of thousands of welfare workers into the low-wage sector of the labour market may place downward pressure on wages in that sector, particularly if participants include those who would not otherwise have been job-seekers, such as recipients of the DPB or widow's benefit. As with displacement, the wage effects of workfare are under-researched. Only a small number of studies touching on this subject have emerged from the United States (Mishel and Schmitt, 1995; Tilly, 1996; Hout, 1997). These suggest that if sufficient workfare participants enter the labour market, even in the public sector, wages in both the public and private sectors may be depressed. It is important to appreciate, as Tilly observes, that even the ring-fencing of workfare within the public sector may not prevent an impact on wages in the private sector. This is because workers compete for jobs in both sectors. If fewer jobs become available in the public sector because of an influx of workfare workers, competition in the private sector becomes more intense, creating an environment in which wages in that sector may be driven down.

It can be argued that the benefits of work experience for the long-term unemployed outweigh the problems of both displacement and wage distortion. The impact on wages may be tiny if the workfare population is not large, and the advantages to those who find work (and therefore increase their incomes) through their involvement in workfare may outweigh any small depression in wages for the whole low-wage working population. It can likewise be argued that although the displacement of non-subsidised by subsidised workers puts some people out of work, it spreads the burden of unemployment and leads to a reduction in long-term unemployment. This argument is more difficult to sustain in the case of workfare than in the case of wage-subsidy programmes generally, because the former involves the displacement of waged workers by welfare workers paid at a very low hourly rate. Thus a section of the low-wage labour market may shift permanently into the realm of workfare, leading to a drop in wages and conditions of employment as these become 'welfare' jobs.

Alongside arguments that the advantages of work experience for some outweigh the potential disadvantages for the larger group, it is important to consider the likelihood that the effects of displacement and wage distortion may be concentrated among particular groups rather than spread throughout the working population. In New Zealand, as elsewhere, many low-wage workers belong to groups that experience disproportionately high rates of unemployment. Māori, Pacific Islanders, school-leavers and some categories of older workers will feature heavily in the workfare programme. Because they are more likely than others to be represented in low-wage work, they will also be more affected by any displacement or wage distortion generated by workfare. The result may be a 'churning' of low-wage workers between workfare, the unemployment queue and low-paid work. Will this process assist participants by improving their employment options? To answer this question we must look to evaluations of workfare programmes overseas.

Programme Evaluation

The impact of workfare and welfare-to-work programmes on participants has been extensively researched, particularly in the United States (Gueron and Pauly, 1991; Friedlander and Burtless, 1995; Rose, 1995).[11] These studies have evaluated workfare programmes according to a range of criteria, including the potential for workfare to cut welfare rolls, reduce welfare expenditure, increase the likelihood of employment for participants, improve the incomes of participants, and reduce poverty. Caution must be exercised, however, in interpreting these evaluations for New Zealand conditions. We cannot assume that because a programme elsewhere has had a particular impact, positive or otherwise, it will have the same impact here. There are a number of reasons for this caution.

First, the programmes themselves are highly specific in terms of the forms of assistance they offer, the sanctions they apply, and the groups they target. Most are a mix of unpaid work experience, job-search assistance, education, training, and case-management, together with a variety of sanctions for failure to participate in any of these prescribed activities. This makes evaluation of any single factor difficult. For example, in the United Kingdom a mandatory work-experience programme known as Project Work had significant success in clearing the unemployment register; that is, in removing from the register those who were not entitled to an unemployment benefit. However, this successful outcome is unlikely to be repeated with a similar programme in New Zealand, because this country's much stricter job-search requirements (noted earlier) are already successful in identifying and removing people who should not be receiving the unemployment benefit (State Services Commission, 1996b).

As well, target groups for these programmes differ. Sole parents are the main target of many US programmes, which means that childcare provision is a key element. For example, in the GAIN programme in California, which is targeted at sole parents, childcare is free for children under twelve, participation in the programme is voluntary unless childcare is available, parents must have a choice of at least two childcare providers, and assistance continues to be offered for one year after the participant has moved into paid employment. In New Zealand, on the other hand, the provision of extra childcare assistance has not been a feature of the community wage proposals (State Services Commission, 1996b), although the 1998 Budget did announce some additional childcare assistance for low-income families. This lack of attention to childcare may have arisen because the programme is targeted at the unemployed, and policy designers have made the rather dubious assumption that childcare is not necessary for this group.

Other reasons why overseas evaluations must be treated with caution can be stated more briefly. In addition to the specificity of various programmes, it is important to remember that these programmes exist within wider welfare regimes (that is, other benefits, programmes and sanctions), which are themselves highly specific and will influence the choices of participants and case-managers, and therefore the programme outcomes. Obviously, labour market contexts differ from state to state and from nation to nation. Wisconsin provides a good example. The state has a stringent workfare programme and is often lauded as an example of successful welfare reform. Certainly, Wisconsin's welfare caseload declined significantly (by 22.5 per cent) between 1987 and 1995. But it is misleading to consider this success in isolation from its context. In 1995 Wisconsin had an unemployment rate of 3.2 per cent, compared with the national figure of 5.8 per cent. Crucially, this buoyant employment scene has included significant growth in manufacturing employment (including work in unskilled and semi-skilled jobs) since the mid-1980s (Wiseman, 1995). For this and other reasons, Wiseman observes that 'if one were to select an ideal economic environment for operating welfare-to-work programs, this is it' (p.4). Elsewhere in the United States, however, opportunities for job-seekers are generally less promising, prompting Bernstein (1996, p.4) to remark that 'the realities of the low wage labor market should serve to temper expectations of welfare reform'.

Finally, the results that emerge from workfare evaluation studies are modest at best and often equivocal. Interpreting programme outcomes for the New Zealand context must therefore be a tentative exercise, particularly when many variables are involved in producing only modest outcomes.

Some Tentative Results

Bearing these caveats in mind, a cautious reading of overseas evaluations of both workfare and welfare-to-work programmes suggests the following points (OECD, 1988; Gueron and Pauly, 1991; Friedlander and Burtless, 1995; Institute of Fiscal Studies, 1997; State Services Commission, 1996b):

- Mandatory unpaid work experience does not contribute to consistent employment, increased earnings, or a decline in welfare receipt for the majority of the unemployed population. There is some evidence that mandatory work experience may be helpful for the very long-term unemployed.
- Active job-search assistance appears to be the most important component of welfare-to-work programmes in terms of producing a modest increase in the incomes of participants and some movement off the welfare rolls.
- Job-search assistance alone is not enough, however, to get people into better-paying jobs in the long term and to contribute to the alleviation of poverty. For this, education and training assistance is required. Job-based training is particularly useful.

These findings suggest a result well known in the employment literature (cf. Windolf and Wood, 1988; Raffe, 1990); namely, that job-search assistance that enables job-seekers to establish connections into the local labour market is vitally important. This may seem obvious, but taking the local labour market seriously has not always been a feature of employment policy in New Zealand (Higgins, 1995). To do so means that job-search and training assistance should be locality-specific in:

- offering job-seekers access to employers' recruitment channels, both formal and informal;
- offering job-seekers training in skills that are required in the local labour

market and/or offering assistance for employers to train them on the job;

- taking a long-term perspective on local skill development (which may involve employers, trainers and workers' organisations working together to establish training programmes and qualifications that are useful and in which they can have confidence); and
- paying attention to mechanisms that segment the local labour market (which may require the introduction of affirmative action procedures in training and recruitment).

All of this requires ongoing research to investigate the occupational structure and skill requirements of local labour markets, so that employment assistance programmes can have a genuine connection with what is happening locally.

The importance of 'the local' has been an underlying theme of employment debates for some time, as submissions to the Employment Promotion Conference of 1985 and the Employment Task Force of the early 1990s indicate. It is therefore noteworthy that as part of the Coalition government's employment strategy, Employment Minister Peter McCardle proposed the appointment of Regional Employment Commissioners. At the time of writing it is not clear what the role of these individuals will be, but the proposal is a step towards acknowledging the significance of locality in employment creation.[12]

Of course, supply-side policy in relation to local labour markets is insufficient to deal with unemployment unless local economies are able to generate jobs. Dalziel's comment (Chapter 4) about the importance of analysing the distribution as well as the growth of aggregate demand may be pertinent here, as economic growth may become concentrated regionally as well as in various groups, as Dalziel suggests. Rapid economic growth in Auckland, for example, may make job-growth figures for the country look encouraging, but the incorporation of other regions and cities in economic development is vital for the employment prospects of the labour force as a whole. Hence, policymakers who are serious about improving employment options for the unemployed cannot be content with policy that is directed solely at economic growth without regard to its distribution.

Returning to the earlier question of whether workfare will improve the employment options of participants, this discussion suggests that better alternatives are available, except in the case of some very long-term unemployed.[13] A reduction in the number of long-term unemployed was one of the stated objectives of the government's proposed workfare programme (Coalition Agreement, 1996), but for most unemployed, workfare is not indicated as a successful option. Nominal reductions in unemployment may be achieved by 'churning' the unemployed from workfare to the benefit and back again, but this is surely an unsatisfactory result. The possibility that workfare may

displace a significant number of waged workers, thereby raising unemployment levels, should also be considered.

Officials advising the Minister have echoed some of these arguments.
Drawing on findings such as those discussed above, they concluded that:

> The available evaluation evidence is clear that, in order to be cost effective,
> mandatory work experience should not be a first intervention. Instead
> mandatory work experience should be targeted at long-term beneficiaries for
> whom mandatory job search, job search assistance and other interventions on
> their own do not appear to have been successful. Targeting to a small group
> reduces the likelihood of displacement and the difficulties in obtaining
> meaningful placements for participants. Given the level of disadvantage of such
> participants, the primary objectives of such a programme would be enhancing
> motivation, testing willingness to work and re-establishing a work record, rather
> than moving the participants directly from the programme into unsubsidised
> employment (State Services Commission, 1996b, pp.21-2).

This conclusion presented the government with an interesting dilemma. The
evaluations indicate that a general work-for-the-dole scheme is neither useful
nor efficient for moving people into employment. But for the government,
workfare is more than simply an employment assistance policy. The second of
its objectives, alongside a reduction in long-term unemployment, was to
maximise the involvement of job-seekers in 'community work' or training.
Together with other Coalition policies such as the proposed Code of Social
Responsibility, this was intended to enforce an overt form of reciprocal
obligation on those receiving state assistance. The government's dilemma is
that, according to its officials, workfare would benefit only a tiny number of
people, while the objective of imposing reciprocal obligation requires that the
programme be extended to as many beneficiaries as possible. This is because
the discourse of reciprocal obligation is characterised by universality: it
proposes a model of citizenship in which *all* people receiving state assistance
are drawn into a relationship with the state in which an overt and immediate
return is required of them. The attraction of a general, mandatory work-for-
the-dole scheme is that it achieves this in a very obvious way. Unfortunately
for the government, such a scheme offers a very inefficient way of pursuing its
employment objective.

Reciprocal Obligation and the Social Contract

'Reciprocal obligation' has become a key concept in neo-liberal welfare
reform. It gained popularity in the United States and the United Kingdom
during the Reagan and Thatcher years, and has received considerable support
in political and public sector circles in New Zealand since the National

government was elected in 1990 (Green, 1996; Department of Social Welfare, 1996b; Bolger et al., 1990). Its importance in this discussion arises from the departure that workfare represents from the social contract that has under-written the delivery of state assistance in New Zealand in the post-war period.

The Social Security Act 1938, the Royal Commission on Social Security in 1972 and the Royal Commission on Social Policy in 1987 all indicate that New Zealand's modest post-war attempt at universal welfare provision was intended to foster a collective notion of the social contract (Cheyne et al., 1997). The 1938 Act refers to safeguarding 'the people of New Zealand from disabilities arising from age, sickness, widowhood, orphanhood, unemploy-ment, or other exceptional conditions', and providing 'such other benefits as may be necessary to maintain and promote the health and general welfare of the community'.

Neo-liberals maintain that in passing legislation such as this, post-war welfare states stressed the rights of citizenship at the expense of responsibili-ties. This is debatable. In New Zealand's case, the 1938 Act must be seen in the context of a welfare history in which the importance of achieving well-being by earning a living had been built into legislation for half a century (Castles, 1985; Bryder, 1991; Du Plessis, 1993). The 1938 Act balanced this focus on paid employment with a commitment by the state, on behalf of the community, to assist those excluded from employment, for whatever reason. The social contract implicit in this arrangement involved what might be termed 'deferred obligation' (in contrast to the immediate forms of obligation required under workfare). According to this social contract, those being assisted by welfare payments or services either had been or would be taxpayers at some stage and able to repay the state and the community for the assistance they were receiving, while those who were paying taxes would be assisted in their turn when their employment disappeared or when illness or age constrained their ability to work.[14]

Two comments should be made about this form of social contract. The first is that it was social, and obviously so. The whole community experienced the benefits of subsidised health care, free compulsory education and income support in times of difficulty and old age. Everyone benefited in some way and was seen to do so. Second, a person's obligations under this system could be fulfilled over time according to their life stage and employability (hence the concept of deferred obligation). In the 1990s, the situation has changed. As the welfare state has been rolled back, the social policy agenda has favoured targeting via user-pays, cuts to services that were formerly tax-funded, and tighter eligibility criteria for many forms of assistance. Targeting has thus encroached on the universality of key forms of welfare. This has encouraged a perception, among the middle class in particular, that welfare is something for which workers pay but from which they do not benefit (Papadakis, 1994).

This perception is unlikely to be accurate, particularly in terms of health and education (Bryson, 1992; Esping-Andersen, 1990; Jamrozik, 1994). But as eligibility for state assistance narrows, lengthy hospital waiting lists have encouraged individuals to consider private health insurance, and changes to Accident Compensation have prompted those who can afford it to seek private income insurance. In this environment the concept of a collective social contract has, understandably, become strained.

It is therefore not surprising that the individualisation of the social contract has grown in popularity, and with it an argument that the terms of the contract be apparent. The proposed Code of Social Responsibility explicitly rejected the notion of deferred obligation: 'In future we hope to provide beneficiaries with a plan that details what the government expects of them in exchange for the help they receive from taxpayers ... a form of contract between a welfare recipient and the State' (Peters, 1997a, p.11).

There are significant dangers in this approach. In particular, it ignores both the obligations that those receiving benefits already fulfil (such as job-search activity and childcare), and the assistance that those not receiving welfare benefits get from the state, such as income assistance (family support, the independent family tax credit) and subsidised access to education, health and public amenities. As well, it increases state surveillance on a group already heavily stigmatised. This has serious implications for the well-being of this group and for the social cohesion of the whole community.

Elsewhere the issue of reciprocal obligation is dealt with in different ways. In Europe and the United States, contribution-based social insurance schemes operate whereby workers, employers and the state pay into trust funds from which workers can draw when they retire or become unemployed. In this situation, reciprocal obligations are made very clear. Workers draw on funds to which they have contributed, and thus can be seen to 'deserve' the assistance they receive. But only those who have contributed to a scheme—that is, those who have been employed—can be involved. Such schemes do not recognise the contribution to society of those who perform unpaid work, particularly child-raising. In addition, some categories of paid work are excluded from social insurance. In the United States, for example, those who are ineligible to participate in contributory social insurance schemes include part-time workers, pregnant women, domestic workers and others in the informal economy. Those entering the labour market for the first time are also unable to draw on such schemes because they have not yet contributed to them. These groups, and those outside the labour market who do not have access to a scheme through a paid worker (sole parents, for example), must rely on meagre forms of means-tested 'public assistance'. This is a heavily stigmatised form of welfare, vulnerable to cuts because it lacks the support of many taxpayers whose own insurance against misfortune lies in contribution-based schemes. The result is a two-tier society in which those eligible for social insurance are considerably better off than those receiving public assistance, both in terms of income and status (Fraser, 1989; Fraser and Gordon, 1992).

There are two ways of implementing systems of social insurance that may avoid these problems. One is to extend employment to as many people as possible, so that most people are able to contribute to a social insurance scheme. This is the policy path followed in Scandinavia, where employment creation by the state, especially in the public sector, has enabled high female participation rates and low unemployment (Esping-Andersen, 1996). The second option is to extend social insurance to those who are not employed, recognising that beneficiaries who are actively searching for work and parents who are involved in child-rearing do contribute to the well-being of society and so participate in a network of reciprocal obligations. Instead of being based on individual contributions, this form of social insurance could be tax-funded (see Chapter 5).

Conclusions

Workfare constituted a major component of the employment strategy of the National/New Zealand First coalition. It is debatable, however, whether workfare will achieve the objectives of that strategy, as stated by Peters (1998a, p.12):

> The key goal of the Government's employment strategy is to reduce long-term unemployment among all working age beneficiaries by getting job-seekers into real work as quickly and cost effectively as possible. A complementary goal is maximising the involvement of job-seekers in community work or training.

This chapter has argued that workfare is not an effective way of reducing unemployment, even long-term unemployment. Problems of displacement, of shuffling people between workfare and low-paid work, and the manifest failure of unpaid work experience to improve employment options for participants in overseas programmes, all suggest that the community wage is ineffective as a genuine employment assistance mechanism. If the policy objectives are to assist job-seekers to find work that offers some hope of permanency with reasonable earnings, then the state's resources for employment assistance should be turned elsewhere, towards effective job-search assistance, training for actual jobs, and a genuine concern for the level and distribution of employment opportunities.

Workfare also raises a broader issue concerning appropriate ways to achieve a balance of rights and obligations in modern welfare states. This is an issue that requires further consideration. Whether it is possible to maintain a genuinely social contract in a highly targeted welfare state is unclear. What can be said, however, is that a social contract based on the concept of deferred obligation represented an assumption that the unemployed would find work before long and become taxpayers in their turn. Workfare represents an admission that this can no longer be expected, and as such, the defeat of full employment as a realistic goal.

Endnotes

1 The Social Security Act 1964 instituted a work-test requiring active job search by unemployment beneficiaries.

2 This included recipients of all forms of the unemployment benefit, including the young job seeker's allowance, 55 Plus, the work-tested independent youth benefit and the training benefit. In the 1998 Budget, recipients of the domestic purposes and widow's benefits (with a youngest child aged six or more) and the sickness and invalid's benefits were made eligible for work-testing. It is unclear, however, whether this makes them subject to the community wage.

3 According to a Ministerial press release, these hours were set to ensure that job-seekers had time to engage in job-search activity, and that no workfare participant would work for less than the minimum wage for hours worked.

4 A Māori Access scheme (MAccess) was introduced at the same time, as were a number of minor schemes in the years following to address specific forms of labour market disadvantage.

5 The exigencies of rising unemployment in the early 1990s saw the re-emergence of small-scale wage-subsidy schemes (Task Force Green and Job Plus). These schemes, which intervene in the labour market in a limited way, suggest some discrepancy between the practice and the rhetoric of employment policy. They are, however, exceptions in a broader programme that is otherwise dedicated to training and labour discipline.

6 For the remainder of this chapter, unless otherwise specified, 'workfare' will refer to mandatory unpaid work experience, while 'welfare to work' programmes refer to a more general combination of either voluntary or mandatory measures that may include job-search assistance, education, training and work experience.

7 The Coalition Agreement proposed an increased budget of $60 million in 1997/98 and $80 million in 1998/99 for the Coalition government's employment initiatives, including the community wage programme. The 1998 Budget (Peters, 1998b, p.13) announced an increase in the overall level of resources available for implementing the employment strategy of $142 million in 1998/99 and $125 million in 1999/2000, but this included the transfer of the Training Opportunities Programme budget of $121 million (*Budget Economic and Fiscal Update 1998*, Doc. B.3, Table 4.13, p.108).

8 By the time the community wage scheme was officially announced, almost one year later, official unemployment had increased from 6.7 per cent to 7.1 per cent. The 1997 Option Two estimates are, therefore, at least comparable to the numbers that may be involved in the scheme from 1998.

9 The legal status of workfare participants became a topic of debate following the April 1998 announcement, which declared that they would not be eligible for holiday pay or sick pay, and would not be covered by the Employment Contracts Act, so personal grievance procedures would not be available to them.

10 This chapter is too brief to consider the response of the voluntary sector to the workfare proposals, or the possible effects of workfare on that sector, but see Adams (1997) and the

New Zealand Federation of Voluntary Welfare Organisations' newsletter *Dialogue*, for discussion on this matter.

11 These offer extensive reviews of workfare evaluations carried out across the United States. There is also a host of useful web sites on workfare, including programme evaluations, such as those of the Welfare Information Network and Workfare Watch.

12 The Minister also instigated a major restructuring of the Employment Service and Income Support—combining these into a single institution to provide a 'one-stop shop' dealing with all employment and income support matters relating to working-age beneficiaries.

13 This category is usually defined as those unemployed for five years or more. In New Zealand at the end of 1997, this group accounted for about 2 per cent of the unemployed population (*The Jobs Letter*, November 1997).

14 It was a highly gendered form of social contract since women were expected to partake of it primarily by virtue of dependency on male employment (Bryder, 1991; Bryson, 1992; Du Plessis, 1993; Fraser, 1997).

CHAPTER FIFTEEN

SUPERANNUATION IN THE 1990S: WHERE ANGELS FEAR TO TREAD?

SUSAN ST JOHN

While most countries are struggling with their retirement income policies in light of the ageing of their populations, few have endured the degree of political rancour that has surrounded the pension debates in New Zealand. Yet despite the furore, which reached a further crescendo in 1997, the actual framework of retirement policies has proved remarkably durable. The foundation of these policies has been a tax-funded state pension supplemented by voluntary saving. Other schemes have been proposed from time to time, but all have been rejected for one reason or another.

This chapter reviews the way these policies have been developed since the 1970s, and the challenge posed to them by the political environment of the late 1990s. Policies for the elderly have a particular cogency as the ageing of the population becomes more pronounced. It is argued that society must confront the issue of the role of the state in a much more direct way than it has hitherto, and that it can no longer maintain the illusion that self-reliance is a politically realistic, equitable and sustainable solution to the income needs of the retired.

It must be acknowledged, however, that it is difficult to retain one part of the welfare state without regard to how others, such as families, students and the sick, are treated. In an increasingly low-tax, user-pays environment, the idea of a full, tax-funded, universal pension, regardless of circumstances, seems anachronistic and unjust. The urgent task is to find some middle ground where the pension is still provided as a basic income, but there is also sensitivity to concerns about intergenerational equity. Such a balance may better reflect the reality of a country like New Zealand in the 1990s, while not succumbing to the New Right prescription of pensions 'only for the poor'.

Table 15. 1 Chronology of Superannuation Events, 1974 to 1997

1974	New Zealand Superannuation Act 1974 passed. Compulsory contributions from employers and employees. Final annuity (inflation-proofed by the state) to be based on contributions and earnings of the fund for each person. State-run scheme with opting out.
1975	New Zealand Superannuation Act 1974 implemented.
1976	New Zealand Superannuation Act 1974 repealed.
1977-8	National Superannuation introduced. Universal taxable pension at 80% of the average ordinary-time wage for a couple.
1984	25% surcharge on superannuitant's other income announced.
1986	Surcharge rate reduced to 18% from October.
1988	Options for state pension reviewed (e.g. social insurance, compulsory saving). Surcharge rate raised to 20% from October.
1989	State pension to remain, but now called the Guaranteed Retirement Income (GRI). Funded by a dedicated tax. The age to be raised to 65 over 20 years.
1988-90	Tax neutrality for saving for retirement implemented.
1991	Bipartisan conference (March) fails to reach agreement on GRI. Budget announcement changes the GRI into a welfare benefit with harsh abatement on joint incomes. Age to be raised over ten years to 65.
1992	Budget legislation repealed. 'National Superannuation' returns. Surcharge tightened: lower threshold, and rate increased to 25%. Task Force on Private Provision for Retirement recommends a voluntary regime (i.e. no tax incentives, no compulsion).
1993	Multi-party talks. The three major political parties sign the Accord, which establishes: – State pension, to be called New Zealand Superannuation; – Voluntary private provision (enhanced); – Link provided by the surcharge, or progressive tax with equivalent effect.
1995	United Party signs the Accord.
1996	New, more liberal rules for the surcharge announced. Coalition government agrees to referendum on a compulsory saving scheme and announces that the surcharge will be removed.
1997	Surcharge exemption raised significantly. The Periodic Report Group (PRG) begins the first review of the policies under the Accord. The White Paper on compulsory saving is released on 1 July. The PRG interim report supports the status quo, with long-term modifications. The referendum (September) is lost with a 91.8% 'no' vote. The final report of the PRG (December) suggests a new multi-party agreement is needed. Options for the integration of public and private provision are set out for debate.
1998	Surcharge abolished from 1 April.

Table 15.1 provides a chronology of the major events in superannuation policy in New Zealand from the early 1970s. New Zealand is unusual in the simplicity of its retirement income policies, and in the lack of comprehensive, mandatory, employment-based saving schemes. The current arrangements are for a tax-funded, universal, individually based, state pension called New Zealand Superannuation (NZS), supplemented by voluntary savings without tax incentives or compulsion.

The Economics of Ageing

Early next century will be a period of rapid demographic change for many nations, including New Zealand. Projections indicate that by the year 2050, one in four New Zealanders will be over the age of 65, and almost one in four of these people will be over the age of 85 (Statistics New Zealand, 1997c, p.14). There will be approximately 2.5 working-age people for each retired person, compared with around five to one in the mid-1990s. This represents a considerable 'greying' of the population, and a doubling of the old-age dependency ratio to around 40 per cent.

The pressures implied by this structural ageing on current output next century may be moderated by having fewer dependent children in the population. If we include the very young in with the old, the overall total dependency ratio is not expected to reach the levels of the 1960s until the middle of next century.[1] In the 1960s, the baby boom placed considerable pressure on resources, yet society managed to cope. But even if the total pressure on resources is no different from that experienced by the youthful population of the 1960s, the implications for redistribution are significantly different. The costs of pensions and health care for the elderly are largely met by direct tax funding, while apart from education and health care, most of the costs of the young are met directly by their parents.

It is also likely that the average productivity of each working-age person will increase, not only because of improved technology but also because of increased participation in the workforce and reduced unemployment, although there are unpredictable factors here.[2] In crude terms, an increase of 1.5 per cent in productivity per working-age person per annum would mean that the quantum of goods and services produced by five people of working age should double by the middle of next century. Thus it should be possible for those five workers to support *two* retired people from this output, compared with only one now, without the standard of living of the retired people falling at all. This conclusion, however, overlooks the fact that as living standards rise among the working-age population, pensions must rise in real terms if the relative living standards of the elderly are not to reduce their capacity to participate in society.

Regardless of how income in retirement is funded, the consumption of both the economically inactive population and the working-age population is constrained by the overall volume of currently produced goods and services. If one group consumes more, there is less for the other to consume. The claims the retired make on current output, by utilising the income from wealth accumulated during their working lives, are at the expense of higher wages and retained profits enjoyed by those not retired. If those claims on resources come from sales of assets such as shares, the working-age population must reduce their disposable income to buy the assets, or use part of their wealth to do so. Thus either their claims on output are reduced directly by higher savings, or they are constrained by the prospect (and eventuality) of lowered inheritances.

Even funded retirement schemes, whether state or private, do not guarantee access to resources but only to claims on resources. Indeed, funded schemes are no panacea (Barr, 1994; St John and Ashton, 1993; Stephens, 1997). To the extent that such funds begin to run down as withdrawals by the retired exceed current contributions and fund earnings, workers must either save more voluntarily, or contribution rates (taxes) have to rise if inflationary pressures are to be contained.

It remains for more direct methods of redistribution, in the form of tax-funded benefits and tax-funded health care, to supplement (or to provide the major part of) living standards for the retired. Currently, the majority of people aged 65 and over receive most of their income from NZS.[3] There is little to suggest that the picture will change markedly in the future, even if exhortations to save privately result in some changed behaviour. Instead, it is likely that more volatile work patterns, a widening income distribution, the imposition of student debt and other user charges will reduce rather than enhance the ability of most of the working-age population to save for their retirement. The top two deciles of income earners will continue to do dramatically better than the rest, however, reflecting a highly skewed income distribution (see PRG, 1997b, p.78).

Background

While a non-contributory state pension, funded from tax revenue, has been an enduring feature of the New Zealand system, the idea of compulsory saving is one that has surfaced in the debate from time to time. In the post-war period, the first major foray into the muddied waters of compulsory saving was in the early 1970s under the third Labour government. In 1975 the New Zealand Superannuation Act 1974 was implemented, introducing a fully funded, state-run, employment-based contributory scheme.[4] Once it matured, New Zealand would have had a two-tier scheme, consisting of a basic state pension supplemented by an inflation-adjusted annuity to be purchased from the balance in a contributor's account at age 65.

Despite rigorous scrutiny of the Bill at the select committee stage (Collins, 1977) and marathon efforts to overcome various perceived deficiencies before the Act was passed, criticism of the scheme quickly emerged in the political environment of election year (Booth, 1977). Among many controversial issues, there was deep concern at the prospect of state control over a vast pool of investment capital. Women were particularly concerned that their lower earnings would result in a smaller annuity than for men, leaving them vulnerable to the state's provision of the first tier, which over time might diminish in relative value. The scheme proved politically unstable, and was vulnerable to the attack mounted by the opposition National Party, which promised a simpler, more generous scheme that was particularly attractive to women. After being in place for only nine months, the compulsory scheme was abolished and employees received back their own and their employer's contributions.

As a measure of the complexity of such schemes, it is interesting to note that in 1997 there were still 30,000 accounts (administered by the National Provident Fund) containing $11 million of unclaimed funds as a legacy from the 1975 scheme. The Superannuation Guarantee established in Australia in 1992 is another example of an employment-based scheme that has resulted in many small accounts whose owners are untraceable. As a general observation, compulsory schemes based on employer and employee payroll contributions are complicated to manage in an environment of job mobility and casualised work practices.

National Superannuation

The old age pension and universal superannuation provisions of the early 1970s were replaced in 1977 by a tax-funded state pension (National Superannuation), set at 80 per cent of the gross average ordinary-time wage for a married couple, payable at age 60 if residential requirements were met. This pension was an individual and taxable entitlement, so each married person received half the gross married rate, taxed in their own name. While there was no income test, there was a high top marginal tax rate which reduced the net payment substantially for the better-off.

Over the next decade a succession of adjustments reduced the generosity of the pension, including in 1985 the introduction of a controversial surcharge of 25 per cent on a superannuitant's other income over an exempt amount. The introduction of the surcharge was hardly a model of policymaking (St John, 1992). It followed an election campaign in which the Labour Party promised 'not to water down National Superannuation in any way'. By imposing a surcharge on 'other income' rather than a direct abatement of the pension itself, Labour could argue that it had kept to the letter of the promise, leaving the public to decry the flouting of the spirit.

When the top tax rate was reduced from 66 per cent to 48 per cent in 1986, and then to 33 per cent in 1988, the well-off would have retained a much greater share of the gross pension had there been no surcharge. Thus, while the chief justification for the surcharge was cost reduction, in effect it restored some tax progressivity for those over 60 with significant other income. Unfortunately, it had the appearance of a highly discriminatory tax, paid only by the elderly. Regardless of the original justification, the surcharge was to prove the single most significant cause of political instability and public rancour over the next decade. The pivotal role played by the surcharge is discussed in later sections.

In 1988 the various options for the state pension were canvassed, including compulsory saving and social insurance. The following year the Labour government decided that the existing arrangements were the most suitable, although the state pension would now be called the Guaranteed Retirement Income (GRI); the age of eligibility would rise to 65 over the next twenty years; and the pay-as-you-go pension would be funded by a dedicated tax.[5]

National came to power in late 1990 with a different agenda, despite an election promise to protect superannuitants. The pledge to repeal the controversial surcharge, which had acted as a modest income test for the better-off, was abandoned. Instead, the 1991 Budget announced changes to GRI that would turn it into a welfare benefit only.[6] At this point it looked as though New Zealand, alone among OECD countries, would have no special policy for the provision of retirement income over and above a subsistence-level, tightly targeted safety net for the poor (St John, 1992). Retired people around the country were shocked and outraged, with many facing substantially reduced incomes. The legislation was forced through the House in an all-night sitting so that it 'could not be undone'. But after a period of intense lobbying, the changes were overturned the following year. This episode was one of a number that ultimately delivered a new electoral system to New Zealand voters.

In announcing the back-down in late 1991, the government stated that the age of eligibility would still be raised in a series of steps to reach 65 by the year 2001, and that a much tighter version of the surcharge would be in place by 1 April 1992. In the meantime, the abatement regime associated with the aborted 1991 changes had heightened awareness of the impact of targeting, and the scramble to find avoidance schemes to thwart the surcharge continued as before. This in turn undermined the integrity of the surcharge system, and gave its critics ample ammunition to discredit it.

Private Provision for Retirement
The fourth Labour government had been determined to reform the tax system by flattening the tax scale and removing all kinds of special tax privileges

(Scollay and St John, 1996, pp.364-75). This thinking was driven by concerns about efficiency and the quality of investment, and reflected a belief in the ability of market signals to guide investment to where the greatest returns could be reaped. Between 1987 and 1990 all tax incentives for retirement savings were abolished. By 1990, saving for retirement via a superannuation scheme was treated no differently for tax purposes from putting money in the bank (see St John and Ashton, 1993, pp.21-45). In the aftermath of these changes, many superannuation schemes were closed to new members; some closed down altogether, paying out existing members; and other employers hesitated to set up new schemes (St John and Ashton, 1993). The exercise was not specifically designed to ensure adequacy of provision through combined public and private sources; nor did it represent a coherent set of retirement income policies. It was inevitable, then, that the issue of the nature of the state pension would be revisited.

After the debacle of the 'Mother of all Budgets' in 1991, the government still felt the need to reduce the state's role in the provision of retirement income, but now saw private provision as the saviour. If only people could be forced or persuaded to save for their own retirement, the government's role could safely diminish. To get advice on how this could be achieved, it established the Task Force on Private Provision for Retirement (known as the Todd Task Force after its chairman, Jeff Todd, a senior partner in Price Waterhouse).

The task force renegotiated its terms of reference to include public provision, after finding that it was impossible to consider private provision for retirement in isolation from public provision. Its final report (1992) looked at three broad frameworks. The first became known as the 'enhanced voluntary option', in which a basic state pension was integrated with private provision by means of a surcharge. Private provision was to be encouraged by education and other improvements to the saving environment, in a tax-neutral regime. It was this option that found favour, while the other two (the reintroduction of tax incentives, and a private compulsory scheme integrated with the state pension) were rejected. Once again, the disadvantages of compulsory saving schemes were thoroughly canvassed, and few, if any, advantages for New Zealand emerged from the debate.

The Accord 1993

The final report of the Todd Task Force was the impetus for the signing of a multi-party agreement, known as the Accord, by the three main parliamentary parties, National, Labour and the Alliance. New Zealand First remained outside the negotiations and did not sign the Accord, but the United Party became a signatory in 1995 shortly after its formation. The Accord was attached to the Retirement Income Act 1993, and although it lacked the force of law it enjoyed considerable moral and political stature. Its agreed framework for retirement income policies had, in essence, six main features:

- an 'adequate and equitable amount' of income for every eligible retired New Zealander, provided from public funds, supplemented by voluntary private tax-neutral provision;
- the state pension to be called New Zealand Superannuation (NZS), and to be indexed to the Consumer Price Index, as long as the net rate for a married couple was within a band of 65.0 and 72.5 per cent of the net average ordinary-time earnings;
- the amount provided from public funds to reduce, through either the surcharge or a progressive tax, as the person's total income increased;
- an environment of enhanced education and information about saving;
- political consensus obtained through the Accord process; and
- periodic reviews at six-yearly intervals.

During the Accord negotiations, the Alliance's position was that the surcharge was a discriminatory tax, based on age, and therefore unacceptable. In its view, an appropriately progressive tax on all taxable income would provide the extra revenue for both universal pensions and other social provision for those of working age. To accommodate this position, the Accord allowed for a surcharge or a 'progressive tax that has equivalent effect'. This wording was somewhat loose, and was to prove problematic later on. In particular, it was unclear whether the total revenue from an increase in the top marginal tax rate on all taxpayers was to provide revenue equivalent to the surcharge, or just the extra revenue paid by superannuitants. Labour took the first view, while the Alliance took the second.

The signing of the Accord was hailed as a major victory, with the kudos for creating consensus largely appropriated by National. Prime Minister Jim Bolger claimed that, at last, the Accord had provided certainty and security for people saving for their retirement.

Peace in our Time?

For over two years there was comparative peace in superannuation policy. It did not feature as an election issue in 1993, and it appeared that the Accord had provided a forum for the parties to raise concerns, albeit with limited progress on most issues. In 1995 the Accord parties agreed to lift the surcharge exemption slightly, which removed 20,000 superannuitants from its effects in two stages, from 1 July 1996 and 1 July 1997.[7]

However, rumblings began to be felt early in 1996 as another election year loomed. One critical issue was the future of the surcharge. In early March, despite the changes already in train, Labour announced its own superannuation policy, which in several respects placed it outside the Accord. In particular, the surcharge would be abolished and the top rate of tax increased to 39 per cent for incomes greater than $60,000. Labour claimed that the revenue raised would equal the forgone surcharge, and thus the policy did not contravene the Accord.[8] But in the eyes of United, this was mere sophistry. Its leader, Clive Matthewson, was reported to have exclaimed that Labour had 'stuffed the Accord' and contravened both its letter and its spirit (*The Press*, 13 March 1996). He believed that the only way to prevent superannuation from becoming a 'political football' again was for the government to dump the surcharge.[9] On 20 March 1996, United duly brought a proposal to the Accord that would abolish the surcharge and replace it with an abatement regime for those with incomes above $40,000.[10]

National was under pressure to compromise on this issue, as Labour's position had left it vulnerable as the only defender of the surcharge status quo.[11] A press release from the Minister of Social Welfare and Senior Citizens, Peter Gresham (29 May 1996), stressed the government's commitment to the Accord in order to maintain certainty, sustainability and security of policy for those in retirement. He went on to say that 'all parties except the government have now signalled a range of moves are necessary beyond those contained in the Tax Reduction and Social Policy Bill'. The government thus proposed a modification of United's suggestion. A married couple would become subject to an abatement of 25 per cent of the net pension once their income exceeded 1.1 times the average ordinary-time wage.[12] The idea was to increase the exemption dramatically and remove most superannuitants from its impact, while giving more transparent effect to the principle of reducing superannuation as net income rose (as required by the Accord).[13] At the same time, the intention was also to make it clear that to go further would benefit only the very well-off.

The abatement proposal was problematic, as it required shifting the income test from Inland Revenue to the Department of Social Welfare (DSW). An income test that was vastly different from the one DSW applied to all other benefits might become incongruous over time. Unlike the surcharge, the standard DSW income test involves joint assessment for a married couple, a low exemption, and a high abatement rate, to say nothing of the more intrusive way income is determined. Women, by virtue of their lower income and consequent lower ability to save, would have been more affected than men by a DSW income test, and some women would have lost all their entitlement because of their spouse's income. Labour and the Alliance, who felt they were being used to 'rubber stamp' government policy, immediately opposed the abatement idea, claiming it would turn NZS into a welfare benefit.

In the absence of agreement among the Accord parties, it appeared that the government would attempt to push through the change to the surcharge exemption, and refer the income test to the 1997 review of the Accord.[14]

Table 15.2 Surcharge Details, 1985/86—1997/98

Income Year Ending March	Value of Surcharge Assessed ($ million)	Number Assessed (000s)	Superannuitants Subject to Surcharge (%)	Exemption Threshold		Rate of Surcharge (%)
				Single ($ p.a.)	Couple ($ p.a.)	
1985/86	167	107	21.9	6,240	10,400	25
1986/87	175	106	22.4	7,202	12,012	22.5
1987/88	209	136	28.3	7,800	13,000	18
1988/89	257	147	30.3	7,800	13,000	19
1989/90	314	171	34.5	7,202	12,012	20
1990/91	306	136	26.7	7,202	12,012	20
1991/92	287	129	25.0	7,202	12,012	20
1992/93	347	152	31.1	4,160	6,240	25
1993/94	311	141	27.9	4,160	6,240	25
1994/95	289	134	28.5	4,160	6,240	25
Estimates and forecasts						
1995/96	320	145	31.5	4,160	6,240	25
1996/97	324	145	32.0	4,550	6,825	25
1997/98	222	72	16.1	10,296	15,444	25
1998/99	*Surcharge abolished*					

Source: PRG (1997a, p.48).

Accord meetings were tense. Grey Power, the lobby group representing the more affluent retired, did not support the government's proposal, and called for nothing less than the full abolition of the surcharge. The Alliance was particularly bitter about the proposal as it did nothing for people who were entirely dependent on the state pension. These people had been excluded from the benefits of the tax package of 1996, the effect of which was to reduce net superannuation as a proportion of the net average wage. As the 'floor' of 65 per cent of the average ordinary wage for a married couple had not been breached, there were no official grounds for an adjustment.[15]

On 3 June 1996, the *Evening Post* headline proclaimed: 'Super accord on last legs'. The *Dominion* editorial of the same day stated that 'the near disinte-gration of the Accord' was 'predictable as it is disappointing'. The surcharge proposal was described as a bribe to voters, 'giving to those who need it least'. Yet the essence of both the Alliance and Labour positions was that the change to the surcharge did not go far enough, so they were seen as scarcely more creditable.[16]

All the Accord partners wanted to prevent the issue becoming a political hot potato because of the opportunity it would present to the fledgling New Zealand First Party. Amid bitterness, and facing the real possibility that the Accord could be finished, the other parties reluctantly acquiesced to the government's proposal for a substantial reduction in the impact of the surcharge, and the bill implementing the change was passed by Parliament.

There was no doubt that decision-making in this situation was proving very difficult.

The adjusted surcharge was implemented on 1 April 1997. Table 15.2 shows the marked increase in the exempt income allowed, although the rate of surcharge remained at 25 per cent. It was calculated that only 16 per cent of superannuitants would be affected by the test, with fewer still in the position of losing all their pension. In effect, the real value of the surcharge exemption that applied before the 1991 Budget had been restored, but not the rate, which remained at 25 per cent. Nevertheless, the marginal tax rate applicable to the majority of surcharge payers was lowered from 28 per cent to 24 per cent in 1996 (and to 21 per cent from July 1998), so that the typical effective marginal tax rate over this period for those paying the surcharge fell from 53 to 49 per cent and would have fallen to 46 per cent in 1998.

Despite the liberalisation of the surcharge, superannuitants on the whole understood little of what had happened. Tensions were apparent as the 1996 election approached. The leader of the New Zealand First Party, Winston Peters, played on the genuine disgust, at times bordering on paranoia, that surrounded the surcharge, and pledged that National's failed 1990 promise to remove it would be honoured. Ironically, the Accord, which had been hailed as the model for the way the new MMP electoral system should work, now appeared (to some at least) to be dead.

The fact that Labour had entered the election year with its own policies on superannuation (to remove the surcharge and to introduce a more progressive tax rate and a dedicated tax to partly pre-fund the Crown's NZS liabilities) was regarded by National as evidence that the Accord had been breached. Bolger later used this to justify National's post-election position on superannuation, which included the referendum on compulsory saving discussed below. However, Labour, the Alliance and United were firmly convinced that it was National that had breached the Accord, and passed a resolution to the effect that National be outside the Accord for as long as it appeared to support compulsory saving.

Developments in 1997

The 1996 election night results gave New Zealand First a major role in determining who would make up the next government. The party had campaigned on getting rid of National, stamping out corruption, and promoting national sovereignty. One of the mechanisms it proposed for achieving this latter goal was a second-tier compulsory saving scheme designed to supplement the state pension. It also promised to abolish the surcharge, claiming that National's reneging on this issue demonstrated the underlying untrustworthiness of politicians. It is not clear why neither National nor Labour stood their ground in the coalition talks and refused to negotiate on issues they had promised to leave to the Accord (see Boston and McLeay, 1997). One of the shortcomings of the Accord was the lack of sanctions on such behaviour, either legally or by way of public opprobrium towards politicians who did not respect the Accord (PRG, 1997a, p.138).

The Coalition Agreement

The coalition negotiations New Zealand First conducted with both National and Labour hinged in part on the way Winston Peter's preference for a compulsory saving scheme was handled. The final agreement with National cut across any vestiges of the latter's attachment to the Accord, first by the unilateral decision to remove the surcharge in 1998, and second by the agreement to hold a referendum on a retirement saving scheme (RSS). As discussed earlier, the decision on the surcharge was a full frontal attack on both the spirit and the letter of the Accord.

After the coalition announcement, Prime Minister Jim Bolger claimed somewhat disingenuously that the removal of the surcharge had made the current state pension unsustainable, and thus justified the entirely different approach of the RSS. Confusingly, he then repeatedly advocated the need for an income test, despite the abolition of the surcharge, arguing that it was not sensible to pay a full universal pension to very well-off retirees. The fiscal pressure the Coalition government was under, together with a dawning realisation that the surcharge had provided some useful additional revenue, may have prompted these views. The baggage associated with the surcharge would also have been uppermost in Bolger's mind. However, his public comments clearly indicated that he had not moved from the 1991 Budget night position that the role of the state pension was to provide little more than a safety net for those in genuine need.

The agreement to hold a referendum in September 1997 led to a flurry of activity in the Treasury, as a design team took on the daunting task of preparing a retirement saving scheme by the beginning of July. It seemed that few of the lessons of the 1974 scheme would be heeded. At the same time, the Periodic Report Group began their separate review of the framework set out in the Accord, despite the apparent fracturing of the Accord by the Coalition Agreement. In response to a request from the government, the group agreed to make an interim report by 31 July 1997.

The Retirement Saving Scheme

When the White Paper on the RSS emerged in early July 1997 (New Zealand Government, 1997b), the scheme originally proposed by New Zealand First was barely recognisable. Winston Peters had wanted increased national savings to 'buy back the family farm', and to make New Zealanders better off in retirement by having access to a pension in addition to NZS. Instead, it was clear that the primary aim of the RSS was to save the state money, and to reduce state involvement by partially privatising the state pension. The result was a one-tier scheme, or a replacement for NZS, not a supplement to it. The regressive nature of the RSS quickly became apparent, and the realisation soon took hold that the scheme would do little to make the average retiree better off next century, while enriching the wealthy.[17]

The RSS had the following features:

- The base for contributions was to be all taxable income, not just employment income as is the case in Australia and Chile.
- The initial contribution rate was 3 per cent, broadly matched by planned tax cuts in 1998, increasing to 8 per cent in the future, with matching tax cuts foreshadowed.[18]
- Most existing employment-based schemes were unlikely to meet the criteria for a RSS fund and were unlikely to adapt to do so. For the employer's contribution to count, it needed to be fully vested or attributed to the employee at the time the contribution was made. In addition, the funds were not to be accessed prior to age 65, when they had to be used to buy an annuity rather than taken as a lump sum. In addition to these restrictions, the funds could not be borrowed against and were required to be invested in a diversified way.
- Once a target level of saving had been achieved, contributions could cease.[19] The White Paper suggested that, in 1997 terms, the capital sum needed to buy an annuity approximating the value of New Zealand Superannuation (that is, 33 per cent of the net average wage for a married person) would be about $120,000. This figure would be revised each year.
- Those people (estimated at 85 per cent of all women and 60 per cent of all men) who were not expected to be able to generate sufficient saving in their RSS accounts to meet the capital requirements would be 'topped up' by the state. As annuities would be provided by the private sector, gender equity would be ensured by a special additional capital top-up for all women.[20]
- The RSS included a guaranteed ten-year period of annuity payments, insurance against the collapse of a provider, and adjustment for any inflation of up to 3 per cent per annum, with any inflation adjustment above this to be met by the state.

The actuarial calculations were based on an arguably optimistic real after-tax return on invested funds, and a likely serious under-estimation of the costs associated with private provision of annuities of the type set out in the RSS. There was to be a long period of transition, during which a taxable NZS would be paid together with the net RSS annuity based on a required capital sum, which would gradually increase until sufficient to fund a full annuity. By the year 2038, all NZS payments would cease for new retirees and the RSS annuity would have replaced the state pension completely. However, it is clear that the state would still have a major funding role in the provision of top-ups.[21] In addition, there was an unquantified liability for taxpayers, as the scheme required the state to be responsible for protecting all existing annuities from any inflation above 3 per cent.

In all this, it was not clear what was the alternative against which the RSS should be compared. For example, the Statement from the Prime Minister and Deputy Prime Minister that prefaced the White Paper contained a diagram contrasting the costs of the RSS with those of the existing scheme. This gave the impression that the tax burden for public payments for retirement would be lower under the RSS from around the year 2017, and would fall sharply as a proportion of GDP after that. But the NZS figures were the *gross* cost of the *wage-adjusted* NZS, while the RSS data were based on the cost of funding an annuity that is tax-free, and adjusted from point of retirement only by prices. By 2051, these two factors would have accounted for a difference in cost of 4 per cent of GDP (New Zealand Government, 1997b, p.10). It could further be argued that the NZS cost in the diagram did not include the surcharge, which was to be removed by the proponents of the RSS, and thus should also have been factored in for a fair comparison.

In addition, the RSS contributions themselves should have been added to the tax cost for the RSS, since the contributions for most workers would have been equivalent to a tax. For workers in the first 30 years of next century, these contributions would have prevented them from using the tax cuts to pay off their mortgages or increase their other savings for retirement; nor could they enjoy the government spending that the tax revenue might have funded. Depending on assumptions about the balance of these factors, taxpayers on average would not have been better off until around 2039.[22] By that stage, the children of the baby-boom generation would themselves be starting to retire, and facing a much less generously indexed pension than the one they had funded for their parents. 'Pay more now to get less later' was one apt description of the way members of the so-called Generation X were to be affected.

One of the arguments for privatising the state pension under the RSS was that it would encourage individual responsibility and give more certainty, security and freedom from state interference. As people would have contributed their 'own' money to the fund that paid for their basic annuity, it was claimed that the government would be less able to interfere with it. Such an argument is highly suspect. For the majority of people, the size of the capital top-up provided by the state would totally determine the size of their annuity, hardly making them less vulnerable to shifts in policy. In the event of premature death, only the personal contributions would become part of the contributor's estate. But had there been no RSS, the tax cuts might have been saved anyway. To promote the RSS as being one's 'own money' was hardly a winning card.[23]

The Periodic Report Group

On 31 July 1997, as promised, the Periodic Report Group published its assessment. The review had not convinced its members that the Accord was dead, nor that the current superannuation framework was in need of radical change. Among the conclusions they presented to the four Accord parties were some stern words about the loss of the link between public and private provision that the surcharge had provided. The essential conclusion of the report was that the existing framework was sound. Projections for government expenditure made by the first task force in 1992 were updated to reflect new demographic data and a sounder initial fiscal position.[24] The repayment of government debt by 2015 was recommended to put government finances in a stronger position once the baby-boomers started to retire in large numbers. The report showed that this was possible, while still meeting all other planned government expenditure.[25] Combining income-testing with either a gradual increase in the age of eligibility to 67 or modified indexation provisions was shown to be an effective mechanism in principle for reducing the final tax:GDP ratio to its level in the early 1990s of around 36 per cent, should that be desired (PRG, 1997a).

The Referendum

The promise that New Zealanders would have the democratic right to vote on the RSS was to prove an expensive one.[26] A 'yes' vote, regardless of the size of the turnout, was to bind the Coalition government to introducing enabling legislation. While there was no guarantee of its final passage, it is clear that unless the public had indicated a strong preference for the scheme, dissident National MPs might not have supported it.[27] In the event, the referendum achieved an astonishing 80.3 per cent voter response in a postal ballot, and sent a resounding 91.8 per cent 'no' vote to the politicians. The size of the turnout and the extent of the rejection were unprecedented in New Zealand's electoral history of nine previous referenda. The support for the scheme was slightly higher in some Māori constituencies and in affluent areas where the ACT Party, which had supported the scheme, might have had some influence.[28]

International Approaches

Every country chooses a mix of retirement income policies to effect the desired access to resources by the retired. Other OECD countries have mixes of basic pensions, social insurance programmes, compulsory saving schemes and tax-subsidised private saving (St John and Ashton, 1993; Littlewood, 1997). New Zealand's arrangements are unique among OECD countries. There are no tax incentives and few regulations for private saving. NZS is paid out of general tax revenue without a contributory link to taxes paid or wages earned, and there are no compulsory contributions to state or private schemes.

International comparisons can be misleading. In other countries, contributions to compulsory private saving schemes are not counted as taxes, and the pensions paid are not counted as state expenditure. It must be remembered too that expenditure on pensions in other countries is seriously understated by the omission of the cost of tax incentives, including the cost of regulations surrounding their use. Nevertheless, OECD countries on average spend nearly 10 per cent of GDP on public pensions. Japan, Germany, France and Italy face ratios of between 14 and 20 per cent of GDP in the first two decades of next century (PRG, 1997a, p.103). Thus the cost of the current state pension in New Zealand seems moderate at a net 4 per cent of GDP, rising to 9 per cent by the middle of next century.

Many OECD countries are concerned that their policies are ill-suited to the problems of ageing, and are trying different methods to reduce the potential claims on resources by the retired population. These include raising the age of eligibility, reducing the generosity of social insurance pensions, and pushing for more private pensions. In the United Kingdom, for example, there have been recent moves to encourage people to opt out of the State Earnings Related Pension Scheme and company plans, and to invest in personal plans. This is despite the historical experience of the high risk and insecurity of such saving, and the propensity of governments to change the rules.[29]

If the objective is to provide an adequate minimum income for all retired people, the New Zealand approach is a highly cost-effective and equitable way of doing it. Littlewood (1997), for example, argues that New Zealand provides a model for other countries to follow. However, its strength—simplicity and fairness—may also be its weakness. There are no clear links between contributions (in the form of taxes paid) and NZS received that might give notions of security and entitlement. There is only a moral obligation based on the idea of an intergenerational contract. The clear link provided by individual contributions to social insurance schemes in other countries makes the resulting pensions more difficult to debase.[30]

The danger in New Zealand is that the state pension could be vulnerable, as it was in 1991, to being reduced to a welfare benefit only. If the state is involved only to the extent of providing a means-tested safety net for those who have not saved, none of the failures of private markets for saving and pensions are addressed (Ashton and St John, 1988). Under such a system, many middle-income people will find their aspirations for a comfortable retirement unmet, while the less affluent face stigmatising abatement regimes that inhibit saving and work effort.

Issues for the Future

In the wake of the referendum, New Zealand is left clinging once more to its traditional approach of a basic, taxable, individually based state pension, with its virtues of simplicity, flexibility and fairness. Nonetheless, the broader issue of how different generations are faring suggests that conflict lies ahead (Thomson, 1996). There are no tax incentives, no compulsion for private provision, and now no mechanism to claw back the state pension from the very well-off. In the context of low tax rates and high user charges for the working-age population, a universal pension sufficient to meet the needs of people with no other saving (except perhaps their own home) raises profound issues of intergenerational equity.[31]

Adjustments to NZS

In the absence of an income test of any kind, there will doubtless be more pressure over time for a sharp lowering of the level of NZS or a raising of the age of entitlement. Yet the interests of the vast majority of retirees, who have only modest additional resources, would be better served by re-imposing a surcharge-like income test. Raising the age would be particularly harsh for many people whose ability to earn has been limited, for example by caregiving or redundancy.

It is clear that simply re-imposing the surcharge is untenable in the current political environment. It is unfortunate that few people, including those in Grey Power, understood the possibility of less attractive alternatives such as a DSW income test. The parameters of the surcharge in 1997/98, as set out in Table 15.2, meant that few people would expect to be affected by it at all, especially the more elderly superannuitants.[32]

While Labour and the Alliance have reiterated their support for a full universal state pension, prominent National MPs have talked about a universal part-pension and a tightly targeted top-up. It is clear that without the stability provided by the Accord, the voices of those who would prefer the state pension to be a minimal welfare benefit will become more strident. Economic commentator Gareth Morgan expressed such a preference, somewhat unfeelingly, as follows:

> Simplicity, minimal intervention and addressing real need is the only rationale for state payouts. This means leave it to self provision but then provide a superannuation annuity of last resort to those who fall short of the means to provide for themselves. Most importantly this safety net should be slung so low

that nobody would aspire to such a measly income. If it is not set that low the hazard of people deliberately seeking to qualify for the state pension will boost the burden on the rest of us taxpayers unnecessarily. Further to qualify the applicant must be both income and asset tested (New Zealand Herald, 5 August 1997).

The Political Process for Policy Decision-Making: A New Accord?

The 1993 Accord represented a unique compromise between the Left and the Right, in which the surcharge played a crucial role. It is difficult to see a new multi-party agreement being forged in the current political environment, especially now that the ACT Party, not a signatory to the Accord, is a significant force in Parliament. Easton (1997c), for example, has argued that the very nature of the competitive electoral system now in place under MMP makes a stable Accord unlikely. The first-past-the-post system favoured the dominance of two large established parties, akin to an oligopoly. An effective Accord was possible because it could be in the interests of the main parties to collude in removing retirement support as a contentious political issue, thereby reducing fiscal pressures. Easton's argument is illustrated by New Zealand First's refusal to join the Accord, and its subsequent electoral success based in part on attracting the older vote. Easton suggests, however, that it may be possible to get a majority of the parties to agree on some common fundamental features of retirement policy, with each party offering variations on top of the agreed base. Thus there may still be a place for a successful Accord process, providing the expectations are not for total agreement by all parties.

The PRG's (1997b) concluding report set out a new process for establishing a multi-party agreement, and identified many thorny issues. For example, what should now be the starting point when there are so many different views on the appropriate nature of NZS? Who should chair the Accord? Should it have its own secretariat? How should decisions be taken? What should constitute a breach of the Accord? Should there be sanctions? How much freedom should individual·parties have to promote their own policies in elections? What should be the role of the Retirement Commissioner? However difficult these challenges may seem, the alternative of returning to the political machinations of the past decade is bound to be worse.

Conclusion

New Zealanders made it clear in the 1997 referendum that they prefer the collective arrangements for NZS and do not want a fundamental reform of the basic pension. Women in particular expressed their support for the current system, and its individual, non-contributory nature. With good reason, they have been uneasy about suggestions that it might be tightly targeted as a way of reducing state spending (St John, 1997b).

It is also evident that a universal pension that is high enough to remove those with no other income from the poverty statistics, together with low tax rates in a user-pays, targeted environment for the working-age population, is a recipe for intergenerational conflict. If the surcharge had remained in place, it might have been possible to convince elderly New Zealanders that their state pension was a genuine entitlement, but to an income 'floor', not a flat-rate pension. As they aged and used up their own resources, they could expect to get an increased share from the state in a simple, dignified manner.[33] The failure to find this middle way between a universal entitlement and a targeted welfare payment bodes ill for the future sustainability of New Zealand's unique retirement income policies.

Endnotes

1 The dependency ratio is the number of people aged 65 and over as a percentage of the working-age population (aged 15-64). The total dependency ratio measures those aged 65 and over plus those under 15 as a percentage of those aged 15-64.

2 Workforce participation rates for those aged 15 and over have increased from 29.6 per cent to 57.9 per cent for women, and decreased from 83.8 per cent to 73 per cent for men in the period 1961-1996 (Statistics New Zealand, 1997c). For those aged 45 and over, participation rates in the full- and part-time workforce have almost doubled among women, while remaining much the same for men. The PRG (1997a, p.28) noted a significant increase in participation rates for those over 60, in line with the lifting of the age of eligibility for NZS.

3 In 1995/96, 72 per cent of women and 54 per cent of men over 65 received at least three-quarters of their income from NZS.

4 'Funded' in the sense that contributions from employer and employee were to be accumulated and invested, with the fund earnings added to the balance. 'Full funding' of schemes ensures actuarial soundness and conformity to private insurance and investment principles. There was an opportunity to contract out for those in suitable private schemes.

5 It was to be about 8 per cent of the current personal income tax base, marked off as a notional tax, not a new one. It was not accumulated separately, but rather used to pay current benefits.

6 It was to be income-tested on a family basis, with the same low level of exemption for both a married couple and a single person. The effective marginal tax rate for a married couple was 92.8 per cent over the income range of $4,160—$23,740. For those over 70, half of the benefit would have become a universal, non-income-tested payment, but in essence the only beneficiaries were the wealthiest older retirees. Some married retirees, with incomes from other sources of around $23,000, for example, found to their horror that the income test would leave them as much as $10,000 worse off.

7 The Accord had provided for the exemption to be inflation-adjusted from time to time. The changes that were agreed as necessary were set out in the Tax Reduction and Social Policy Bill, February 1996.

8 The 39 per cent tax did not nearly approximate the 53 and 58 per cent marginal rates paid through the surcharge from the low exemption, as it was in 1993 (see Table 15.2).

Moreover, the 39 per cent rate would have affected very few superannuitants, as only a tiny number have incomes over $60,000. However, as Labour's tax scale implied no tax on NZS for those with no other income, NZS would have been reduced by 15 per cent to retain its parity. Thus, a gross pension of $10,000 would fall to $8,500 after the Labour tax changes. A retiree on the 33 per cent tax rate would pay $2,805 tax, making the effective tax rate on the original gross pension 43 per cent. This range of effective marginal tax is not too dissimilar to the rates that would have applied for most surcharge payers from 1998, had the surcharge been retained.

9 In the midst of the confusion, Labour and the Alliance had convened an unofficial Accord meeting. Among the issues decided was the right to rotate the chair and for any two parties to have the right to call a meeting.

10 This was received with 'good spirit', but the issue was not resolved. The Accord parties agreed not to comment on the issue outside the Accord.

11 For example, the *New Zealand Herald* trumpeted: 'Verge of collapse as only National supports surcharge' (15 March 1996).

12 The 1.1 factor was to reflect timing problems, as the intention was to relate this to 100 per cent of the average wage. The change was expected to cost $85-100 million per annum, affecting 66,000-69,000 pensioners (13-15 per cent).

13 This provision would give superannuitant couples $34,900 a year, and singles $23,000, before any pension was lost. The effect would be to raise the cut-out point for a married couple (assuming equal earnings) to $71,512, and $45,920 for a single person.

14 To be carried out under the chairmanship of Jeff Todd and known as the Periodic Report Group.

15 The gross married person rate of NZS was only just above the first tax threshold, which was unadjusted by the tax reductions.

16 Nevertheless, the Alliance's objection to National's proposal was that it reduced the surcharge but did not propose a progressive income tax in its stead, as required by the Accord. The Alliance eventually indicated that it would agree to Labour's proposal for a marginal rate of 39 cents in the dollar above $60,000, to be introduced along with the abolition of the surcharge.

17 The Council of Trade Unions mounted a vigorous campaign, co-ordinating opposition from many diverse factions (including the New Zealand Business Roundtable) through the Internet.

18 For those on low incomes and those on high incomes, the contributions would exceed the tax cuts. For some, with incomes in the high $30,000s or low $40,000s, the tax cuts exceeded the contributions. Future tax cuts were likely to involve the reduction of the top marginal tax rate, thus benefiting the better-off.

19 The idea of a cap on saving is unusual and would doubtless have proved problematic. There are no examples in other countries of schemes that have a similar provision, although some have other restrictions on contributions.

20 The higher capital sum was to reflect their greater longevity. While this apparently ensured gender equity—as it allowed private insurers to pay the same pension to women as to men—it was viewed by many women as another instance of having to go 'cap in hand' to the government.

21 Even at full maturity, tax-based funding of the RSS (through 'top-up' contributions to the annuity providers) accounted for as much as 40 per cent of the scheme's cash-flow.

22 It was clear that better-off income earners who reached the capital goal quickly would be better off, as they would then enjoy tax cuts. On the other hand, low income earners could

contribute for a lifetime and not end up with a higher than basic RSS annuity. The impact of funding and payouts was highly regressive.

23 New Zealand First promoted the scheme as good for Māori, because of their lower life expectancy. On death before 75, the balance of personal contributions in the RSS fund would be able to pay for the tangi. It appeared difficult to find much more to say in the scheme's favour.

24 This included improved life-expectancy data and revised health costs for older people. These factors altered the projections for tax as a percentage of GDP out to the year 2051, but not markedly so.

25 The baseline projection includes the tax cuts of 1998 but does not prescribe or project future tax burdens. In the next decade or so, the government could have higher taxes and higher spending, and also run surpluses that are sufficient to repay debt.

26 The costs of developing the White Paper, the independent referendum panel, the public education programme and the final postal ballot were perhaps as high as $20 million.

27 Jenny Shipley, for example, campaigned vigorously against the RSS—unlike Jim Bolger.

28 It is clear that for many very well-off voters, the RSS was almost an irrelevance except to the extent that such a constituency believes there is moral virtue in requiring the less affluent to save.

29 The Maxwell scheme is often cited as an example of how private pensions can go wrong, although no pensioner has actually lost out as a result of Maxwell's actions. There are other concerns in the United Kingdom, including the high costs of private arrangements, poor returns, and the lack of ability to protect against the ravages of inflation. Under reforms to the State Earnings Related Pension Scheme (SERPS), many people were mis-sold personal plans and there are now billions of pounds of compensation to be paid.

30 Not completely so, however, as rises in the contributions and the age of eligibility in many countries attest.

31 Asset- and income-tests for public hospitals and asset-tests for private geriatric care are also to be removed in 1998. The better-off older population have also benefited from personal tax reductions since 1986 and the introduction of the more regressive Goods and Services Tax. Those of young working age are increasingly disadvantaged by the abandonment of universal welfare provisions of all kinds and the introduction of student loans.

32 For example, a couple would need over $1 million in the bank earning 7 per cent before they lost all entitlement.

33 One of the options canvassed by the PRG (1997b) would achieve the same effect as the surcharge but have a more acceptable presentation. It would involve paying NZS as a tax rebate, abated through the tax system: in effect, a negative income tax.

PART III

SUMMARY AND CONCLUSION

CHAPTER SIXTEEN

REBUILDING AN EFFECTIVE WELFARE STATE

JONATHAN BOSTON, PAUL DALZIEL
AND SUSAN ST JOHN

Soon after its landslide victory in the 1990 general election, the National government created a series of task forces to examine a wide range of social policies under the direction of a special Ministerial Committee on the Reform of Social Assistance (Bolger et al., 1990, p.11). The policy reforms produced by that process were then unveiled in Ruth Richardson's 1991 Budget, along with the following justification (Richardson, 1991, p.7):

> The redesign of the welfare state is integral to our strategy for growth. We cannot make economic progress without reforming our social systems, nor can social and economic policy be divorced from one another. The only sustainable welfare state is one that is fair and affordable. Our current system is neither.

The contributors to this volume have documented and analysed the policy changes that were introduced over the next seven years in industrial relations, health, accident compensation, education, housing, social welfare, employment assistance and superannuation. Their unanimous assessment is that the Richardson reforms failed or fell short in many important respects. Overall, New Zealanders are not 'more confident, more prosperous, more self-reliant, and more secure' (Richardson, 1991, p.5). Poverty and social exclusion have intensified, income disparities have widened and unemployment remains a serious problem. The social problems associated with these trends are imposing new economic costs on the individuals concerned, and also on the government in the form of new prisons, a larger police force and rising numbers of people receiving income support, despite the savage benefit cuts in April 1991. In short, the objective of producing a fair and affordable welfare state has not been realised.

The following sub-sections briefly summarise our contributors' major criticisms of the post-1990 reforms in the eight policy areas addressed in this book. Each sub-section begins with a relevant quote from the 1991 Budget, drawing attention to the gap between rhetoric and outcomes that has bedevilled social policy during the 1990s. The chapter then picks up the challenge made in the government's 1998 discussion booklet, *Towards a Code of Social and Family Responsibility*, to look for answers to these problems. Our response to this challenge does not share the booklet's strong individualist approach, nor do we accept its claim that the fundamental problems are social and not economic. This leads us to a lengthier discussion about the role of full employment in rebuilding an effective welfare state, before the final section examines the implications of this for future public policy.

Industrial Relations

> We had three urgent objectives. The first was to reform the labour market to give New Zealand one of the most dynamic industrial relations frameworks in the world. That reform is now in place. (Richardson, 1991, p.20)

In Chapter 7, Walsh and Brosnan draw on workplace surveys undertaken in May 1991 and May 1995 to assess the impact the Employment Contracts Act 1991 has had on labour conditions. They find little change in the overall structure of the workforce. The proportion of workers in permanent employment was remarkably stable in the two surveys (83.8 and 83.5 per cent respectively, albeit with some increase in part-time employment among permanent staff). Although the percentage of fixed-term and temporary appointments increased, there was a comparable fall in casual employment (see Table 7.1). Trade union membership, however, dropped precipitately under the Act. Walsh and Brosnan estimate that only 19 per cent of workplaces have any union members at all (Table 7.3), and that unions have very little role in workplace change decisions in those that do (Table 7.4). There is a much wider dispersion of wage settlements than under previous legislation, and the overall trend of falling real wages has continued. The Act may have provided opportunities for employers and employees to negotiate more appropriate working conditions in some workplaces, and may have allowed employee exploitation in others. This is hard to measure, however, since employment contracts are private documents which are not published (unlike the former award documents). Most importantly, the Act has failed to deliver higher productivity growth or lower unemployment than was being achieved in the period before New Zealand's economic reforms began in 1984 (see Figures 4.1 and 10.1).

Health

> The changes we have announced are far reaching, but nothing less will provide an affordable health system that works. The Government will carefully manage the changes over the next three years to ensure services are fully maintained. (Richardson, 1991, p.12)

Ashton in Chapter 8 records how some of the changes to the health system announced in the 1991 Budget turned out to be problematic, and how one key element (the proposal for individuals or groups to have the ability to choose alternative health care plans) had to be abandoned. Such policy U-turns have been a common experience internationally with market-oriented reforms in health. In New Zealand, real health expenditure per capita has continued to rise (driven largely by increased expenditure in the private sector—see Figure 8.2), and public hospitals are treating more patients who on average are experiencing shorter stays (Table 8.1). The hospitals are not keeping within budget, however, and surgical waiting lists increased between 1990 and 1996 (Figures 8.3 and 8.4). Ashton summarises her assessment with a passage from the Ministry of Health (1996b, p.16) acknowledging the disappointing health sector performance: 'costs have not been constrained in line with planned funding growth; both CHEs and RHAs have experienced deficits; although total output has increased, access to some services appears to have reduced; and only 35 percent of public health targets are expected to be achieved.' The Ministry continues with the observation that there is 'widespread lack of confidence in the ability of the sector to meet performance expectations and in the credibility of policy settings'.

Accident Compensation

The Government is reforming accident compensation to reduce costs and to spread the cost of the scheme more fairly. (Richardson, 1991, p.13)

Accident Compensation is the only social insurance initiative in New Zealand that is primarily funded by earmarked levies and taxes. In Chapter 9, St John records the erratic funding policies that have been implemented with respect to ACC over the years, reflected in widely fluctuating deficits/ surpluses and financial reserves (see Table 9.2). A major reform of the Act in 1992 narrowed the definition of personal injury by accident, and reduced compensation levels in some cases, particularly by removing lump-sum payments for pain, suffering and loss of enjoyment of life. The responsibility for funding the non-work accidents of workers was passed to a new levy on employee wages—the earners' premium. In November 1997, a work-capacity assessment procedure was introduced, with the intention of shifting long-term claimants deemed fit for 30 hours of paid employment per week onto income support (provided by the Department of Social Welfare) if they are unable to find work. These initiatives have slowed the growth of ACC expenditure (Table 9.2), but St John argues that they have also undermined the social contract on which ACC was established; namely, that accident victims give up the right to sue in return for *comprehensive* accident insurance.

Education

> Education is a key investment in our economic future. The Government is determined to provide an environment that enables businesses and individuals to develop internationally competitive and innovative skills. . . . We will improve the quality of our education system from pre-school through to university. (Richardson, 1991, pp.20-21)

The National government elected in 1990 inherited a compulsory education system that had already been subject to far-reaching reforms as a result of the Picot Report and *Tomorrow's Schools*. It carried on those reforms through the development of the National Qualifications Framework set up in the Education Act 1989, launching the new National Curriculum and the National Certificate in 1991. The government also abolished school zoning in 1991. It is, perhaps, too early to judge the impact of the National Qualifications Framework (which has both strong advocates and detractors), but Peters and Olssen in Chapter 10 cite research that shows the end of school zoning is producing socio-economic segregation between schools that is likely to enhance the divisions already existing in the wider society.

In Chapter 11, Boston reports that the government has increased its spending on tertiary education, but inflation-adjusted public expenditure per equivalent full-time student was reduced by almost 10 per cent between 1992 and 1997. By the end of 1997, when the student loan scheme had been operating for six years, around 230,000 people had loans, of whom 100,000 were still borrowing. The average amount borrowed was approximately $10,000, representing a large debt burden at a stage in the life cycle when young people are likely to be looking for loans to finance the beginning of a career or the purchase of their first home.

Housing

> The Government is making changes that will provide a fairer, more effective service to people in need of accommodation assistance. (Richardson, 1991, p.16)

The government's reform of housing policy involved transforming the management of the public housing stock into a commercial business, with all housing assistance delivered through an income-targeted accommodation supplement. Murphy records in Chapter 12 that the cost of the supplement has been considerably higher than expected, and continues to grow (see Figure 12.1). Despite this, 80 per cent of the 33,000 special benefit payments made in 1996 were due to high housing costs, including 9,000 payments to tenants of Housing New Zealand. Foodbanks have reported that poverty related to the cost of housing is an important factor for their clients. The move to market rates has significantly raised rents for Housing New Zealand tenants, particularly in the Auckland area. The rent differentials in different suburbs of Auckland, and the subsequent reconfiguration of the public housing stock towards cheaper areas, are beginning to reinforce a ghettoisation of state tenants on the urban periphery, with all the social costs associated with this type of socio-spatial polarisation.

Social Welfare

The Government believes that protecting and improving the position of low-income families is a key priority. That is why we favour targeting more of the available assistance to those in genuine need and asking those who are better-off to pay more for the social services they use. (Richardson, 1991, p.8)

Stephens observes early in Chapter 13 that the immediate impact of the April 1991 benefit cuts was a substantial increase in the level and severity of poverty and hardship, with many beneficiaries having to supplement their family finances with food parcels from mainly church-based foodbanks. This is not surprising, since Figure 13.2 shows that income support, adjusted for inflation, is now back to what the Royal Commission on Social Security (1972) described as a subsistence level. On an international scale, New Zealand in 1993 ranked sixteenth out of eighteen OECD countries in terms of the average generosity of its family assistance package. The New Zealand Poverty Measurement project, of which Stephens is a member, has estimated that using a focus-group defined absolute poverty measure, the number of people living in poverty increased from 159,000 in 1984 to 393,000 in 1993 (see also Table 13.3). The number of children in poor households also more than doubled, from 82,000 in 1984 to 186,000 in 1993. Social security expenditure has become more tightly targeted, but rather than providing more resources to those who need it most, many low-income families have been forced into increasing levels of financial hardship.

Employment Assistance

Many people will be encouraged to take greater responsibility for themselves where they had previously relied on the state. Others will be excited by a greater range of choices and opportunities opening up for them. Others again will be reassured by the Government's clear commitment that those most in need receive a fair deal from our social services. (Richardson, 1991, p.20)

Over the last two decades, more stringent work-tests have been applied to those receiving social assistance. In 1991, formal rules were introduced in which sanctions were applied if a recipient turned down a second offer of 'suitable employment' or a second job interview. Since 1997, the sanctions have applied if any offer of suitable employment or training opportunity is refused. The government is going further down this track with the introduction of a work-for-the-dole scheme. Higgins analyses the proposed change in Chapter 14. Even if only the long-term unemployed were targeted, this would involve nearly 87,000 people a year, which would inevitably interfere with the operation of the labour market (especially through displacement of people already in employment and through downward pressure on wages in the low-wage sector). Further, Higgins argues that this form of reciprocal obligation on the part of beneficiaries represents an admission by policymakers that full employment is no longer a realistic goal.

Superannuation

> The new National Superannuation scheme we are announcing tonight owes much to the work of the Royal Commission on Social Policy. However, in many respects, the new provisions are more generous than the Royal Commission's recommendations. (Richardson, 1991, p.17)

The superannuation reforms announced in the 1991 Budget created a storm of protest, and were very quickly repealed in favour of a return to the old National Superannuation, with a higher surcharge and a lower threshold. The increase in the age of eligibility from 60 to 65, phased in over ten years, remained. When New Zealand First gained the balance of power in the 1996 election, it effectively held National to its 1990 promise to remove the controversial surcharge. Unfortunately, this policy is expensive ($253 million per annum), and represents a large redistribution of income towards the households of the wealthiest older New Zealanders. Policies that provide pensions on a universal basis, while other age groups face tighter targeting and user-pays, are likely to be perceived as unfair, thus creating political tensions between younger and older members of the electorate. While the compulsory Retirement Saving Scheme was rejected by 91.8 per cent of voters in the referendum of September 1997, the lack of clear political leadership on alternatives has undermined the former agreement on superannuation policy effected in the 1993 Accord. In 1998 there appears to be little appreciation of why the state needs to be involved in the provision of retirement income. In the absence of a clear philosophy, the universal state pension now seems vulnerable to future change, with a clear risk that the burden of any future fiscal adjustments may fall on the poorest of older New Zealanders.

The Code of Social and Family Responsibility

The failure of the Richardson reforms of 1991 was implicitly acknowledged by the present Prime Minister (Shipley, 1998) when she made the following observations in her opening address to Parliament on 17 February 1998:

Economic policy and social policy can't stand alone. They must be dealt with together as part of the whole. In this context most would agree the big outstanding challenge New Zealand faces is to reverse the trends that show too many New Zealanders not realising their full potential, not receiving income from paid work, not coping with the demands of modern society. We can turn this round. We can put it right. For this reason the National/New Zealand First Government believes that social policy must be on top of the agenda for every New Zealander in 1998.

This is a clear echo of the Richardson paragraph cited at the beginning of this chapter. In contrast to the policy process of strict budget secrecy that produced the Richardson reforms, however, the Prime Minister and Deputy Prime Minister launched a public discussion booklet and survey, calling on all citizens 'to work with other New Zealanders as we look for the answers' (New Zealand Government, 1998, p.1).[1] The essays in this volume are written in precisely that spirit of co-operative inquiry in the face of what are recognised as serious policy problems. There are, however, two aspects of the approach taken in the government's booklet, *Towards a Code of Social and Family Responsibility*, that stand in stark contrast to the approach adopted by our contributors. First, the booklet invokes a strongly individualist approach to what it calls 'social responsibility'. Indeed, Boston (1998) points out that seven of its eleven expectations are primarily concerned with parental responsibilities, while the other four focus on the responsibilities individuals have to look after themselves. Boston suggests that these expectations might therefore be more accurately described as making up a 'Code of Parental and Individual Responsibility'.

Part I of this volume discussed 'social responsibility' from two very different perspectives. In Chapter 2, Boston drew on Western philosophical traditions concerned with the tension between individual liberty and social justice, while Henare in Chapter 3 drew on traditional Māori values, particularly as expressed in his own region of Muriwhenua, to discuss what is authentic to Māori for sustainable social development. Despite their different starting points, both authors reach a similar conclusion in their assessment of what is the key moral value underpinning the welfare state; namely, the social responsibility of the community to work towards ensuring that all its members are able to live in dignity and to participate in the life and culture of their society. Boston quotes with approval the famous statement by the Royal Commission on Social Security (1972, p.65): 'The community is responsible for giving dependent people a standard of living consistent with human dignity and approaching that enjoyed by the majority, irrespective of the cause of dependency.' For Henare, taking action to implement this principle is a basic element in his definition of a tribe. He argues, for example, that urban Māori

authorities such as Te Waipareira Trust should be included among the beneficiaries of the Treaty of Waitangi Fisheries Commission, precisely because their
work in promoting the economic and social development of their members
entitles the authorities to call themselves modern Māori tribes.

This interpretation of social responsibility, which is defended by Boston
against market-liberal objections in Chapter 2 and connected to other Māori
cultural values by Henare in Chapter 3, leads to the rejection of an individualist 'safety net' approach to social policy. Resources beyond subsistence level
are required to reintegrate people into community participation if family
responsibilities, unemployment, illness, accident, disability or retirement
threaten to push them to the margins of society for any length of time. This
view of social responsibility has been regarded as 'fair' by generations of
New Zealanders.

The second point of issue we take with the government's approach
concerns the claim made in the opening sentence of *Towards a Code of Social
and Family Responsibility* that 'New Zealand has a strong economy and is
competitive internationally', with the implication (developed in the
remainder of the discussion booklet) that New Zealand's problems are
primarily social rather than economic. Such an approach excludes economic
policy from the parameters of the debate, and in our view is fundamentally
misplaced. The remainder of this chapter defends our claim that the search for
solutions to New Zealand's social problems must include a critical analysis of
the government's economic framework.

The Central Role of Productive Employment

[The Social Security Fund] is now being used for all those miscellaneous
payments included under the heading of Social Security. One of these payments
is sustenance for those unable to find employment. This fund can only meet
sustenance payments while there are comparatively few in need of it. *This means
the continuation of full employment by other means*. If it is not provided by private
enterprise, it must be provided by the State, either out of other taxation or by
financing from the government's Reserve Bank or from public borrowing.
(Sutch, 1941, p.140, emphasis added)

The founding of the modern welfare state in New Zealand took place with the
passing on 13 September 1938 of the Social Security Act—described by
Michael Joseph Savage's biographer as 'the crowning achievement of the
first Labour Government and probably the most important single piece of
legislation in New Zealand's history' (Gustafson, 1986, p.221). Sutch's
comments (quoted above) illustrate how that landmark initiative was
designed around the assumption that full employment would be maintained

'by other means'. Full employment was necessary not only to ensure fair access to market incomes by all workers (thus guaranteeing low demands on the social security budget), but also to generate the income required to afford universal provision of health care and other social services. Hence, from the very beginning, full employment was the keystone of New Zealand's welfare state.

This feature, which was shared by Australian developments, has led more recent commentators such as Bryson (1992), Du Plessis (1993) and Castles (1996) to describe the Antipodean systems as 'male wage-earners' welfare states' (see Chapter 14, note 14). The increase in female participation rates that occurred from the mid-1960s, accompanied by equal pay legislation and other important policy changes, increased the available labour supply considerably and broke down aspects of the former system's male orientation. These developments did not, however, diminish the importance of the fundamental principle that economic policies had to sustain full employment for the country's social policies to be fair and affordable.

Figure 16.1 Registered Unemployment in New Zealand, 1960-1997

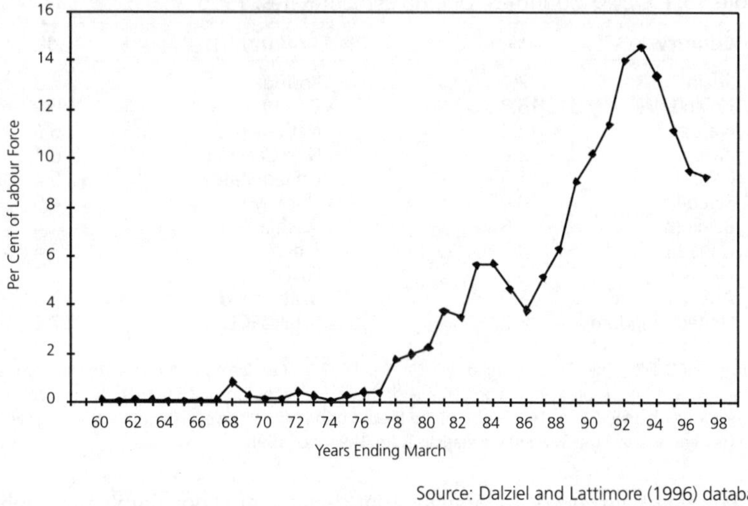

Source: Dalziel and Lattimore (1996) database.

Consider, therefore, Figure 16.1, which presents a graph of New Zealand's registered unemployment rate for the financial years (ending March) 1960 to 1997. Throughout the post-war period until the late 1970s, unemployment was remarkably low, threatening to reach one per cent of the labour force only in the recession of 1967/68.[2] By 1980, however, unemployment was above 2 per cent, rising above 3.5 per cent the following year and beyond 5.5 per cent in 1983 and 1984. By 1987, registered unemployment was on the rise again, to

6.3 per cent in 1988, to 10.2 per cent in 1990, and peaking at 14.6 per cent in 1993. There has been some improvement since, with the rate falling back to 9.3 per cent in 1997, but this is still far too high for a welfare system that was most effective when the registered unemployment rate was less than one per cent (see Rosenberg, 1977, for an expression of this view two decades ago, when unemployment was first emerging as a problem in the post-war period). The loss of full employment, in our view, is a fundamental cause of the higher taxes needed to maintain New Zealand's welfare state at the end of the 1990s, compared with two decades earlier.

The experience of high and persistent unemployment is not unique to New Zealand. Table 16.1 presents standardised unemployment data for OECD countries. Most OECD countries have higher rates of unemployment than New Zealand, despite New Zealand's rate being enormously higher than it was in the 1960s. Mass unemployment is a global problem, which some economists suggest will require global policies to solve; for example, through changes to the international monetary system, and internationally co-ordinated stabilisation policies (Arestis and Sawyer, 1998, pp.189, 191-3).

Table 16.1 OECD Countries' Unemployment Rates, 1996

Country	%	Country	%
Spain	22.1	Portugal	7.3
Finland	15.3	Denmark	6.9
France	12.4	Netherlands	6.3
Italy	12.0	New Zealand	6.1
Ireland	11.6	United States	5.4
Sweden	10.0	Norway	4.9
Belgium	9.8	Austria	4.4
Canada	9.7	Japan	3.4
Germany	8.9	Luxembourg	3.3
Australia	8.6	Switzerland	3.3
United Kingdom	8.2	Total OECD	7.6

Source: OECD Economic Outlook, vol.62, December 1997, Annex Table 22. All data are standardised unemployment rates expressed as a percentage of the civilian labour force. Note that the New Zealand figure is lower than in Figure 16.1, because the table is using official survey data rather than registered data (see endnote 2). The Switzerland statistic is for 1995, not 1996.

The point also needs to be made that the answer is not simply more jobs, regardless of the quality of those jobs. If further growth in expenditure in health and education is to be affordable—not to mention the pressures of meeting the retirement needs of New Zealand's ageing population over the next half century—the workforce must be engaged in *high productivity* employment. This is why the result reported in Chapter 4 of this volume, that there is still no obvious increase in labour productivity growth after the decade of radical economic reform between 1984 and 1993 (see Figure 4.1), is so worrying. High unemployment and low productivity growth will inevitably create fundamental economic and social problems for New Zealand, regardless of the outcome of current debates about the proper division between private and public sector provision of goods and services. Against this background, policies that reduce income support through social welfare simply shift the economic burden of high unemployment and low productivity growth from taxpayers in general to individuals who very often are the least able to cope with the consequences. Again, this is not unique to New Zealand. Western welfare states everywhere are struggling to design suitable economic and social policies in response to the mass unemployment and widespread low-wage employment that emerged during the last three decades of the twentieth century (see, for example, Esping-Andersen, 1996b, pp.24-7).

The quote from Sutch at the beginning of this section illustrates another important issue. Policymakers in the late 1930s accepted that if full employment 'is not provided by private enterprise, it must be provided by the State, either out of other taxation or by financing from the government's Reserve Bank or from public borrowing'. Space does not permit a discussion here of the protectionist policies that were initiated in the middle of this century to create an employment-rich light industry sector to achieve that goal; of how the logic of that strategy broke down with the loss in 1973 of the guaranteed agricultural markets in the United Kingdom; of how the government responded in the late 1970s and early 1980s with temporary work schemes and the ill-fated Think Big projects; or of how most of this was swept away by Rogernomics after 1984. Nor is there room to discuss why the policy framework of the mid-twentieth century is no longer appropriate, given New Zealand's obligations under international and regional trading agreements and the likely reaction of the global financial markets. But we believe an important point of principle has been lost over the last decade and a half, which needs to be recovered as the first step towards rebuilding an effective welfare state.

The economic forces creating mass global unemployment are far beyond the power of any individual to control. Certainly, the sudden and steep rise in unemployment during the period of New Zealand's economic reforms points to structural rather than individual explanations. Once this is accepted, it is unrealistic to define social responsibility solely in terms of expectations that 'people will take responsibility for developing the skills and knowledge they need to help them get a job, or take on a new job', and that 'people receiving income support will seek full-time or part-time work (where appropriate), or take steps to improve their chances of getting a job' (New Zealand Government, 1998). On their own, these expectations simply blame the victims of global economic change for an outcome over which they have no influence. As social responsibility was originally understood by the architects of New Zealand's modern welfare state, these expectations must be matched by a commitment to use the powers of the state to achieve and maintain productive full employment.

This is all the more important in the context of the downturn in economic growth experienced by New Zealand in 1997 and 1998. The 1994-95 recovery from the depressed years of the early 1990s ran out of steam (the downturn reinforced by domestic drought and Asian currency crises), with New Zealand data revealing very high current account deficits and record levels of private sector overseas debt. Domestic real interest rates were pushed up to become the highest in the OECD, while unemployment again rose above 7 per cent, further eroding the opportunities available to low-income households. If the costs of adjustment to this downturn are not to be imposed on the most vulnerable members of New Zealand society (as happened in 1991), future economic and social policies must be designed around the government accepting a role in achieving and maintaining full employment.

This is not idle speculation. The city of Auckland, for example, has been under enormous strain during the mid to late 1990s, with its transport and other public systems stretched to capacity and beyond by rapid population and economic growth. Public investment in infrastructure could create large returns to the city's population, and at the same time create new industries, provide productive employment for workers (who would thus have an incentive to invest in acquiring the necessary skills), and allow regional development in some industry-starved regions of the North Island. The planning and co-ordination required to achieve this should be (and once would have been) accepted as the social responsibility of central government.

In this context, the 1998 Budget was a bitter disappointment. Instead of promoting state involvement in regional and infrastructure development, the government persevered with its previously announced work-for-the-dole programme and its plans to work-test all working-age people receiving benefits (see Chapter 14). In a continuation of the 1991 benefit cuts, the brunt of the fiscal costs of adjustment was borne by beneficiaries, while the better-off received significant income tax cuts. With few exceptions, all invalid's, sickness, domestic purposes and widow's benefits became work-tested. Thus a large number of new competitors for scarce part-time jobs will be forced into the job market. The sickness benefit was frozen for existing claimants, and reduced to the level of the unemployment benefit for new beneficiaries after 1 July 1998 (Peters, 1998b, p.14). While these measures will increase employment for social welfare administrators and enforcers, this is not the high-quality employment growth New Zealand needs.

There is no shortage of worthwhile work to be done in New Zealand. We have already mentioned the need for infrastructure and regional development. As the population ages, there are increasing demands for caregiving and health services of all kinds. Quality childcare and education are two other areas where many more people could be gainfully employed. Affordable housing remains in short supply in the main centres. Expenditure on research and development is low by OECD standards. In our view, the challenge faced by government is to find appropriate ways to co-ordinate the creation of worthwhile jobs out of these work opportunities.

The Way Forward

The previous section has highlighted the need to reaffirm New Zealand's earlier commitment to a policy of full employment as a critical step in the process of rebuilding the welfare state. Such a commitment will entail, among other things, significant additional public investment in education and training, in research and development, and in physical infrastructure, together with the strengthening of social institutions and social capital. We are aware, of course, that any additional public expenditure must be paid for, and that this in turn raises important questions about tax policy, the proper size of the state, and the potential for 'government failure'. While it is not possible to address such issues in detail here, a number of broad principles and considerations need to be emphasised.

First, the making of public policy inevitably entails trade-offs; no society can have every desirable good simultaneously. Accordingly, priorities must be set. Second, in rebuilding an effective welfare state, careful attention must be given to the issue of economic incentives. High marginal tax rates, for example, create incentives for avoidance and evasion, while at the same time reducing the incentive to seek employment or engage in economic activity. Third, having endured a comprehensive and far-reaching programme of economic and social policy reform since the mid-1980s, New Zealand arguably needs a period of relative policy stability. This does not mean simply living with the status quo, but it does suggest that significant policy initiatives should not be embarked on unless they are based on sound research, proper public consultation and a reasonably broad measure of political support. There seems little point, for example, in pursuing substantial and disruptive policy changes in the absence of a secure and enduring level of parliamentary support.

Fourth, it must be a priority over the coming years to ensure that all New Zealanders have a genuine stake in their society and economy; otherwise there is a risk of greater alienation, social division and anti-social behaviour, with all the costs that these entail. Addressing the issue of social exclusion will require action on a number of policy fronts, not least in the areas of education, employment and income support. Fifth, we acknowledge that, as a general principle, individuals should not be taxed without good reason to provide goods and services they could have purchased for their own benefit in the private sector (see Chapter 4). But we argue that there are good reasons for the government to finance and/or provide what Dalziel and St John call 'social goods and services' (see Chapter 5). These include merit goods, goods with externalities, public goods, poverty relief and social insurance.

Of these, social insurance is probably the least familiar in New Zealand debates, but it has been very important in the design of many European welfare states (see Chapter 1). For certain services that society agrees should not be denied to anyone who needs them (health care, for example, or retirement income), social insurance is more efficient than private insurance because it eliminates problems of sample bias and adverse selection; it permits economies of scale in service delivery; it involves lower transaction costs in revenue collection; and it allows lower budgets for advertising and promotion. This still leaves us with the issue of whether social insurance schemes should provide, or simply fund, the relevant services. Often it will be efficient to allow private sector firms to compete for their state-funded clients; however, serious problems emerge if it is not easy to define the details of the required service contract, or if the market is not *perfectly* competitive. It is perhaps not widely appreciated that if a market departs from perfect competition (or perfect contestability), even to only a small degree, then the negative impact on efficiency can be severe. In particular, we argue that a more accurate industry model for many public services is 'monopolistic competition', whereby each firm competes for market share by distinguishing its product from that of other firms, leading to economic inefficiency and social waste. In such circumstances, it can be considerably more efficient for the government to provide, as well as fund, the services in question.

Another critical issue for the future of the welfare state concerns the extent to which social assistance is targeted. Many market liberals argue that high income earners should be directly responsible for most of the costs of their social services (see, for example, Richardson, 1990, p.20) This not only increases their incentive to earn more income to pay these costs, but also allows government expenditure to be directed to those who most require assistance. In line with this argument, for example, New Zealand's universal family benefit was abolished in 1991 and amalgamated with the targeted family support scheme. Yet a heavy reliance on targeting is open to many objections. Targeted welfare programmes are often more vulnerable to cuts in government expenditure, compared with programmes that also provide benefits to the middle class (see Chapter 6). Furthermore, policies targeted on the basis of income usually produce very high effective marginal tax rates at low to middle income levels. Table 6.2 records the wide range of abatement rates over different income bands in New Zealand's social assistance pro-grammes, and the accompanying text illustrates how these can combine to produce effective marginal tax rates approaching 100 per cent or higher. Given that the top income tax rate has been set at 33 cents in the dollar to minimise disincentive effects for high income earners, this outcome is both inefficient and inequitable for many low- and middle-income earners.[3]

Thus, there is a fundamental choice to be made for the future of the welfare state in New Zealand concerning the core public services such as health, education and income support. New Zealand's post-war system was based on the universal provision of these services, funded from a progressive tax system. It is possible to create an alternative private user-pays system, with the lower taxes allowed by such an approach subsidising only those citizens who cannot provide for themselves. In our view, however, the traditional approach has considerably more merit than this alternative. We have already made the point that there are economies of scale and other advantages to be gained from universal social insurance schemes, and that targeted assistance creates high effective marginal tax rates for low-income households. Furthermore, because a tightly targeted system creates financial incentives for people to represent themselves as eligible for the public subsidies, either the public system must be made so unattractive that nobody would choose to use it unless forced to do so by circumstance, or participation in a certified private scheme must be made compulsory. Hence, a low-tax, tightly targeted policy regime with private insurance for unemployment relief, health, ACC, pensions and so forth is likely to be less efficient and less equitable than the current policy regime or, indeed, a policy regime in which most forms of social assistance are funded via the tax system on a more or less universal basis.

Contributors to this volume have made particular suggestions in their areas of expertise, which need not be repeated here. We do observe, however, that in contrast to fiscal and monetary policy, there is no legislation setting out an overall framework for social policy. Two of the present editors, in association with Robert Stephens, have proposed that the government introduce a 'Social Responsibility Bill' to fill this gap. Such legislation might extend to listing a set of agreed principles for social policy, but would at a minimum strengthen the government's reporting and monitoring responsibilities in relation to social policy outcomes (see Boston, St John and Stephens, 1996, for further discussion). As indicated by the quotes from the 1991 Budget in this chapter's opening section, it is our view that inadequate requirements for transparency and accountability for social policy outcomes have been a significant weakness in New Zealand's policymaking framework (see also Higgins, 1997b).

Finally, a particular word must be said about poverty. In Chapter 5, 'poverty relief' was given its own heading under 'Social Goods and Services' on the basis that even those who advocate a very small role for the state accept that the state should provide a minimal safety net for those in genuine need. The evidence continues to show that there are tens of thousands of New Zealanders in genuine and serious need. The dominant view in policy design since 1990 has been that income support should be reduced to increase the incentives for people to look after themselves. The April 1991 benefit cuts were expected to reduce income support by $1.3 billion in a full fiscal year (approximately the same amount as was returned in *each* round of the 1996 and 1998 tax cuts), and from 1 July 1998 new sickness beneficiaries had their income support reduced to the level of the unemployment benefit. In contrast, we agree with George Akerlof (1998, p.308) that 'welfare is a response to poverty and not its cause', and support his conclusion that, 'insofar as poverty comes from causes other than the provision of welfare itself, the reduction of each dollar for the poor takes resources away from those who need it most'. To deny people adequate income support in the face of over-whelming economic and social trends is unjust and inefficient. As a matter of urgency, social welfare benefits must be restored to a level that removes the need for foodbanks and other charities to meet the basic living requirements of thousands of New Zealand citizens.

Endnotes

1 At the time of writing (March 1998), the value of the government's mechanism for public consultation—its discussion booklet and survey, *Towards a Code of Social and Family Responsibility*—is very doubtful (see, for example, Boston, 1998). Not only do social scientists have better methods available for obtaining representative views, but there is some doubt about how much impact the survey will have in practice on the development of government policy. The Budget Policy Statement of 4 February 1998, for example, made no reference to the survey, but nonetheless contained detailed statements about the government's intentions to reduce welfare benefit costs in a number of ways.

2 The recession was associated with a collapse in the price of wool, which at the time produced nearly a third of New Zealand's export earnings (see Dalziel and Lattimore, 1996, p.12; Easton, 1997a, pp.73-4). Note that registered unemployment data are being used in this section because New Zealand's official Survey Unemployment series began only in December 1985, which is too recent to reveal the trends under discussion. Registered unemployment data are typically higher than survey data, because the latter series is based on international conventions that require a person to be actively searching for work and immediately available for employment to be counted as officially unemployed. Also, a person is counted as employed in the survey data if he or she works for pay for as little as one hour in a week.

3 While effective marginal tax rates are so high at the bottom of the income scale, we believe that moves to reduce the progressivity of the tax system further by lowering the top rate of tax are inequitable. It is noteworthy that the well-received 1998 Budget in the United Kingdom reversed the trends of recent decades by significantly increasing the universal child benefit and implementing other important redistributive measures for low-income families.

REFERENCES

Adams, K. (1997), 'Workfare: A Discussion Paper.' Wellington: New Zealand Council of Christian Social Services.

Akerlof, G. (1998), 'Men Without Children: The 1997 Johnson Lecture.' *Economic Journal*, 108 (447), pp.287-309.

Anderson, G., P. Brosnan and P. Walsh (1996), 'The New Public Management and Human Resource Management Policies: Numerical Flexibility in the New Zealand Public Sector.' *International Journal of Employment Studies*, 4 (1), pp.37-56.

ARCIC (1992), *Employer Guide to Experience Rating.* Wellington: Accident Rehabilitation and Compensation Insurance Corporation.

ARCIC (1997a), *Annual Report 1997.* Wellington: Accident Rehabilitation and Compensation Insurance Corporation.

ARCIC (1997b), *Injury Statistics 1997.* Wellington: Accident Rehabilitation and Compensation Insurance Corporation.

Arestis, P. and M. Sawyer (1998), 'Keynesian Economic Policies for the New Millennium.' *Economic Journal*, 108 (446), pp.181-95.

Armitage, C. (1996), 'Survey of Employment Contracting under the Employment Contracts Act.' Paper presented to the Seventh Labour, Employment and Work Conference, Victoria University of Wellington, 28-29 November.

Arrow, K. (1950), 'A Difficulty in the Concept of Social Welfare.' *Journal of Public Economy*, 58 (3), pp.328-46.

Arrow, K. (1992), 'Moral Thinking and Economic Interaction.' In *Social and Ethical Aspects of Economics*. Vatican City: Pontifical Council for Justice and Peace.

Ashton, T. (1992a), 'Reform of the Health Services: Weighing Up the Costs and Benefits.' In J. Boston and P. Dalziel, Eds, *The Decent Society? Essays in Response to National's Economic and Social Policies*. Auckland: Oxford University Press.

Ashton, T. (1992b), 'User Charges: An Assessment of the Interim Targeting Regime.' Paper prepared for the Department of Health.

Ashton, T. (1996), 'Health Care Systems in Transition: New Zealand. Part 1: An Overview of New Zealand's Health Care System.' *Journal of Public Health Medicine*, 18 (3), pp.269-73.

Ashton, T. (1998), 'Contracting for Health Services in New Zealand: A Transaction Cost Analysis.' *Social Science and Medicine*, 46, pp.357-67.

Ashton, T. and S. St John (1988), *Superannuation in New Zealand: Averting the Crisis.* Wellington: Institute of Policy Studies.

Atkinson, A. (1993), 'On Targeting Social Security: Theory and Western Experience with Family Benefits.' Discussion Paper WSP/99. London: London School of Economics.

Atkinson, A. (1995), 'The Welfare State and Economic Performance.' Discussion Paper WSP/109. London: London School of Economics.

Auckland Unemployed Workers' Rights Centre (1997), *Mean Times*. Various issues. Auckland: AUWRC.

Austin, P., B. Hucker and J. Lunday (1996), *Rent Rises, Housing Sales and Relocation.* Auckland: Department of Planning, University of Auckland.

Bacon, D. (1996), 'Racing to the Bottom: Workfare May Make Things Tougher All Right—For Those Who Already Have Jobs.' *Jinn*, 17 December. Cited in Institute for Women's Policy Research, *Welfare Reform Network News*. Issue 5, 30 April 1997.

Ballard, C.L. and D. Fullerton (1992), 'Distortionary Taxes and the Provision of Public Goods.' *Journal of Economic Perspectives*, 6 (3), pp.117-31.

Barker, G. (1996), *Income Distribution in New Zealand*. Wellington: Institute of Policy Studies.

Barker, G. (1997), 'Social Capital and Policy Development.' In D. Robinson, Ed, *Social Capital and Policy Development*. Wellington: Institute of Policy Studies.

Barr, N. (1989), 'Social Insurance as an Efficiency Device.' *Journal of Public Policy*, 9, pp.59-82.

Barr, N. (1990), 'Economic Theory and the Welfare State: A Survey and Reinterpretation.' Discussion Paper WSP/54. London: London School of Economics.

Barr, N. (1994), *The Economics of the Welfare State*, 2nd Edition. London: Weidenfeld and Nicolson.

Barrett, M. (1988), 'Standards and Foundations for Social Policy.' In *Future Directions*, Vol. III, Part I of *Report of the Royal Commission on Social Policy*. Wellington: Government Printer.

Barry, B. (1973), *The Liberal Theory of Justice*. Oxford: Clarendon Press.

Barry, B. (1989), *Theories of Justice*, Vol. I. Berkeley: University of California Press.

Barry, B. (1990), 'The Welfare State versus the Relief of Poverty?' In A. Ware and R. Goodin, Eds, *Needs and Welfare*. London: Sage.

Bates, R. (1990), 'Educational Policy and the New Cult of Efficiency.' In S. Middleton, J. Codd and A. Jones, Eds, *New Zealand Education Policy Today: Cultural Perspectives*. Wellington: Allen and Unwin.

Beaglehole, R. and R. Bonita (1997), *Public Health at the Crossroads*. Cambridge: Cambridge University Press.

Beck, P., A. Walters and N. Francisco (1990), *The Sacred—Ways of Knowledge, Sources of Life*. Arizona: Northland Publishing.

Bernstein, J. (1996), 'The Challenge of Moving from Welfare to Work: Depressed Labor Market Awaits Those Leaving the Rolls.' Washington: Economic Policy Institute.

Bertram, G. (1988), 'Middle Class Capture: A Brief Survey.' In *Future Directions*, Vol. III, Part II of *Report of the Royal Commission on Social Policy*. Wellington: Government Printer.

Bertram, G. (1997), 'Macroeconomic Debate and Economic Growth in Postwar New Zealand.' In C. Rudd and B. Roper, Eds, *The Political Economy of New Zealand*. Auckland: Oxford University Press.

Birch, W.F. (1990), 'Statement by the Minister of Labour and State Services.' *Economic and Social Initiative—December 1990*. Wellington: Government Printer.

Birch, W.F. (1991), *Accident Compensation: A Fairer Scheme*. Wellington: Government Printer.

Birch, W.F. (1994), *Economic and Fiscal Outlook 1994*. Wellington: New Zealand Treasury.

Birch, W.F. (1996a), *Tax Reduction and Social Policy Programme: Details*. Wellington: New Zealand Treasury.

Birch, W.F. (1996b), *Budget Economic and Fiscal Update*. Wellington: New Zealand Treasury.

Blakeley, R. and D. Suggate (1997), 'Public Policy Development.' In D. Robinson, Ed, *Social Capital and Policy Development*. Wellington: Institute of Policy Studies.

Blaug, M. (1972), *An Introduction to the Economics of Education.* Harmondsworth: Penguin.

Bolger, J. (1990), 'Statement by the Prime Minister'. In *Economic and Social Initiative—December 1990.* Wellington: New Zealand Government.

Bolger, J. (1997), 'Sound Economics, Good Politics.' Speech to the New Zealand Institute of Economic Research Qantas Economic Awards, 15 October.

Bolger, J., R. Richardson and W. Birch (1990), *Economic and Social Initiative—December 1990.* Statements to the House of Representatives. Wellington: New Zealand Government.

Boon, B. (1992a), 'Remedies for Unjustifiable Dismissal under the Labour Relations Act.' *New Zealand Journal of Industrial Relations,* 17 (1), pp.101-7.

Boon, B. (1992b), 'Procedural Fairness and the Unjustified Dismissal Decision.' *New Zealand Journal of Industrial Relations,* 17 (3), pp.301-17.

Booth, C. (1977), 'The National Party's 1975 Superannuation Policy.' In G. Palmer, Ed, *The Welfare State Today: Social Welfare Policy in New Zealand in the Seventies.* Wellington: Fourth Estate Books.

Boston, J. (1988), *The Future of New Zealand Universities.* Wellington: Victoria University Press.

Boston, J. (1991), 'The Theoretical Underpinnings of Public Sector Restructuring in New Zealand.' In J. Boston, J. Martin, J. Pallot and P. Walsh, Eds, *Reshaping the State.* Auckland: Oxford University Press.

Boston, J. (1992a), 'Targeting: Social Assistance for All or Just for the Poor?' In J. Boston and P. Dalziel, Eds, *The Decent Society? Essays in Response to National's Economic and Social Policies.* Auckland: Oxford University Press.

Boston, J. (1992b), 'The Funding of Tertiary Education: Rights and Wrongs.' In J. Boston and P. Dalziel, Eds, *The Decent Society? Essays in Response to National's Economic and Social Policies.* Auckland: Oxford University Press.

Boston, J. (1993), 'Is Social Democracy Morally Defensible?' *Reshaping Social Democracy.* Wellington: Gamma Foundation Occasional Paper No. 4.

Boston, J. (1994), 'Grand Designs and Unpleasant Realities: The Fate of the National Government's Proposals for the Integrated Targeting of Social Assistance.' *Political Science,* 46, pp.1-21.

Boston, J. (1995), *The State Under Contract.* Wellington: Bridget Williams Books.

Boston, J. (1997), 'The Ownership, Governance, and Accountability of Tertiary Institutions in New Zealand.' *New Zealand Annual Review of Education,* 6, pp.5-28.

Boston, J. (1998), 'The Proposed Code of Social and Family Responsibility.' *Stimulus,* 6(2), pp.43-7.

Boston, J. and A. Cameron (1994), Eds, *Voices for Justice: Church, Law and State in New Zealand.* Palmerston North: Dunmore Press.

Boston, J. and F. Cooper (1989), 'The Treasury: Advice, Co-ordination and Control.' In H. Gold, Ed, *New Zealand Politics in Perspective,* 2nd Edition. Auckland: Longman Paul.

Boston, J. and P. Dalziel (1992), Eds, *The Decent Society? Essays in Response to National's Economic and Social Policies.* Auckland: Oxford University Press.

Boston, J., S. Levine, E. McLeay and N. Roberts (1996), *New Zealand Under MMP: A New Politics?* Auckland: Auckland University Press/Bridget Williams Books.

Boston, J., S. Levine, E. McLeay and N. Roberts (1997), Eds, *From Campaign to Coalition.* Palmerston North: Dunmore Press.

Boston, J., J. Martin, J. Pallot and P. Walsh (1991), Eds, *Reshaping the State: New Zealand's Bureaucratic Revolution.* Auckland: Oxford University Press.

Boston, J., J. Martin, J. Pallot and P. Walsh (1996), *Public Management: The New Zealand Model*. Auckland: Oxford University Press.

Boston J. and E. McLeay (1997), 'Forming the First MMP Government: Theory, Practice and Prospects.' In J. Boston, S. Levine, E. McLeay and N. Roberts, Eds, *From Campaign to Coalition*. Palmerston North: Dunmore Press.

Boston, J., S. St John and R. Stephens (1996), 'The Quest for Social Responsibility.' *Social Policy Journal of New Zealand*, 7 (December), pp.2-16.

Boxall, P. and P. Haynes (1997), 'Strategy and Trade Union Effectiveness in a Neo-liberal Environment.' *British Journal of Industrial Relations*, 35 (4), pp.567-91.

Bradford, M. (1993), 'The Future of the Employment Court and Tribunal: The Government View.' Paper presented to a New Zealand Institute of Industrial Relations Research Seminar, 23 April 1993, Wellington.

Bradford, M. (1997), 'What Happens Now?' Labour–Management–Government Relations Seminar, Industrial Relations Centre, Victoria University of Wellington, 20 March.

Bradshaw, J., J. Ditch, H. Holmes and P. Whiteford (1993), *Support for Children: A Comparison of Arrangements in Fifteen Countries*. Department of Social Security Research Report, No.21. London: HMSO.

Bradshaw, J., S. Kennedy, M. Kilkey, S. Hutton, A. Corden, T. Eardley, H. Holmes and J. Neale (1996), *Policy and the Employment of Lone Parents in 20 Countries*. York: European Observatory on National Family Policies, University of York.

Brash, D. (1997), 'How Fast Can the New Zealand Economy Grow?' Address to the Auckland Rotary Club. *Reserve Bank Bulletin*, 60 (4), pp.309-14.

Brashares, E. (1993), 'Assessing Income Adequacy in New Zealand,' *New Zealand Economic Papers*, 27 (2), pp.185-207.

Brennan, G. and C. Walsh (1990), Eds, *Rationality, Individualism and Public Policy*. Canberra: Centre for Research on Federal Financial Relations.

Brook-Cowen, P. (1993), 'Labour Relations Reform in New Zealand: The Employment Contracts Act and Contractual Freedom.' *Journal of Labor Research*, 14 (1), pp.69-83.

Brosnan, P., F. Horwitz and P. Walsh (1997), 'Non-Standard Employment: Results from a Workplace Survey in Three Countries.' In J. Wickham, Ed, *The Search for Competitiveness and its Implications for Employment*. Proceedings of the Fifth European Industrial Relations Congress. Dublin: Oak Tree Press.

Brosnan, P. and D. Rea (1991a), 'Rogernomics and the Labour Market.' Working Paper 3/91. Wellington: Industrial Relations Centre, Victoria University of Wellington.

Brosnan, P. and D. Rea (1991b), 'An Adequate Minimum Code: A Basis for Freedom, Justice and Efficiency in the Labour Market.' *New Zealand Journal of Industrial Relations*, 16 (2), pp.143-58.

Brosnan, P., D. Smith and P. Walsh (1990), *The Dynamics of New Zealand Industrial Relations*. Auckland: Wiley.

Brosnan, P. and P. Walsh (1997), 'Why are New Zealand Unions Stronger at the Workplace Under the Employment Contracts Act Than Australian Unions Under the Accord?' In T. Bramble, B. Harley, R. Hall and G. Whitehouse, Eds, *Current Research in Industrial Relations*. Proceedings of the Eleventh AIRAANZ Conference, Brisbane, 30 January—1 February.

Brosnan, P., M. Wilson and D. Wong (1989), 'Welfare Benefits and Labour Supply: A Review of the Empirical Evidence.' *New Zealand Journal of Industrial Relations*, 14 (1), pp.17-35.

Brown, C. and P. Jackson (1990), *Public Sector Economics*. Oxford: Basil Blackwell.

Bryant, R. (1996), 'Central Bank Independence, Fiscal Responsibility, and the Goals of Macroeconomic Policy: An American Perspective on the New Zealand Experience.' Wellington: Victoria University of Wellington Foundation.

Bryder, L. (1991), 'A Social Laboratory: New Zealand and Social Welfare, 1840-1990.' *British Review of New Zealand Studies*, 4, pp.37-48.

Bryson, L. (1992), *Welfare and the State: Who Benefits?* London: Macmillan.

Bushnell, P. and G. Scott (1988), 'An Economic Perspective.' In J. Martin and J. Harper, Eds, *Devolution and Accountability*. Wellington: GP Books.

Butterworth, R. and N. Tarling (1994), *A Shakeup Anyway: Government and the Universities in New Zealand in a Decade of Reform*. Auckland: Auckland University Press.

Campbell, I. (1996), *Compensation for Personal Injury in New Zealand: Its Rise and Fall*. Auckland: Auckland University Press.

Capper, P. (1992), 'Curriculum 1991.' *New Zealand Annual Review of Education*, 1, pp.15-27.

Caragata, P. (1997), 'Response to New Zealand "Critics" Comments on the Tax and Growth Papers Produced for the Inland Revenue Department, New Zealand.' Mimeo. Wellington: McCallum Petterson Forensic.

Caragata, P. and J. Small (1996), 'Tax Burden Effects on Output Growth in New Zealand: A Non-Linear Dynamic Model.' *Working Papers on Monitoring the Health of the Tax System*, No.24. Wellington: Inland Revenue New Zealand.

Casey, B. (1986), 'Back to the Poor Law? The Emergence of "Workfare" in Britain, Germany and the USA.' *Policy Studies*, 7 (1), pp.52-64.

Castles, F. (1985), *The Working Class and Welfare: Reflections on the Political Development of the Welfare State in Australia and New Zealand, 1890-1980*. Wellington: Allen and Unwin/Port Nicolson Press.

Castles, F. (1996), 'Needs-Based Strategies of Social Protection in Australia and New Zealand.' In G. Esping-Andersen, Ed, *Welfare States in Transition: National Adaptations in Global Economics*. London: Sage Publications.

Castles, F. and S. Dowrick (1990), 'The Impact of Government Spending Levels on Medium-Term Economic Growth in the OECD, 1960-85.' *Journal of Theoretical Politics*, 2, pp.173-204.

Castles, F. and D. Mitchell (1990), 'Three Worlds of Welfare Capitalism or Four?' Discussion Paper No.21. Canberra: Public Policy Program, Australian National University.

Chapple, S. (1997), 'One From the X-Files? A Critical Assessment of Professor Scully's "Taxation and Economic Growth in New Zealand".' Research Contract No.1282. Wellington: New Zealand Institute of Economic Research.

Chapple, S. and J. Yeabsley (1994), *Cycles of Disadvantage: A Summary*. Wellington: New Zealand Institute of Economic Research.

Cheyne, C., M. O'Brien and M. Belgrave (1997), *Social Policy in Aotearoa New Zealand: A Critical Introduction*. Auckland: Oxford University Press.

Chiao, Y-S. and I. Walker (1992), 'Labour Market Behaviour of Prime Age Individuals.' In M. Prebble and P. Rebstock, Eds, *Incentives and Labour Supply: Modelling Taxes and Benefits*. Wellington: Institute of Policy Studies.

Christensen, J.G. (1997), 'The Scandinavian Welfare State: The Institutions of Growth, Governance, and Reform. Review Article.' *Scandinavian Political Studies*, 20, pp.367-86.

Chubb, J. and T. Moe (1990), *Politics, Markets and America's Schools*. Washington D.C.: Brookings Institution.

Clark, M. (1990), 'The Legislative Framework and the Reality.' Address to the New Zealand Business Roundtable Labour Market Media Seminar, Wellington, 29 May.

Coalition Agreement (1996), Agreement between New Zealand First and the New Zealand National Party, December.

Coase, R.H. (1937), 'The Nature of the Firm.' Reprinted as Chapter 2 in *The Firm, the Market, and the Law*. Chicago: Chicago University Press, 1988.

Codd, J. (1990a), 'Policy Documents and the Official Discourses of the State.' In J. Codd, R. Harker and R. Nash, Eds, *Political Issues in New Zealand Education*. Palmerston North: Dunmore Press.

Codd, J. (1990b), 'Educational Policy and the Crisis of the New Zealand State.' In S. Middleton, J. Codd and A. Jones, Eds, *New Zealand Educational Policy Today*, Wellington: Allen and Unwin.

Codd, J. (1993), 'Neo-Liberal Education Policy and the Ideology of Choice.' *Educational Philosophy and Theory*, 24 (2), pp.31-48.

Codd, J. (1997), 'NZQA and the Economic Rationalisation of Education.' *Access*, 16 (2), pp.1-13.

Collins, D. (1977), 'Formulating Superannuation Policy: The Labour Party Approach.' In G. Palmer, Ed, *The Welfare State Today: Social Welfare Policy in New Zealand in the Seventies*. Wellington: Fourth Estate Books.

Commission on Social Justice (1993), *Social Justice in a Changing World*. London: Institute for Public Policy Research.

Commission on Social Justice (1994), *Social Justice: Strategies for National Renewal*. London: Vintage.

Coney, S. (1992), *Accident Compensation: A Women's Issue*. Federation of Women's Health Councils Aotearoa-New Zealand.

Coney, S. (1996a), 'Political Prognosis.' *Sunday Star Times*, 15 September, p.C1.

Coney, S. (1996b), 'Fund-Holding and Managed Care: Ethical Issues in the Patient-Provider Relationship.' Paper presented at the conference on Managed Care: Options for New Zealand, May 2-4, Wellington.

Contract Monitoring (1994/95), *Purchasing for Your Health: 1994/95*. Wellington: Ministry of Health.

Coote, A. (1992), Ed, *The Welfare of Citizens: Developing New Social Rights*. London: Institute for Public Policy Research.

Copp, D. (1992), 'The Right to an Adequate Standard of Living: Justice, Autonomy, and Basic Needs.' *Social Philosophy and Policy*, 9 (1), pp.231-61.

Court of Appeal (1987), 'New Zealand Māori Council and Latimer v Attorney General and Others (CA 54/87).' *NZAR*, Vol. 6, Part 12.

Council of Trade Unions (1994), 'Submission to the Regulations Review Panel.' Wellington: CTU.

Craig, A., N. Brosnahan, C. Briar and M. O'Brien (1992), *Neither Freedom Nor Choice*. Palmerston North: People's Select Committee.

Crawford, A., R. Harbridge and K. Hince (1997), 'Unions and Union Membership in New Zealand: Annual Review for 1996.' *New Zealand Journal of Industrial Relations*, 22 (2), pp.209-16.

Crocombe, G.T., M. Enright and M. Porter (1991), *Upgrading New Zealand's Competitive Advantage*. Auckland: Oxford University Press.

Crosland, C. (1956), *The Future of Socialism*. London: Jonathan Cape.

Crown Company Monitoring Advisory Unit (1996), *Crown Health Enterprises: Briefing to the Incoming Minister*. Wellington: CCMAU.

Culyer, A. (1971), 'Merit Goods and the Welfare Economics of Coercion.' *Public Finance*, 26, pp.546-72.

Culyer, A. (1980), *The Political Economy of Social Policy*. Oxford: Martin Robertson.

Dale, R. and J. Jesson (1992), 'Mainstreaming Education: The Role of the State Services Commission.' *Annual Review of Education*, 2, pp.7-34.

Dalziel, P. (1992a), 'National's Macroeconomic Policy.' In J. Boston and P. Dalziel, Eds, *The Decent Society? Essays in Response to National's Economic and Social Policies*. Auckland: Oxford University Press.

Dalziel, P. (1992b), 'Policies for a Decent Society.' In J. Boston and P. Dalziel, Eds, *The Decent Society? Essays in Response to National's Economic and Social Policies*. Auckland: Oxford University Press.

Dalziel, P. (1996), 'Poor Policy.' A Report on the 1991 Benefit Cuts and the 1996 Tax Cuts for the New Zealand Council of Christian Social Services, Wellington.

Dalziel, P. (1997), 'Setting the Reserve Bank's Inflation Target: The New Zealand Debate.' *Agenda*, 4 (3), pp.285-96.

Dalziel, P. (1998a), 'New Zealand's Economic Reforms, 1984-95: Comment,' *Victoria Economic Commentaries*, 15(1), pp.1-6.

Dalziel, P. (1998b), 'New Zealand's Experience with an Independent Central Bank Since 1989.' In P. Arestis and M. Sawyer, Eds, *The Political Economy of Central Banking*. Cheltenham: Edward Elgar.

Dalziel, P. and R. Lattimore (1996), *The New Zealand Macroeconomy: A Briefing on the Reforms*. Auckland: Oxford University Press.

Dannin, E. (1997), *Working Free: The Origins and Impact of New Zealand's Employment Contracts Act*. Auckland: Auckland University Press.

Davidson, A. (1994), *A Home of One's Own: Housing Policy in Sweden and New Zealand from the 1840s to the 1990s*. Stockholm: Almqvist and Wiksell International.

Davis, P., B. Gribben, R. Lay Yee and B. McAvoy (1994), 'The Impact of the New Subsidy Regime in General Practice in New Zealand.' *Health Policy*, 29 (1-2), pp.113-25.

Davis, R. (1998), Ed, *Social Capital and Strong Communities*. Proceedings of a conference organised by Capital City Forum, Wellington, 14 November 1997.

de Raad, J-P. (1997), 'The Duration and Repeat of Unemployment Benefit Spells: A Study of a Cohort of New Zealand Unemployment Beneficiaries 1992-1995.' MA thesis, Victoria University of Wellington.

Dearing, Sir Ron (1997), *Higher Education in the Learning Society*. London: National Committee of Inquiry into Higher Education.

Deeks, J., J. Parker and R. Ryan (1994), *Labour and Employment Relations in New Zealand*. Auckland: Longman Paul.

Deloitte Touche Tohmatsu (1996), 'Trends in AHB/CHE Performance.' Wellington: Deloitte Touche Tohmatsu.

Department of Labour (1985), *Labour Employment Gazette*, June. Wellington: Department of Labour.

Department of Labour (1991), 'Employment Contracts Bill: Outstanding Policy Issues.' Paper to the Minister of Labour, 29 January.

Department of Labour (1996), *Post Election Brief*. Wellington: Department of Labour.

Department of Labour (1997a), 'Survey of Labour Market Adjustment Under the Employment Contracts Act.' Wellington: Industrial Relations Service.

Department of Labour (1997b), 'ILO Employment Conventions: New Zealand Obligations.' Wellington: Department of Labour.

Department of Social Welfare (1992), *Statistical Information Report*. Wellington: Department of Social Welfare.

Department of Social Welfare (1996a), *From Welfare to Well-being: Statistics Report, Fiscal Year 1996*. Wellington: Department of Social Welfare.

Department of Social Welfare (1996b), *Strategic Directions: Post Election Briefing Papers*. Wellington: Department of Social Welfare.

Dewey, J. (1916), *Democracy and Education*. New York: Macmillan.

Diewert, W.E. and D.A. Lawrence (1994), *The Marginal Costs of Taxation in New Zealand*. Wellington: New Zealand Business Roundtable.

Diewert, W.E. and D.A. Lawrence (1996), 'The Deadweight Costs of Taxation in New Zealand.' *Canadian Journal of Economics*, 29 (S), pp.S658-S673.

Dods, J. and E. McCann (1995), 'A Latent Variables Approach to the Estimation of the Deadweight Loss of Taxation in New Zealand.' *Working Papers on Monitoring the Health of the Tax System*, No.17. Wellington: Inland Revenue New Zealand.

Douglas, R. (1984), *Budget Speech*. Parliamentary Paper B.6.

Drumbl, M.A. (1994), 'Exploring the Constitutional Limits to Workfare and Learnfare.' *Journal of Law and Social Policy*, 10, pp.107-54.

Du Plessis, R. (1993), 'Women, Politics and the State.' In B. Roper and C. Rudd, Eds, *State and Economy in New Zealand*. Auckland: Oxford University Press.

Duncan, G. (1995), 'Accident Compensation—1995 and Still Languishing.' *New Zealand Journal of Industrial Relations*, 20 (3), pp.237-53.

Duncan, G. (1996), 'Whatever Happened to No-Fault Compensation?' *Employment Today*, 26 (September).

Duncan, G. and J. Nimmo (1993), 'Accident Compensation and Labour Relations: The Impact of Recent Reforms,' *New Zealand Journal of Industrial Relations*, 18 (3), pp.288-305.

Duncan, I. and A. Bollard (1992), *Corporatization and Privatization: Lessons from New Zealand*. Auckland: Oxford University Press.

Durie, M. (1988), 'Social Policy Perspectives.' In J. Martin and J. Harper, Eds, *Devolution and Accountability*. Wellington: GP Books.

Durie, M. (1995), *Principles for the Development of Māori Policy*. Paper presented to the Māori Policy Development Conference, Wellington, April.

Dworkin, R. (1989), 'Equality of Resources.' *Philosophy and Social Affairs*, 19, pp.283-345.

Eardley, T., J. Bradshaw, J. Ditch, I. Gough and P. Whiteford (1996), *Social Assistance in OECD Countries: Synthesis Report*. Department of Social Security Research Report, No.46. London: HMSO.

Easton, B. (1980), *Social Policy and the Welfare State in New Zealand*. Auckland: Allen & Unwin.

Easton, B. (1990), 'Policy as Revolution: Two Case Studies.' Paper presented at the New Zealand Political Studies Association Annual Conference, Dunedin.

Easton, B. (1995a), 'Properly Assessing Income Adequacy in New Zealand,' *New Zealand Economic Papers*, 29 (1), pp.89-102.

Easton, B. (1995b), 'Poverty in New Zealand: 1981-1993.' *New Zealand Sociology*, 10 (2), pp.182-213.

Easton, B. (1996a), 'Income Distribution.' In B. Silverstone, A. Bollard and R. Lattimore, Eds, *A Study of Economic Reform: The Case of New Zealand*. Amsterdam: North-Holland.

Easton, B. (1996b), 'The Post-War Welfare State.' *Social Policy Journal of New Zealand*, 7 (December), pp.17-28.

Easton, B. (1997a), *In Stormy Seas: The Post-War New Zealand Economy*. Dunedin: University of Otago Press.

Easton, B. (1997b), *The Commercialisation of New Zealand*. Auckland: Auckland University Press.

Easton, B. (1997c), 'Divided We Stand.' *New Zealand Listener*, 15 September.

Education Directions Ltd (1997), 'Entitlements in Education: Empowering Student Demand: A Literature Review Prepared for the Treasury.' Wellington.

Edwards, D. (1991), 'A Study in Conflict: Inside the Porter Project.' *New Zealand Listener*, 23 September, pp.39-42.

Ernst and Young (1996), *Housing New Zealand Review of Rent Setting Process*. Wellington: Ernst & Young Real Estate Consulting Group.

ESC Secretariat (1984), *A Briefing on the New Zealand Economy*. Wellington: Government Printer.

Esping-Andersen, G. (1990), *The Three Worlds of Welfare Capitalism*. Princeton and Cambridge: Princeton University Press and Polity Press.

Esping-Andersen, G. (1996a), Ed, *Welfare States in Transition: National Adaptations in Global Economies*. London: Sage.

Esping-Andersen, G. (1996b), 'After the Golden Age? Welfare State Dilemmas in a Global Economy.' In G. Esping-Andersen, Ed, *Welfare States in Transition: National Adaptations in Global Economics*. London: Sage Publications.

Evans, L., A. Grimes and B. Wilkinson, with D. Teece (1996), 'Economic Reform in New Zealand 1984-95: The Pursuit of Efficiency.' *Journal of Economic Literature*, 34 (4), pp.1856-902.

Falkingham, J., J. Hills and C. Lessof (1993), 'William Beveridge versus Robin Hood: Social Security and Redistribution over the Lifecycle.' Discussion Paper WSP/88. London: London School of Economics.

Feinberg, J. (1973), *Social Philosophy*. Englewood Cliffs: Prentice-Hall.

Ferge, S. (1997), 'The Changed Welfare Paradigm: The Individualization of the Social.' *Social Policy and Administration*, 31 (1), pp.20-44.

Ferguson, G. (1994), *Building the New Zealand Dream*. Palmerston North: Dunmore Press.

Fergusson, D., L. Harwood and M. Lynsley (1993), 'The Effects of Conduct Disorder and Attention Deficit in Middle Childhood on Offending and Scholastic Ability at Age 13.' *Journal of Child Psychology and Psychiatry*, 34, pp.899-916.

Finn, D. (1987), *Training Without Jobs: New Deals and Broken Promises*. London: Macmillan.

Finnigan, A. (1997), 'The Role of Private Providers in Tertiary Education: Funding, Ownership and Competition.' MPP 503 Project. Wellington: Victoria University of Wellington.

Fitzsimons, P. (1997), Ed, *Perspectives on the New Zealand Qualifications Authority*. Special edition of *Access*, 16 (2).

Fitzsimons, P. and P. Frater (1996), 'The Seamless Education System and Private Training Establishments: An Investigation of the Consequences for Private Training Establishments of Possible Changes to the EFTS Funding System.' Report to Te Puni Kōkiri, Wellington, 28 June.

Forrest, R. and A. Murie (1991), *Selling the Welfare State: The Privatisation of Council Housing*. London: Routledge.

Franklin, J. (1997), Ed, *Equality*. London: Institute for Public Policy Research.

Fraser, N. (1989), 'Women, Welfare and the Politics of Need Interpretation.' In *Unruly Practices: Power, Discourse and Gender in Contemporary Social Theory*. Cambridge: Polity Press.

Fraser, N. (1997), 'After the Family Wage: A Postindustrial Thought Experiment.' In *Justice Interruptus: Critical Reflections on the Postsocialist Condition*. New York: Routledge.

Fraser, N. and L. Gordon (1992), 'Contract vs. Charity: Why is There No Social Citizenship in the United States?' *Socialist Review*, 22 (3), pp.45-67.

Freyer, L. (1997), 'Unjustifiable Dismissal: Procedural Fairness and the Employer.' *New Zealand Journal of Industrial Relations*, 22 (2), pp.143-58.

Friedlander, D. and G. Burtless (1995), *Five Years After: The Long Term Effects of Welfare-to-Work Programs*. New York: Russell Sage Foundation.

Friendship House (1997), *The Impact of the Accommodation Supplement on South Auckland Housing Markets 1993-1997*. Manukau City: Friendship House.

Fullerton, D. (1991), 'Reconciling Recent Estimates of the Marginal Welfare Cost of Taxation.' *American Economic Review*, 81 (1), pp.302-8.

Galster, G. (1997), 'Comparing Demand-side and Supply-side Housing Policies: Sub-market and Spatial Perspectives.' *Housing Studies*, 12, pp.561-77.

Garret, E.M. and R.J. Bates (1977), 'Education: Socialisation, Social Welfare and Social Control.' In A.D. Trlin, Ed, *Social Welfare and New Zealand Society*. Wellington: Methuen.

Gibson, D., R. Goodin and J. Le Grand (1985), '"Come and Get It": Distributional Biases in Social Service Delivery Systems.' *Policy and Politics*, 13, pp.109-25.

Giles, D. (1995), 'Measuring the Size of the Hidden Economy and the Tax Gap in New Zealand: An Econometric Analysis.' Working Paper No.5. Wellington: Department of Inland Revenue.

Giles, D. (1997), 'Testing for Asymmetry in the Measured and Underground Business Cycles in New Zealand.' *Economic Record*, 73 (222), pp.225-32.

Gleeson, D. (1989), *The Paradox of Training: Making Progress out of Crisis*. Milton Keynes: Open University Press.

Glennerster, H. (1992), 'Paying for Welfare: Issues for the Nineties.' Discussion Paper WSP/82. London: London School of Economics.

Goddard, T. (1993), 'The Role of the Employment Court.' Paper presented to a New Zealand Institute of Industrial Relations Research Seminar, 23 April, Wellington.

Golder, Q. (1997), 'A Limited Option Out of ACC.' *The Employer*, Official Journal of the Employers Federation, November.

Goodger, K. (1997), 'Employment of Sole Parents Increases.' Mimeo. Wellington: Social Policy Agency.

Goodin, R. (1982), 'Freedom and the Welfare State: Theoretical Foundations.' *Journal of Social Policy*, 11, pp.149-76.

Goodin, R. (1988), 'Reasons for Welfare: Economic, Sociological, and Political but Ultimately Moral.' In D. Moon, Ed, *Responsibility, Rights and Welfare: The Theory of the Welfare State*. Boulder: Westview Press.

Goodin, R. (1990), 'Liberalism and the Best-Judge Principle.' *Political Studies*, 38, pp.181-95.

Goodin, R. and J. Le Grand (1986), 'Creeping Universalism in the Welfare State: Evidence from Australia.' *Journal of Public Policy*, 6, pp.255-74.

Goodin, R. and J. Le Grand (1987), *Not Only the Poor: The Middle Classes and the Welfare State*. London: Allen and Unwin.

Gordon, L. (1992), 'The State, Devolution and Educational Reform in New Zealand.' *Journal of Education Policy*, 7 (2), pp.187-203.

Gordon, L. (1994), 'Is School Choice a Sustainable Policy for New Zealand? A Review of Recent Research Findings and a Look to the Future.' *New Zealand Annual Review of Education*, 4, pp.9-24.

Goulet, D. (1995), *Development Ethics: A Guide to Theory and Practice*. New York: Apex Press.

Graham, D. (1995), *Crown Proposals for the Settlement of Treaty of Waitangi Claims*. Two volumes, Detailed Proposals and Summary. Wellington: Office of Treaty Settlements, Department of Justice.

Graham, D. (1997), *Trick or Treaty?* Wellington: Institute of Policy Studies.

Gray, J. (1992), *The Moral Foundations of Market Institutions*. London: IEA Health and Welfare Unit.

Green, D. (1996), *From Welfare Society to Civil Society: Towards Welfare That Works in New Zealand*. Wellington: New Zealand Business Roundtable.

Gueron, J. and E. Pauly (1991), *From Welfare to Work*. New York: Russell Sage Foundation.

Gunby, J. (1996), *Housing the Hungry: The Third Report*. Wellington: New Zealand Council of Christian Services and the Salvation Army.

Gustafson, B. (1986), *From the Cradle to the Grave: A Biography of Michael Joseph Savage*. Auckland: Reed Methuen.

Hall, R.E. and C.I. Jones (1997), 'Levels of Economic Activity Across Countries.' *American Economic Review*, 87 (2), pp.173-7.

Hall, V. (1997), 'Economic Growth.' In B. Silverstone, A. Bollard and R. Lattimore, Eds, *A Study of Economic Reform: The Case of New Zealand*. Amsterdam: North-Holland.

Hammond, S. and R. Harbridge (1993), 'The Impact of the Employment Contracts Act on Women at Work.' *New Zealand Journal of Industrial Relations*, 18 (1), pp.15-30.

Hanson, E.A. (1975), 'The Social Security Story: A Study of the Political Origins of the 1938 Social Security Act.' MA thesis, University of Auckland.

Harbridge, R. (1994), *Labour Market Regulation and Employment: Trends in New Zealand*. Wellington: Industrial Relations Centre, Victoria University of Wellington.

Harbridge, R., A. Crawford and P. Kiely (1997), *Employment Contracts: Bargaining Trends and Employment Law Update 1996/97*. Wellington: Graduate School of Business and Government Management, Victoria University of Wellington.

Harbridge, R. and P. Kiely (1995), *Dynamism and Conservatism: The Role of the Judiciary in New Zealand's Employment Contracts Act*. Wellington: Industrial Relations Centre, Victoria University of Wellington.

Harbridge, R. and S. McCaw (1992), 'Award, Agreement or Nothing? A Review of the Impact of S132(a) of the Labour Relations Act 1987 on Collective Bargaining.' *New Zealand Journal of Industrial Relations*, 17 (2), pp.175-83.

Harloe, M. (1988), 'The Changing Role of Social Rented Housing.' In M. Ball, M. Harloe and M. Martens, Eds, *Housing and Social Change in Europe and the USA*. London: Routledge.

Harloe, M. (1995), *The People's Home?* Oxford: Blackwell.

Hart, O. (1995), *Firms, Contracts, and Financial Structure*. Oxford: Oxford University Press.

Hawke, G. (1988), *Report of the Working Group on Post Compulsory Education and Training*. Wellington: Office of the Associate Minister of Education.

Hayek, F. (1976), *Law, Legislation and Liberty. Vol. 2: The Mirage of Social Justice*. London: Routledge and Kegan Paul.

Head, J. (1974), *Public Goods and Public Welfare*. Durham: Duke University Press.

Henare, Sir James (1981), 'Address to the Auckland District Law Society.' 4 July.

Henare, Sir James (1987), 'Foreword.' In J. McRae, Ed, *He Pepeha, He Whakatauki, Nō Tai Tokerau*. Auckland: Government Print.

Henare, M. (1988), 'Ngā Tikanga me ngā Ritenga o te Ao Māori. Standards and Foundations of Māori Society.' In *Future Directions*, Vol. III, Part I of *Report of the Royal Commission on Social Policy*. Wellington: Government Printer.

Henare, M. (1990), 'Christianity: Māori Churches.' In P. Donovan, Ed, *Religions of New Zealanders*. Palmerston North: Dunmore Press.

Henare, M. (1995a), 'Human Labour as a Commodity.' In P. Morrison, Ed, *Labour, Employment and Work in New Zealand 1994: Proceedings of the Sixth Conference*. Wellington: Department of Geography, Victoria University of Wellington.

Henare, M. (1995b), 'Te Tiriti, te Tangata, te Whānau: The Treaty, the Human Person, the Family.' In *Rights and Responsibilities: Papers from the International Year of the Family Symposium on Rights and Responsibilities of the Family, held in Wellington 14 to 16 October 1994*. Wellington: International Year of the Family Committee in association with the Office of the Commissioner for Children.

Henare, M. (1996), Compiler, *Te Whākaputanga o Te Rangatiratanga o Nu Tireni 1835-1839 (Māori text). The Declaration of Independence of New Zealand 1835-1839 (Busby's Explanation in English)*. Auckland: Department of Management and Employment Relations, The University of Auckland.

Henare, M. (1997a), 'Globalisation: An Indigenous Religious/Cultural Perspective.' Paper presented to the Regional Conference on 'Globalisation—The Perceptions and Responses of Religious Traditions and Cultural Communities in the Asia Pacific Regions.' Just World Trust with the co-operation of the International Christian Peace Movement (Pax Christi) Australia, 4-6 July, Shah Alam, Malaysia.

Henare, M. (1997b), 'The Mana of Whangaroa.' In D. Urlich Cloher, Ed, *Sustainable Development in Tai Tokerau. Case Study 3—Whangaroa*. Auckland: University of Auckland.

Henare, M. (1998), 'Mana, Tapu, Mauri, Hau: A Māori Philosophy of Vitalism.' In J. Grimm, Ed, *Indigenous Traditions and Ecology*. Cambridge, MA: Centre for the Study of World Religions, Harvard University, forthcoming.

Henare, M. (forthcoming), 'Religion and Changing Images of the 19th Century Māori Society—From Tribe to Nation.' PhD thesis, Victoria University of Wellington.

Henare, M. and E. Douglas (1988), 'Te Reo o Te Tiriti Mai Rā Anō: The Treaty Always Speaks.' In *Future Directions*, Vol. III, Part I of *Report of the Royal Commission on Social Policy*. Wellington: Government Printer.

Henderson, D. (1996), *Economic Reform: New Zealand in an International Perspective*. Wellington: New Zealand Business Roundtable.

Henning, J. (1995), 'The Employment Contracts Act and Work Stoppages.' *New Zealand Journal of Industrial Relations*, 20 (1), pp.77-92.

Higgins, J. (1995), 'Skills and Schemes: The Training Response to Youth Unemployment.' In P. Morrison, Ed, *Labour, Employment and Work in New Zealand: Proceedings of the Sixth Conference*. Wellington: Department of Geography, Victoria University of Wellington.

Higgins, J. (1997a), 'No Longer a Burning Social Issue? Employment Assistance Policy and the Closure of the Unemployment Debate in New Zealand.' *Australian and New Zealand Journal of Sociology*, 33 (2), pp.137-52.

Higgins, J. (1997b), 'Policy Trade-offs in Social Service Contracting: A Case for Transparency in Policy Discourse.' *Social Policy Journal of New Zealand*, 9 (November), pp.1-15.

Hills, J. (1995), *Inquiry into Income and Wealth*, Vol. 2. London: Joseph Rowntree Foundation.

House of Representatives (1997a), *Parliamentary Debates, Questions for Written Answers, Lodged 17 March to 27 March 1997*. Hansard Supplement 5.

House of Representatives (1997b), *Parliamentary Debates, Questions for Written Answers, Lodged 21 April to 23 May 1997*. Hansard Supplement 7.

Housing New Zealand (1996), *Housing New Zealand Briefing Paper*. Wellington: HNZ.

Housing New Zealand (1997), *Statement of Corporate Intent 1997-2000*. Wellington: HNZ.

Hout, M. (1997), 'Inequality at the Margins: The Effects of Welfare, the Minimum Wage, and Tax Credits on Low-Wage Labor Markets.' Working Paper, March. New York: Russell Sage Foundation.

Hughes, J. (1991), 'The Employment Tribunal and the Employment Court.' *New Zealand Journal of Industrial Relations*, 16 (2), pp.175-83.

Hughes, J. (1992), 'The "Freedom" to Enforce Contracts.' In *Industrial Law Bulletin*, 5 (August), p.46.

Hunt, P. (1993), 'Reclaiming Economic, Social and Cultural Rights.' *Waikato Law Review*, 1, pp.141-63.

Hyman, P. (1994), *Women and Economics: A New Zealand Feminist Perspective*. Wellington: Bridget Williams Books.

Income Distribution Group (1990), *Who Gets What? The Distribution of Income and Wealth in New Zealand*. Wellington: New Zealand Planning Council.

Industry Commission (1993), *Public Housing*, Vol. 1. Canberra: Australian Government Publishing Service.

Industry Commission (1997), *Submission to the Review of Higher Education Financing and Policy*. Canberra: Australian Industry Commission.

Institute of Fiscal Studies (1997), *Green Budget*. London: Institute of Fiscal Studies.

International Labour Organisation (1995), *Final Report of the Committee on Freedom of Association on the Complaint against the Government of New Zealand presented by the New Zealand Council of Trade Unions*. Case No.1698. Geneva: International Labour Organisation.

Irwin, J. (1984), *An Introduction to Māori Religion*. Adelaide: Australian Association for the Study of Religions, Flinders University.

Irwin, M. (1997), 'The National Qualifications Framework: Where to Now?' *Access*, 16 (2), pp.14-30.

Jackson, F. (1997), 'Taxation and Economic Growth: A Critique of Scully.' Mimeo. Wellington: Victoria University of Wellington.

Jamrozik, A. (1994), 'Social Class and Community Services: The Paths to Privilege.' In M. Wearing and R. Berreen, Eds, *Welfare and Social Policy in Australia: The Distribution of Advantage*. Sydney: Harcourt Brace.

Jensen, J. (1988), 'Income Equivalences and the Estimation of Family Expenditures on Children.' Mimeo. Wellington: Department of Social Welfare.

Jonathon, R. (1997), 'Illusory Freedoms: Liberalism, Education and the Market.' *Journal of the Philosophy of Education*, 31 (1), Special Issue, pp.1-221.

Jones, M. (1996), 'Full Steam Ahead to a Workfare State? Analysing the UK Employment Department's Abolition.' *Policy and Politics*, 24 (2), pp.137-57.

Jones, M. (1997), *Reforming New Zealand Welfare: International Perspectives*. Policy Monograph No.37. St Leonards: Centre for Independent Studies.

Kahne, J. (1996), *Reframing Educational Policy: Democracy, Community and the Individual*. New York: Teachers College Press.

Keat, R. and N. Abercrombie (1991), Eds, *Enterprise Culture*. London: Routledge.

Kelsey, J. (1993), *Rolling Back the State: Privatisation of Power in Aotearoa/New Zealand*. Wellington: Bridget Williams Books.

Kelsey, J. (1997a), *The New Zealand Experiment: A World Model for Structural Adjustment?* 2nd Edition. Auckland: Auckland University Press/Bridget Williams Books.

Kelsey, J. (1997b), 'The Globalisation of Tertiary Education: The Implications of GATS.' In M. Peters, Ed, *Cultural Politics and the University in Aotearoa/New Zealand*. Palmerston North: Dunmore Press.

Kemp, P. (1990), 'Shifting the Balance Between State and Market: The Reprivatisation of Rental Housing Provision in Britain.' *Environment and Planning* A, 22, pp.793-810.

Kemp, P. (1994), 'Housing Allowances and the Fiscal Crisis of the Welfare State.' *Housing Studies*, 9, pp.531-42.

Kernot, B. (1997), 'Preface.' In S. Mead, *Māori Art on the World Scene*. Wellington: Āhua Design & Illustration Ltd/Matau Associates.

Kerr, R. (1993a), 'A Court for Employment or Unemployment?' *The Independent*, 7 May, pp.6, 8.

Kerr, R. (1993b), 'Employment Contracts Act Undermined by Judicial Activism.' *The Independent*, 14 May, pp.6, 8.

Kerr, R. (1994), 'Why Taxes Should Not Be Increased.' Wellington: New Zealand Business Roundtable.

Kerr, R. (1996a), 'The Business Experience of Economic Reform in New Zealand.' Speech to the Japan/New Zealand Business Council 23rd Joint Meeting. Reprinted in *MMP Must Mean Much More Progress*. Wellington: New Zealand Business Roundtable, 1996.

Kerr, R. (1996b), 'New Zealand's ACC Scheme: Time for a Burial.' Wellington: New Zealand Business Roundtable.

Kerr, R. (1997), 'Seven Deadly Economic Sins of the Twentieth Century.' New Zealand Post—College of Business Jubilee Lecture, Massey University, 6 August. Reprinted in *The Trouble with Teabreaks*. Wellington: New Zealand Business Roundtable, 1998.

Kerr, R. (1998), 'Private Sector has a Role to Play in ACC.' *Evening Post*, 7 January.

Kesselman, J. (1980), 'Pitfalls of Selectivity in Incomes Security Programs.' *Canadian Taxation*, 2, pp.154-63.

Keynes, J.M. (1936), *The General Theory of Employment Interest and Money*. London: Macmillan.

Kim, K., R. Buckle and V. Hall (1995), 'Dating New Zealand Business Cycles.' *New Zealand Economic Papers*, 29 (2), pp.143-71.

King, D.S. (1992), 'The Establishment of Work-Welfare Programs in the United States and Britain: Politics, Ideas and Institutions.' In S. Steinmo, K. Thelen and F. Longstreth, Eds, *Restructuring Politics: Historical Institutionalism and Comparative Analysis*. Cambridge: Cambridge University Press.

King, J. (1996), 'A Time Limit for the Dole?' *Social Policy Journal of New Zealand*, 6 (July), pp.92-109.

Koopman-Boyden, P. (1990), 'Social Policy: Has There Been One?' In M. Holland and J. Boston, Eds, *The Fourth Labour Government: Politics and Policy in New Zealand*. Auckland: Oxford University Press.

Koopman-Boyden, P. and C. Scott (1984), *The Family and Government Policy in New Zealand*. Sydney: Allen and Unwin.

Krishnan, V. (1995), 'Modest but Adequate: An Appraisal of Changing Household Income Circumstances in New Zealand.' *Social Policy Journal of New Zealand*, 4 (July), pp.76-97.

Kwon, H-J. (1997), 'Beyond European Welfare Regimes: Comparative Perspectives on East Asian Welfare Systems.' *Journal of Social Policy*, 26 (4), pp.467-84.

Labour Market Policy Group (1997), 'Labour Market Context.' *Context Papers: Beyond Dependency*, Wellington: Department of Labour.

Lange, D. (1989), *The Crown and the Treaty of Waitangi. A Short Statement of the Principles on which the Crown Proposes to Act*. Wellington: Department of Justice.

Lauder, H. (1994), *The Creation of Market Connections for Education in New Zealand: An Empirical Analysis of a New Zealand Secondary School Market 1990-1993*. Wellington: Ministry of Education.

Laugesen, R. (1997), 'PM-Elect Tips Overhaul of Benefit System.' *Sunday Star Times*, 9 November.

Law, J. (1996), 'Businesses Not Governments Create Wealth.' Speech to the Wanganui Chamber of Commerce and Industry. Reprinted in *MMP Must Mean Much More Progress*. Wellington: New Zealand Business Roundtable.

Le Grand, J. (1982), *The Strategy of Equality*. London: Allen and Unwin.

Le Grand, J. (1987), 'The Middle Class and the Use of British Social Services.' In R. Goodin and J. Le Grand, Eds, *Not Only the Poor*. London: Allen and Unwin.

Lebacqz, K. (1986), *Six Theories of Justice*. Minneapolis: Augsburg.

Lepper, J. (1997), 'On Scully's "Taxation and Economic Growth in New Zealand".' Mimeo. Wellington: Integrated Economic Services Ltd.

Levine, M., H. Wyn and L. Asiaiga (1993), *Lone Parents and Paid Work: A Study of Employment Patterns and Barriers and Options for Change*. Wellington: Social Policy Agency.

Littlewood, M. (1997), *Will You Still Need Me? A Retirement Income Primer for Politicians, Employers and Meddlers*. Auckland: Planit Services.

Lovell, K. and J. Branson (1997), 'A Growth Maximising Tax Structure for New Zealand.' *Working Papers on Monitoring the Health of the Tax System*, No.30. Wellington: Inland Revenue New Zealand.

Luxton, J. (1991), *Housing and Accommodation: Accommodation Assistance*. Wellington: Government Printer.

Maaka, R. (1994). 'The New Tribe: Conflicts and Continuities in the Social Organisation of Urban Māori.' *The Contemporary Pacific*, 6 (2), pp.311-36.

Maani, S. (1996), 'The Effect of Fees on Participation in Higher Education: A Survey of OECD Countries.' *New Zealand Economic Papers*, 30 (1), pp.55-86.

Maani, S. (1997), *Investing in Minds: The Economics of Higher Education in New Zealand*. Wellington: Institute of Policy Studies.

Mackay, R. (1994), *Foodbanks in New Zealand: Patterns of Growth and Usage*. Wellington: Social Policy Agency.

Mackay, R. (1995), 'Foodbank Demand and Supplementary Assistance Programmes: A Research and Policy Case Study.' *Social Policy Journal of New Zealand*, 5 (December), pp.129-41.

Malcolm, L. (1997), 'GP Budget Holding in New Zealand: Lessons for Britain and Elsewhere.' *British Medical Journal*, 314, pp.1890-92.

Maloney, T. (1997), *Benefit Reform and Labour Market Behaviour in New Zealand*. Wellington: Institute of Policy Studies.

Marsden, M. (1991) 'Pastoral Plan—Some Reflections.' Reflection given at Roman Catholic Hui Whakaminenga, Papa o Te Aroha Marae, Tokorua. 16 March. Manuscript in Manuka Henare's possession.

Marshall, J.D. (1992), 'Principles and the National Curriculum: Centralised Development.' Paper presented to the New Zealand Council for Teacher Education Conference, Auckland College of Education.

Marshall, J.D. (1995), 'Skills, Information and Quality for the Autonomous Chooser.' In M. Olssen and K. Morris Matthews, Eds, *Education, Democracy and Reform*. Auckland: Auckland University, New Zealand Association of Research in Education/Research Unit for Māori Education.

Marshall, P. (1996), 'Rights Talk and Welfare Policy.' In S. Carlson-Thiers and J. Skillen, Eds, *Welfare in America: Christian Perspectives on a Policy in Crisis*. Grand Rapids: Eerdmans.

Marshall, S. (1993), 'The Future Structure and Operation of the Employment Court and Tribunal.' Paper presented to a New Zealand Institute of Industrial Relations Research Seminar, 23 April, Wellington.

Massey, P. (1995), *New Zealand: Market Liberalisation in a Developed Economy*. London: Macmillan.

Mbiti, J.S. (1975), *Introduction to African Religion*. London: Heinemann Educational.

McCully, M. (1997a), 'McCully Announces Stronger Social Mandate for HNZ.' New Zealand Executive Government News Release Archive, 12 November.

McCully, M. (1997b), 'Hon Murray McCully, Minister of Housing.' New Zealand Executive Government News Release Archive, 14 November.

McCully, M. (1997c), 'Auckland Housing NZ Rent Reductions Announced.' New Zealand Executive Government News Release Archive, 2 December.

McGurk, T. (1997), 'Submission on Social Security Amendment Bill (No 2) to the Social Services Select Committee.' Wellington.

McKenzie, A. (1997), 'Workfare: The New Zealand Experience and Future Directions.' *Social Policy Journal of New Zealand*, 8 (March), pp.97-110.

McKeown, P.C. and A.E. Woodfield (1995), 'The Welfare Cost of Taxation in New Zealand Following Major Tax Reforms.' *New Zealand Economic Papers*, 29 (1), pp.41-62.

McLeay, E. (1992), 'Housing Policy.' In J. Boston and P. Dalziel, Eds, *The Decent Society? Essays in Response to National's Economic and Social Policies*. Auckland: Oxford University Press.

Mead, L. (1997), 'Raising Work Levels Among the Poor.' *Social Policy Journal of New Zealand*, 8 (March), pp.1-28.

Mendelson, M. (1980), 'The Selectivity Mistake.' *Canadian Taxation*, 2, pp.167-9.

Menzies, P. (1991), 'Why New Zealand Needs a Responsible Budget.' Speech to New Zealand Credit and Finance Institute.

Miller, D. (1976), *Social Justice*. Oxford: Clarendon Press.

Miller, D. (1992), 'Review Article: Recent Theories of Social Justice.' *British Journal of Political Science*, 21, pp.371-91.

Miller, D. (1997), 'What Kind of Equality Should the Left Pursue?' In J. Franklin, Ed, *Equality*. London: Institute for Public Policy Research.

Miller, R. (1997), Ed, *New Zealand Politics in Transition*. Auckland: Oxford University Press.

Minister of Health (1994), *Policy Guidelines for Regional Health Authorities 1994/95*. Wellington: Ministry of Health.

Ministerial Consultative Group (1994), *Funding Growth in Tertiary Education and Training* (known as the Todd Report). Wellington: Ministry of Education.

Ministerial Planning Group (1991), *Ka Awatea*. Wellington: New Zealand Government.

Ministry of Education (1994a), *Education for the Twenty First Century*. Wellington: Ministry of Education.

Ministry of Education (1994b), *The Education Gazette*, February.

Ministry of Education (1997a), 'Tertiary Education Review: Proposals and Key Decisions.' 17 July. Wellington: Ministry of Education.

Ministry of Education (1997b), *A Future Tertiary Education Policy for New Zealand: Tertiary Education Review (Green Paper)*. Wellington: Ministry of Education.

Ministry of Health (1992), *Policy Guidelines to Regional Health Authorities*. Wellington: Ministry of Health.

Ministry of Health (1996a), *Healthy New Zealanders: Briefing Papers for the Minister of Health 1996*, Volume 1. Wellington: Ministry of Health.

Ministry of Health (1996b), *Sustainable Funding Package for the Health and Disability Sector*. Wellington: Ministry of Health.

Ministry of Health (1996c), *Progress on Health Outcome Targets: Te Haere Whakamua Ki Ngā Whāinga Hā Mō Te Hauora, 1996*. Wellington: Ministry of Health.

Ministry of Housing (1996), *Post-election Briefing to the Minister of Housing*. Wellington: Ministry of Housing.

Ministry of Women's Affairs (1991), 'Change Team Proposals on the Targeting of Social Assistance.' 2 May. Wellington: Ministry of Women's Affairs.

Mishel, L. and J. Schmitt (1995), 'Cutting Wages by Cutting Welfare: The Impact of Reform on the Low-Wage Labor Market.' Briefing Paper No.58. Washington DC: Economic Policy Institute.

Moore, D. and S. Davenport (1990), 'Choice: The New Improved Sorting Machine.' In W.L. Boyd and H.L. Walberg, Eds, *Choice in Education: Potential and Problems*. Berkeley: McCutchan.

Moore, M. (1996), *Children of the Poor*. Christchurch: Canterbury University Press.

Morgan-Thomas, E. (1997), 'Is This the End of Public Housing.' In R. Coles, Ed, *The End of Public Housing?* Canberra: Urban Research Program, Research School of Social Sciences, Australian National University.

Morrison, P. (1995), 'The Geography of Rental Housing and the Restructuring of Housing Assistance in New Zealand.' *Housing Studies*, 10, pp.39-56.

Morrison, P. and L. Murphy (1996), 'The Geography of the Housing Reforms.' In R. Le Heron and E. Pawson, Eds, *Changing Places: New Zealand in the Nineties*. Auckland: Longman Paul.

Mulgan, R. (1991), 'Targeting the Welfare State—A Theoretical Overview.' Paper prepared for the Change Team on Targeting Social Assistance. Wellington: Department of the Prime Minister and Cabinet.

Murie, A. (1997), 'The Social Rented Sector, Housing and the Welfare State in the UK.' *Housing Studies*, 12, pp.437-61.

Murphy, L. (1996), 'Whose Interests Rates? Issues in the Development of Mortgage-Backed Securitisation.' *Housing Studies*, 11, pp.581-9.

Murphy, L. (1997), 'New Zealand's Housing Reforms and Accommodation Supplement Experience.' *Urban Policy and Research*, 15, pp.247-56.

Murphy, L. and R.A. Kearns (1994), 'Housing New Zealand Ltd: Privatisation by Stealth.' *Environment and Planning A*, 26, pp.623-37.

Musgrave, R.A. (1957), 'A Multiple Theory of Budget Determination.' *Finanz Archiv*, 17 (3), pp.333-43.

Musgrave, R.A. (1987), 'Merit Goods.' In J. Eatwell, M. Milgate and P. Newman, Eds, *The New Palgrave: A Dictionary of Economics*, Vol. 3. London: Macmillan.

Musgrave, R.A. (1997), 'Reconsidering the Fiscal Role of Government.' *American Economic Review*, 87 (2), pp.156-9.

Musgrave, R.A. and P. Musgrave (1980), *Public Finance in Theory and Practice*. New York: McGraw Hill.

National Advisory Committee on Core Health and Disability Support Services (1992), *Core Services for 1993/94*. Wellington: Ministry of Health.

National Advisory Committee on Core Health and Disability Support Services (1994), *Core Services for 1995/96*. Wellington: Ministry of Health.

National Business Review (1997), 'Higher ACC Levies to Cover Treasury's Blunders?' 17 October.

National Party (1990), *Election Manifesto*. Wellington: National Party.

New Zealand Business Roundtable (1987), *Better Value for Public Money: The Government's 1987 Budget and Medium-Term Fiscal Policy*. Wellington: NZBR.

New Zealand Business Roundtable (1988), *Reforming Tertiary Education in New Zealand*. Wellington: NZBR.

New Zealand Business Roundtable (1990), *Choice in the Workplace: A Better Framework for Labour Law*. Wellington: NZBR.

New Zealand Business Roundtable (1991), 'Submission on the Policy Statement Accident Compensation: A Fairer Scheme.' Wellington: NZBR.

New Zealand Business Roundtable (1996), *Moving into the Fast Lane*. Wellington: NZBR.

New Zealand Business Roundtable/New Zealand Employers' Federation (1992), *A Study of the Labour/Employment Court*. Wellington: NZBR/NZEF.

New Zealand Business Roundtable/New Zealand Employers' Federation (1996), *The Employment Contracts Act and Unjustifiable Dismissal—The Economics of an Unjust Employment Tax*. Wellington: NZBR/NZEF.

New Zealand Church Leaders (1993), *Social Justice Statement*. Wellington, 11 July.

New Zealand Employers' Federation (1995), *A New Prescription for Accident Compensation*. Wellington: NZEF.

New Zealand Engineering Union (1991), 'Submissions to the Labour Select Committee on the Employment Contracts Bill.' NZEU, February.

New Zealand Federation of Voluntary Welfare Organisations (1997), *Dialogue: Newsletter of the NZFVWO*. Various issues. Wellington: NZFVWO.

New Zealand Government (1984), *A Review of Employment Subsidy Programmes: A Framework for Consultation*. Wellington: Government Printer.

New Zealand Government (1985), *Industrial Relations: A Framework for Review*. Wellington: Department of Labour.

New Zealand Government (1997a), *Review of the Holidays Act 1981: Consultation Paper— Options for Review*. Wellington: Department of Labour.

New Zealand Government (1997b), *You and Your Retirement Savings: The Proposed Compulsory Retirement Savings Scheme*. Wellington: The Treasury.

New Zealand Government (1998), *Towards a Code of Social and Family Responsibility*. Public Discussion Document, February 1998.

New Zealand Law Society (1988), *Personal Injury: Prevention and Recovery. Report on the Accident Compensation Scheme*. Report No.4. Wellington: Law Commission.

New Zealand Vice-Chancellors' Committee (1997), 'Submission on the Green Paper.' Wellington: NZVCC.

Ngata, A. and I.L.G. Sutherland (1940), 'Religious Influences.' In I.L.G. Sutherland, Ed, *The Māori People Today*. Wellington: New Zealand Institute of International Affairs/New Zealand Council for Educational Research.

Nowland-Foreman, G. (1997), 'Can Voluntary Organisations Survive the Bear Hug of Government Funding Under a Contracting Regime? A View From Aotearoa/New Zealand.' *Third Sector Review*, 3, pp.5-39.

Nozick, R. (1974), *Anarchy, State and Utopia*. Oxford: Basil Blackwell.

Obler, J. (1981), 'Private Giving in the Welfare State.' *British Journal of Political Science*, 11, pp.17-48.

O'Brien, M. and C. Briar (1997), Eds, *Beyond Poverty: Conference Proceedings*. Auckland: The People's Centre.

O'Dea, D.J., K. Szeto, S. Dovey and M. Tilyard, 'The Effect of Changes in User Charges on Visits to New Zealand GPs.' Unpublished.

O'Higgins, M. (1985a), 'Inequality, Redistribution and Recessions: The British Experience 1976-1982.' *Journal of Social Policy*, 14, pp.279-307.

O'Higgins, M. (1985b), 'Welfare, Redistribution and Inequality: Disillusion, Illusion and Reality.' In P. Bean, J. Ferris and D. Whynes, Eds, *In Defence of Welfare*. London: Tavistock.

O'Higgins, M. (1987), 'Egalitarians, Equalities and Welfare Evaluation.' *Journal of Social Policy*, 16, pp.1-18.

Oliver, W.H. (1989), 'The Labour Caucus and Economic Policy Formation, 1981-1984.' In B. Easton, Ed, *The Making of Rogernomics*. Auckland: Auckland University Press.

Olssen, M. and K. Morris Matthews (1997), *Education Policy in New Zealand: The 1990s and Beyond*. Palmerston North: Dunmore Press.

Onyx, J. (1996), 'The Measure of Social Capital.' Paper presented to the Australia and New Zealand Third Sector Research Conference on 'Social Cohesion, Justice and Citizenship: The Role of the Voluntary Sector.' Victoria University of Wellington.

Orange, C. (1987), *The Treaty of Waitangi*. Wellington: Allen & Unwin, and Port Nicholson Press.

Organisation for Economic Co-operation and Development (1988), *Measures to Assist the Long Term Unemployed: Recent Experience in Some OECD Countries*. Paris: OECD.

Organisation for Economic Co-operation and Development (1990a), *Financing Higher Education: Current Patterns*. Paris: OECD.

Organisation for Economic Co-operation and Development (1990b), *The Tax/Benefit Position of Production Workers*. Paris: OECD.

Organisation for Economic Co-operation and Development (1996), *Economic Surveys: New Zealand 1996*. Paris: OECD.

Organisation for Economic Co-operation and Development (1997), 'Thematic Review of the First Years of Tertiary Education: New Zealand.' Paris: OECD.

Oxenbridge, S. (1997), 'Organizing Strategies and Organizing Reform in New Zealand Service Sector Unions.' *Labor Studies Journal*, 22 (3), pp.3-27.

Oxenbridge, S. (1998), 'The Individualisaton of Employment Relations in New Zealand: Trends and Outcomes.' Paper presented to the Individualisation and Union Exclusion in Employment Relations conference, University of Melbourne, 3–4 September.

Papadakis, E. (1994), 'Public Opinion, Redistribution and the Welfare State.' In M. Wearing and R. Berreen, Eds, *Welfare and Social Policy in Australia: The Distribution of Advantage*. Sydney: Harcourt Brace.

Parker, M. (1997), 'The Industry Commission's Approach to Housing Assistance.' In R. Coles, Ed, *The End of Public Housing?*. Canberra: Urban Research Program, Research School of Social Sciences, Australian National University.

Parks, C.D. (1996), 'A Study of Community Services Cards in Five Primary Health Care Practices in Auckland Region.' MHSc thesis, Department of Community Health, University of Auckland.

Patterson, G. (1991), 'New Zealand Universities Under the Fourth Labour Government.' Occasional Papers No.5. Palmerston North: Department of Management Systems, Massey University.

Peddie, R. and B. Tuck (1995), Eds, *Setting the Standards: Issues in Assessment for National Qualifications*. Palmerston North: Dunmore Press.

Performance Management Unit (1995/96), *Purchasing for Your Health 1995/96*. Wellington: Ministry of Health.

Performance Management Unit (1996/97), *Purchasing for Your Health 1996/97*. Wellington: Ministry of Health.

Performance Monitoring and Review (undated), *Review of 1994/95 RHA Contracting*. Wellington: Ministry of Health.

Periodic Report Group (1997a), *1997 Retirement Income Report: A Review of the Current Framework—Interim Report*. 31 July. Wellington: PRG.

Periodic Report Group (1997b), *Concluding Report*. 18 December. Wellington: PRG.

Perkins, R.J., K.J. Petrie, P.G. Alley, P.C. Barnes, M.M. Fisher and P.J. Hatfield (1997), 'Health Service Reform: The Perceptions of Medical Specialists in Australia (New South Wales), the United Kingdom and New Zealand.' *Medical Journal of Australia*, 167, pp.201-4.

Peston, M. (1966), 'The Theory of Spillovers and its Connection with Education.' *Public Finance*, 21, pp.184-99.

Peters, M. (1992), 'A Critique of the Porter Report.' *Delta*, 46, pp.3-14.

Peters, M. (1997), Ed, *Cultural Politics and the University in Aotearoa/New Zealand*. Palmerston North: Dunmore Press.

Peters, M., J. Marshall and G. Smith (1991), 'The Business Roundtable and the Privatisation of Education: Individualism and the Attack on Māori.' In L. Gordon and J. Codd, Eds, *Education Policy and the Changing Role of the State*. Palmerston North: Delta Studies in Education, Massey University.

Peters, W. (1997a), *Budget Speech and Fiscal Strategy Report*. Parliamentary Paper, B2.

Peters, W. (1997b), *Treasurer's Statement and Overview, Economic and Fiscal Forecast, Summary*. Wellington: The Treasury.

Peters, W. (1998a), *Budget Policy Statement*. Wellington: New Zealand Government.

Peters, W. (1998b), *Budget Speech and Fiscal Strategy Report*. Parliamentary Paper, B2.

Pharmac (1996), *Pharmac Annual Review 1995/96*. Wellington: Pharmac.

Philpott, B. (1991), 'Review of *Upgrading New Zealand's Competitive Advantage*.' *New Zealand Economic Papers*, 25, pp.275-82.

Plant, R. (1985), 'Welfare and the Value of Liberty.' *Government and Opposition*, 20, pp.297-314.

Plant, R. (1990), 'Citizenship and Rights.' In *Citizenship and Rights in Thatcher's Britain: Two Views*. London: IEA Health and Welfare Unit.

Plant, R. (1992a), 'Citizenship, Rights and Welfare.' In A. Coote, Ed, *The Welfare of Citizens: Developing New Social Rights*. London: Institute for Public Policy Research.

Plant, R. (1992b), 'Autonomy, Social Rights and Distributive Justice.' In *The Moral Foundations of Market Institutions*. London: IEA Health and Welfare Unit.

Player, M. (1994), 'From Welfare to Well-Being: Communicating a Vision.' *Social Policy Journal of New Zealand*, 3 (December), pp.77-81.

Pool, I. (1987), 'New Zealand Universities Until 2007: Demographic Structures and Changes.' Wellington: New Zealand Vice-Chancellors' Committee.

Poole, W. (1991), 'Employers' View.' IPSO Conference on Accident Compensation Reform, Wellington.

Prebble, M. (1990), *Information, Privacy and the Welfare State: An Integrated Approach to Redistribution*. Wellington: Victoria University Press.

Prebble, M. (1992), 'Introduction to the Study.' In M. Prebble and P. Rebstock, Eds, *Incentives and Labour Supply: Modelling Taxes and Benefits*. Wellington: Institute of Policy Studies.

Prebble, M. and P. Rebstock (1992), Eds, *Incentives and Labour Supply: Modelling Taxes and Benefits*. Wellington: Institute of Policy Studies.

Prebble, M. et al. (1991), *Report of the Change Team on Targeting Social Assistance*. Wellington: Department of Prime Minister and Cabinet.

Preston, D. (1996), 'Reducing Benefit Dependence.' *Social Policy Journal of New Zealand*, 6 (July), pp.69-91.

Preston, D. (1997), 'Welfare Benefit Reform.' *Social Policy Journal of New Zealand*, 8 (March), pp.29-36.

Priemus, H. (1997), 'Growth and Stagnation in Social Housing: What is "Social" in the Social Rented Sector.' *Housing Studies*, 12, pp.549-60.

Public Health Commission (1994), *A Strategic Direction to Improve and Protect the Public Health: The Public Health Commission's Advice to the Minister of Health 1993-94*. Wellington: Public Health Commission.

Public Health Referendum (1997), Media Statement, 16 October.

Putnam, R.D. (1993a), with R. Leonardi and R.Y. Nanetti, *Making Democracy Work: Civic Traditions in Modern Italy*. Princeton NJ: Princeton University Press.

Putnam, R.D. (1993b), 'The Prosperous Community: Social Capital and Public Life.' *The American Prospect*, 13 (Spring), pp.35-42.

Putnam, R.D. (1996), 'Bowling Alone: America's Declining Social Capital.' *Journal of Democracy*, 6 (1), pp.65-78.

Raffe, D. (1990), 'The Context of the Youth Training Scheme: An Analysis of its Strategy and Development.' In D. Gleeson, Ed, *Training and its Alternatives*. Milton Keynes: Open University Press.

Rankin, K. (1991), 'The Universal Welfare State, Incorporating Proposals for a Universal Basic Income.' Policy Discussion Paper No.12. Auckland: Economics Department, University of Auckland.

Rawls, J. (1972), *A Theory of Justice*. Oxford: Oxford University Press.

Raz, J. (1986), *The Morality of Freedom*. Oxford: Clarendon Press.

Rennie, D. (1994), 'ACC and the Common Law.' *Employment Today*, 4 (April), pp.16-18.

Rennie, D. (1996), 'Employers are Misled in their Call to Privatise ACC.' *National Business Review*, 9 August.

Report of the Social Policy Committee of the Board for Social Responsibility (1986), *Not Just For The Poor: Christian Perspectives on the Welfare State*. London: Church House Publishing.

Richardson, R. (1990), 'Statement by the Minister of Finance.' *Economic and Social Initiative—December 1990*. Wellington: Government Printer.

Richardson, R. (1991), *Budget 1991*. Parliamentary Paper, B6.

Richardson, R. (1995), *Making a Difference*. Christchurch: Shoal Bay Press.

Riddell, M. (1997), 'Bringing Back Balance: The Role of Social Capital in Public Policy.' In D. Robinson, Ed, *Social Capital and Policy Development*. Wellington: Institute of Policy Studies.

Roberts, C. (1992), 'Accommodation Supplement: New Zealand's Experiment in Housing Policy.' Auckland: New Zealand Council of Christian Social Services.

Robertson, B. (1997), *Economic, Social and Cultural Rights: Time for a Reappraisal*. Wellington: New Zealand Business Roundtable.

Robertson, S., R. Dale and M. Thrupp (1997), *Report on Education Review Office*. Wellington: Post-Primary Teachers' Association.

Robinson, D. (1997), Ed, *Social Capital and Policy Development*. Wellington: Institute of Policy Studies.

Rochford, M. (1993), *A Profile of Sole Parents from the 1991 Census*. Research Report Series No.15. Wellington: Social Policy Agency.

Roper, B. (1991), 'From the Welfare State to the Free Market: Explaining the Transition.' *New Zealand Sociology*, 6 (1), pp.38-63.

Roper, B. (1992), 'A Level Playing Field? Business Political Activism and State Policy Formulation.' In B. Roper and C. Rudd, Eds, *State and Economy in New Zealand*. Auckland: Oxford University Press.

Roper, K. (1991), 'Towards a New Unionism: The Response of the New Zealand Public Service Association to the Fourth Labour Government.' In *Labour Movement Strategies for the 21st Century*. Sydney: Evatt Foundation.

Rose, N. (1995), *Workfare or Fair Work: Women, Welfare and Government Work Programs*. New Brunswick: Rutgers University Press.

Rosenberg, W. (1977), 'Full Employment: The Fulcrum of the Welfare State.' In A.D. Trlin, Ed, *Social Welfare and New Zealand Society*. Wellington: Methuen.

Rothstein, B. (1993), 'The Crisis of the Swedish Social Democrats and the Future of the Universal Welfare State.' *Governance*, 6 (4), pp.492-517.

Royal Commission of Inquiry into Workers' Compensation (1967), *Compensation for Personal Injury in New Zealand*. Wellington: Government Printer.

Royal Commission on Social Policy (1988a), *The April Report*. Wellington: Government Printer.

Royal Commission on Social Policy (1988b), *Summary Report*. Wellington: Government Printer.

Royal Commission on Social Security (1972), *Report on Social Security in New Zealand*. Wellington: Government Printer.

Rudd, C. (1997), 'The Welfare State.' In C. Rudd and B. Roper, Eds, *The Political Economy of New Zealand*. Auckland: Oxford University Press.

Rudd, C. and B. Roper (1997), Eds, *The Political Economy of New Zealand*. Auckland: Oxford University Press.

Ryan, R. (1994), *A Survey of Labour Market Adjustments under the Employment Contracts Act 1991: Gender Analysis of the Employee Survey*. Wellington: National Advisory Council on the Employment of Women.

Sala-i-Martin, X. (1997), 'I Just Ran Two Million Regressions.' *American Economic Review*, 87 (2), pp.178-83.

Sale, E.V. (1986), Compiler, *Whangaroa*. Kaeo: Whangaroa Books Committee.

Salmond, A. (1985), 'Māori Epistemologies.' In J. Overing, Ed, *Reason and Morality*. London: Tavistock.

Saltman, R.B. and C. von Otter (1995), *Implementing Planned Markets in Health Care*. Buckingham: Open University Press.

Saunders, P. (1994), *Welfare and Inequality: National and International Perspectives on the Australian Welfare State*. Melbourne: Cambridge University Press.

Scheffler, S. (1976), 'Natural Rights, Equality and the Minimal State.' *Canadian Journal of Philosophy*, 6, pp.59-76.

Schrempp, G. (1992), *Magical Arrows: The Māori, the Greeks and the Folklore of the Universe*. Madison: University of Wisconsin.

Scollay, R. and S. St John (1996), *Macroeconomics and the Contemporary New Zealand Economy*. Auckland: Longman.

Scott, C. (1994), 'Reform of the New Zealand Health System.' *Health Policy*, 29 (1-2), pp.25-40.

Scott, G. and P. Gorringe (1989), 'Reform of the Core Public Sector: The New Zealand Experience.' *Australian Journal of Public Administration*, 48 (1), pp.81-92.

Scott, G. and S. Smelt (1995), 'Ownership of Universities.' A paper prepared for consideration by the New Zealand Vice-Chancellors' Committee. Wellington: Graham Scott New Zealand.

Scott, G.C. (1996), *Government Reform in New Zealand*. Occasional Paper No.140. Washington DC: International Monetary Fund.

Scully, G.W. (1996a), 'Taxation and Economic Growth in New Zealand.' Working Papers on Monitoring the Health of the Tax System No.14. Wellington: Inland Revenue New Zealand.

Scully, G.W. (1996b), 'Taxation and Economic Growth in New Zealand.' *Pacific Economic Review*, 1 (2), pp.169-77.

Scully, G.W. (1997a), 'Reply to Formal Review by E. Sieper.' Mimeo. Dallas: University of Texas.

Scully, G.W. (1997b), 'Reply to Jackson Critique of Scully Paper.' Mimeo. Dallas: University of Texas.

Sector Analysis Section (undated), *Health Expenditure Trends in New Zealand 1980-1996*. Wellington: Ministry of Health.

Sexton, S. (1991), *New Zealand Schools: An Evaluation of Recent Reforms and Future Directions*. Wellington: New Zealand Business Roundtable.

Shannon, P. (1991), *Social Policy*. Auckland: Oxford University Press.

Sharp, A. (1994), Ed, *Leap into the Dark: The Changing Role of the State Since 1984*. Auckland: Auckland University Press.

Sheeran, G. (1997), 'Private Health Costs Sure to Rise.' *Sunday Star Times*, 1 June, p.D1.

Shipley, J. (1991), *Social Assistance: Welfare That Works*. Wellington: GP Print.

Shipley, J. (1996), *Advancing Health in New Zealand*. Wellington: Ministry of Health.

Shipley, J. (1998), 'Speech to Open 1998 Session of Parliament.' Wellington: New Zealand Government.

Shirley, I., P. Koopman-Boyden, I. Pool and S. St John (1997), *Family Change and Family Policy: New Zealand*. New Zealand's contribution to the twenty country International Study on Family Policy, co-ordinated by the Mannheim Institute. Oxford: Oxford University Press.

Shirres, M. (1997), *Te Tangata. The Human Person*. Auckland: Accent Publications.

Sieper, E. (1997), 'Review of Gerald W. Scully "Taxation and Economic Growth in New Zealand".' Mimeo. Wellington: New Zealand Treasury.

Silverstone, B., A. Bollard and R. Lattimore (1996), Eds, *A Study of Economic Reform: The Case of New Zealand*. Amsterdam: North-Holland.

Skocpol, T. (1991), 'Targeting within Universalism: Politically Viable Policies to Combat Poverty in the United States.' In C. Jencks and P. Peterson, Eds, *The Urban Underclass*. Washington: The Brookings Institution.

Smith, G. (1991), 'Reform and Māori Educational Crisis: A Grand Illusion.' Keynote Speech at the PPTA Conference, Ōtautahi.

Smith, J. and M. Oxley (1997), 'Housing Investment and Social Housing: European Comparisons.' *Housing Studies*, 12, pp.489-507.

Smith, L. (1991), *Education Policy: Investing in People, Our Greatest Asset*. Wellington: Government Printer.

Smith, S. and S. Mallinson (1997), 'Housing for Health in a Post-Welfare State.' *Housing Studies*, 12, pp.173-200.

Snively, S. (1995), 'The New Zealand Economic Cost of Family Violence.' *Social Policy Journal of New Zealand*, 4 (July), pp.98-110.

Solow, R.M. (1997), 'Is There A Core of Usable Macroeconomics We Should All Believe In?' *American Economic Review*, 87 (2), pp.230-32.

Sowry, R. (1997), 'From Welfare to Well-being.' Address to Business Breakfast, Wellington, 14 October.

St John, S. (1979), 'Cost Allocation in the New Zealand Accident Compensation Scheme.' Masters thesis, University of Auckland.

St John, S. (1981), 'Safety Incentives in the New Zealand Accident Compensation Scheme.' *New Zealand Economics Papers*, 15, pp.111-26.

St John, S. (1991), 'The Core Family Unit: The Implications of the 1991 Budget for Women.' *Women's Studies Journal*, 7 (2), pp.1-13.

St John, S. (1992), 'Superannuation Policy: or How Not to Make Policy.' In J. Boston and P. Dalziel, Eds, *The Decent Society? Essays in Response to National's Economic and Social Policies*. Auckland: Oxford University Press.

St John, S. (1996a), 'The Policy Framework Which Has Driven the Massive Increase in Poverty.' In K. Hackwell, Ed, *Eradicating Poverty in New Zealand: Notes from the Second National Food Bank Conference*. Wellington: Downtown Community Ministry.

St John, S. (1996b), 'The Welfare Mess Revisited.' Policy Discussion Paper No.21. Auckland: Department of Economics, University of Auckland.

St John, S. (1997a), 'The Measure of Success for Beyond Dependency: Aims, Methods and Evaluation.' *Social Policy Journal of New Zealand*, 8 (March), pp.61-66.

St John, S. (1997b), 'Retirement Policies: Issues for Women—The 1997 Retirement Income Report.' Paper given to the Seminar on Women and Retirement, Women's Health Action, Ellen Melville Hall, Auckland, 30 August.

St John, S. and T. Ashton (1993), *Private Pensions in New Zealand: Can They Avert the Crisis?* Wellington: Institute of Policy Studies.

Standing, G. (1996), 'Social Protection in Central and Eastern Europe: A Tale of Slipping Anchors and Torn Safety Nets.' In G. Esping-Andersen, Ed, *Welfare States in Transition: National Adaptations in Global Economies*. London: Sage.

State Services Commission (1996a), 'Policy Costing—Requiring Unemployed Job Seekers to be Employed in Community Work and/or Training.' Document GF No.504/1. Wellington: SSC.

State Services Commission (1996b), 'Information Supplied by the Public Service in Response to Requests Made by Political Parties Taking Part in Coalition Formation Talks.' Document GF No.512. Wellington: SSC.

Statistics New Zealand (1996), *Demographic Trends 1996*. Wellington: Statistics New Zealand.

Statistics New Zealand (1997a), *Key Statistics: November 1997*. Wellington: Statistics New Zealand.

Statistics New Zealand (1997b), *Labour Market 1996*, Wellington: Statistics New Zealand.

Statistics New Zealand (1997c), *Ageing and Retirement in New Zealand*. Wellington: Statistics New Zealand.

Statistics New Zealand (various editions), *Hot Off the Press: Crown Health Enterprises Statistics*. Wellington: Statistics New Zealand.

Steering Group (1997), *Implementing the Coalition Agreement on Health*. Report of the Steering Group to Oversee Health and Disability Changes to the Minister of Health and the Associate Minister of Health. May.

Stephens, R. (1987), 'Social Policy Reform: In Retrospect and Prospect.' In A. Bollard and R. Buckle, Eds, *Economic Liberalisation in New Zealand*. Wellington, Allen and Unwin.

Stephens, R. (1990), 'Flattening the Tax Rate Scale in New Zealand.' In J. Head and R. Krever, Eds, *Flattening the Tax Rate Scale*. Melbourne: Longman.

Stephens, R. (1991), 'Who Gets What? Income Distribution and Redistribution in New Zealand, 1987-88.' Unpublished paper. Wellington: Public Policy Group, Victoria University of Wellington.

Stephens, R. (1992), 'Budgeting with the Benefit Cuts.' In J. Boston and P. Dalziel, Eds, *The Decent Society? Essays in Response to National's Economic and Social Policies*. Auckland: Oxford University Press.

Stephens, R. (1993), 'Poverty in New Zealand: An Interim Report.' Seminar paper presented to the Social Policy Agency, Wellington.

Stephens, R. (1994), 'Financing Education.' *New Zealand Annual Review of Education*, 3, pp.9-35.

Stephens, R. (1996a), 'Housing and Poverty in New Zealand.' Paper prepared for a conference on 'Housing and Social Change', Wellington, February.

Stephens, R. (1996b), 'Social Services.' In B. Silverstone, A. Bollard and R. Lattimore, Eds, *A Study of Economic Reform: The Case of New Zealand*. Amsterdam: North-Holland.

Stephens, R. (1997), 'Funded or Pay-As-You-Go?' *Victoria Economic Commentaries*, 14 (2), pp.10-17.

Stephens, R. and J. Boston (1995), 'Financing Tertiary Education: An Evaluation of the Todd Taskforce.' *New Zealand Annual Review of Education*, 4, pp.109-35.

Stephens, R. and J. Bradshaw (1995), 'The Generosity of New Zealand's Assistance to Families with Dependent Children: An Eighteen Country Comparison.' *Social Policy Journal of New Zealand*, 4 (July), pp.53-75.

Stephens, R., C. Waldegrave and P. Frater (1995), 'Measuring Poverty in New Zealand.' *Social Policy Journal of New Zealand*, 5 (December), pp.88-112.

Stocks, P. (1993), 'Changes in Health Targeting.' *Social Policy Journal of New Zealand*, 1 (November), pp.60-73.

Sutch, W.B. (1941), *Poverty and Progress in New Zealand*. Wellington: Modern Books.

Sutch, W.B. (1966), *The Quest for Security in New Zealand, 1840-1966*. London: Oxford University Press.

Sutch, W.B. (1971), *The Responsible Society in New Zealand*. Christchurch: Whitcombe and Tombs.

Szaszy, M. (1993), *Rapua Te Purapura E Ora Ai Te Iwi: Seek the Seeds for the Greatest Good of All People*. Wellington: School of Māori Studies, Victoria University of Wellington/Huia Publishers.

Taggart, M. (1990), 'Corporatisation, Privatisation and Public Law.' Publication No.31. Auckland: Legal Research Foundation, University of Auckland.

Tanzi, V. and L. Schuknecht (1997), 'Reconsidering the Fiscal Role of Government: The International Perspective.' *American Economic Review*, 87 (2), pp.164-68.

Task Force on Private Provision for Retirement (1992), *The Way Forward*. Wellington: The Task Force on Private Provision for Retirement.

Tawney, R. (1931), *Equality*. London: Allen and Unwin.

Tertiary Review Group (1991), *Review of Study Right*. Wellington: Ministry of Education.

The Jobs Letter (1997), Various issues. P.O. Box 428, New Plymouth.

Thomson, D. (1991a), *Selfish Generations? The Ageing of New Zealand's Welfare State*. Wellington: Bridget Williams Books.

Thomson, D. (1991b), 'Society and Social Welfare.' In C. Davis and P. Lineham, Eds, *The Future of the Past: Themes in New Zealand History*. Palmerston North: History Department, Massey University.

Thomson, D. (1996), *Selfish Generations? How Welfare States Grow Old*. Cambridge: White Horse Press.

Thomson, J. (1992), 'Personal Grievance Outcomes: Have There Been Any Changes?' Diploma in Industrial Relations Research Paper, Industrial Relations Centre, Victoria University of Wellington.

Thorns, D. (1986), 'New Zealand Housing Policy: Continuities and Changes.' *Housing Studies*, 1, pp.182-91.

Tilly, C. (1996), 'Workfare's Impact on the New York City Labor Market: Lower Wages and Worker Displacement.' Working Paper No.92 (March). New York: Russell Sage Foundation.

Tilyard, M.W., D.E. Phillips, S.M. Dovey and R.K. Whitney (1991), 'The Health Services Utilisation of a General Practice Population.' *New Zealand Medical Journal*, 104, pp.463-65.

Titmuss, R.M. (1974), *Social Policy: An Introduction*. London: Unwin Hyman.

Tobin, J. (1970), 'On Limiting the Domain of Inequality.' *Journal of Law and Economics*, 13, pp.363-78.

Treasury (1984), *Economic Management*. Wellington: Government Printer.

Treasury (1987a), *Government Management: Volume I*. Wellington: Government Printer.

Treasury (1987b), *Government Management: Volume II—Education Issues*. Wellington: Government Printer.

Treasury (1990), *Briefing to the Incoming Government: 1990*. Wellington: New Zealand Treasury.

Treasury (1991), 'Employment Contracts Bill: Outstanding Policy Issues.' Paper to Minister of Finance, 22 March.

Treasury (1996), *Briefing to the Incoming Government: 1996*. Wellington: New Zealand Treasury.

Tylor, E. (1873), *Primitive Cultures*, 2 Vols, 2nd Edition. London: John Murray.

University of Auckland (1997), 'Submission on the Green Paper on Tertiary Education.' Auckland.

Upton, S. (1991), *Your Health and the Public Health: A Statement of Government Health Policy*. Wellington: Government Printer.

van Oorschot, W. (1995), *Take It or Leave It: A Study of Non-take-up of Social Security Benefits*. Aldershot: Avebury.

Victoria University of Wellington (1997a), 'Report of the Working Party on Governance.' Wellington: VUW.

Victoria University of Wellington (1997b), 'Submission on the Green Paper on Tertiary Education.' Wellington: VUW.

Vowles, J., P. Aimer, H. Catt, J. Lamare and R. Miller (1995), *Towards Consensus? The 1993 General Election in New Zealand and the Transition to Proportional Representation*. Auckland: Auckland University Press.

Waitangi Tribunal (1988), *Muriwhenua Fishing Report*, Wai 22. Wellington: Government Printer.

Waitangi Tribunal (1997), *Muriwhenua Land Report*, Wai 45. Wellington: GP Publications.

Waldegrave, C. (1997), 'Talk of Dependency Inaccurate.' *Dominion*, 28 April.

Waldegrave, C. and P. Frater (1991), Eds, *The National Government Budgets of the First Year in Office: A Social Assessment*. Wellington: The Family Centre and Business and Economic Research Limited.

Waldegrave, C., S. Stuart and R. Stephens (1996), 'Participation in Poverty Research: Drawing on the Knowledge of Low Income Householders to Establish an Appropriate Measure for Monitoring Social Policy Impacts.' *Social Policy Journal of New Zealand*, 7 (December), pp.191-206.

Walsh, P. (1989), 'A Family Fight? Industrial Relations Reform Under the Fourth Labour Government.' In B. Easton, Ed, *The Making of Rogernomics*. Auckland: Auckland University Press.

Walsh, P. and R. Ryan (1993), 'The Making of the Employment Contracts Act.' In R. Harbridge, Ed, *Employment Contracts: New Zealand Experiences*. Wellington: Victoria University Press.

Walzer, M. (1983), *Spheres of Justice*. Oxford: Martin Robertson.

Ward, A. (1978), *A Show of Justice: Racial 'Amalgamation' in New Zealand*. Auckland: Auckland University Press.

Ware, A. (1990), 'Meeting Needs Through Voluntary Action: Does Market Society Corrode Altruism?' In A. Ware and R. Goodin, Eds, *Needs and Welfare*. London: Sage.

Ware, A. and R. Goodin (1990), Eds, *Needs and Welfare*. London: Sage.

Waring, M. (1988), *Counting for Nothing: What Men Value and What Women are Worth*. Wellington: Allen and Unwin/Port Nicholson Press.

Waslander, S. and M. Thrupp (1995), 'Choice, Competition and Segregation: An Empirical Analysis of a New Zealand Secondary School Market, 1990-1993.' *Journal of Education Policy*, 10 (1), pp.1-26.

Watts, R., J. Herbison, T. Johnston and R. Meyers (1987), *New Zealand Universities: Partners in National Development*. Report of the Universities Review Committee. Wellington: New Zealand Vice-Chancellors' Committee.

West, R. (1997), *Learning for Life: Review of Higher Education Financing and Policy–A Policy Discussion Paper*. Canberra: Australian Government Publishing Service.

Wetere, K. (1988), *Te Urupare Rangapū. Te Rārangi Kaupapa—Partnership Response. Policy Statement*. Wellington: Office of The Minister of Māori Affairs.

Whale, A. (1993), 'Voluntary Welfare Provision in a Landscape of Change: The Emergence of Food Banks in Auckland.' MA thesis, University of Auckland.

Williams, D.V. (1989), 'Te Tiriti o Waitangi: A Unique Relationship Between Crown and Tangata Whenua?' In I.H. Kawharu, Ed, *Waitangi: Māori and Pakeha Perspectives on the Treaty of Waitangi*. Auckland: Oxford University Press.

Williams, H.W. (1975), *A Dictionary of the Māori Language*, 7th Edition. Wellington: Government Printer.

Wilson, M. (1996), 'Institutional Labour Economics, Benefit Levels and Unemployment.' *Social Policy Journal of New Zealand*, 6 (July), pp.2-22.

Wilson, R. (1994), 'ACC on the Cheap.' *Employment Today*, 3 (February), pp.18-19.

Wilson, R. (1995), 'Cost Smoke Screen Does Not Obscure Need for Reform.' *Employment Today*, 12 (March), pp.22-23.

Wilson, R. (1996), 'Too Little Too Late?' *Employment Today*, 20 (February), pp.25-26.

Wilson, R. (1997), 'Casualties of the Social Contract.' *Employment Today*, 36 (December), pp.28-30.

Windolf, P. and S. Wood, with H.W. Hohn and T. Manwaring (1988), *Recruitment and Selection in the Labour Market*. Aldershot: Avebury.

Winiata, M. (1967), *The Changing Role of the Leader in Māori Society*. Auckland: Blackwood and Janet Paul.

Wiseman, M. (1995), 'State Strategies for Welfare Reform: The Wisconsin Story.' Discussion Paper No.1066-95. Madison: Institute for Research on Poverty, University of Wisconsin.

Woodhouse, O. (1996), 'Costly Misconceptions.' *Employment Today*, 21 (March), pp.20-22.

World Commission on the Environment and Development (1987), *Our Common Future*. Melbourne: Oxford University Press. Reprinted and cited from the Australian Edition with *A Sustainable Future for Australia*. Produced by the Australian Commission for the Future, 1990.

Wylie, C. (1994), *Self-Managing Schools in New Zealand: The Fifth Year*. Wellington: New Zealand Council for Educational Research.

Yeabsley, J. and J. Savage (1996), *What Do We Know About the Economic Impacts of the Employment Contracts Act?* Wellington: New Zealand Institute of Economic Research.

Young, A. (1996), 'Patient Safety Audit Planned.' *New Zealand Herald*, 7 December, p.A21.

INDEX